1 HABITAT

revista das artes no Brasil

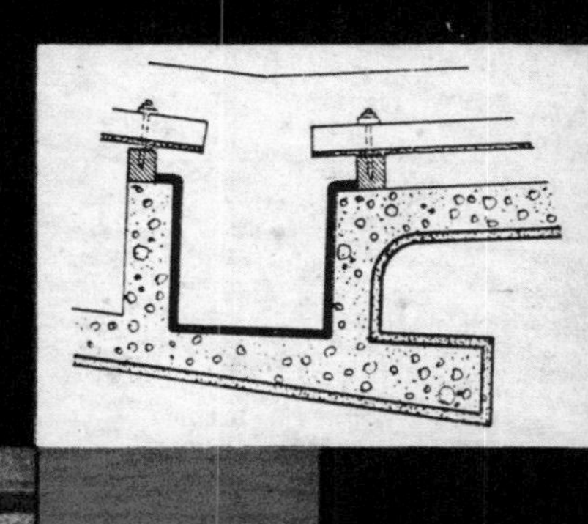

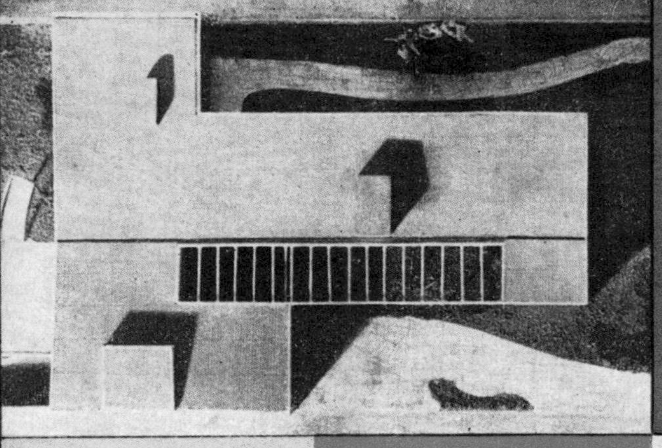

HABITAT 1

(OUTUBRO-DEZEMBRO DE 1950)

Diretor: ARQ. LINA BO BARDI

SUMÁRIO

Diretor responsavel: Geraldo Serra
Propriedade: HABITAT EDITORA LTDA.
R. 7 de Abril, 230, 8.º, Sala 820, São Paulo

Administração e Publicidade:
HABITAT EDITORA LTDA.
R. 7 de Abril, 230, 8º, Sala 820, Fone, 4-4403

Assinatura (4 números anuais):
Brasil ... Cr$ 100,00 Exterior .. US$ 5,00
C/registro. Cr$ 115,00 C/ registro US$ 6,00
N. avulso Cr$ 30,00 Exterior . US$ 1,50
N. atrazd. Cr$ 50,00 Exterior . US$ 2,50

Cliches: Funtymod Ltda., Rua Florencio de Abreu, 762, 2º, São Paulo

Impressão: Empresa «O PAPEL» Ltda. Rua Lavapés, 538, Tel. 6-3689, São Paulo

FIGS. 1–2
Habitat: Revista das Artes no Brasil, no. 1 (October–December 1950): cover and table of contents

FIGS. 3–4
Habitat: Revista das Artes no Brasil, no. 2 (January–March 1951): cover and table of contents

2 HABITAT

revista das artes no Brasil

HABITAT 2

(JANEIRO - MARÇO DE 1951)

Diretor : ARQ. LINA BO BARDI

SUMÁRIO

Diretor responsável : GERALDO SERRA
Propriedade: HABITAT EDITORA LTDA.
R. 7 de Abril, 230, 8.º, Sala 820, São Paulo

Administração e Publicidade:
HABITAT EDITORA LTDA.
R. 7 de Abril, 230, 8.º, Sala 820, Fone, 34-4403

Assinatura (4 números anuais):

Brasil	Cr$ 150,00	Exterior	US$ 6,00
c/registro ..	Cr$ 165,00	c/registro ..	US$ 7,00
N.º avulso .	Cr$ 40,00	Exterior	US$ 1,75
N.º atrazado	Cr$ 60,00	Exterior	US$ 2,75

Clichês: Funtimod — Fundição de Tipos Modernos S. A., Secção Clicheria, Rua Florêncio de Abreu, 762, 2.º — Fone, 34-8773 - S. Paulo

Impressão: Arco - Artusi Gráfica — Rua Apa, 45 — Fone, 52-7886 — São Paulo

FIGS. 5–6
Habitat: Revista das Artes no Brasil, no. 3 (April–June 1951): cover and table of contents

3 HABITAT

revista das artes no Brasil

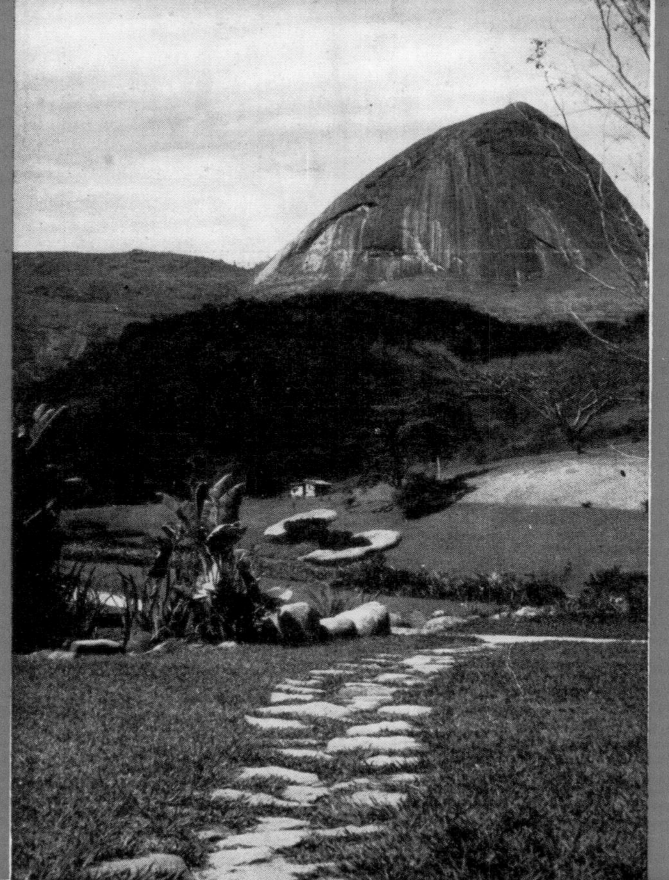

HABITAT 3

Diretor: ARQ. LINA BO BARDI

SUMARIO

ALENCASTRO 

Fotografias de: Roberto Maia, Peter Scheier, P. M. Bardi, Gregory Warchavchik, Ivo Ferreira da Silva, Eduardo Salvatore, Geraldo Barros, Vasari, Roma; Camponeri, Chianciano; Berzin, Recife; Julius Scherb, Viena; Goern Schisav, Oslo.

Diretor responsável: GERALDO N. SERRA
Propriedade: HABITAT EDITORA LTDA.
R. 7 de Abril, 230, 8º, Sala 820, São Paulo

Administração e Publicidade:
HABITAT EDITORA LTDA.
R. 7 de Abril, 230, 8º, Sala 820, Fone, 34-4493

Assinatura (4 números anuais):

Brasil	Cr$ 150,00	Exterior	US$ 6,00
c/registro .	Cr$ 165,00	c/registro ..	US$ 7,00
Nº avulso .	Cr$ 40,00	Exterior	US$ 1,75
Nº atrazado	Cr$ 60,00	Exterior	US$ 2,75

DISTRIBUIDORES NO RIO DE JANEIRO:
Livros de Portugal, Rua Gonçalves Dias, 62

Clichês: Funtimod - Fundição de Tipos Modernos S. A., Secção Clicheria, Rua Florêncio de Abreu, 762, 2º - Fone, 34-8773 - S. Paulo

Impressão: Emprêsa «O PAPEL» Ltda. Rua Lavapés, 538, Fone, 36-3689, São Paulo

FIGS. 7–8
Habitat: Revista das Artes no Brasil, no. 4 (July–September 1951): cover and table of contents

4 HABITAT

revista das artes no Brasil

HABITAT 4

Diretor: ARQ. LINA BO BARDI

SUMÁRIO

Fotografias: Chico Vizzoni, Peter Scheier, Marcel Cautherot, Roberto Maia, Sacha Harnisch, Felippe Quartiermeister, Alice Brill, P. M. Bardi, F. Krauss, Gustav Werner, Marc Vaux, S. Londynski, André Kertész, Soichi Sunami, Matthiesen Ltd. Knoedler Ltd., Diarios Associados, Fredi Kleemann, Farabola, Publifoto, Bruno Schuch, Zygmunt Haar, Jaques Pires, Foto Kurt, C. G. Stillman.

Diretor responsável: GERALDO N. SERRA
Propriedade: HABITAT EDITÔRA LTDA.
R. 7 de Abril, 230, 8.º, Sala 820, São Paulo

Administração e Publicidade:
HABITAT EDITÔRA LTDA.
R. 7 de abril, 230, 8.º, Sala 820, Fone, 34-4403

Assinatura (4 números anuais):

Brasil	Cr$ 150,00	Exterior ...	US$ 6,00
c/registro.	Cr$ 165,00	c/registro .	US$ 7,00
N.º avul. .	Cr$ 40,00	Exterior ...	US$ 1,75
N.º atraz.	Cr$ 60,00	Exterior ...	US$ 2,75

DISTRIBUIDORES NO RIO DE JANEIRO:
Livros de Portugal, Rua Gonçalves Dias, 62

Clichês: Funtimod - Fundição de Tipos Modernos S. A., Secção Clicheria, Rua Florêncio de Abreu, 762, 2.º - Fone, 34-8773 - S. Paulo

Impressão: Emprêsa Gráfica Editôra Guia Fiscal - Rua da Glória, 653, Fone, 3-3307 São Paulo, Brasil.

FIGS. 9–10
Habitat: Revista das Artes no Brasil, no. 5 (October–December 1951): cover and table of contents

5 HABITAT

revista das artes no Brasil

HABITAT 5

Diretor: ARQ. L I N A B O B A R D I

SUMÁRIO

Fotografias: Diários Associados, Zygmunt Haar, Peter Scheier, Alice Brill, Giacomelli, Flieg, Eduardo Tanon, C. de Boer, E. M. Czakó, Becherini, Louise Leiris, Paul Bijtebier, A.S.A.C., Marc Vaux, Leão Rosemberg, Tibor Örkényi, Halfeld

Diretor responsável: GERALDO N. SERRA
Propriedade: HABITAT EDITORA LTDA.
R. 7 de Abril, 230, 8.º, Sala 820, São Paulo

Administração e Publicidade:
H A B I T A T E D I T O R A L T D A .
Rua Sete de Abril, 230, 8.º
Sala 820, Fone 35-2837, São Paulo

Assinaturas: (4 números anuais)

Brasil	Cr$ 150,00	Exterior	US$ 6,00
c/registro	Cr$ 165,00	c/registro	US$ 7,00
Nº avulso	Cr$ 40,00	Exterior	US$ 1,75
Nº atrazado	Cr$ 60,00	Exterior	US$ 2,75

DISTRIBUIDORES NO RIO DE JANEIRO:
Livros de Portugal, Rua Gonçalves Dias, 62

Clichês: Clicheria e Estereotipia «Planalto»
Avenida Brigadeiro Luís Antônio, 153,
fones 33-4921 e 35-4048, São Paulo.

Impressão: Emprêsa «O PAPEL» Ltda.
Rua Lavapés, 538, Fone, 36-3689, São Paulo.

FIGS. 11–12
Habitat: Revista das Artes no Brasil, no. 6 (January–March 1952): cover and table of contents

6 HABITAT

revista das artes no Brasil

HABITAT 6

Diretor: ARQ. LINA BO BARDI

SUMÁRIO

	O centenário
	Um artigo do semanal "Arts"
ASSIS CHATEAUBRIAND	Obras de arte recebidas como personagens
	Ticiano
	Cézanne
	O retrato francês no Museu de Arte
	Steinberg no Brasil
SERAFIM	Retrato de Yan
TARSILA DO AMARAL	Recordações de Paris
B. CENDRARS	Saint-Paul
	Fundar
J. VALLADARES	A pintura popular na Bahia
ROGER BASTIDE	Art et religion: le culte des jumeaux
	Ourivesaria
	Grupo de móveis
M. BERKOWITZ	Sascha Harnisch, fotógrafo
	Pintores
	Juventude
P. M. BARDI	A cultura figurativa da infância
M. DA SILVA	O carro em frente dos bois
	Corpus do Barroco
	Arquitetura: Redig de Campos; Mathias e Palanti; Duarte e Carvalho Mange; Coelho Cardozo e Osborn Coelho
FLAVIO MOTTA	Verde em São Paulo
	Cartazes
	Um livro sôbre de Fiori
	Ver e compreender
	Arte religiosa
	O Indio na Bienal
	Um xilógrafo
A. CAVALCANTI	**Cinema:** A nova etapa
	Música: A Orquestra sinfônica juvenil do Museu de Arte
EDINO KRIEGER	Koellreutter e nosso meio musical
W. P.	**Teatro:** Cenografia
M. DA S.	Maria della Costa
ALENCASTRO	
Fora texto	Quatro gravuras
Fotografias:	Casa Wildenstein, P. M. B., Zygmunt Haar, Sascha Harnisch, R. Klein, Coelho Cardozo, Diários Associados, Pierre Verger, Marc Vaux, Alice Brill, E. e D. Gibbs, P. Scheier, Manoel Ribeiro, Flieg, G. Tamarski, Roger Bezombes, Roberto Maia, Halfeld, Edoardo Tanon

Propriedade: HABITAT EDITORA LTDA.
Diretor responsável: GERALDO N. SERRA
Rua 7 de Abril, 230, 8.º, Sala 820, São Paulo

Administração e Publicidade:
HABITAT EDITORA LTDA.
Rua Sete de Abril, 230, 8.º
Sala 820, Fone 35-2837, São Paulo

Assinaturas: (4 números anuais)

Brasil	Cr$ 150,00	Exterior	US$ 6,00
c/ registro .	Cr$ 165,00	c/ registro ..	US$ 7,00
N.º avulso .	Cr$ 40,00	Exterior	US$ 1,75
N.º atrazado	Cr$ 60,00	Exterior	US$ 2,75

DISTRIBUIDORES NO RIO DE JANEIRO:
Livros de Portugal, Rua Gonçalves Dias, 62

Clichês: Clicheria e Estereotipia "Planalto" Avenida Brigadeiro Luis Antônio, 153, fones 33-4921 e 35-4048, São Paulo

Impressão: Arco - Artusi Gráfica Ltda. R. Marquês de Itú, 282/284, Fone: 35-5797, São Paulo

FIGS. 13–14
Habitat: Revista das Artes no Brasil, no. 7 (April–June 1952): cover and table of contents

7 HABITAT

revista das artes no Brasil

HABITAT 7

Diretor: ARQ. LINA BO BARDI

SUMÁRIO

Fotografias: Gilberto de Biasi, Roberto Maia, E. Tannon, F. Albuquerque, Alice Brill, P. M. Bardi, Sascha Harnisch, G. Ocker, Oscar Savio, Jurno, De Beausacq, Zanella e Moscardi, Barratt, Foto Técnica Milan, T. Abresch

Propriedade: HABITAT EDITORA LTDA.
Diretor responsável: GERALDO N. SERRA
Rua 7 de Abril, 230, 8.º, Sala 820, São Paulo

Administração e Publicidade:

HABITAT EDITORA LTDA.

Rua Sete de Abril, 230, 8.º
Sala 820, Fone 35-2837, São Paulo

Assinaturas: **(4 números anuais)**

Brasil	Cr$ 150,00	Exterior	US$ 6,00
c/registro .	Cr$ 165,00	c/ registro ..	US$ 7,00
N.º avulso .	Cr$ 40,00	Exterior	US$ 1,75
N.º atrazado	Cr$ 60,00	Exterior	US$ 2,75

DISTRIBUIDORES NO RIO DE JANEIRO:
Livros de Portugal, Rua Gonçalves Dias, 62

Clichês: Clicheria e Estereotipia "Planalto"
Avenida Brigadeiro Luís Antônio, 153,
Fones 33-4921 e 35-4048, São Paulo

Impressão: Arco - Artusi Gráfica Ltda.
R. Marquês de Itú, 282/284, Fone: 35-5797,
São Paulo

FIGS. 15–16
Habitat: Revista das Artes no Brasil, no. 8 (July–September 1952): cover and table of contents

8 # HABITAT

revista das artes no Brasil

HABITAT 8

Diretor: ARQ. L I N A B O B A R D I

SUMÁRIO

Fotografias: Rachel Esther Prochnik, Albuquerque, P. M. Bardi, Flieg, Sascha Harnisch, P. C. Scheier, Janari, A. Feichtenberger, Fotoptica

Propriedade: HABITAT EDITORA LTDA.
Diretor responsável: GERALDO N. SERRA
Rua 7 de Abril, 230, 8.º, Sala 820, São Paulo

Administração e Publicidade:
H A B I T A T E D I T O R A L T D A .
Rua Sete de Abril, 230, 8.º
Sala 820, Fone 35-2837, São Paulo

Assinaturas: **(4 números anuais)**

Brasil	Cr$ 150,00	Exterior	US$ 6,00
c/registro .	Cr$ 165,00	c/ registro ..	US$ 7,00
N.º avulso .	Cr$ 40,00	Exterior	US$ 1,75
N.º atrazado	Cr$ 60,00	Exterior	US$ 2,75

DISTRIBUIDOR NO RIO DE JANEIRO: Walter Simoni, Rua Santa Luzia, 799, 18.º andar, Fone: 22-3005, Rio de Janeiro

Clichês: Clicheria e Estereotipia "Planalto" Avenida Brigadeiro Luís Antônio, 153, Fones 33-4921 e 35-4048, São Paulo

Impressão: Arco - Artusi Gráfica Ltda. R. M. de Itú, 282/284, Fone: 35-5797, S. Paulo

FIGS. 17–18
Habitat: Revista das Artes no Brasil, no. 9 (October–December 1952): cover and table of contents

9 HABITAT

revista das artes no Brasil

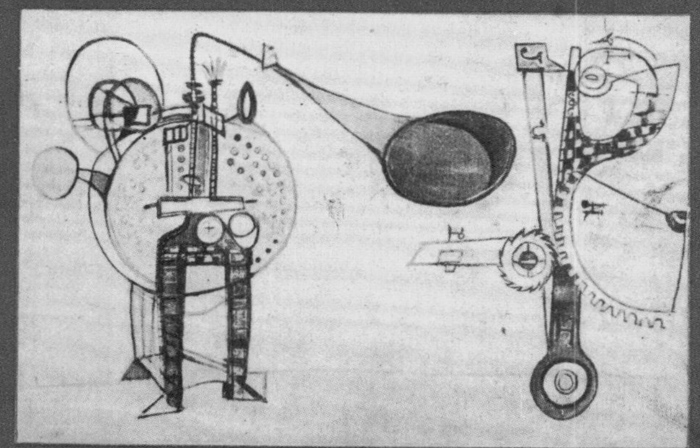

HABITAT 9

Diretor: ARQ. L I N A B O B A R D I

NOSSA CAPA: Desenhos de Saul Steinberg Hedda Sterne

SUMÁRIO

Fotografias: Casa Durand-Matthiesen, L. Liberman, A. P. de Albuquerque, Odorico Tavares, Ernesto Mandowsky, C. Biaghetti, E. Tanon, Cassius, P. Scheier, Voltaire Fraga, Nelson

Propriedade: HABITAT EDITORA LTDA.
Diretor responsável: GERALDO N. SERRA
Rua 7 de Abril, 230, 8.º, Sala 820, São Paulo

Administração e Publicidade:
H A B I T A T E D I T O R A L T D A .
Rua Sete de Abril, 230, 8.º
Sala 820, Fone 35-2837, São Paulo

Assinaturas: (4 números anuais)

Brasil	Cr$ 150,00	Exterior	US$ 6,00
c/registro .	Cr$ 165,00	c/registro ..	US$ 7,00
N.º avulso .	Cr$ 40,00	Exterior	US$ 1,75
N.º atrazado	Cr$ 60,00	Exterior	US$ 2,75

DISTRIBUIDOR NO RIO DE JANEIRO: Walter Simoni, Rua Santa Luzia, 799, 18.º andar, Fone: 22-3005, Rio de Janeiro

Papel: Murray Simonsen S. A., Rio de Janeiro, Av. Rio Branco, 85 e São Paulo, R. Barão de Itapetininga, 224, 7.º, s. 73.

Clichês: Clicheria e Estereotipia "Planalto" Avenida Brigadeiro Luís Antônio, 153 Fones 33-4921 e 35-4048, São Paulo

Impressão: Arco - Artusi Gráfica Ltda. R. M. de Itú, 282/284, Fone: 35-5797, S. Paulo

FIGS. 19–20
Habitat: Revista das Artes no Brasil, no. 10 (January–March 1953): cover and table of contents

10 HABITAT

revista das artes no Brasil

HABITAT 10

Diretor: **FLAVIO MOTTA**

SUMÁRIO

Propriedade: HABITAT EDITORA LTDA.

Diretor responsável: GERALDO N. SERRA

Administração e Publicidade:

HABITAT EDITORA LTDA.

Rua Sete de Abril, 230, 8.º
Sala 820, Fone 35-2837, São Paulo

Assinaturas: (4 **números anuais)**

Brasil	Cr$ 150,00	Exterior	US$ 6,00
c/registro .	Cr$ 165,00	c/registro ..	US$ 7,00
N.º avulso .	Cr$ 40,00	Exterior	US$ 1,75
N.ºatrazado	Cr$ 60,00	Exterior	US$ 2,75

DISTRIBUIDOR NO RIO DE JANEIRO: Walter Simoni, Rua Santa Luzia, 799, 18.º andar, Fone: 22-3005, Rio de Janeiro

DISTRIBUIDOR NA ARGENTINA: Galeria Bonino, Maipu, 962 - Buenos Aires

Impressão: Arco - Artusi Gráfica Ltda. R. M. de Itú, 282/284, Fone: 35-5797, S. Paulo

FIGS. 21–22
Habitat: Revista das Artes no Brasil, no. 11 (April–June 1953): cover and table of contents

11 HABITAT

revista das artes no Brasil

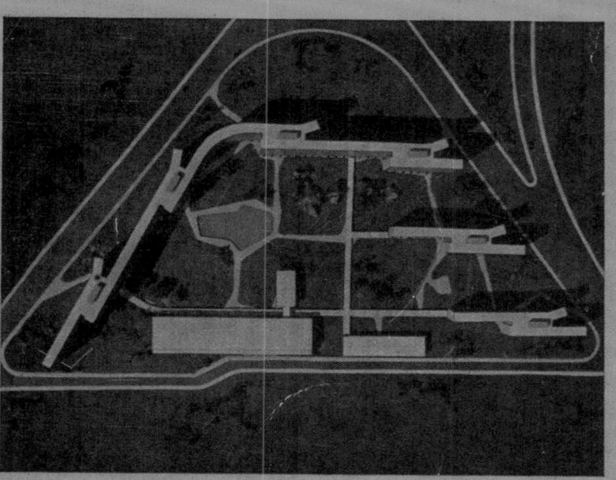

HABITAT 11

Ano III; Junho de 1953

Diretor: **FLAVIO MOTTA**

SUMÁRIO

Fotografias: Alice Brill, Giacomo Brogi di Lauranti, Diários Associados, Usa Borchert, José Medeiros, F. Albuquerque, Odorico Tavares, Peter Scheier, Leon Liberman, Fiorenza, Flieg, Lise Modern, Carlos, Germano, Edson, Leão Rozemberg, Sasso

Na capa: um desenho de Cuoco; uma pintura de Plattner; conjunto residencial do estudante, Arq. Rino Levi; estádio do S. P. F. C., Arq. Icaro de Castro Mello

Propriedade: HABITAT EDITORA LTDA.
Diretor responsável: GERALDO N. SERRA

Administração e Publicidade:
HABITAT EDITORA LTDA.
Rua Sete de Abril, 230, 8.º andar
Conj. 837/8, Fone 35-2837, São Paulo

Assinaturas: (4 números anuais)

Brasil	Cr$ 150,00	Exterior	US$ 6,00
c/registro .	Cr$ 165,00	c/registro ..	US$ 7,00
N.º avulso .	Cr$ 40,00	Exterior	US$ 1,75
N.º atrazado	Cr$ 60,00	Exterior	US$ 2,75

DISTRIBUIDOR NO RIO DE JANEIRO: Importadora e Exportadora BRASITODO Ltda. Avenida Almirante Barroso, 54, térreo (Edifício Valparaiso). Correspondência: Cx. P. 4057

DISTRIBUIDOR NA ARGENTINA: Galeria Bonino, Maipu, 962 - Buenos Aires

DISTRIBUIDOR PARA PORTUGAL E ESPANHA: ARICIE Ltda. Rua Antônio Maria Cardoso, 19 - 3.ª D - LISBOA

Impressão: Arco - Artusi Gráfica Ltda.
R. Marques de Itú, 282/4, Fone 35-5797, S. Paulo

FIGS. 23–24
Habitat: Revista das Artes no Brasil, no. 12 (July–September 1953): cover and table of contents

12 HABITAT

revista das artes no Brasil

HABITAT 12

Ano III; Setembro de 1953

Diretor: **FLAVIO MOTTA**

SUMÁRIO

FOTOGRAFIAS: L. Albuquerque, Zanella & Moscardi, Alice Brill, Leon Liberman, Haar Studios, Carlos, Wonneberger, G. Lorca, Casali, Publifoto, L. Modern, Sascha Harnisch, Kinofilmes, Estudios Amador, Mandowsky, F. Albuquerque, Hugo Zanella, Lula, Edson, Diarios Associados, Berzin, P. Scheier, Odorico Tavares, Marri, R. E. Prochnik

Na capa: Um desenho de Lula Cardoso Ayres

Propriedade: HABITAT EDITORA LTDA.

Diretor responsável: GERALDO N. SERRA

Administração e Publicidade:
HABITAT EDITORA LTDA.
Rua Sete de Abril, 230, 8.º andar
Conj. 837/8, Fone 35-2837, São Paulo

Assinaturas: (4 números anuais)

Brasil	Cr$ 150,00	Exterior	US$ 6,00
c/registro	Cr$ 165,00	c/registro	US$ 7,00
N.º avulso	Cr$ 40,00	Exterior	US$ 1,75
N.º atrazado	Cr$ 60,00	Exterior	US$ 2,00

DISTRIBUIDOR NO RIO DE JANEIRO: Importadora e Exportadora BRASITODO Ltda. Avenida Almirante Barroso, 54, térreo (Edifício Valparaiso). Correspondência: Cx. P. 4057

DISTRIBUIDOR PARA PORTUGAL E ESPANHA: ARICIE Ltda. Rua Antônio Maria Cardoso, 19 - 3.ª D - LISBOA

Impressão: Arco - Artusi Gráfica Ltda.
R. Marques de Itú, 282/4, Fone 35-5797, S. Paulo

FIGS. 25–26
Habitat: Revista das Artes no Brasil, no. 13 (October–December 1953): cover and table of contents

13 HABITAT

revista das artes no Brasil

Beaux-Arts

L'Orangerie accueille 60 chefs-d'œuvre du musée de SAO-PAULO

Germain BAZIN

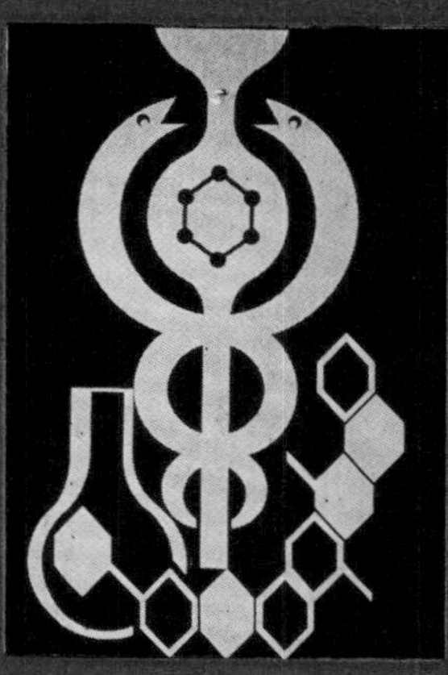

HABITAT 13

Ano IV; Dezembro de 1953

Diretor: FLAVIO MOTTA

SUMÁRIO

FOTOGRAFIAS: Aertsens Michel, Alice Brill, Boer, "Diários Associados", F. Albuquerque, F. Federighi. Freddy Kleemann, Foto Jerry, G. Cruz, Hugo Zanella, Jean Lecoq, Odorico Tavares, Peter Scheier, Publifoto (Paris), Roberto Maia, Sascha Harnisch, V. Vaitekunas

Propriedade: HABITAT EDITORA LTDA.
Diretor responsável: GERALDO N. SERRA

Administração e Publicidade:
HABITAT EDITORA LTDA.
Rua Sete de Abril, 230, 8.º andar
Conj. 837/8, Fone 35-2837, São Paulo

Assinaturas: (4 números)

Brasil	Cr$ 150,00	Exterior	US$ 6,00
c/registro .	Cr$ 165,00	c/registro ..	US$ 7,00
N.º avulso .	Cr$ 40,00	Exterior	US$ 1,75
N.º atrazado	Cr$ 60,00	Exterior	US$ 2,00

DISTRIBUIDOR NO RIO DE JANEIRO: Importadora e Exportadora BRASITODO Ltda. Avenida Almirante Barroso, 54, térreo (Edifício Valparaiso). Correspondência: Cx. P. 4057

DISTRIBUIDOR PARA BAHIA: Deposito de Livros CONTINENTAL, Florencio Mattos, Pr. Barão do Rio Branco, 5A, 2.º - SALVADOR

DISTRIBUIDOR PARA PORTO ALEGRE E. C. Martins - Caixa Postal, 2457, Porto Alegre

DISTRIBUIDORA NOS EE.UU.: Galeria Sudamericano, 866 Lexington Avenue, New York 21

DISTRIBUIDOR PARA PORTUGAL E ESPANHA: ARICIE Ltda. Rua Antônio Maria Cardoso, 19 - 3.ª D - LISBOA

Clichês: Clicheria Universal, F. Grabenweger & Cia. Ltda., Rua Aurora, 186, São Paulo

Impressão: Arco - Artusi Gráfica Ltda.
R. Marques de Itú, 282/4, Fone 35-5797, S. Paulo

FIGS. 27–28
Habitat: Revista das Artes no Brasil, no. 14 (January–February 1954): cover and table of contents

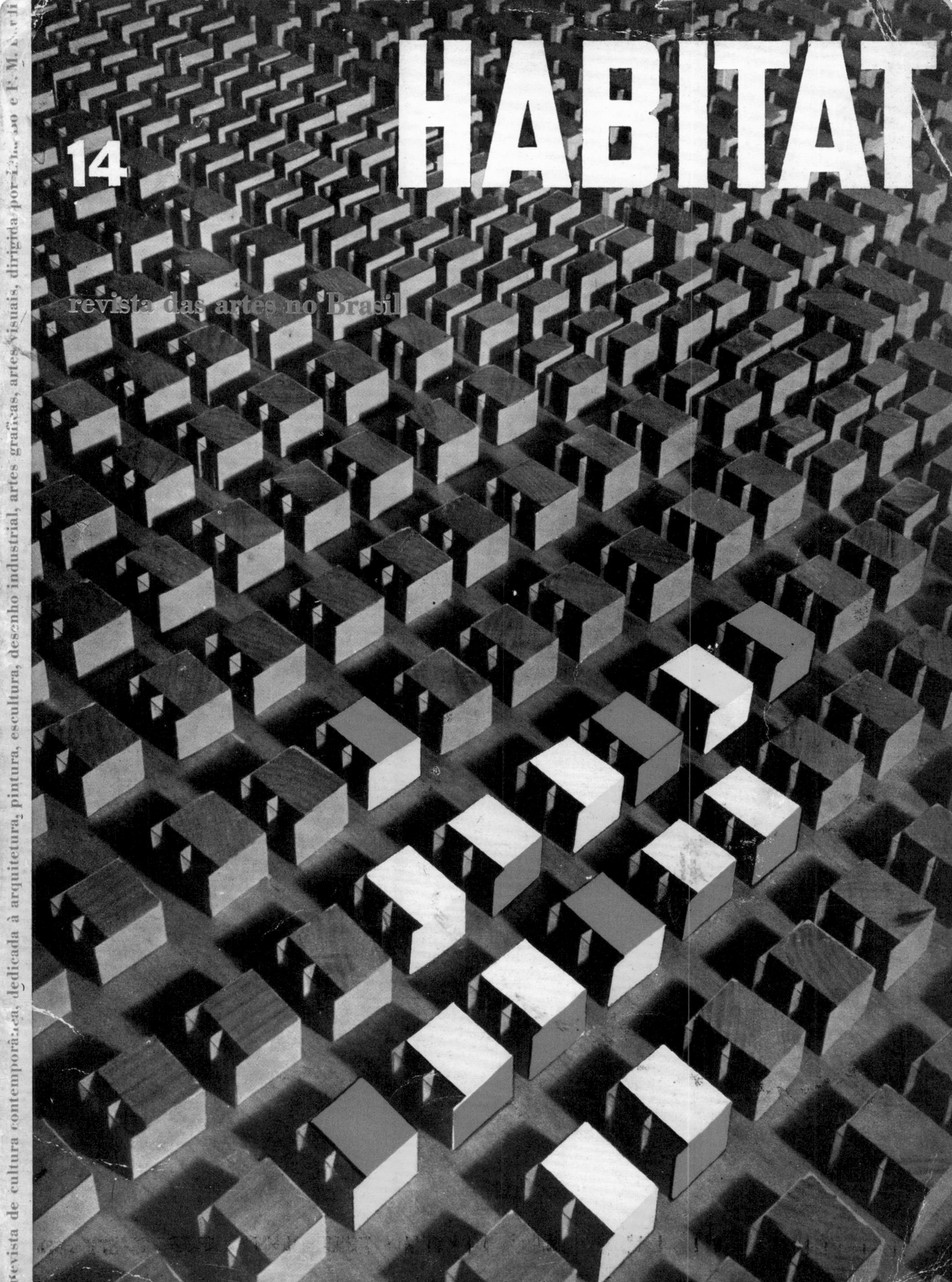
HABITAT
14
revista das artes no Brasil
Revista de cultura contemporânea, dedicada à arquitetura, pintura, escultura, desenho industrial, artes gráficas, artes visuais, dirigida por

Janeiro - Fevereiro de 1954

Revista de cultura contemporânea, dedicada à arquitetura, pintura, escultura, desenho industrial, artes gráficas, artes visuais, dirigida por Lina Bo e P. M. Bardi

Propriedade: Habitat Editôra Ltda.; Diretor responsável: Geraldo N. Serra; Editor: Rodolfo Klein; Departamento de Publicidade: Walter Simoni; Redação: Rua 7 de Abril, 230, 13.o andar, Fone: 34-5648; Administração e Publicidade: Habitat Editôra Ltda., rua 7 de Abril, 230, 8.o andar, conjunto 837-38, Fone: 35-2837, São Paulo.
Fotografias: Marcel Gautherot, Peter Scheier, Alice Brill, Roberto Maia, Sa-

FIGS. 29–30
Habitat: Revista das Artes no Brasil, no. 15 (March–April 1954): cover and table of contents

Revista de cultura contemporânea, dedicada à arquitetura, pintura, escultura, desenho industrial, artes gráficas, artes visuais, dirigida por Lina Bo e P. M. Bardi

HABITAT

15

revista das artes no Brasil

Neste número:

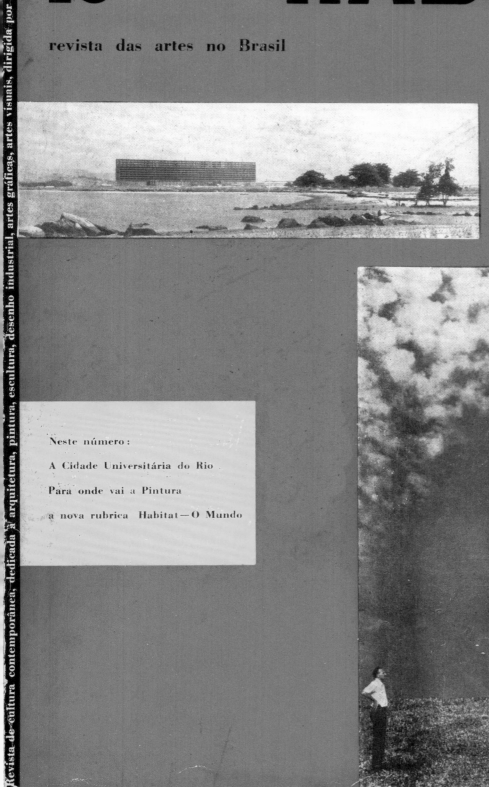

A Cidade Universitária do Rio

Para onde vai a Pintura

a nova rubrica Habitat — O Mundo

Março - Abril de 1954

Revista de cultura contemporânea, dedicada à arquitetura, pintura, escultura, desenho industrial, artes gráficas, artes visuais, dirigida por Lina Bo e P. M. Bardi

Propriedade: Habitat Editôra Ltda.; Diretor responsável: Geraldo N. Serra; Editor: Rodolfo Klein; Departamento de Publicidade: Walter Simoni; Redação: Rua 7 de Abril, 230, 13.º andar, Fone: 34-5648; Administração e Publicidade: Habitat Editôra Ltda., rua 7 de Abril, 230, 8.º andar, conjunto 837-38, Fone: 35-2837, S. Paulo. Fotografias: Marcel Gautherot, José Medeiros,

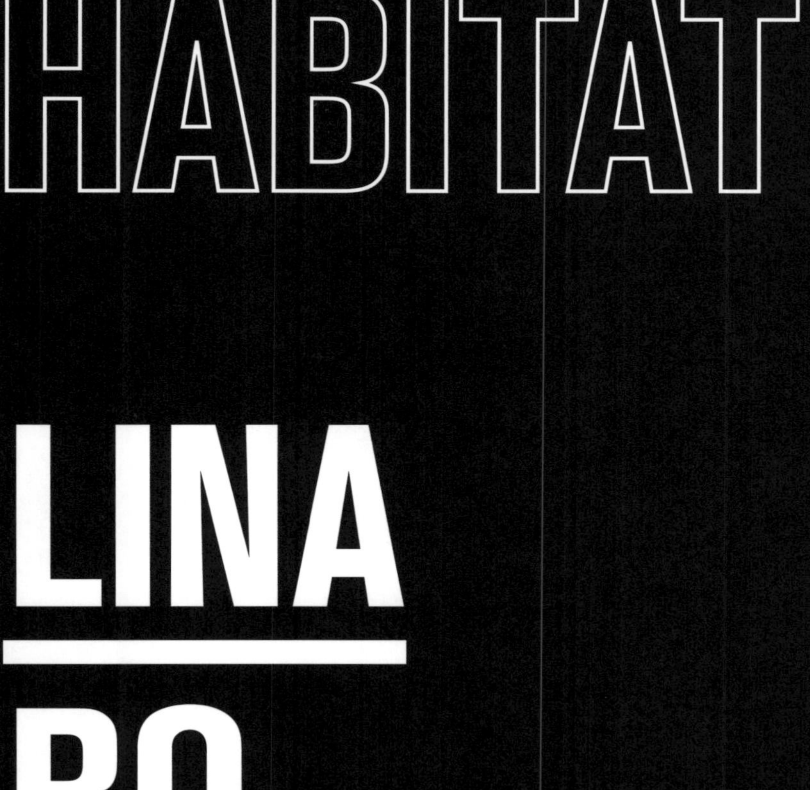

BO
BARDI

EDITORS
Adriano Pedrosa
José Esparza Chong Cuy
Julieta González
Tomás Toledo

ESSAYS
Adriano Pedrosa
Antonio Risério
Beatriz Colomina and Mark Wigley
Denis Joelson
Esther da Costa Meyer
Guilherme Giufrida
Guilherme Wisnik
Jane Hall
José Esparza Chong Cuy
Julieta González
Lina Bo Bardi
Luis. M. Castañeda
Tomás Toledo
Vanessa Mendes

STRATEGIC PARTNERS

SPONSORS

SUPPORTER

CULTURAL SUPPORTER

PRODUCTION

HABITAT

LINA BO BARDI

MASP
Museu de Arte de São Paulo Assis Chateaubriand

FUNDACIÓN JUMEX
ARTE CONTEMPORÁNEO

DelMonico Books · Prestel Munich, London, New York

FOREWORD ITAÚ

A characteristic aspect of the thought of architect, designer, editor, set designer, and illustrator Lina Bo Bardi was her emphasis on "potentiality"; that is, whether in relation to historical events, social contexts, or the material resources at hand, the artist and intellectual always kept in mind where all the elements fit, which paths they suggested to avoid, and what experiences they might elicit.

One way of illustrating this is with Lina's own words: "The past, viewed as a historical present, is still alive, a gift that helps to avoid pitfalls . . . In the face of the historical present, our task is to forge another present, [one that is] 'true.'" We can see how what took place in the past is not a mere accumulation of information; it is something that remains active and which we must take up again, both to avoid mistakes and to forge new futures.

The activities to which Lina devoted herself were not restricted to the highly educated: "The deep knowledge of specialists is not necessary," she asserted, "but rather an ability to historically understand the past, to distinguish what will serve today's new situations as they present themselves, and this is not learned only in books." There are multiple possibilities for understanding one another in time, thus becoming truly contemporary.

Another way of defending this interpretation is to recall Lina's conceptions of architecture—considered "as a collective service and as poetry, something that has nothing to do with art, a kind of alliance between duty and scientific practice" (again, knowledge, social understanding, and intervention are connected). Or to mention her efforts to develop an industry based on artisanal production, on national creativity.

Above all, we can find the concretization of all these presuppositions in the artist's work, an experience made possible by the exhibition *Lina Bo Bardi: Habitat*. Organized in one of Lina's great achievements, the Museu de Arte de São Paulo Assis Chateaubriand (MASP)—a project about which she observed, "I did not seek beauty, I sought freedom"—this is a broad retrospective. Itaú Cultural invites the public to delve deeper into this work, which considers "culture as conviviality."

The exhibition is also a chance to discover more about Brazilian modern architecture. Such an opportunity will be offered at our headquarters as well: from April to June 2019, we will hold the exhibition *Ocupação Gregori Warchavchik* (Gregori Warchavchik Occupation). Like Lina, Warchavchik was an artist, architect, immigrant, modernist, and pioneer. The *Occupation* program, focused on foundational names in Brazilian art, features three other honorees from the field of architecture: Vilanova Artigas, Paulo Mendes da Rocha, and Flávio Império. Materials from these exhibitions—analysis, documents, interviews—are available at itaucultural.org.br/ocupacao.

Other events at Itaú Cultural will focus on architects, such as *Oscar Niemeyer: clássicos e inéditos* and *Ser estar: Sergio Rodrigues* (in this case, a more design-oriented show). At issuu.com/itaucultural—our collection of digital publications—you can get to know the works that were produced for these exhibitions. You can also access our schedule of cultural activities and related content at itaucultural.org.br.

FOREWORD IGUATEMI

Lina Bo Bardi, an Italian who became a naturalized Brazilian, found in São Paulo the place for her modernist conceptions of architecture. Here, she built unconventional structures, such as the ones we see at MASP, Sesc Pompeia, and the Glass House where she lived for over forty years with her husband, Pietro Maria Bardi.

Considered one of the most important architects in Latin America, Bo Bardi was also an urban planner, designer, illustrator, set designer, writer, and curator. In Brazil in the 1960s, her pioneering force paved the way for women in what were then considered masculine domains, such as politics and architecture.

For Lina, architecture should be simple. Although her approach could be quite conceptual, she sought to create designs with social impact that immediately communicated with the public, with the people, thus imbuing them with a sense of collectivity.

It was Lina who chose MASP's site at the Trianon Belvedere, on Avenida Paulista. Moreover, it is interesting to note that a condition imposed by São Paulo's City Hall—that the vista from Avenida Paulista down Avenida 9 de Julho toward downtown remain open—became an act of freedom. Out of it came the creation of MASP's free span, which is 74 meters long and 8 meters high from the ground.

Today, MASP, the Museo Jumex, and the Museum of Contemporary Art Chicago host this grand panoramic exhibition featuring works that epitomize Lina's cultural legacy. Visitors will be able to follow a careful investigation of how her editorial, pedagogical, museographical, and curatorial endeavors influenced her architectural projects.

We at Iguatemi São Paulo are proud to support and to be part of such an important project highlighting the recent history of our country. Following Lina Bo Bardi's life trajectory reinforces our commitment to promoting culture, women, and the vision to transform society.

FOREWORD LEFOSSE

One might find it ugly and say: the São Paulo Museum of Art is not beautiful, it has never been beautiful. I did not seek beauty, I sought freedom. The intellectuals didn't like it; the people liked it. Really liked it. Do you know who did this? It was a woman!

LINA BO BARDI, in the documentary *Lina Bo Bardi*, directed by Aurélio Michiles, 1993

Lina Bo Bardi was born in Rome in 1914, naturalized as a Brazilian citizen in 1951, and lived here until her death in 1992.

As an architect, she designed one of the most iconic buildings in São Paulo and Brazil: MASP, the instantly recognizable structure along Avenida Paulista, with its red columns and vast free span.

But Lina Bo Bardi did much more. She created the Glass House, Sesc Pompeia, and the famous glass easels that display MASP's collection; she worked as an illustrator, a set designer, a writer, and a furniture designer.

In a catalogue of women's achievements, Lina Bo Bardi remains to this day an exemplary figure.

Lefosse Advogados supports this exhibition as a way to promote art, especially women's art in Brazil.

This support is part of Lefosse Plural, an initiative by Lefosse Advogados to discuss and implement alternatives that will generate an increasingly plural and inclusive environment, through proposals that reinforce our commitment to respect for diversity and LGBT+ rights, to measures for racial inclusion, and of course, to reducing gender inequality.

Lefosse is not just a law firm; it is a firm formed by people who believe that they can contribute to our society, with the increasing presence of independent women, entrepreneurs who tirelessly seek professional fulfillment.

Lefosse Advogados seeks to internally realize its values and to connect with movements in society that reflect its initiatives.

FOREWORD PWC

PwC began its activities in Brazil in 1915. A year earlier, Lina Bo Bardi was born in Rome.

Throughout our first decade of existence, we witnessed the country's nascent industrialization, as well as the manifestos and events that culminated in the 1922 Modern Art Week—a symbolic landmark of the Brazilian modernist movement.

Over the following decades, following Brazil's growing participation in the international economic order, we expanded our operations, focusing primarily on providing services to foreign companies in the areas of auditing, tax consultancy, and business consulting.

It was a period of rapid progress, marked by the emergence of our most important state-owned enterprises. PwC's presence in the country was consolidated during this period, and our performance gained enormous momentum.

Meanwhile, national architecture acquired modernist traits, with new aesthetic conceptions and techniques in construction. Buildings that stand out for their functionality, rationalism, and well-defined geometric forms projected names such as Lúcio Costa and Oscar Niemeyer onto the international scene.

Amidst this scenario, Lina Bo Bardi landed in 1946 in Rio de Janeiro, then the country's capital. The architect's work quickly gained prominence. In less than ten years, Lina would begin designing MASP's ultimate home on Avenida Paulista. It was not long before she became one of the most important names in modern Brazilian architecture, capable of combining aesthetic avant-garde conceptions with our cultural and popular traditions to create an entirely new language.

In its 104 years of existence, PwC has actively participated in the key milestones of the economic life of our republic, closely following and often contributing to our cultural and artistic evolution—either through sponsorship and support for specific actions and events, or collaborations with the management of leading entities in the world of arts, culture, and education.

Sponsorship of *Lina Bo Bardi: Habitat* at MASP is one of the most recent examples of our contributions.

FOREWORD NOVA ENERGIA

It is an honor for Nova Energia Comercializadora to sponsor the exhibition *Lina Bo Bardi: Habitat*, about this visionary architect who, among so many works, left us the masterpiece of MASP, with its unique architecture and iconic crystal easels.

Nova Energia believes that art is the true expression of the soul, and the clarity and inventiveness of Lina's works corroborate this belief. Access to culture is unquestionably essential to the intellectual development of a country, and this is how a better and fairer society is built. The architecture of MASP, with its great, partition-free galleries, is living proof of Lina's commitment to democratic art. The arrangement of the second-floor works on crystal easels further underlines the idea that works of art should be accessible to all, part of people's daily lives.

As a sponsor, Nova Energia hopes that everyone can enjoy the treasures of this exhibition and benefit from the innovative and liberating essence of Lina, always present in her projects, in her life and personal dreams, contributing to the construction of a better world.

FOREWORD INSTITUTO BARDI/ CASA DE VIDRO

SONIA GUARITA
Chair of the Board, Instituto Bardi/Casa de Vidro

SOL CAMACHO
Cultural Director, Instituto Bardi/ Casa de Vidro

Habitat: it signifies environment, dignity, convenience, morality of life, and therefore spirituality and culture; this is why we have chosen for the title of our magazine a word closely related to architecture, which we value and interpret as not only an artistic but also an artistically social function.

With these words, Lina Bo Bardi launched the first issue of *Habitat: Revista das Artes no Brasil* in 1950, bridging diverse themes with an emphasis on architecture, museography, graphic and furniture design, popular and avant-garde art.

On the present occasion, in which three major museums, the Museu de Arte de São Paulo Assis Chateaubriand (MASP), the Fundación Jumex Arte Contemporáneo, and the Museum of Contemporary Art Chicago (MCA), have organized an international exhibition dedicated to Lina Bo Bardi entitled *Habitat*, the term once again stands out in relation to the architect's work, synthesizing her legacy in its entirety, just as Lina and her husband, Pietro Maria Bardi, looked at life. Everything, on any scale, was for them a cultural project.

Thus, intertwining life, art, and architecture, Lina Bo Bardi built a career that positioned her as one of the most relevant figures of the twentieth century, not only for the work she undertook in Brazil, but also for the universality of her thinking, which was always rooted in social life.

Presenting the ideas of a vanguard woman to a wide audience is today very pertinent in the sociopolitical context of Brazil, her country by choice. Equally opportune is to expose the facts of Italian-Brazilian coexistence within and outside of museums, in Mexico and in the United States, countries where the Instituto Bardi's rich collection has not been seen for decades and where this show will now be presented.

The Instituto Bardi/Casa de Vidro, as it is known, was founded in 1990 by the couple Lina Bo and Pietro Maria Bardi, to promote the study and research of Brazilian culture, especially in the fields of architecture, design, and art. In its more than twenty-five years of activities, headquartered at the Glass House, that emblematic residence and first structure built by Lina, the institute has become ubiquitous on the national cultural scene, as was the wish of Lina and Pietro, offering the public access to relevant and little-known aspects of the country's artistic and cultural thinking and production through exhibitions, publications, lectures, and conferences.

The institute, which holds in its collection precious testimonies to the Bardis' life, is pleased to have the opportunity to contribute to the enrichment of the content of this important exhibition and its catalogue. Thus, through the perspectives of José Esparza Chong Cuy, Tomás Toledo, and Julieta González, the institute was able to reevaluate and reflect upon its own collection, consisting of thousands of drawings, photographs, documents, works, objects, and furniture that, over the years, Lina designed, created, and collected, becoming, through her architecture, a major promoter of the arts in Brazil.

TABLE OF CONTENTS

1

LINA BO BARDI'S HABITAT

2

RETHINKING THE MUSEUM

3

FROM GLASS HOUSE TO HUT

LINA BO BARDI IN SÃO PAULO, MEXICO CITY, AND CHICAGO

JULIETA GONZÁLEZ
Curator of the exhibition at
Museo Jumex, Mexico City

MADELEINE GRYNSZTEJN
Pritzker Director, Museum of
Contemporary Art Chicago—MCA

ADRIANO PEDROSA
Artistic Director, Museu de Arte de
São Paulo Assis Chateaubriand—
MASP

We are honored to present the work of designer, architect, writer, and curator Lina Bo Bardi (1914–1992), a radical thinker who formulated a new language of modernism with her unique vision. As an Italian émigré in Brazil, Bo Bardi immersed herself in the local context with the understanding that widespread modernist ideas in Europe would not translate exactly to the conditions and customs of Latin America. Bo Bardi's alternative drew less upon the promises of machines creating a universal vocabulary of forms than it did on the popular artisanal traditions that she encountered in her adopted home country of Brazil.

The intersection of high and low, of so-called popular art and fine art, is central to Bo Bardi's practice. As the architect of the Museu de Arte de São Paulo—MASP's building and as a curator of various exhibitions at the museum, Bo Bardi highlighted the work of designers and artists of so-called popular, vernacular, or outsider art alongside established canonical figures in the history of art, thus profoundly shaping cultural discourse in modern Brazil. The layout of MASP's inaugural exhibitions in 1969 is emblematic: canonical art displayed on glass easels in the second-floor gallery, *A mão do povo Brasileiro* (The Hand of the Brazilian People) on the first floor. It is with great excitement that we engage this history by re-creating the installations of Bo Bardi's most significant curatorial projects. Her editorial contributions to *Habitat*, the magazine she launched with her husband Pietro Maria Bardi, founding director of MASP, form a fulcrum in this exhibition and publication, lending the show its title.

Forward-thinking exhibitions not only celebrate the accomplishments of the finest artists and cultural practitioners, but also change the course of art history and its institutional embodiment, museums. The history of architecture at large—and of modernism in particular—has for too long been dominated by male voices, and we are delighted to shed light on the work of a pioneering woman at a scale and with the depth that it merits. We believe that contemporary audiences will benefit greatly from a deeper familiarity with Lina Bo Bardi's achievements, with the purpose of meaningfully altering the landscape of modernism and indeed the fields of architecture and design.

This publication likewise expands the understanding of Bo Bardi's life and work, in essays by leading scholars, curators, and historians of architecture and art: Beatriz Colomina and Mark Wigley, Esther da Costa Meyer, José Esparza Chong Cuy, Julieta González, Jane Hall, Antonio Risério, Tomás Toledo, and Guilherme Wisnik. This anthology of texts about Bo Bardi is accompanied by a selection of writings by Bo Bardi herself, most of which have been translated into English for the first time.

While Bo Bardi's esteemed legacy lives on in her buildings, designs, and texts that survive today, her importance to the global history of art and design has not yet been fully acknowledged internationally, and this is also one of the aims of our project. The collaboration between MASP, the Museo Jumex, and the Museum of Contemporary Art Chicago (MCA) in organizing this exhibition is therefore one of the most significant aspects of *Lina Bo Bardi: Habitat*. The three institutions are equal partners in its conception; that the exhibition is first being shown in São Paulo before traveling to Mexico City and Chicago is a reversal of the typical direction of global cultural circulation.

It is a testament to the dedication of each institution involved in this project that we are also able to undertake a large-scale exchange of works from the permanent collections of MASP, the Museo Jumex, and MCA. In each venue, key pieces from each museum's collections are presented on Bo Bardi's iconic glass easels, offering visitors the rare opportunity to experience her radical curatorial vision while appreciating treasures from museums that span the Americas. The exhibition and this publication exemplify cultural exchange in the truest sense. It is an honor to share *Lina Bo Bardi: Habitat* with our audiences in celebration of the life and legacy of a truly visionary figure—in São Paulo, in Mexico City, and in Chicago.

INTRODUCTION

JULIETA GONZÁLEZ
Curator of the exhibition at
Museo Jumex, Mexico City

JOSÉ ESPARZA CHONG CUY
Chief Curator, Storefront for Art
and Architecture, New York

TOMÁS TOLEDO
Chief Curator, MASP, São Paulo

Lina Bo Bardi: Habitat, an exhibition co-organized by the São Paulo Museum of Art (MASP), the Museum of Contemporary Art Chicago (MCA), and the Museo Jumex, Mexico City, addresses the life, work, and legacy of Italian-Brazilian architect Lina Bo Bardi (1914–1992). In addition to a review of Bo Bardi's many contributions to the fields of architecture, design, curatorship, and museum studies, this exhibition seeks to position her as a critical thinker who re-evaluated the culture of her time through the *unlearning* of knowledge and Western perspectives, a process that she undertook in Brazil and that included research trips throughout the country's Northeast—a watershed in her career.

This approach allows us to read Bo Bardi's museological and architectural practice as a means of rethinking place, human relations, community formation, modes of co-existence, and solidarity that transcended the boundaries of the traditional narrative of modern museums and architecture, expanding epistemologically by incorporating additional vocabularies and knowledges, including popular, indigenous, and Afro-Brazilian perspectives. Such a vantage also inscribes Bo Bardi within a constellation of thinkers, artists, architects, and designers who questioned modernity: from Paulo Freire and Ivan Illich, in the fields of philosophy and pedagogy, to Aldo van Eyck and Peter and Alison Smithson, of Team 10, in architecture, among others. Like those of her peers, Bo Bardi's approach required new ways of thinking and doing that would center human beings, in the process making room for other forms of knowledge and ecologies, breaking from modernity and capitalism's logic of progress and profit.

Titled *Habitat*, like the magazine she edited between 1950 and 1953 with her husband, Pietro Maria Bardi, the exhibition features a significant selection of Bo Bardi's greatest achievements in the fields of architecture, industrial design, and curatorship, as well as critical examples of her museological, editorial, and pedagogical practices and her collaborations in theater and cinema. It is informed by the recognition that the construction of a pluralistic and inclusive culture was key to her intellectual and professional development from the time of her arrival in Brazil in 1946.

The exhibition and catalogue are organized into three sections—Lina Bo Bardi's Habitat, Rethinking the Museum, and From Glass House to Hut. The first is dedicated to the presentation of her intellectual habitat, with republications of her fundamental writings, from *Habitat*'s initial texts to final reflections in her posthumously published book, *Tempos de grossura: o design no impasse* (Times of Thickness: Design at an Impasse). The second section focuses on the fields of museum studies and curatorship, which Bo Bardi explored from a position that sought new approaches to the traditional—linear, hermetic, and segmented—history of art. The section covers museum projects such as MASP, the Museum of Modern Art of Bahia, and the Museum of Popular Art (the latter two which she founded and directed); curatorial projects, including *Bahia no Ibirapuera* (Bahia in Ibirapuera), Nordeste (Northeast), *A mão do povo brasileira* (The Hand of the Brazilian People), and *Caipiras, capiaus: pau-a-pique* (Countryfolk, Rustics: Wattle-and-Daub); and exhibition designs, such as for *Cem obras-primas de Portinari* (One Hundred Portinari Masterpieces) and MASP's iconic glass easels. The final section illustrates Bo Bardi's trajectory from modern to vernacular and popular with several architectural projects, theater and set designs, and furniture designs focusing on chairs.

Each section is complemented by essays from the curators and guest authors—Luis M. Castañeda, Beatriz Colomina and Mark Wigley, Esther da Costa Meyer, Jane Hall, Adriano Pedrosa, Antonio Risério, and Guilherme Wisnik—as well as commentaries on the projects written by Guilherme Giufrida, Denis Joelson, Vanessa Mendes, Adriano Pedrosa, and Tomás Toledo.

Over the past decade, renewed interest in Bo Bardi's work has manifested in exhibitions, research, and scholarly texts. MASP has been at the forefront of many of these initiatives, and has devoted the last few years of its programming to restoring and revisiting Bo Bardi's important contributions in the field of museum studies. These projects include the reinstallation of her glass easels in MASP's picture gallery, the application of her design principles in exhibition installations, and the 2016 reenactment of *The Hand of the Brazilian People*, MASP's first temporary exhibition at its new location on Avenida Paulista in 1969.

In this context of renewed attention to Bo Bardi's work, this book and exhibition seek to present the architect's approach and achievements based on her particular mix of modern ideas and the crossovers and dialogues with the Brazilian sociocultural context, into which she dove deeply, generating from this South American *habitat* the creative environment for her unique and radical language and thought.

LINA BO BARDI'S HABITAT

BECOMING LINA BO BARDI: AN IDEOLOGICAL ODYSSEY

1. For Bo Bardi's life and oeuvre, see Zeuler R. M. de A. Lima, *Lina Bo Bardi* (New Haven: Yale University Press, 2013).

FIG. 32
Inauguration of MASP, Rua 7 de Abril, São Paulo, 1947

It was never going to be an easy journey. Lina Bo Bardi spent her life straddling fault lines between cities—Rome and Milan, São Paulo and Salvador—and countries, Italy and Brazil. Coming to grips with fast-paced social, political, and economic change, absorbing often contradictory cross-cultural currents, and seeking to achieve a coherent and creative synthesis out of such disparate experiences meant she was constantly recalibrating her approach. There were also challenges that arose from her multiple activities, including architecture, design, preservation, curatorial and editorial practices, and work for theater and film. How did she forge a unity out of so many discontinuities, and make sense of her conflicted identities—as an Italian, a Brazilian, a woman practicing in a male-dominated profession, and, after the military coup of 1964, as a leftist increasingly isolated from her former professional activities? Bo Bardi's capacity to start afresh from unanticipated premises and in difficult circumstances was impressive. And yet, an intellectual of her stature could not simply divest herself of previous intellectual baggage every time she embraced new ideas. Rather, new ideas were brought into fruitful—if sometimes strained—tension with the old. Bo Bardi's cultural capital is usually taken for granted. In fact, it was a work in progress, requiring constant reconfiguration.

In 1946, when Bo Bardi arrived in Brazil at the age of thirty-two, she had a strong architectural background from the Sapienza University of Rome (though with no built projects) and considerable editorial experience gleaned in modernist circles in Milan.[1] After an initial period in Rio de Janeiro, her husband Pietro Maria Bardi was tapped by the newspaper magnate Assis Chateaubriand to create an art museum for São Paulo, which would take form as MASP, the Museu de Arte de São Paulo. Chateaubriand was a king-maker. Trained as a lawyer, he founded a powerful network of newspapers and radio stations, and involved himself in a number of cultural and philanthropic initiatives. The couple's early years in São Paulo were spent among the politically conservative circles of the haute bourgeoisie, and they plunged into their new surroundings with enthusiasm (fig. 32).

The early MASP was a pathbreaking institution with few precedents. Bo Bardi redesigned the interiors of a preexisting modern building by French architect Jacques Pilon. Initially a modest affair occupying a single floor, it soon expanded, taking over three additional floors. Both Bardis understood that education had to be a priority, and they set about organizing a series of important shows beginning with *Exposições didáticas de história da arte* (Didactic Exhibition of the History of Art). Rejecting the distinction between ancient and modern art, their exhibition spanned centuries with numerous photographs and explanatory wall texts. MASP became a cultural and educational center where students could take courses in industrial design, drawing, sculpture, dance, art appreciation for both adults and children, fashion, and even gardening. Nevertheless, conditioned by the socioeconomic framework of São Paulo's elites, the classes reflected the city's social and ethnic fractures (fig. 33).

Bo Bardi's achievements were remarkable. By 1953, then a Brazilian citizen, she had mastered Portuguese, published in important newspapers and magazines, and made notable contributions to MASP in the form of interior design, exhibitions, and pedagogical initiatives. Nevertheless, she was aware of the dangers of exile and immigration. As she noted in 1967, moving to North America had "drained Gropius and Mies, inhibited the inventiveness of [George] Grosz, and the violence of Kurt Weill—who became a composer of saccharine film melodies."[2] Taking stock of her situation, Bo Bardi realized that her own efforts at adapting had paid off. In a striking letter to her husband, dated April 30, 1956, she wrote: "Now that the fear of no longer having roots has vanished, I feel epiphytic roots sprouting, and I think they will do just fine: I was born for this."[3]

It is important to probe Bo Bardi's early writings in Brazil to understand her extraordinary evolution from an Italian architect looking at Brazil top-down, to someone who came to see herself as part of her adoptive country. In *Habitat*, the museum's magazine launched in 1950 and initially edited by the Bardis, she found an ideal platform for her ideas. Her articles are witty, aphoristic, and biting. Some focus on preoccupations linked to her life in Italy: rationalism, furniture, housing, but she was also genuinely interested in both modern architecture in Brazil and the indigenous practices in the Amazon and the Northeast that would play such a key role in her later work. At the same time, some of these early writings are laced with a strong dose of European condescension. An essay published in 1951—sympathetic but patronizing—describes Brazil as a new country without a history that needed to be guided by Europeans: "Brazilian architecture was born as a beautiful child; we do not know why it was born beautiful, but we must now educate it, heal it, guide it, and follow its evolution."[4] Eight years after the exhibition *Brazil Builds* (1943), organized by the Museum of Modern Art (MoMA) in New York, and seven years after Niemeyer's beautiful architectural complex at Pampulha (1942–44), this assertion betrays the familiar stereotypes of the Old World faced with the complex realities of what we now call the Global South. Bo Bardi admired the astonishing headquarters of the Ministry of Education and Culture in Rio de Janeiro (1943), where her husband had organized two exhibitions, yet this appreciation coexisted with older, preconceived notions.[5] As she observed in 1956, "The Brazilian

2. Lina Bo Bardi, "Na América do Sul: após Le Corbusier, o que está acontecendo?," *Mirante das Artes*, no. 1 (January–February 1967): 10.

3. Quoted in Anna Carboncini, "Lina Bo e Pietro Maria Bardi: un'alleanza fortunata," in Alessandra Criconia, ed., *Lina Bo Bardi: Un'architettura tra Italia e Brasile* (Milan: FrancoAngeli, 2017), 108.

4. Lina Bo, "Bela criança," *Habitat*, no. 2 (January–March 1951): 3.

5. The Ministério de Educação e Saúde, or MES, now the Edifício Gustavo Capanema, was designed by Lúcio Costa, Carlos Leão, Oscar Niemeyer, Affonso Eduardo Reidy, Ernani Vasconcellos, and Jorge Machado Moreira.

FIG. 33
Figure drawing class at MASP, Rua 7 de Abril, São Paulo, 1948

architect is a young man called to battle suddenly, engaging with courage and generosity without understanding the 'mechanism' very well."[6] Bo Bardi's assessment of Brazilian modernism's penchant for formalism was often on target but could also fall short of objective appraisal.

In São Paulo, Bo Bardi produced her first nonjournalistic piece of writing: "Preliminary Contribution to the Teaching of Architectural Theory," presented to the School of Architecture in support of her candidacy for the chair of Theory of Architecture at the University of São Paulo (FAU-USP).[7] This learned but labored text, completed in 1957, was intended to demonstrate her credentials in the field. Sweeping through 2,000 years of largely Western architecture, it reveals a strong grasp of the history of architecture that Bo Bardi had received in Rome and on her own. From the great Renaissance theoreticians through those of the twentieth century—including Sebastiano Serlio, Andrea Palladio, Claude Perrault, Jacques-François Blondel, Eugène-Emmanuel Viollet-le-Duc, Geoffrey Scott, Rudolf Wittkower, and Heinrich Wölfflin—the range of citations shows an impressive literacy in historiography. As scholarship, however, the text is problematic. Foreign quotations, not always transcribed verbatim and riddled with spelling mistakes, are not always discussed in depth. Brazil, mentioned occasionally in the text, is represented mainly in a few illustrations, and appears largely as a recipient of European culture—unavoidably, given its colonial past.

Salvador

In 1958, Bo Bardi was invited by Edgard do Rêgo Santos, president of the University of Bahia, to teach a three-month course in architectural theory at the School of Fine Arts in Salvador, where she would live intermittently until 1964. In his effort to raise the cultural level of the city, Santos invited a number of notable figures known for their cutting-edge approach to music, dance, theater, film, and architecture.[8] Bo Bardi found a vibrant climate full of promise and excitement, open to experimentation—and to foreigners. At first she was able to keep up her editorial work publishing a weekly cultural page in the *Diários de Notícias* of the ubiquitous Chateaubriand: "Crônicas de arte, de historia, de costume, de cultura da vida." This required covering not only modern art and architecture, but also the cultural specificities of the Northeast.

Bo Bardi arrived full of self-confidence. In the notes from her very first lecture at the university, she argued that "the true architect can solve, when called upon, the realities of any country. If he is a genuine architect, he can reach an understanding that sometimes architects from the country

6. Lina Bo Bardi, "Lettera dal Brasile," *L'Architettura: Cronache e Storia*, no. 9 (July 1956): 186–87.

7. *Contribuição propedêutica ao ensino da teoria da arquitetura: um inédito de Lina Bo Bardi* (São Paulo: Instituto Lina Bo e P. M. Bardi, 2002). The text must have been translated by a professional; Bo Bardi never departed from her idiosyncratic Portuguese sprinkled with Italianisms.

8. For the important role of Santos, see Antonio Risério, *Avant-garde na Bahia* (São Paulo: Instituto Lina Bo e P. M. Bardi, 1995), 31–63.

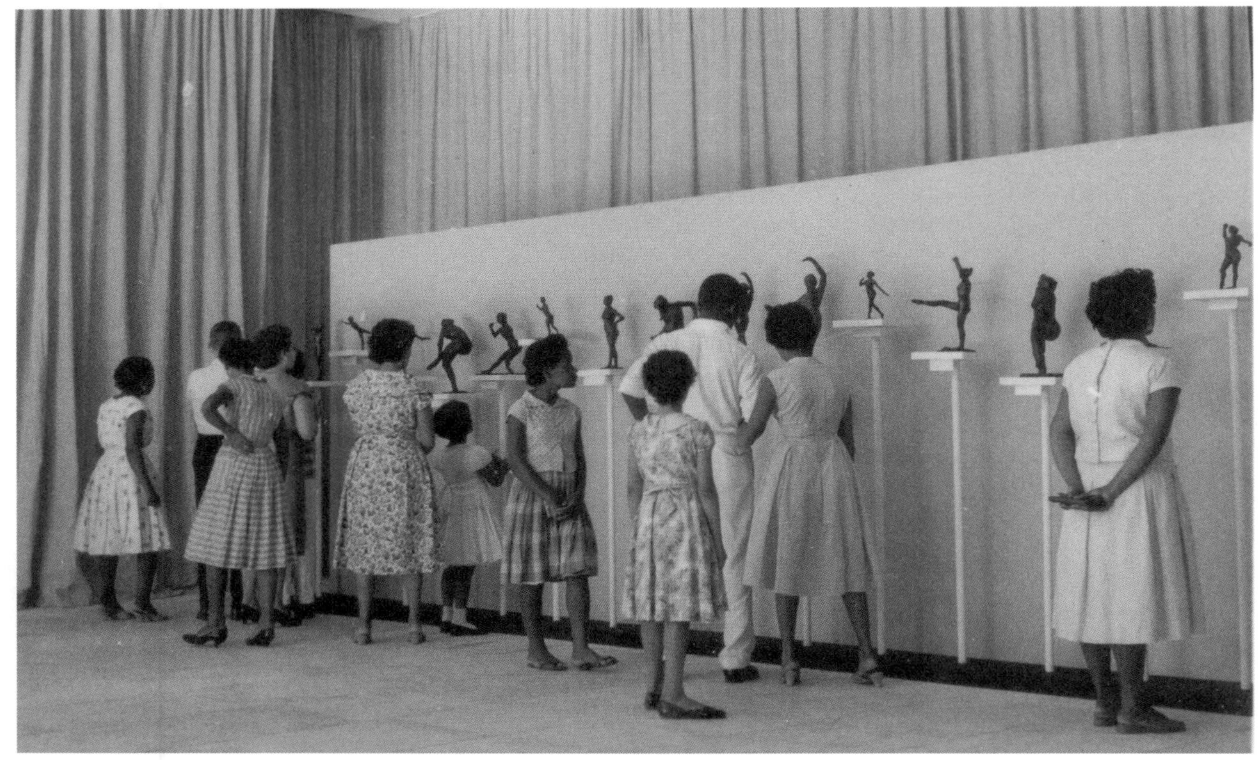

9. Lina Bo Bardi, "The Theory and Philosophy of Architecture," in Olivia de Oliveira, ed., *Lina Bo Bardi: obra construída / Built Work* (Barcelona: 2G, 2002), 213.

10. Lina Bo Bardi, "Casas ou museus?," *Diário de Notícias*, no. 5 (October 1958): 100.

11. Lina Bo Bardi, "Cinco anos entre os 'brancos,'" *Mirante das Artes*, no. 6 (November–December 1967): 1. See also Caetano Veloso, *Verdade Tropical* (São Paulo: Companhia das Letras, 1997), 59.

12. Caetano Veloso, in Aurélio Michiles' film *Lina Bo Bardi*, script by Isa Grinspum Ferraz, 1993.

in question have not been able to formulate or understand. This is the case of Le Corbusier in India."[9] Today we shy away from such universalist claims. Several first-rate Indian architects worked alongside Le Corbusier in Chandigarh; they understood the political, economic, and social situation of the Punjab better than he. Nevertheless, she realized that she had a steep learning curve ahead of her and set about taking stock of the city and its hinterland. She put down more epiphytic roots.

The experience in Salvador turned out to be transformative—an intense apprenticeship in teaching, building, directing museums, engagement in historic preservation, as well as curatorial and pedagogical activities. Bo Bardi found a freedom hitherto unknown to her, but it also forced her into unexpected situations, setting her on the path to different forms of self-discovery that prompted her to question many assumptions of her work in São Paulo. Intellectual growth paid handsome dividends particularly in 1959, when the governor of Bahia, Juracy Magalhães, invited her to direct the Museum of Modern Art of Bahia (MAM-BA), temporarily located in the foyer of the Castro Alves Theater, after being badly damaged by fire just before its inauguration in 1958.

As MAM-BA had almost no art collection, Bo Bardi saw it as a "museu-escola" that focused on education. "The modern museum," she explained in 1960, "has to be a didactic museum; has to wed conservation to the capacity to transmit the message that works must be placed in evidence, with an educational purpose."[10] Perplexed and excited by her new surroundings for which nothing had prepared her, she tried to break class-specific barriers in the museum by introducing a variety of courses at different levels, organizing unusual exhibitions, and tearing down distinctions between high art and the everyday. MAM-BA was both a continuation and a trenchant institutional critique of her work at MASP: the public she now tried to attract had to reflect Salvador's ethnic diversity (fig. 34). In the damaged auditorium, she built a small semicircular theater where she helped Martim Gonçalves, the new head of the Drama School, to stage Bertolt Brecht's *Threepenny Opera* (figs. 359–362) and Albert Camus' *Calígula*. Bo Bardi also carved out space for a small Cine Club, thanks to her collaboration with the film critic Walter da Silveira.[11] She galvanized the intellectual scene in Salvador with her interventions. In an interview, Caetano Veloso credits "dona Lina" with the renaissance of the arts in Bahia; he and his elder brothers would station themselves near the Hotel da Bahia where she stayed just to see her pass by.[12] In 1963, Bo Bardi moved MAM-BA to the Solar do Unhão, a colonial sugar mill on a spectacular waterfront location that she restored, which housed as well the Museum

FIG. 34
View of Edgar Degas' bronze ballerinas, from MASP's collection; installation design by Lina Bo Bardi, for the inauguration of the Museum of Modern Art of Bahia at its temporary location at the Castro Alves Theater, Salvador, 1960

of Popular Art that she founded to showcase artifacts from the Northeast.

It was in Salvador that Bo Bardi got to know important members of the Brazilian intelligentsia—writers, film directors, musicians, artists, and social scientists—who had fascinating backgrounds and stimulating ideas. Working with so many intellectuals from different fields—the atonal composer Hans-Joachim Koellreutter, the choreographer Yanka Rudzka, the musician and sculptor Walter Smetak, the young Glauber Rocha, who launched Cinema Novo—freed Bo Bardi from the overbearing shadow of Chateaubriand's tutelage (fig. 35). She became more daring, leaving her comfort zone in the cultures of modernism, familiar since her youth in Italy and her work in São Paulo, to embrace the historical avant-gardes. Her lectures and articles were now peppered with names such as Brecht, Vladimir Mayakovsky, Kurt Weill, Antonin Artaud, Alfred Jarry, Erwin Piscator, and Antonio Gramsci. Bo Bardi also met and befriended major anthropologists such as Pierre Verger and Roger Bastide, two Frenchmen who specialized in Afro-Brazilian culture, as well as Vivaldo da Costa Lima, among others. She got to know Darcy Ribeiro, who worked on indigenous culture, and was acquainted with Gilberto Freyre's work on slavery.[13] Anthropology challenged her attitude to form, materiality, and the body. It gave her an intellectual armature that prepared her for a deeper engagement with two interlocking cultures that would have an indelible impact on her built and written work: Africa and the Northeast.

The city's rich Afrocentric cultures were a revelation that would lead her to study, and later exhibit, African and Afro-Brazilian art, in both Salvador and São Paulo. "I believe that Brazil is not part of the West," she declared excitedly. "It is Africa!"[14] Her contribution to the city was all the more notable since Salvador's white elites downplayed the significance of the city's African heritage.[15] And there was the Northeast with its unique culture, patriarchal structure, and endemic environmental problems. Bo Bardi's eagerness to learn took her to the parched, impoverished hinterlands of Polígono das Secas (Polygon of Drought), to poverty-stricken villages haunted by hunger but "rich in fantasy," as she later observed.[16] Social abstractions—the *sertão* (backlands), the Nordestinos, and their way of life—assumed corporeality. No Brazilian architect of her stature had anything comparable to her deep exposure to the Northeast, or her commitment to understand and appreciate it.

13. Several books by Claude Lévi-Strauss were found in the Glass House. Renato Anelli, "Annotazioni sulla formazione intellettuale di Lina Bo Bardi," in Criconia, ed., *Lina Bo Bardi*, 130.

14. Lina Bo Bardi, quoted in Marcelo Carvalho Ferraz, ed., *Lina Bo Bardi* (São Paulo: Instituto Lina Bo e P.M. Bardi, 1996), 203.

15. Risério, *Avant-garde na Bahia*, 54–55.

16. Lina Bo Bardi, "Terapia intensiva," in Silvana Rubino and Marina Grinover, eds., *Lina por escrito: textos escolhidos de Lina Bo Bardi, 1943–1991* (São Paulo: Cosac Naify, 2009), 159.

FIG. 35
Filming of *Tocaia no asfalto* (Ambush on the Asphalt), directed by Roberto Pires, at the Museum of Modern Art of Bahia, Castro Alves Theater, Salvador, 1961

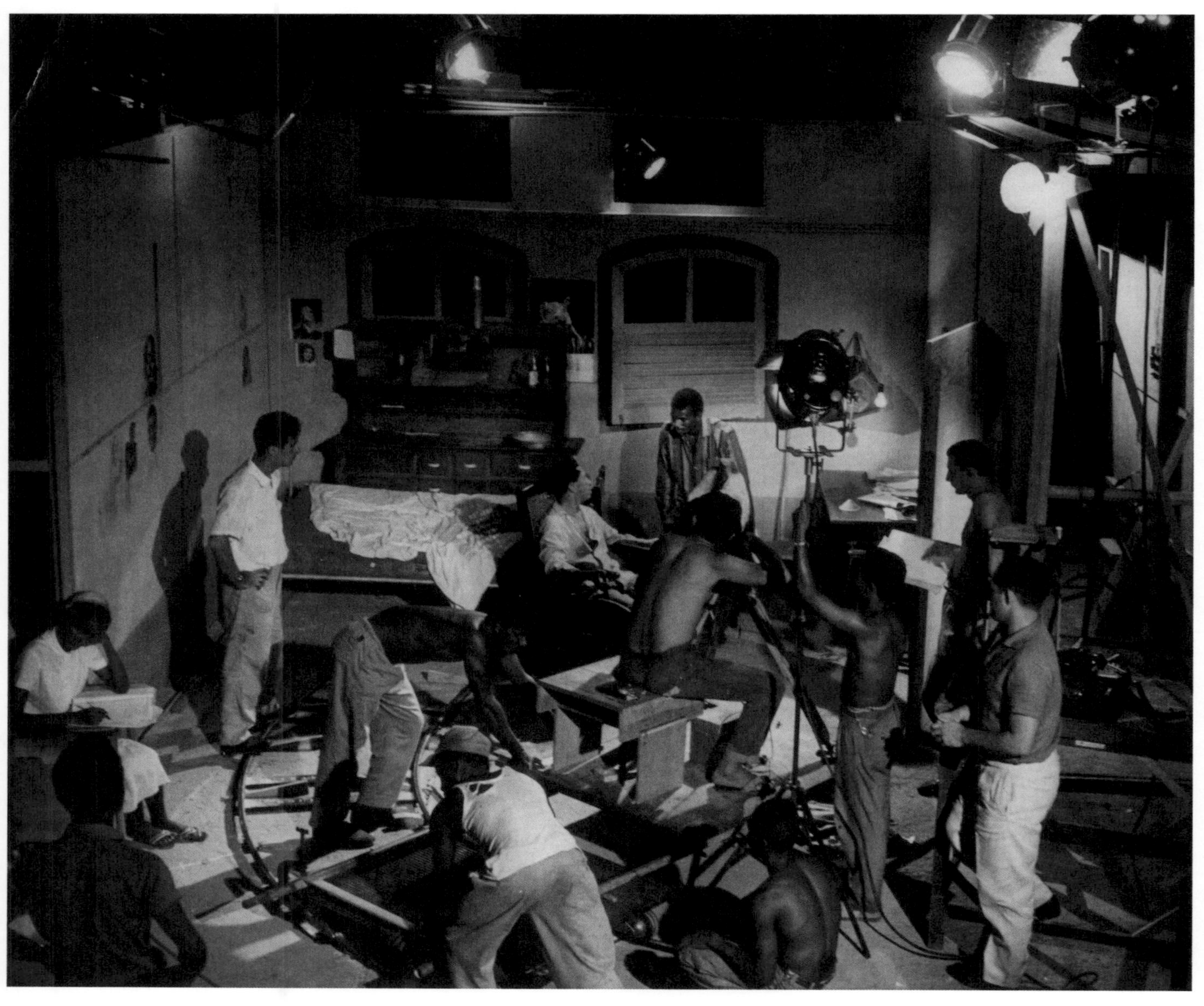

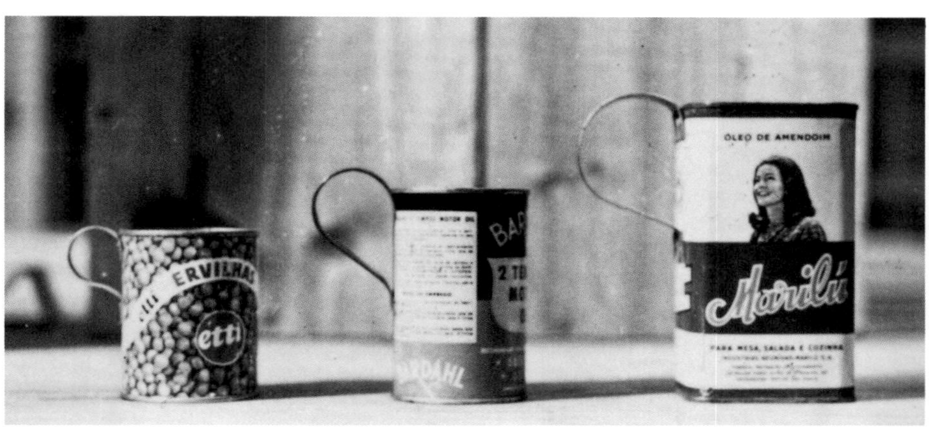

FIG. 36
Mugs made from oil cans, at the Feira de Santana (Santana Market), Bahia, shown in the exhibition *The Hand of the Brazilian People*, MASP, São Paulo, 1969

Design

Bo Bardi's encounter with the Northeast was a long epiphany that triggered a reevaluation of her architectural culture, casting a different perspective on her postwar experiences in Milan concerning popular housing, design, and material culture, and on her writings in *Habitat*. In the vernacular artifacts found along dusty roads and villages, she discovered something vital that had not been coopted by administered culture: not a lesser modernity, but a lean, imaginative, and minimalist approach, responsive to the environment, sustainable, and reliant on salvaged materials (fig. 36). Confrontation with the handicraft of disenfranchised populations revealed an *Existenzminimum* very different from that of middle-class European architects. These nonauratic objects, made with leftover scraps—tin, wood, cardboard, string—contained the germ of a new theory of design that led her to question the presumed universality of International Style dogma. Its apparent formal autonomy, she realized, hid partisan, power-charged relations and political positions. "No one can save themselves by *design*," she wrote movingly in 1990. "Can a beautiful glass save us from thirst? Can a very beautiful dish or a beautiful plate save us from hunger, misery, illness, and unemployment?"[17] But the old world still struggled with the new, and Bo Bardi often implied that Brazil's culture was still inchoate. Finding it, she argued in 1961, required seeking "wearily amid the *meager* inheritance of a new and passionately cherished land, the roots of *a culture as yet unformed*."[18] There was a lot to un-learn.

The years in Salvador radicalized Bo Bardi culturally and politically.[19] Armed with her newfound ethnographic sensibility, and refusing to ignore use value, a common casualty in art museums, Bo Bardi learned to reject the aestheticization of poverty, which treated popular artifacts as art and ignored the misery that helped shape them: "Ex-votos are presented as useful objects and not as 'sculptures,'" she wrote; they were not to be judged with the "means of art criticism."[20] Mindful of the exaltation of the countryside by Fascist Italy's rabid, antimodernist forces, she was careful not to idealize rural life. On the other hand, she shared with her times an essentialist and romanticized view of the *Povo*, the People, a word she often used in the upper case: "A Nation based on the culture of the People, is a Nation of enormous possibilities."[21] Bo Bardi's concept of the simple man of the people, Silvana Rubino pointed out, "was also an intellectual and political construction of Lina, the Bardi couple, and of *Habitat*."[22]

17. Lina Bo Bardi, "Uma aula de arquitetura," *Revista Projecto*, no. 133 (1990): 107. Emphasis hers.

18. Lina Bo Bardi, *Brennand cerâmica*, exh. cat. (Salvador: Museu de Arte Moderna da Bahia, 1961). Italics mine.

19. Alessandra Criconia, "Un'architetta romana in Brasile," in Criconia, ed., *Lina Bo Bardi*, 42.

20. Lina Bo Bardi, "A arte popular nunca é kitsch," in Marcelo Suzuki, ed., *Tempos de grossura: o design no impasse* (São Paulo: Instituto Lino Bo e P. M. Bardi, 1994), 33.

21. Lina Bo Bardi, "Discurso sobre a significação da palavra artesanato," in Suzuki, ed., *Tempos de grossura*, 16.

22. Silvana Rubino, "A escrita de uma arquiteta," in Rubino and Grinover, eds., *Lina por escrito*, 34.

The Coup

23. Lina Bo Bardi, "Uma aula de arquitetura," 105, and "Currículo literário," in Ferraz, ed., *Lina Bo Bardi*, 11.

The military coup of 1964 meant something very different to the Bardis than it did to Brazilians. Although it bore little resemblance to Italian Fascism of the 1920s and 1930s, it brought up a chapter of their lives they thought had been closed forever. In Salvador, Edgard Santos had already been forced out of the university in 1962, followed by some of his protégés. Faced with mounting opposition, Bo Bardi resigned her position as head of MAM-BA. Back in São Paulo, she found herself in a difficult situation. Her social and political alignments had changed; the Bo Bardi who finished MASP in 1968 was not the same as the one who started it. And yet, to build, restore, and manage museums, one needed the backing of cultural and political power. Both Bardis were able to achieve most of their goals thanks to their relations with financial and political elites, rubbing elbows with right-wing industrialists such as Chateaubriand and Matarazzo, politicians like Magalhães, Adhemar de Barros, and Carlos Lacerda, or powerful philanthropists with a conservative political agenda like Nelson Rockefeller. All of them supported the coup that brought the generals to power. Although Bo Bardi's contact with them gradually ended, the experience in the Northeast opened up a growing rift between her past and her present. Her contradictions and compromises, which she was far too intelligent to ignore, weighed on her. Whereas some of her friends in Italy had been anti-Fascist, others, including family members and her husband, had supported the regime. As her ideological leanings moved further left, she reinvented her past to make it square with present beliefs, claiming, with a penchant for self-dramatization, to have been a member of the armed resistance in Italy, and to have been persecuted by the Gestapo.[23]

After 1968, architectural commissions dried up until the mid-1970s. Bo Bardi poured her creativity into other fields—film, theater, and exhibitions at MASP—working with young collaborators. She traveled the world, broadening her horizons. A decade and a half before her death, she was finally able to bring together her praxis and political beliefs, working for impoverished Catholic communities in the interior of São Paulo and Minas Gerais (fig. 37). Her masterpiece, SESC Pompeia (1977–86), and the late work in the historic center of Salvador (1986–90), are a visionary testament to the lessons of a lifetime, wedding the raw immediacy and unrefined materials encountered in the Northeast to her experience as an architect on the cusp of her profession.

In the end, there was no seamless synthesis, no way of dissolving European-ness into a newfound Brazilian identity. Bo Bardi

FIG. 37
Lina Bo Bardi with children at the construction of the Church of Espírito Santo do Cerrado, Uberlândia, Minas Gerais, 1981

remained a hyphenated identity, attached to the dialectics of creative friction (and fiction) between Italy and Brazil, the Salvador of her heart and her home in São Paulo. It was just this unresolved dualism that allowed her to soar above particularisms, to transcend critical regionalism, and to be both Italian and Brazilian, a sophisticated modernist profoundly responsive to the needs and challenges of the disenfranchised of her chosen country.

Esther da Costa Meyer is professor emerita in the history of architecture at Princeton University. She has published countless articles exploring the work of architects such as Lilly Reich, Charlotte Perriand, and Lina Bo Bardi. Her recent curatorial projects include exhibitions of Frank Gehry's drawings and the work of Pierre Chareau.

A IS FOR ANXIETY: LINA BO'S WAR

LA BOMBA ATOMICA

pone nuovi problemi di cultura

Ci puoi far nulla?

FOSSIMO ALMENO DEI PAZZI

FIG. 39
Article by Bruno Zevi in *A: Attualità Architettura Abitazione Arte*, no. 1, February 1946

Amputated Life

"A is for Anxiety," wrote Lina Bo about the biweekly magazine *A* that she edited with Carlo Pagani and Bruno Zevi between February and June of 1946.[1] *A* was also for Atomic Bomb. In the first issue, a close-up photograph of a shocked and frightened child's face is juxtaposed with images of the atomic bomb exploding in Hiroshima and the first atomic test in the Jornada del Muerto desert of New Mexico (fig. 39). The accompanying text by Zevi, "La bomba atomica pone nuovi problemi di cultura" (The Atomic Bomb Poses New Cultural Problems), suggests that the new madness of humanity takes the form of collective suicide, when the whole of humanity could be incinerated in an hour.[2] The issue documented the wartime decimation of Italy. It was illustrated with images from Bo's 1945 tour of the south with her professional and once personal partner Pagani and photographer Federico Patellani (fig. 38). The reportage, commissioned by the antifascist newspaper *Milano Sera* a few days after the end of the war,[3] was originally meant to cover housing conditions. The newspaper declined to publish their ultimate record of devastation. Traveling along ruined roads, encountering unexploded bombs, confronted by the retreating US Army, and at a certain point surrounded by soldiers and tanks, Bo feared for her life.[4] Destruction and the housing condition had become the same thing. The ruins were now a frightening form of housing.

The images in *A*, many by Patellani, reflect the cataclysmic environment in which the magazine was conceived: minefields, denuded trees and landscapes, shelled buildings, bomb shelters, improvised war cemeteries with row upon row of simple crosses, provisional homes in caves, completely furnished bedrooms without roofs, children playing in shacks that resembled collages of wreckage, and portraits of desperately vulnerable yet dignified people. On the cover of the third issue (March 15, 1946), the amputated fingers of the hand of a Bernini statue, apparently vandalized by soldiers, polemically represent the four *A*'s of the magazine's subtitle: *Attualità Architettura Abitazione Arte* (News, Architecture, Home, Art; fig. 40). But in the context of the immediate postwar years, it also evoked the countless amputated hands of soldiers and citizens. The new starting point for the architect would be the body and brain violated by war. The magazine is above all about reconstruction, beginning with the collective reconstruction of the human, as the cover of the first issue announces:

We have to start anew, from the letter *A*, to generate a happy life for everyone. We propose to create in every man and every

1. *A* was subtitled *Attualità Architettura Abitazione Arte* (News, Architecture, Home, Art) for the first six issues, and *Cultura della Vita* (Culture of Life) for the last three. The magazine was published by the editorial house Domus and closed after the ninth issue.

2. Bruno Zevi, "La bomba atomica pone nuovi problemi de cultura," *A: Attualità Architettura Abitazione Arte*, no. 1 (February 1946): 4.

3. Gabriella Cianciolo Consentino, "Early Years and Wartime," in Andres Lepik and Vera Simone Bader, eds., *Lina Bo Bardi 100: Brazil's Alternative Path to Modernism* (Munich: Hatje Cantz, 2014), 58.

4. Olivia de Oliveira, "Interview with Lina Bo Bardi," in *Lina Bo Bardi: obra construida / Built Work* (Barcelona: 2G, 2002), 236.

FIG. 38
Lina Bo Bardi in Milan, days after the end of World War II, May 1945

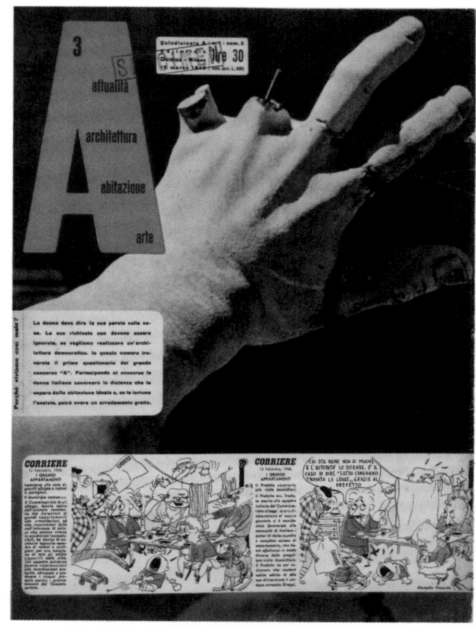

FIG. 40
Cover of *A: Attualità Architettura Abitazione Arte*, no. 3, March 15, 1946, showing the amputated fingers of the hand of a Bernini statue, apparently vandalized by soldiers

woman the consciousness of that which is the house, the city; it is necessary to make known to everyone the problems of reconstruction so that everyone—not only the technicians—can collaborate in the process.[5]

A was itself a product of war. While the first issue appeared in February 1946, the magazine had been prepared in secrecy, even mocked-up, two years before, awaiting the right moment, according to a letter sent by Lina Bo to Zevi on July 6, 1945, when she was trying to convince him to join her and Pagani on the project.[6] Zevi eventually joined as the "American correspondent,"[7] and many of the magazine's articles and images present optimistic American-based ideas for domestic design and furniture—symptomatically accompanied by advertisements for Italian sparkling wine. Bo wanted *A* to be optimistic and found American postwar attitudes to be both rational and uplifting. But this urgent desire for optimism was itself a child of the war.

Bo had lived through periods of intense bombardment in Milan. Mussolini entered the war on June 10, 1940, a month or so after her arrival in Milan, and the city was bombed ten times between then and December—a time "when nothing was built, only destroyed," in Bo's words.[8] In 1943, Milan was again the target of air bombardments. Bo described the city in flames, crumbling buildings, and the terror of constantly running to bomb shelters: "Years that should have been ones of sunshine, blue skies, and happiness, I spent underground, running and taking shelter from bombs and machine guns."[9] On the morning of August 13, the building where Bo and Pagani had their office on Via Gesù was completely demolished, burying their work in the rubble.

The war made Bo anxious. How could it not? And yet this seems to have baffled some of her closest colleagues, including Pagani, who was deployed to Corsica in 1943 and injured in a torpedo attack that sank his ship. He nevertheless expressed his frustration with Bo's "capricious" and erratic behavior while in charge of the office and the magazine *Lo Stile* that they had been co-editing along with all the other magazines that the duo were working on and contributing articles and designs to—including *Domus*, *Quaderni di Domus*, *Tempo*, *Grazia*, *Vetrina e Negozi*, *Bellezza*, and *Cordelia*. "The tired goddess," Valentino Bompiani, the influential Milan publisher, said of Bo.[10] A goddess then, a powerful figure, a force in a hypermasculine world now threatened by the savagery of war. She was overwhelmed with anxiety, as were so many soldiers and citizens, including countless artists and intellectuals. Should we count this against them?

5. *A: Attualità Architettura Abitazione Arte*, no. 1 (February 1946): cover text. Cited in Marcelo Carvalho Ferraz, ed., *Lina Bo Bardi*, 5th ed. (São Paulo: Instituto Lina Bo e P. M. Bardi, 2018), 30.

6. Letter from Lina Bo to Bruno Zevi, July 6, 1945, archives of the Bruno Zevi Foundation, Rome. We are grateful to Silvia Perea for kindly providing a copy of this letter.

7. See Silvia Perea, "Revista *A*: destrucción y creación en cuatro movimientos," in *Las revistas de arquitectura (1900–1975): crónicas, manifiestos, propaganda: actas preliminares, Pamplona, 3/4 de mayo de 2012* (Pamplona: T6 Ediciones, 2012), 247–54.

8. *Lina Bo Bardi*, directed by Aurélio Michiles, script by Isa Grinspum Ferraz (São Paulo: Museu de Arte de São Paulo, 1993), video, cited in Zeuler R. M. de A. Lima, *Lina Bo Bardi* (New Haven: Yale University Press, 2013), 20.

9. Lina Bo Bardi, "Currículo literário," in Marcelo Carvalho Ferraz, ed., *Lina Bo Bardi* (São Paulo: Instituto Lina Bo e P. M. Bardi, 1993), 11. For Bo Bardi in Milan, see Francesco Tentori, "Una lettera da San Paolo," in Alessandra Criconia, ed., *Lina Bo Bardi: Un'architettura tra Italia e Brasile* (Milan: FrancoAngeli, 2017), 118.

10. Ibid.

Achillina Bo had been an anxious child growing up in Rome, distressed by Rome itself, made uneasy by its damaged beauty, the beauty of its damage: "As a kid I was afraid of all the beauty in Rome and I asked myself, 'Why is everything in ruins?'"[11] All her life, she was obsessed with ruins. Ruins of past civilization, ruins of war, ruins of earthquakes . . . She claimed to have lived through an earthquake when she was still inside her mother: "Fifteen days before my birth, I experienced the earthquake of Avezzano in my mother's womb."[12] She was actually five weeks old when the earthquake occurred in January 1915. Does that change anything? The inaccuracy is repeatedly pointed out in the scholarship about Bo, which, strangely enough, often resembles a police interrogation. Do we ask the same questions of our male architects, who all romanticize their own histories as part of their self-construction, part of the work itself? It is as if poetry is illegal, but if it is, why talk about her work at all?

The association of earthquake and womb is actually what is interesting and takes us to the truth of Bo, not some nervous accounting by contemporary critics. It deepens the emotional and intellectual position. Earthquake as birth. Destruction as a beginning. Bo described what she liked most about Rio de Janeiro when arriving in 1947: "I felt I was in an unimaginable country where everything was possible. I felt happy, and Rio had no ruins."[13] Brazil was her *A*, her new starting point. The Bo of Brazil was born out of the anxiety of a ruined Europe.

A is also for the anxiety that Bo provokes in others. In older male colleagues, for example, who were in love with her but unable to ultimately possess her. They write to her with a combination of deep affection, admiration, and frustration. Gio Ponti, for example, writes about "our life full of nuances, delicacy, and tenderness" and of "missing her presence and lamenting her silence."[14] Marcello Piacentini, her former professor at Sapienza University in Rome, wrote of the "deep and physically intimate friendship" they had when they reconnected and about leaving their feelings "behind veils" as he anticipated "doing great things together."[15] But Bo always remained her own person, which was a big part of the attraction in the first place.

Likewise, for critics today, Bo is all too attractive but ultimately impossible to possess. They anxiously scrutinize the archives, questioning everything she said. She presented a paper at the first national conference on reconstruction in Milan, organized in December 1945 by Ernesto Rogers, for example,[16] about which a historian felt the need to say that "the full authorship of her presentation is unclear."[17] Is there ever evidence of that? Isn't everything ultimately collaborative, including the work of critics? Do we ask the same questions of the rest of the speakers? And who was supposed to have worked with her? And would that have in any way lessened her voice? Especially as she so often insisted on a "collaborative" model, was herself so long neglected, and argued against signing work, preferring the idea of anonymous production by a "commune," as she wrote to Zevi in her letter of July 6, 1945, about the magazine *A*.[18] Contemporary critics also downplay her role in the projects and magazines on which she worked. Conversely, they accept at face value whatever Pagani, her ex-partner and jilted lover, said to minimize Bo's role and expand his own.[19] No doubt, he was a crucial partner to Bo as they motivated each other to elevate their work, as is the secret norm in architecture. It is also the norm to suppress the work of women, so no wonder there was little credit at the time and that, still today, any chance to reduce her contribution is taken.[20]

During the six years that Bo studied architecture, only six women graduated alongside 250 men.[21] Bo's grade of 106 out of 110 was, as Giorgio Ciucci points out, very good, especially given the way women were treated.[22] Writer after writer feels the need to point out today that Bo misrepresented her grade as 108 but "forget" to mention that Pagani's grade was lower than Bo's. Skepticism was even raised as to whether she really participated in the M.S.A. (Movimento di Studi per L'Architettura) in 1944, until archival documents were unearthed that proved she was actually one of the eighteen signers of the group's founding constitution. Likewise, some doubt her

11. Oliveira, "Interview with Lina Bo Bardi," 230.

12. Tentori, "Una lettera da San Paolo," 117.

13. Lina Bo, handwritten note, ca. 1990, ILBPMB. Quoted in Lima, *Lina Bo Bardi*, 38.

14. Quoted in Lima, *Lina Bo Bardi*, 22.

15. Letter from Marcello Piacentini to Lina Bo, October 18, 1942, ILBPMB. Cited in Lima, *Lina Bo Bardi*, 23–24.

16. Lina Bo, "La propaganda per la ricostruzione," lecture published in *Rassegna dal primo convegno nazionale per la ricostruzione* (Milan) (December 1945), 35–38.

17. Lima, *Lina Bo Bardi*, 28.

18. "The magazine should not be the monopoly of the directors . . . there are no 'directors,' only a committee." Letter from Lina Bo to Bruno Zevi, July 6, 1945.

19. In a 1998 interview, Pagani refuted some facts in the autobiographical "literary curriculum" that Lina Bo prepared based on her 1957 curriculum vitae for the catalogue of the first retrospective exhibition of her work that was presented in 1993, a year after her death. Carlo Pagani, "Considerazioni sul *Curriculum Letterario* di Lina Bo Bardi e altri ricordi," in Criconia, ed., *Lina Bo Bardi*, 93–103. Bo ended her personal relationship with Pagani in December 1942, but they continued to work together professionally until 1946. Pagani describes Bo as a very good and intelligent partner with an excellent drawing and writing ability, but he systematically credits himself with all the ideas and leadership role in design, publication, and political activity, even to the extent of claiming that Bo was not involved in projects in which she clearly was. He, for example, takes sole credit for the concept of the magazine *A*, all the production, and the involvement of Zevi. Yet the records show Bo working on the original idea and mockups, and in direct correspondence with Zevi, for instance, penning a very detailed personal and strategic letter referring to their previous meetings. While Bo's story is repeatedly questioned, Pagani's account is symptomatically never even treated as a story.

participation in the resistance, even in texts that also note that the meetings were held at her home.[23] Suspicions are mechanically repeated by others in essay after essay, assuming the force of law. The effect is always to push Bo away from the language of polemics and politics, coded as masculine, toward the language of visual seduction, coded as feminine—and even to push her away from architecture, toward art. The celebration of Lina Bo nervously and defensively redesigns and diminishes her.

Why does Bo make everyone so anxious? In a watercolor self-portrait as an adolescent sitting astride a metal garden chair, a masculine pose common in Mediterranean countries, she wears a delicate, striped dress, pulled up by her posture, her exposed legs swinging out (fig. 41). Short hair, a hint of lipstick, thick horizontal eyebrows. She looks directly at us, focused, knowing. Her arms are crossed over the back of the chair, building a kind of defense. This is Lina, strong and seductive, masculine and feminine, inviting yet distancing.

Fear and defiance are impossible to separate. Bo builds courage out of fear. On the one hand, "I was so frightened from being born, I decided never to have children."[24] On the other hand, "I never wanted to be young. What I really wanted was to have a History. At the age of twenty-five, I wanted to write my memoirs, but I didn't have the materials."[25] She constructed herself retroactively in advance. She imagined writing about that which was yet to happen, and in that way made it happen. She had just graduated from architecture school in Rome, and like so many decisive figures, set about producing work in order to make a narrative—work that is worth telling stories about, work that is itself a story, intimately connected with her personal life. All architects tell stories. The architect *is* a storyteller. In her case, there is a confusion of the deeply personal and the highly public media in which stories are told. In fact, Bo radically sees architecture "not as built work, but as possible means to be and to face situations."[26]

It began with her move to Milan and the traumas of wartime, during which "one year corresponds to fifty years," in her words.[27] Suddenly there was too much to tell, new levels of anxiety and the need to keep the ideas and the body moving. It is with perceptiveness and tenderness that Zevi's reflective essay on Bo is titled "Lina Bo Bardi: An Architect on an Anxious Journey."[28] Anxiety produces movement. From Rome to Milan, back to Rome and to Rio, then São Paulo, Salvador de Bahia, and back to São Paulo. And war can never be left behind. It is hard not to see the irregular, brutal holes that Bo punches through the thick walls of Sesc Pompeia as poignant belated echoes of the traumatized, wounded buildings of war in Italy—the return of the repressed.

Horizontal Theory

In the end, Lina Bo wrote, edited, illustrated, designed, and built for forty-two seemingly breathless years after graduating from architecture school in November 1939 after her first move to Milan. Her work ranged widely across furniture, interiors, buildings, exhibitions, landscapes, urban planning, theater, film, jewelry, and clothing in a kaleidoscopic array of unique and compelling projects—all of which produce a kind of barely veiled jealousy in the field, even in books and exhibitions that ostensibly celebrate the work. Which is not necessarily a negative thing, in the sense that the strongest work challenges even its admirers. Conversely, it is difficult to be interested in any artist whose work provokes unhesitating praise. Bo's work needs to be celebrated for interrupting the way we typically write and think about architecture. To simply absorb her into the pantheon of twentieth-century "masters" or as an icon of Brazilian, feminist, Marxist, transnational, or surrealist counter-hegemony—all of which she is—would be to constrain the work yet again. The strength of Bo's work is precisely the way it irritates complacencies about architecture—its definition, history, modes of production, and reception.

Anyway, Bo's work is not simply waiting to be read and patronized one more time. She wrote extensively on what her work was trying to do, how and why decisions were made, what it means to be treated

20. See, for example, Massimo Martignone in Margherita Guccione, ed., *Lina Bo Bardi in Italia* (Rome: Fondazione Maxxi, 2015), 63–64, where he refers to Pagani's counter-chronology as "elegant" before remarkably and inexcusably asserting: "It is my opinion that the layout, the editorial choices, the texts, the entire written portions, were the work of Pagani, while Lina was responsible for the graphics."

21. Rossana Battistacci, "Achillina Bo nella Regia Scuola Superiore di Architettura di Roma," in Criconia, ed., *Lina Bo Bardi*, 153.

22. Giorgio Ciucci, "Lina Bo 1939–1946," in Criconia, ed., *Lina Bo Bardi*, 184.

23. The nature of Bo's participation is indeed unclear, as is repeatedly pointed out—with some recent speculations by scholars that her main role beyond hosting secret meetings was transporting people and messages between cities—but the point here is simply that Bo only claimed to have joined the resistance associated with the clandestine Communist Party. As with so many others around her, her political associations during the time were evolving and complex—especially given her relationships with figures unambiguously on the right like Piacentini and Bardi. If she became increasingly radicalized in Brazil, the seeds of that radicalization were already there in that moment during the war in Milan—which is precisely what she was saying.

24. Lina Bo Bardi, interview with Fábio Malavoglia, Centro Cultural São Paulo, March 1991, ILBPMB. Quoted in Lima, *Lina Bo Bardi*, 6.

25. Bo Bardi, "Currículo literário," 9.

26. Lina Bo Bardi, "Arquitetura como movimiento," lecture notes, School of Dance, Salvador, August 1958, ILBPMB. Quoted in Lima, *Lina Bo Bardi*, 4.

27. Bo Bardi, "Currículo literário," 10.

28. Bruno Zevi, "Lina Bo Bardi: un architetto in transito ansioso," *Caramelo*, no. 4 (1992): 80–84.

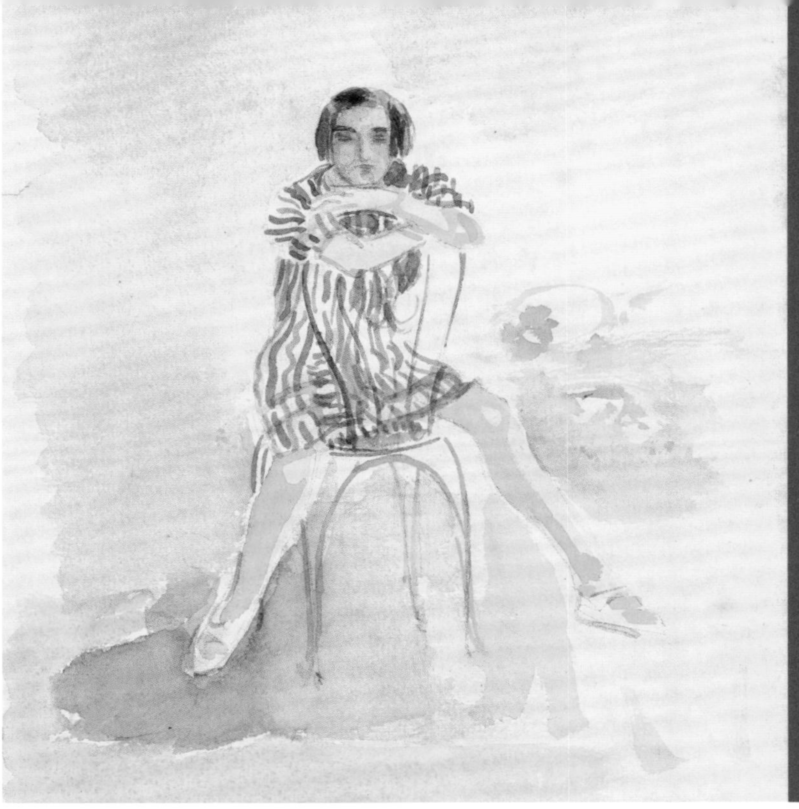

FIG. 41
Lina Bo Bardi, *Untitled (Self-Portrait)*, 1933. Watercolor and graphite on card stock, 28 x 19 cm. Collection of the Instituto Bardi/Casa de Vidro, São Paulo

as a "modern," a "Brazilian," or a "woman" architect (or not), what narratives about contemporary architecture were liberations or constraints, and so on. And she was equally articulate about the work of her colleagues. One of the unique qualities of her work was the care dedicated to that of others, and their reception by the institutional forces in the field. She was especially scathing about the patronizations of the critics and institutions of the north:

With the confidence that comes naturally to the rich, well educated, and handsome, C. Ray Smith, *associate editor* (Features and Interior Design) of the important U.S. [journal] *Progressive Architecture*, presents a panorama of architecture in South America. . . . [He] paternalistically advises South American architects not to copy the "international industrialized" architecture of the developed world but to find inspiration in Indian housing structures, in "ranchitos" and the "favelas" of the poor, befitting of underdeveloped architects operating on an underdeveloped continent . . . Acting under a misconception (we prefer not to think bad faith) . . . the author broadcasts his conviction that the true architecture is North American, and based on a system of industrial mass production to which young Latin American architects do not "yet" have access, on account of their own and their nations' underdevelopment.[29]

Bo was herself a communicator, not only in the sense of guiding an almost continuous stream of magazines and exhibitions, but also through her own conviction that architecture itself is a medium of communication, a "mass architecture" for the age in which "mass media" is treated as a "natural phenomenon."[30] Writing was very much part of her practice. Even if we foolishly put aside her more than 120 co-authored texts, thirty or so co-edited magazine issues, and twelve independently edited magazine issues, all before leaving Italy,[31] she ultimately published a huge number of independent articles in a variety of contexts for different audiences—refusing any simple line between architecture and dance, film, ornament, technology, stones, insects, window displays, animals, space travel, festivals, rituals, and so on. The writings have exactly the kind of expansive breadth one associates with polemical architects like Alison and Peter Smithson, Le Corbusier, Hermann Muthesius, and Adolf Loos. Furthermore, her diverse explorations are interlocked and can be thought of as a single extended project—the invention of Bo that invented Bo.

Perhaps the greatest anxiety Bo produced came precisely from the fact that she was such a self-conscious theorist. She read theory, taught theory, and even theorized the role of theory throughout her career.

29. Lina Bo Bardi, "Na América do Sul: após Le Corbusier, o que está acontecendo?" (1967), in Silvana Rubino and Marina Grinover, eds., *Lina por escrito: textos escolhidos de Lina Bo Bardi, 1943–1991* (São Paulo: Cosac Naify, 2009), 118–22.

30. Ibid.

31. The fact that Pagani was the one officially listed as editor of the thirty-one issues of *Lo Stile* magazine from 1941 through 1943 is not convincing evidence of his leadership of the magazine that was produced in their joint studio space, but more likely a reflection of the routine bias in who gets credit in the field. Bo was the solo editor of all the 1944 issues of *Domus* while Pagani was doing military service, and they co-edited the first five substantial issues of the new publication *Quaderni di Domus* in 1945. Bo then co-edited *A* with Pagani and Zevi in 1946 up to the ninth issue, when the magazine folded.

She wrote her most substantial publication, *Preliminary Contribution to the Teaching of Architectural Theory* (fig. 42), in 1957 to enter a competition for the first chaired professorship in "architectural theory" at the University of São Paulo, where she had already been teaching.[32] It is a remarkable thesis-book, grafting analyses of countless historical texts of architectural theory and projects from ancient to contemporary, while expanding the scope to include objects of everyday life and recent newspaper reports as it quietly but steadily builds up a Gramscian politics of architecture—with even Karl Marx, Friedrich Engels, György Lukács, and Antonio Gramsci included on the reading list of the proposed syllabus. Every page is filled with subtle and precise observations about the "practice" of architectural theory and its complex relationships to education and professional practice.

The argument is rigorous and self-aware, starting with a lengthy footnote that cannily rejects any expectation that she should begin by "theoretically" defining "theory"—since the definition would only remain within a vicious circle of philosophy unable to connect with professional practice and historical life—but then she goes on to elaborate a provisional argument about the status of theory as a practice in its own right, concluding with the thought that no permanently valid theory of architecture exists. Bo insists that specific theories only take their value from history and are surpassed by history.[33] Very few, if any, twentieth-century architects wrote at this level. The book is very much academic, in the best sense, in the precision of citations, commentary, criticism, range of sources and tone, yet it steadily undoes so many of the binary oppositions organizing traditional thinking in the field—theory/practice, history/modern, engineer/architect, science/art, inside/outside, architecture/decoration, artisanship/industrial design, etc.—in its argument for a resolutely anti-hierarchical horizontal view that finally devotes architecture to the always urgent question of everyday life and social justice. The 227 accompanying images, borrowed from classical treatises, sketchbooks, architectural monographs, art, archaeology, anthropology, engineering, commercial catalogues, popular magazines, and newspaper clippings, are not illustrations of the text, but parallel arguments in their own right that work through clusters of images assembled like mini-exhibitions that continuously punctuate the text through to the last footnotes. The dedication to horizontal politics is discretely evident throughout, as communicated by Bo's final sentence insisting that the teacher sits alongside rather than above the student, and her repeated final call for a "rigorous ethics" and the architect's "moral responsibility" to the needs of society.

This is a dramatic work, easily exceeding the requirements of such an academic position and likely demonstrating a wider and deeper understanding of the history and effects of architectural theory than any of the rivals for the position. Bo chose to synthesize all five of the topics offered in the competition instead of addressing one, as requested. In a familiar dance, the outsider looking for membership to a club feels that to even be considered they have to far outperform those who feel entitled to membership—by virtue of their gender, race, class, nationality, skin color, friendships, etc.—but in doing so threaten the very hierarchies by which the club is organized. In fact, the university refused to even consider Bo for the position. She made an official legal complaint—being an insider in so many circles and never simply an outsider. The government in Rio finally agreed after a two-year battle and ordered the university search committee to include her as a candidate. The committee preferred to cancel the competition altogether. Bo would later portray this as a rejection of her being a leftist and a fighter, the fact that she was a "tough cookie."[34] But it would seem that a woman theorist is even more threatening than a woman architect, hence the almost desperate attempts of contemporary scholarship to repeat the historical violence by using the fact that she was a serial collaborator to downplay her words and confine her to the world of forms and images. Yet the sheer quantity of theoretical texts over the years, and the consistency and development of their argument, suggest it was more the other way around, that the collaborators were the real beneficiaries—as seems to have been understood by the most celebrated figures she worked with over the years, but always rankled the

32. Lina Bo Bardi, *Contribuição propedêutica ao ensino da teoria da arquitetura* (São Paulo: Habitat, 1957), translated by Cathrine Veikos as *The Theory of Architectural Practice* (London: Routledge, 2014).

33. Ibid., 8. A year later, Bo wrote: "Let's set aside the idealistic definition . . . which sets up a vicious circle by attempting to define the term 'theory' theoretically as if it were a *theoretical* form somehow distinct from practice." Lina Bo Bardi, "Theory and Philosophy of Architecture" (1958), in Lina Bo Bardi, *Stones Against Diamonds* (London: AA Publications, 2013), 49.

34. "I wanted to participate in the public competition for the Theory of Architecture Professorship at the FAU, but they didn't want me there because I was a leftist, a tough cookie, and the teachers at the time were from engineering: good teachers. It was a tragedy. The students kicked up a huge fuss. There was a competition, and they didn't let me put my name down (I don't know why)." Oliveira, "Interview with Lina Bo Bardi," 249.

less-celebrated collaborators and their contemporary surrogates in the academy.

This anxiety-producing theory is a theory precisely about anxiety. Bo recalled that war necessitated the production of theory: "The outbreak of war . . . presented other problems: one could no longer build, and the field of 'Practice' was replaced by 'Theory.'"[35] The nightmare of war provokes "Theory," polemically capitalized and in quotation marks as a distinct thing. Theory comes first for Bo. As did the nightmare. She literally graduated directly into war. And she also argued that the war never ended, that resistance can never rest. As she put it in 1986:

Conclusion: we are still living under ashen postwar skies. "Tout est permis, Dieu n'existe pas." But we cannot doubt the existence of the war, which still continues, just as the great resistance movements go on.[36]

Theory is therefore always being produced in the face of ongoing horror, trying to establish a foundation for practice that will itself be understood as an attempt to address trauma, even—or especially—when that trauma mistakenly appears to have passed.

It is not by chance that the first image of the 1957 book's preface is one of the series of "cataclysm" drawings by Leonardo da Vinci in which a violent, all-consuming turbulence swallows everything (fig. 43). On little 6 x 8–inch pieces of paper, Leonardo used hundreds of swirling and overlapping black chalk lines to visualize the vertiginous forces dissolving landscapes and cities in a terrifying fury of movement. He had experienced an extremely violent storm as a four-year-old that completely destroyed buildings, trees, animals, and humans in the countryside of Tuscany. He wrote eloquently about this disaster and is thought to have drawn on the experience to produce the apocalyptic renderings of the end of the world toward the end of his own life.[37] But the drawings can also be seen as representations of the violent chaotic force of nature itself, as much about the beginning of the world as its end.[38] Violence as the most basic truth—the generator as much as the degenerator. And it is pointedly below one of these images of violence without limit that Bo lines up Cesare Ripa's late sixteenth-century allegorical figures for "theory," "practice," and "design." Theory is a young woman looking upward with a V-shaped compass lightly perched on top of her head as a kind of antenna with which she picks up ideas from the air. Practice is an older woman of the world focused downward, with the compass now heavier and having moved from head to hand, inverted to apply the ideas to the physical world. Design floats in between the two as a handsome or noble young man looking horizontally, with one of his hands holding the compass turned upward, halfway between ground and air, yet touching neither, and the other holding a mirror. Bo's text doesn't refer to these images directly. They are given the same status as words, conveying the sense that some kind of overwhelming existential threat engenders feminine theory, which in turn acts as the basis for equally feminine practice, mediated or interrupted by the masculine introspection or self-reflection of the designer. Care for the immaterial air and the material ground is contrasted with self-absorption that imagines another world in a book about theory in which the traditional concept of "design" will be repeatedly challenged.

If there was any remaining doubt about this impression, the first chapter of the book begins with a quotation from Geoffrey Scott's 1914 *The Architecture of Humanism: A Study in the History of Taste*, arguing that man is not the center of the world but just "one of her myriad products, more conscious and more perplexed," a "stranger" terrified in the "formidable" face of nature that "remains, in the end, as in the beginning, something alien and inhuman often destructive of his hopes." He may "cower" before this threat like the earliest humans or analyze it dispassionately like the latest scientists, or he can take a third path and "construct, within the world as it is, a pattern of the world as he would have it."[39] Design is a response to existential threat, the "projection," in Bo's words, of "infinitesimal architectures that, once refined, form new architectures all over the world, from the chipped rock to the interplanetary satellite."[40] The level of human anxiety doesn't decrease as the human's apparent domination of the planet through design increases.

35. Bo Bardi, "Currículo literário," 9.

36. Bo Bardi, "The Architectural Project" (1986), in Bo Bardi, *Stones Against Diamonds*, 99.

37. "I have seen movements of the air so violent as to carry away and strew in their course immense forest trees and whole roofs of great palaces; and I have seen this same fury with its whirling movements bore a hole in and hollow out a bank of shingle and carry away in the air gravel, sand, and water for more than half a mile." Leonardo da Vinci, "Of the Movement of Air in Water," 1508 notebook, 1338.

38. Irving Lavin, "Leonardo's Watery Chaos," Institute of Advanced Studies, Princeton University, 2018, at ias.edu/ideas /lavin-leonardo-chaos.

39. Geoffrey Scott, *The Architecture of Humanism: A Study in the History of Taste* (1914), cited in Bo Bardi, *The Theory of Architectural Practice*, 52.

40. Bo Bardi, *The Theory of Architectural Practice*, 60.

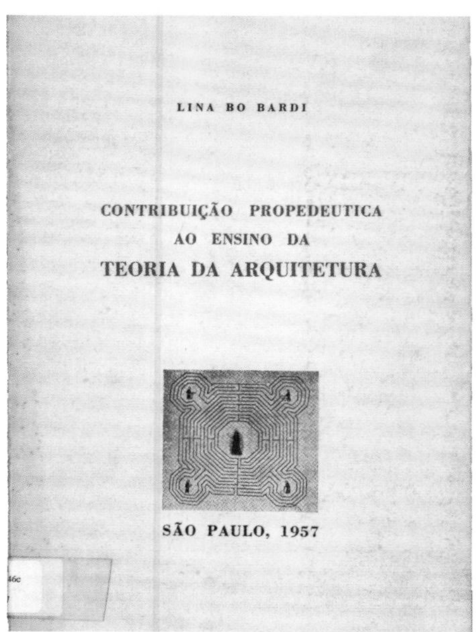

FIGS. 42–43
Lina Bo Bardi, *Contribuição propedêutica ao ensino da teoria da arquitetura* (Preliminary Contribution to the Teaching of Architectural Theory) (São Paulo, 1957): cover and illustrated page of the preface to Bo Bardi's thesis in the teaching course at FAU-USP

On the contrary, the "anxious doubts," the "questions and fears," remain:

> From the intimate space of the house, the family nucleus, to the omnipresent space of nature, the problem of architecture—an activity of man in the contiguous space defined by earth and undefined by air—appears to us full of facts and anxious doubts; of assurances because of what has already been achieved; and simultaneously, questions and fears.[41]

In fact, the ever-expanding all-too-human world of technology has become the contemporary source of anxiety in what Bo described as a time that is, "even in its literary and artistic preferences, agitated and eclectic, innovative, anxious for syntheses and speed, and nearly distraught due to the sheer accumulation of facts, thoughts and actions with which it is palpably overloaded."[42] She insisted that the central question in the always-threatening atomic age remained that of the house for the human, shelter in the face of anxiety that can never be a shelter from anxiety.

Bo's inaugural 1958 lecture for her course on the theory of architecture at the School of Fine Arts of Bahia, titled "Theory and Philosophy of Architecture," extended the argument, again insisting that theory itself is a form of practice, even a form of professional practice that provides the ethical and moral foundation for architectural practice. This must start with making the architect "keenly aware that his humanity does not exist in a vacuum, but extends beyond himself, drawing on other people and on nature"[43] and "understand human beings as they are today—electrified, mechanized, tormented by the progress they have achieved but whose meaning they do not yet fully grasp."[44] The human fear of nature has migrated to a fear of the human itself. Or, more precisely, the human fear of nature and the fear of the human are tied together. In another text written later the same year, Bo argued that man completely dominates nature but is still "staring up at the fruits of his labors with the same startled eyes as he did thousands of years ago." And that fruit?—"the prospect of self-destruction."[45] Her architecture was always that of the atom bomb. She concludes that the only way out is "to build humanity anew"[46] by rediscovering the simplest architectural gesture, for which her model since the early 1950s was a solitary figure in Northeast Brazil reworking the materials of the forest into a minimal shelter—which is not a kind of nostalgia or primitivism, as can be seen in her 1960s writing about computers and the "architecture of a new electronic era."[47] Rather it's a comment on the necessary fragility of shelter and a political attack on all hierarchies.

41. Ibid., 70.

42. Ibid., 78.

43. Bo Bardi, "Theory and Philosophy of Architecture," 51.

44. Ibid., 52.

45. Lina Bo Bardi, "The Moon" (1958), in Rubino and Grinover, eds., *Lina por escrito*, 105.

46. bid., 107.

47. Bo Bardi, "Na América do Sul: após Le Corbusier, o que está acontecendo?," in Rubino and Grinover, eds., *Lina por escrito*, 121.

Trans-Species Architecture

This attitude can be seen everywhere in her work, forming her work, being her work. It is not by chance, for example, that Bo insists in 1953 that the 1951 Glass House for herself and husband Pietro Bardi was "open to everything that is poetic and ethical, even to the wildest storms. . . . bringing it into contact with its 'dangers' without fussing too much with the usual 'protections.'"[48] Such "minimum defenses" against nature mean living with the existential threat rather than trying to cut oneself off from it with technologies that will ultimately be even more threatening. After all, any sealed box that "flees the storms" equally blindly "shies away from the world of men."[49] The radically nonhierarchical approach starts with a refusal to elevate the human. Plants, animals, and insects are the real clients of all Bo's minimal "poor architecture." The plants are even living within the very material of the buildings. The anxious fragile human is but a temporary, awed guest. Bo's relentless documentation of all the different companion species living, growing, and crawling around, under and inside her house, was not a hobby but an architectural philosophy. Her architecture typically consists of a few horizontal planes and a kind of scaffolding placed within the world of plants and animals that invites them to climb up, over, and into it. Her own house polemically wraps itself around a tree and is filled with plants. It is a tree house that houses trees. In photographs, Bo even positions herself as a kind of plant by seemingly attaching herself to one of the polemically thin green columns, with other plants in the foreground as the real protagonists (fig. 44). Her architectural drawings usually have plants in the foreground framing the images, plants in the interior, and plants beyond the interior to reinforce the sense of architecture completely suspended within nature—even when firmly on the ground or within the dense city. The space, in which architecture appears as a minimal set of lines, is alive.

The subordination of human to plant was already clear in the 1940 Casa sul Mare di Sicilia that Bo designed with Carlo Pagani—where her watercolors in the August issue of *Domus* unambiguously present the plants as the real occupants, standing up and looking at us from inside the successive walls of the garden and roof of the building.[50] This uncanny effect conveyed in the first seemingly exotic manifesto project was repeatedly reproduced over the next four years in Bo and Pagani's contributions to *Lo Stile* (which was edited in their studio space) and their weekly suggestions to the readers of women's magazines like *Grazia* about how to recycle

48. Lina Bo Bardi, "House in Morumbi" (1953), in Bo Bardi, *Stones Against Diamonds*, 43.

49. Ibid., 44.

50. Lina Bo and Carlo Pagani, "Casa sul Mare di Sicilia," *Domus*, no. 152 (August 1940): 35.

scarce wartime resources and use furniture, plants, and animals (birds and fish) to dissolve the limits of existing confined urban interiors. Countless drawings strategically positioned plants inside, outside, and at the threshold to turn interiors into exteriors and exteriors into interiors—with a catalogue of meticulously designed micro-architectures for the plants to inhabit (fig. 45). The plants typically blur or conceal the lines defining the floor, ceiling, wall, and especially the window—constructing the illusion of openness in a constrained interior for an increasingly constrained society tormented by war. Any house is first a greenhouse—not by chance the theme of Bo's first individually signed article in May 1941, with one of her images showing such a density of interior plants that the already minimal architecture becomes a shadowy backdrop, even the ruin of a no longer central human life.[51] Humans are rarely shown in this architecture of plants that will become the main point of, for instance, the Valéria Cirell House and the Chame-Chame House from 1958 (figs. 46, 288–291)—where the walls themselves are completely filled with plants that sprout out in all directions. Architecture becomes a simple set of lines floating within plants, with plants also floating within the lines. Humans become just one of the countless species that continuously intrude on yet depend on each other.

Bo's intermingling of species radicalizes the polemical entanglements of plants and buildings in the Mediterranean villas designed by Gio Ponti under the influence of Bernard Rudofsky in the late 1930s that were sometimes published alongside her work in the early 1940s. In one image by Rudofsky, published in the April 1938 issue of *Domus*, plants seemingly rise up from the grassy floor of the central outdoor living room to overwhelm the building and the spaces of the two occupants in a kind of childlike imagination of an animate ever-expanding forest—turning the solid building into a minimal screen.[52] But the wartime step taken by Bo and Pagani, then taken further by Bo in Brazil (without ever losing the survival urgency of minimal gestures and recycling scarce resources), is the surrealist gesture of treating plant and animal life as the real clients and occupants—emphasizing the multiplicity, hybridity, and otherness of species in a kind of counter-domesticity.[53]

The effect was already prophetically captured in Bo's astonishing René Magritte–like rendering of a children's bedroom for a 1942 issue of the woman's magazine *Cordelia* in which all of the walls and the ceiling are painted in such a way that they become barely visible lines among tropical plants and a menagerie of animals, birds, and insects that are very much at home. A hammock is hung from the painted trees, and a green straw carpet becomes an animal-shaped lawn. The interior is a lightly domesticated exterior, or even a mirage, a barely believable space within the completely believable world of plants and animals.[54] Glass House, already.

The tree house, the shack on the forest floor, and the cave are the constant references that reappear in Bo's largest projects: museums, civic centers, performance spaces, and public buildings. And they are usually portrayed in the style of antihierarchical surrealism that Bo employed in her very first published drawings in 1940—where every object, plant, and animal floats, suspended in polemically deep perspectival spaces yet flattened into incongruous avatars of an unknown life. Surrealism, which was born out of the shock and violations of World War I, remains the medium for Bo's architecture of anxiety, with every scene looking as if humanity or some other alien species has departed after a relatively short stay, leaving behind some fossils that could be objects of everyday life or treasured artworks.

The objects in Bo's images appear to have been amputated from some unknown place and time. There is a pervasive sense of animism in which anything might wake up at any moment and take on a life of its own. They are haunted images—perhaps from the dream world of a child or a traumatized artist, or simply evidence of an open mind, a mind that is still open or has been shocked open. At the very least, they are an invitation to open the mind, which might be the most that architecture can do. Architecture as nothing more than a trans-species invitation, a tender form of hospitality.

51. Lina Bo, "Serre," *Lo Stile*, nos. 5–6 (May 1941): 113. Bo would go on to publish a number of articles on the entangled roles of plants and glass with "miniature gardens" within the window itself that frame the exterior landscape and "blend" it with the interior. For example, Lina Bo, "Finestre," *Lo Stile*, no. 16 (April 1942): 18–19.

52. Bernard Rudofsky, " Variazione," *Domus*, no. 124 (April 1938): 14.

53. This wartime surrealist gesture might be related to the fact that the idealized escapist villas in Ponti's magazines were actually the companions of the Fascist regime they might appear to flee. Ponti always acted as if disconnected, as if in his own better world, and his magazines only rarely addressed the regime directly, even though the Fascist government had been controlling all architectural commissions since 1932, and Ponti wrote positive editorials in *Domus* about Mussolini's revival of Italian architecture—as, for example, in the second issue featuring Bo and Pagani (Gio Ponti, "Vocazione archiettonica degli italiani," *Domus*, no. 155 [November 1940]: 25–28). Some of the work he published, including two built projects by Pagani, Bo, and Castiglioni of 1942 that were likely brought to the studio by Pagani—the *War Poster Exhibition* that displayed arrays of the Axis flags (the German swastika, the Italian tricolor with fasces, and the Japanese sun) and the "Wool Collection," a structure covered with Italian flags—were literal celebrations of the regime that have to be considered alongside the commitments to the resistance that Pagani and Bo made soon after. See Sarah Catalano, "Lina Bo [Bardi] in Italy," *RISCO: Revista de Pesquisa em Arquitetura e Urbanismo*, no. 2 (2014): 65–73. Bo did become increasingly concerned and wrote to Pagani a month before they both resigned from Ponti's magazine in June 1943 (which was itself just a month before Mussolini was arrested): "My work with Ponti is morally almost unbearable . . . and his superficiality makes me sick." Letter from Lina Bo to Carlo Pagani, May 10, 1943, cited in Lima, *Lina Bo Bardi*, 24.

54. Lina Bo and Carlo Pagani, "Ambiente per bambini," *Cordelia* 61, no. 1 (February–March 1942): 13–14.

FIG. 44
Lina Bo Bardi at the Glass House,
Morumbi, São Paulo, ca. 1953

FIG. 45
Lina Bo Bardi and Carlo Pagani, illustration from the article "Finestre" (Windows), *Lo Stile*, no. 10 (1941): 25

FIG. 46
Lina Bo Bardi, *Lateral elevation, Valéria Cirell House, São Paulo*, 1958. Graphite and ink on parchment paper, 20 x 40.5 cm. Collection of the Instituto Bardi/ Casa de Vidro, São Paulo

All of this is a way to understand the ever-shocking brilliance of MASP (figs. 116–150), the first designs for which were perhaps not by chance produced at the same time as Bo's thesis-book on architecture theory. The initial versions reworked the drawings and model of her 1952 Oceanfront Museum project (figs. 109–115), which was another suspended box entered from below with plants underneath it, above it, and inside it—where unframed art could be suspended, framed by nature, as rendered in Bo's photocollaged paintings that refused any distinction between art and tree.[55] Bo then radicalized the idea by suspending the box from the ends rather than the sides and removing the one wall of glass. In the early 1960s version, she rendered a dense, closed, primeval suspended block inhabited by plants and animals, as if leaking living organisms, or being itself alive and surrounded only by plants with no sign of the metropolis of São Paulo (figs. 117–120). It was a brutalist manifesto, in the Jean Dubuffet sense, with contemporary and primeval time collapsed into an ambiguity about whether humanity has yet to appear or has just left. Bo gave the renderings an apocalyptic feel. One 1965 image in particular torments and scars the underside of the volume against hints of a radioactive or bloody sky (fig. 135). The feeling persists into 1966, when the solid monolith finally gives way to glass walls late in the construction. All the floating—the building off the ground and the artworks inside it off the floor—emphasized by the empty ground plane and the bunkerlike civic space below, is somehow linked to this sense of devastating threat, and the call to a new horizontal order based on the popular. In the shadow of impending crisis, the idealized museum offers its own threat. It must aim, as Bo wrote in 1950, "to produce a shock that would elicit reactions of curiosity and investigation."[56] It is the rawest of instruments to let society face itself on its own terms and reboot itself.

Once again, the deep perspectival space under the floating volume in Bo's renderings of MASP as a pre- or post-apocalyptic garden is occupied by objects whose exact location and nature are profoundly unclear. No easy distinction between art, animal, and plant is possible. Likewise, the artworks inside the hovering space stand like an assembled army facing visitors, with more or less the same size and proportion as humans, paintings suspended at the same height as faces, paintings themselves as faces on transparent bodies—as if both sides are looking into a mirror. This possibility of facing an object without any frame or explanation, of taking any path through the garden of artworks, and of personally consulting the secrets of any object (the explanations and traces of history, construction,

55. Lina Bo Bardi, "Museu á beira do oceano," *Habitat*, no. 8 (July–September 1952): 11.

56. Lina Bo Bardi, "Função social dos museus," *Habitat*, no. 1 (October–December 1950): 43.

travel, ownership, and damage visible on the back of the easel) is theoretical work—an experiment in refusing to patronize the visitor or the art, which is another kind of visitor. It's a radical experiment in hospitality and agency whose "frightening" effect, in Bo's words, is a tremor still being felt in galleries across the planet.[57]

But how to write about and exhibit Lina Bo herself without simply absorbing her threat? How to avoid making a vitrine for her in which she is frozen as a kind of still life with a too-heavy frame and trivializing explanation? How to allow many paths and the exploration of secrets? How to allow her work to live on, to make us hesitate and, above all, educate? Bo's most substantial theory was written in an attempt to gain acceptance as a teacher, but her work was always and everywhere infused with the mission of education, understood as a political project, an attempt for a horizontal society to realize itself. It is not by chance that her most celebrated work is a huge, floating horizontal that she explicitly presented as a new form of education. What does it mean to really treat Lina Bo as our teacher? What lessons do we have still to learn with her? What is the fate of the horizontal today, when income and opportunity disparity are projected to keep growing? If the anxiety and radical destabilizations and displacements of war provoke theory, there was no peacetime for Bo. Inequity, segregation, arrogance, self-entitlement, clumsiness, and stupidity were the permanent enemies of this self-described "tough cookie," as they should be for us, especially now.

57. "Seeing thousands of people walk among the paintings with an almost familiar, nonauratic air . . . is frightening, like a prophecy of fundamental changes. . . . It was my intention to destroy the aura that always surrounds a museum, to present the work of art as work, as a prophecy of work at everyone's reach." Lina Bo Bardi, "Explanações sobre o museu de arte," in Adriano Pedrosa and Luiza Proença, eds. *Concreto e cristal: o acervo do MASP nos cavaletes de Lina Bo Bardi* (São Paulo: MASP, 2015), 137.

Beatriz Colomina is the Howard Crosby Butler Professor of the History of Architecture at Princeton University. She has written and curated extensively on questions of design, art, sexuality, and media. Her most recent publications include *Are We Human? Notes on an Archaeology of Design* (2016), with Mark Wigley, and *X-Ray Architecture* (2019).

Mark Wigley is professor of architecture at Columbia University. Historian, theorist, and curator, he explores the intersection of architecture, art, philosophy, culture, and technology. His most recent publications are *Buckminster Fuller Inc.: Architecture in the Age of Radio* (2017) and *Cutting Matta-Clark: The Anarchitecture Investigation* (2018).

LINA BO BARDI, THE ORGANIC INTELLECTUAL, AND HABITAT MAGAZINE

Habitat was a magazine made with six hands; two from Lina, two from Pietro, and two from Flávio Motta.[1]

FIG. 48
Lina Bo Bardi, cover layout study for the first issue of *Habitat*, 1950. Ink and collage on paper, 30 x 23.5 cm. Collection of the Instituto Bardi/Casa de Vidro, São Paulo

Information as Weaponry

Habitat magazine was first published in 1951 as the official catalogue for the Museu de Arte de São Paulo (MASP). Its full title, *Habitat: Revista das Artes no Brasil*, signalled its editors' ambition to synthesize cultural discourse in a country defining the terms of its own modern identity. The magazine ran for twenty-five issues until 1965, and although Lina Bo Bardi was its editor, she had direct involvement only in the first ten, returning to edit the fourteenth and fifteenth issues before resigning entirely (fig. 48). Bo Bardi edited the magazine along with her husband Pietro Maria Bardi, who was also the director of MASP. While supporting MASP's program of promoting the arts in Brazil, *Habitat* featured articles addressing a broad range of issues that reflected the couple's parallel ambition to form an integral connection between the institution's museological agenda and the Institute of Contemporary Art (IAC), the design school founded by Bo Bardi in the same year. The IAC was one of Brazil's first schools dedicated to training young designers, with the museum using its cultural capital to foster links with national industry in addition to educating the general public about this new artistic field.[2] An extract from an article published in the newspaper *Diário de São Paulo* describes the IAC as "completing the work of artistic education that the museum has been offering, providing its students with a clearly avant-garde orientation."[3] *Habitat*, launched to create a market for contemporary Brazilian design through the promotion of products in its pages, augmented this tripartite approach. Factory owners at the time did not question design as such, and continued to fabricate replicas of old items or those popularized in Europe, meaning that for the Bardis, change was about making the home a new site of design:

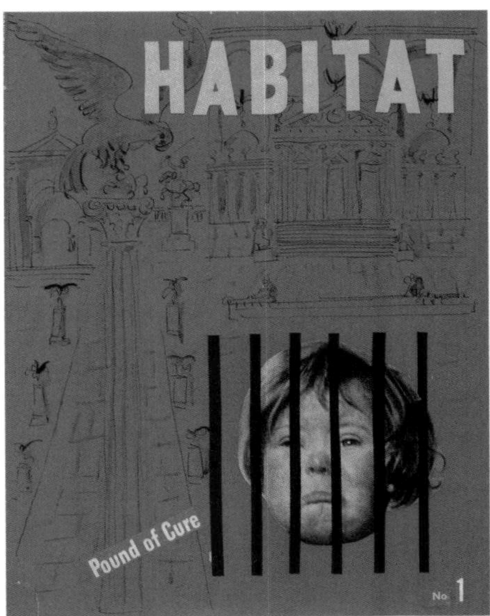

Habitat magazine . . . railed against the ugliness of São Paulo's urban furniture, bourgeois interior decoration, and commercial window displays. After all, there was no point in having a museum with permanent exhibits of Poussin, Tintoretto, and

1. Fabiana Terenzi Stuchi, "Revista *Habitat*: um olhar moderno sobre os anos 50 em São Paulo," Master's thesis, Faculty of Architecture, Universidade de São Paulo, 2006, 61.

2. The school lasted only two years, during which Bo Bardi led the course alongside Flávio Motta and Luiz Hossaka.

3. *Diário de São Paulo*, March 8, 1951, quoted in Adriano Tomitão Canas, "MASP: Museu laboratório: projeto de museu para a cidade: 1947–1957," PhD diss., Universidade de São Paulo, 2010, 63.

FIG. 47
Gustavo Capanema Building, former headquarters of the Ministry of Education and Health, project by Affonso Eduardo Reidy, Carlos Leão, Ernani Vasconcellos, Jorge Machado Moreira, Lúcio Costa, and Oscar Niemeyer, with consultation by Le Corbusier, Rio de Janeiro, ca. 1955

Picasso if the elite went on sitting on Napoleonic thrones and entertaining in rooms in which eclectic upholsterers had been given free rein.[4]

For São Paulo, a city increasingly known for its industrial development, any attempt to address its new culture was underpinned by an integration of art into a market society. As a result, *Habitat* was oriented to create a consumer base for the new type of design taught at the school, while at the same time extending MASP's reach to audiences who were either unable to visit or had not yet visited the collection.[5]

War Positions[6]

By proposing industrial design as an extension of art history, Bo Bardi's role transformed from founder and designer to teacher. Yet with Pietro Maria Bardi as the official director, Bo Bardi has been largely overlooked in the creation of the museum beyond being the architect of its permanent building. This essay therefore explores the construction of Bo Bardi's professional identity during the early stages of her career in Brazil by considering her actions through the lens of the Italian Marxist philosopher Antonio Gramsci's notion of the "organic intellectual." For Gramsci, the task of the organic intellectual was to work as an "organizer of culture" and create class alliances by addressing and articulating the experiences of subaltern groups. Playing a key part in constructing a counter-hegemonic position to capitalist power, such a figure would be actively engaged in a constant struggle to change minds.[7] As a focus for the "making conscious" of the intellectual's role between their private production and public dissemination, *Habitat* is therefore not only a site for challenging cultural norms, but also a space in which the production of Bo Bardi's own role *takes place*. Steeped in Gramsci's tutelage, Bo Bardi's own writing demonstrates an implicit concern for the empowerment of lay audiences, but it also reflects her conscious self-positioning as a designer, artist, and architect—an indication of her personal ambition to enact the Italian philosopher's model of intellectualism.

Publishing was a crucial part of Bo Bardi's design thinking before she left for Brazil in 1946. A well-known editor in Italy working alongside Gio Ponti for *Domus* magazine, she regularly contributed articles to other titles, including Bruno Zevi and Carlo Pagani's short-lived *A* magazine, which was founded at the close of war. *A* was designed to act explicitly as a form of propaganda and further the concerns of art and architecture in the reconstruction of Italy.[8] To this end, Bo Bardi also presented a paper, "La propaganda per la ricostruzione" (Propaganda for Reconstruction), at a conference organized by Pagani in Milan in December 1945. Her speech was focused primarily on her belief in the role of popular media—newspapers, radio, monthly magazines—in the rebuilding debate, insisting "it is necessary to fire up public opinion, creating interest for whatever Italy needs to do . . . it would be useless to create plans . . . without moral participation."[9]

Here, Bo Bardi's words echo that of recent combat, employing polemical language to address culture as if it were a branch of warfare; constructing a new cultural paradigm was as important as the reconstruction of cities physically devastated by war. Since culture had become such a contested territory in the interwar period, the problem was no longer one of documentation in print, but the use of information as weaponry. In this way, Bo Bardi's "war" had no singular enemy, just a discernible direction; she was against the "old" and sought the "new." This linear projection demanded an architecture of reactive opportunism, with a magazine in this instance disseminated more quickly than the planning or construction of a building—which is to say, publishing was faster than architecture. With the developing market itself based on speed and opportunity, the introduction of alternative tactics for the dissemination of design through magazine publishing reflected the emerging culture of the age.

Beautiful Child

Translating this thinking upon her arrival in Brazil, Bo Bardi did not position *Habitat* as a definite manifesto for the direction of art and architecture in her new home; rather,

4. Ethel Leon, "IAC/MASP, a Futurist School in São Paulo," paper delivered at the conference Modernidade Latina: Os Italianos e os Centros do Modernismo, Museu de Arte Contemporânea da Universidade de São Paulo, 2013, at mac.usp.br/mac/conteudo/academico/publicacoes/anais/modernidade/pdfs/ETHEL_ING.pdf.

5. First aimed at a Paulista market, the magazine was also distributed in Rio de Janeiro after three issues and in Argentina after ten, followed by Portugal, Spain, Salvador, Porto Alegre, and the US under the editorship of Flávio Motta. *Habitat*'s ambition was thus to promote Brazilian design abroad, with its positive recognition by foreign audiences a measure against which a local readership assessed its value. See Stuchi, "Revista *Habitat*," 5.

6. "War positions" is a term coined by Antonio Gramsci to refer to the stance oppositional groups must take in order to wrestle hegemonic dominance from one another.

7. This differed from other well-established definitions such as Julien Benda's more conservative one of the intellectual as a superiorly gifted individual with a moral responsibility. See Edward W. Said, *Representations of the Intellectual: The 1993 Reith Lectures* (New York: Vintage, 1996), 3.

8. Zeuler R. M. de A. Lima, *Lina Bo Bardi* (New Haven: Yale University Press, 2013), 30.

9. Lina Bo Bardi, quoted in Lima, *Lina Bo Bardi*, 28.

it was intended to engage the perspective of those who may have a financial stake in the city's claims on modernity. This process provoked an astonished reaction from its readership. Julio Roberto Katinsky, a former student of Bo Bardi's and later an established designer himself, has noted: "*Habitat* magazine was a shock to all of us . . . we looked forward to every issue, even the little notes of 'Alencastro.'"[10]

Bold editorial gestures engendered the shock to which Katinsky referred, particularly through the striking aesthetic of the magazine's covers: high-contrast primary colors and figurative imagery that was collaged with everything from illustrations of tropical fauna and primitive sculpture to plans of buildings and even whole urban designs. With the absence of text and the frequent use of illustration rather than photography as the lead image, the covers give little away about the content inside. Here "newness" is an end in itself, voicing Bo Bardi's ambition to open up the contemporary dialogue as a means to conceive modernity in alternative ways.[11] To achieve this aim, her involvement in producing the magazine varied widely, including the publication of her writing. Her best-known text, "Bela criança" (Beautiful Child), which appeared in the second issue of the magazine, argues for Brazilian architecture to adopt a new position, amplifying the language of resistance that characterized much of her early contributions in print.

Bo Bardi identifies the work of Lúcio Costa and Oscar Niemeyer as the focus of her opposition. Her article disparages both modernists by lauding the vernacular talents "from the house of the rubber tapper," referencing remote regions she considered overlooked by the project of modernity.[12] Niemeyer's architecture, Bo Bardi suggests, accepts Brazil's condition as a colonized subject, with its expression of difference an indication of the alienation of the local context rather than a celebration of it (fig. 47).[13] The Vargas government's patronage of aspirational projects was symptomatic of the state's invention of nationality as a radical tool for consolidating its political agenda both at home and abroad, which would eventually lead to the construction of Niemeyer's project for the continent's first modernist city, Brasília. This reciprocal pattern of political and cultural determinism manifested a monumentality that was employed both as a dialectic conclusion to the country's history and as a statement of its birth. As such, the Cariocas' attempt to attain some power over a modernism impressed upon them was for Bo Bardi just a representation of an official version of "otherness" authorized by the nation-state.

Rejecting this agenda, the article attributes Brazilian modernism's "flaws" to the consequence of the country's youth, "born suddenly, as a *beautiful child*."[14] Despite "Bela criança" simultaneously supporting and deriding the modern project in Brazil, Bo Bardi avoids fully presenting her own position within this binary through her use of language that romanticizes both Brazil's adaption of European modernism *and* lesser-known structures familiar to the *sertão*, the country's "backland" regions in the Northeast. Coming from an architect caught between the two, Bo Bardi's invention of the term "beautiful child" expresses the conditions of cultural and, more widely, social inequalities across Brazilian society, but it is in many ways also a personal reflection of herself. As if evidence of the process of her own acculturation, the description she relates echoes her own experience of emerging in Brazil as a qualified architect yet to build and navigating new social, cultural, and political terrain.

Making Multiple

The frequency of Bo Bardi's self-publication in *Habitat* has led to the perception that as a historical document, it evidences her own unique approach to architecture—the magazine operating as a record of her personal design thinking. Articles incongruous to the broader architectural themes presented in *Habitat* include drawings by Bo Bardi's father Enrico Bo, the most charming of which is a small, untitled sketch of a figure standing in front of a number of cacti with a caption stating: "Enrico Bo, 'The Cactus Collector'" (fig. 49).[15] Bo Bardi's connection to the artist is omitted from the accompanying text, which offers only a simple biography:

10. Julio Roberto Katinsky, quoted in Stuchi, "Revista *Habitat*," 33. "Alencastro" was one of Bo Bardi's pseudonyms, the use of which I address later in this essay.

11. Ibrahim Kaya, "Modernity, Openness, Interpretation: A Perspective on Multiple Modernities," *Social Science Information* 43, no. 1 (2004): 35.

12. Lina Bo Bardi, *Stones Against Diamonds* (London: AA Publications, 2013), 37. It is important to remember that during this period while Bo Bardi traveled around Brazil, her affinity with the Northeast, particularly the region of Bahia, had not yet fully begun.

13. Homi Bhabha, "Of Mimicry and Man: The Ambivalence of Colonial Discourse," *October*, no. 28 (Spring 1984): 125–33.

14. Bo Bardi, "Bela criança," *Habitat*, no. 2 (March 1951): 3. Author's italics.

15. Lina Bo Bardi, "Enrico Bo," *Habitat*, no. 7 (April–June 1952): 36. Enrico Bo was an artist and friend of Giorgio de Chirico, who painted Bo Bardi's portrait as a teenager.

FIG. 49
Enrico Bo, "The Cactus Collector," *Habitat*, no. 7 (April–June 1952): 36

[Enrico Bo is] a painter who began painting at sixty-two years old. For sixty-two years, he stored objects, forms, colors within the repository of his spirit, thoughts, memories, sensations. One day . . . as the world's turmoil crashed and wrecked his city, Enrico Bo . . . opened the repository of his memories and began to paint . . . De Chirico was enchanted before one of his works . . . the Swiss magazine *Graphis* dedicated an article to him.[16]

Bo Bardi "exhibits" her father's drawings through their reproduction in the magazine, and the page itself becomes a new form of picture frame. In giving significance to such works, she sought to question institutionalized systems of meaning not through refutation, but by instead creating multiple sites for discussion. To this end, another notable article argues for the virtues of cats as companions for artists. The short text is richly illustrated with drawings and photographs of a number of cats spread across several pages:

Cats have always been indispensable companions of artists, either as an inspiration or merely as a dear friend. In our days, where figurative art is giving way to abstract art, all a cat really can do in a studio [is] chase rats. With our deepest respect for abstract painting, we reserve three of our pages for painters, sculptors, and photographers who still found interest and inspiration in felines.[17]

Bo Bardi's own love of cats is well documented, with numerous photographs showing her either holding or in the presence of one (fig. 50).[18] Indeed, it is her use of the symbol of cat's eyes under the pseudonym "Alencastro" that reveals her personal opinions about São Paulo and its inhabitants in *Habitat*.[19] Appearing on the opening editorial page and later in a dedicated section devoted entirely to event-based cultural activities, Alencastro acts as both programmer and gossip columnist, at once promoting the activities of high society in the city and bestowing criticism. Appealing to the artistic taste of the local elite, this section allowed *Habitat*'s readership to see themselves represented in its pages, but in its sarcastic tone and juxtaposition with more diverse content across the rest of the publication, the section acts also as a form of mockery intent on revealing disparities in the social system.[20]

However, as European émigrés invited to Brazil, the Bardis were an integral part of the very social group at whom they directed their criticism. *Habitat*, while attempting to speak from the peripheries, did not therefore speak with a marginal voice. This fact is largely elided in historiographies of Bo

16. Ibid.

17. "Alguns Gatos" (Some Cats), *Habitat*, no. 5 (October–December 1951): 37.

18. See also Marcelo Carvalho Ferraz, ed., *Lina Bo Bardi* (São Paulo: Instituto Lina Bo e P. M. Bardi, 1993), 32.

19. The symbol for Alencastro also appears in personal notes and on sketches for projects.

20. Leon, "IAC/MASP."

FIG. 50
Lina Bo Bardi and cat at the Glass House, São Paulo, undated

Bardi, with her marginality as a woman portrayed as somehow equivalent to the ongoing subjugation of peoples living within the conditions of postcoloniality. While she indeed spoke to and of the Southern Hemisphere, she was not representative of it. Still, Bo Bardi's strategy of neatly articulating the Brazilian Northeast as singular—despite its own fractured multilocality—is important because of the strong African roots in its culture. For many in Brazil, the African continent represented the antithesis of the country's modernizing agenda, making it a site of anxiety for the ruling elite. The impact of this simplification allowed Bo Bardi to refute the West as the prototype for social progress, with the idea of *multiple modernities* a means to confront the tendency to promote a single dominant reality over the existence of others (figs. 51–52). Going against established theories of the way in which the world had been and was being made modern, the notion of multiplicity in this context rejects Europe as the origin of development, drawing attention instead to the global history of modernity as a nonlinear process co-constituted by a number of different cultural attributes originating elsewhere.[21]

Fashioning the Subaltern

With a reading public emerging as part of the wider modern project, Bo Bardi recognized the magazine as both a concerted new space for received knowledge and the location of that knowledge's contestation.[22] Unexpected content was made modern through its reproduction, while simultaneously invoking a notion of primitivism that appealed to the constructed artifice of the New World as exotic in the eyes of the Old. This was an unaggressive form of expression, dialogic in its aspiration to attract new audiences, but monological in its reality as a print object. In this way, Bo Bardi used *Habitat* to demythologize the *sertão* by speaking to São Paulo's wealth—conflating opposing value systems in its pages, not to unmask those to whom the art market appealed, but rather to challenge the origin of their values. Without abandoning the culture of Brazil's European inheritance and orientation to Western modernity, Bo Bardi sought to rehabilitate it by appealing to the home as a shared space of critical reflection. In her words, one of the goals of *Habitat* was "to make architecture accessible to everybody so they can realize the kind of house where they want to live . . . [and] to have critical judgment. This is what we plan to do through our magazine."[23]

21. Important to this concept is the notion of transference, embedded in the complicated history of flow of both people and ideas across national borders. See Shmuel N. Eisenstadt, ed., *Multiple Modernities* (New Brunswick, N.J.: Transaction, 2002), 1.

22. Kaya, "Modernity, Openness, Interpretation," 35.

23. Lina Bo Bardi, quoted in Lima, *Lina Bo Bardi*, 29.

FIG. 51
Karajá Indian, Bananal Island, Goiás, ca. 1946

FIG. 52
"Amazônas: o povo arquiteto" (Amazon: The People as Architect), *Habitat*, no. 1 (October–December 1950): 68

In increasing the simultaneity of different cultures through their side-by-side exhibition in its pages, *Habitat* forced their interrelation, positing a version of modernity that situated the *sertão* alongside Brazil's established cultural center, if not yet necessarily within it.[24] Eschewing an appeal to middle-class tastes, Bo Bardi invoked the culture of the *sertão*, thereby providing a visual language by which to talk about Brazil's constituent cultures and recognizing the dislocation of modern identities from its coastal regions. She thus expanded the contents of the museum and geographies beyond its own walls and into the private space of the home.[25]

Bo Bardi used marginal content as a means to empathize with those from peripheral regions while simultaneously appropriating it to develop her role as a public figure, demonstrating her agency as a European to speak from a privileged location and to audiences from which intellectual others are excluded. In deterritorializing spaces of privilege, her polyvocal approach choreographed Brazil's hybridity to argue for the coexistence of difference. Yet there was little evidence that the craftspeople in the Northeast, whom Bo Bardi featured, desired assimilation with societies geographically distinct from their own. As Arjun Appadurai has suggested, the "collective memories and desires" of the diaspora are shaped by their plurality rather than their ability to be defined by others.[26] In reality, the incorporation of these groups into an official sphere only anaesthetized Brazil's *sertão* for the palatability of the rich, instead of empowering a culture of the poor. However, the argument Bo Bardi made with *Habitat* was not one of replacement, subjugating Western modernity to a nascent and seemingly more "authentic" Brazilian alternative; rather, she attempted to upend the inequality in the relationship of power between the two. In addressing this rebalance—and by giving equal voice to the aesthetic and material forms of both—she highlighted the West as an idea as much as it is a geographical fact.[27] *Habitat*, therefore, must be viewed not simply as a project of design, but also as a political tool. Through unusually passive but nonetheless provocative means, Bo Bardi instrumentalized the magazine format to combat and challenge broader social relations with the intention of making the bourgeoisie the principal agent of their own decline.

24. Nestor Garcia Canclini, *Hybrid Cultures: Strategies for Entering and Leaving Modernity* (Minneapolis: University of Minnesota Press, 1995).

25. There are interesting parallels between *Habitat* and Le Corbusier's *L'Esprit Nouveau*, which ran between 1920 and 1925. Le Corbusier also understood his magazine as a vehicle for subverting the interests of his readership, stating, "*L'Espirit Nouveau* is read calmly. You surprise your client into calmness, far from business, and he listens to you because he doesn't know you are going to solicit him." Le Corbusier, quoted in Beatriz Colomina, *Privacy and Publicity: Modern Architecture as Mass Media* (Cambridge, Mass.: MIT Press, 1996), 185. It is likely that Bo Bardi would have been familiar with this influential publication, not least because of the personal friendship between Le Corbusier and Pietro Maria Bardi.

26. Arjun Appadurai, ed., *The Social Life of Things: Commodities in Cultural Perspective* (Cambridge: Cambridge University Press, 1988), i.

27. Stuart Hall, "The West and the Rest: Discourse and Power," in Bram Gieben and Stuart Hall, eds., *Formations of Modernity: Understanding Modern Societies, an Introduction, Book 1* (Cambridge: Polity Press, 1993), 275–332.

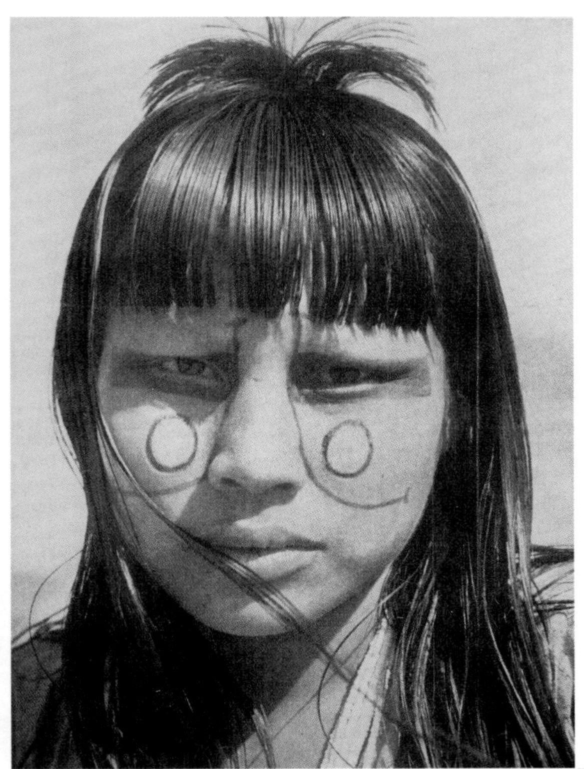

Botequins flutuantes das ruas liquidas de Manaus.

Amazônas: o povo arquiteto

Quando se fala em sociedade, pensa-se sempre, sem saber porque, num cocktail ou numa daquelas festas onde as mulheres vão com as costas despidas e os homens com os sapatos laqueados.

Mas a sociedade é outra coisa; é o conjunto dos cidadãos, e compreende todas as classes sem distinções. É verdade que, para fazer confissão, a sociedade das soirées se faz chamar de "sociedade"; mas esta denominação é errônea: parece-me jamais ter visto, nestas reuniões, figuras de excepcional importância fisica ou intelectual. Estas distinções, medidas com a escala da solidariedade humana, vão sendo aos poucos reduzidas, e os ultimos saudosistas que desejam conservar estas divisões, e a assim chamada "esféra aristocrática", baseados em argumentos históricos fragilissimos e tão absurdos hoje em dia — mais parecem pessoas senis já vividas, do que sêres realmente vivos.

Sociedade, então, significa todos os cidadãos, de Einstein ao fazendeiro do Arizona, de Cocteau ao carteiro de Albi, de Mac Arthur a um soldado raso coreano, enfim, o homem com suas caracteristicas ideológicas ou nacionais ou municipais. (O conceito verdadeiro do Brasil trabalhador, país de cimento, espaços e riquezas, sua atividade generosa — esse conceito, dizia, deveria ser baseado inicialmente nas camadas sociais do interior, ao longo de rios fabulosos, nos cafezais, nas fazendas de algodão, e nos seringais, nas pontes e oficinas. O milagre de uma sociedade que fala uma só lingua há séculos, que se criou numa amalgama de elementos históricos provindos de continentes tão diversos — o Brasil, deve ser compreendido através de imagens reais e não através dos falsos instantâneos das boites).

É porisso que reproduzimos aqui o habitat de nossa gente no Amazônas, com sua casa de uma arquitetura extremamente funcional e muito estética, agradável, com cenas da vida cotidiana, que se manifestam através das alegrias do homem simples.

De vez em quando aparece na cidade um filósofo, por vezes verdadeiro, outras apenas filósofo da universidade — e que, mesmo sem ser iniciado em Sartre, dá sua conferência sôbre o existencialismo, pois esta palavra é mágica. Quando se trata dum existencialista oficial, tudo é visto através dum prisma de péssimismo desesperado do mundo, de "não vale a pena", etc., quando ao contrário, o criador não é existencialista, limita-se a expor teorias, comentá-las, traduzí-las em docinhos digeríveis pelas senhoras presentes. Disse "senhoras", porquê são êstas ao que parece, as mais interessadas pela filosofia, não pela filosofia em si, como pela moda. As conferências sucedem-se em ordem de importância — : filosofia, estética, critica de arte... A senhora condenada a isto não quer que, no dia seguinte à conferência, a prima lhe telefone pedindo o que pensa sôbre Sartre, sem saber qual é o chapeu mais bonitinho da assistência. Precisa-se, afinal de contas, estar ao par daquilo que acontece no campo das modistas!

Jane Hall is a founding member of the architecture collective Assemble, which won the Turner Prize in 2015 for their work in Granby, Liverpool. Her work on public space, occupation, and collective action in Brazil has been published in *Blueprint Magazine*, *The Architectural Review*, and *Matzine*.

EXCURSIONS ALONG THE PRAIA DE AMARALINA[1]

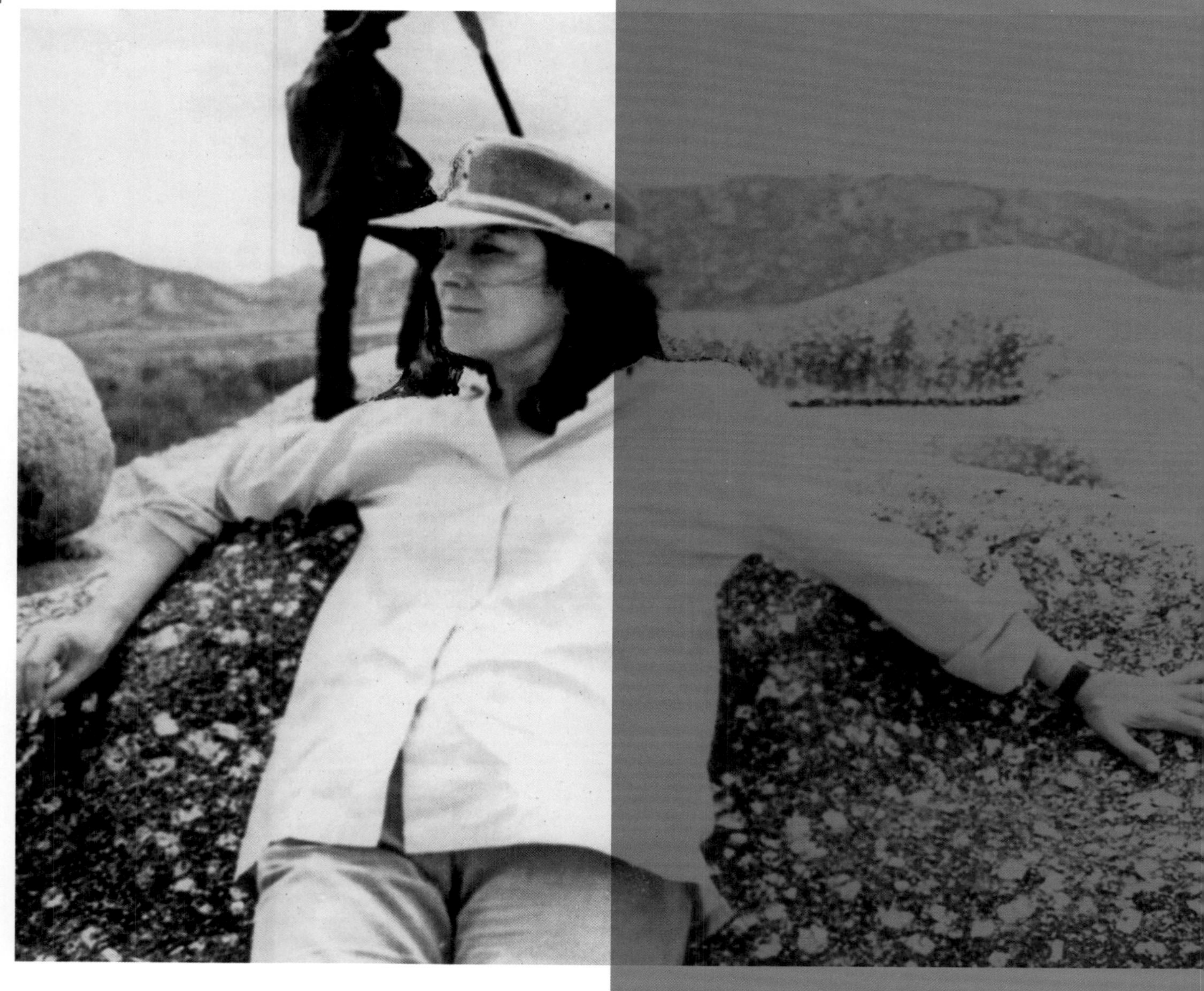

FIG. 53
Lina Bo Bardi during the filming of *A compadecida* (The Compassionate), 1968

1. Praia de Amaralina (Amaralina Beach), on the Bahian coast, is a play on "amar a Lina," or "to love Lina," in Portuguese.

It's easy to recognize the beauty and grandeur of the exhibitions by Lina Bo Bardi, while it is simultaneously difficult to accept the formulations that supposedly support them. True, such an observation remains a truism anytime we venture into the realm of aesthetic creation. But I hope to transcend generic banality, verifying through a close reading, face to face with Lina's work, the manifestation of ambiguities, misconceptions, and contradictions at the theoretical or reflexive level, which in no way diminish the aesthetic results of her achievements. Before celebrating the architect's accomplishments, I will therefore—so to say, schematically—highlight two problems of "Linabobardian" praxis: the *anthropological* misconception and the ideological misconception. Her utopian-ideological predilections are visible in her obsession with making popular northeastern artisanal production a launching pad for her vision of Brazilian industrial design. On the other hand, her anthropological miscalculation took place on two levels: first, in *the fantasy of the northeast* and, second, within it, the inability or unwillingness to objectively recognize—and then try to overcome, thus multiplying—internal differences, characteristic of a merely dualistic understanding of that regional reality.

The formula of the "anthropological gaze" became cliché in writings about the architect's feel-think-do. Lina came from Italy prepared for it, they said. Her anthropological vocation was formed while still on the Italian peninsula, then marked by attention to popular cultural forms, both before and after World War II, under the influence of Antonio Gramsci (the "national-popular"), the concerns of Gio Ponti, and neorealism in cinema, for example. In Brazil, Lina refined and deepened this gaze. "Lina Bardi evolved to [conduct] in-depth research into the Brazilian reality, from the physical to the anthropological," wrote Rogério Duarte in the mid-1960s. And it was along this path that she affirmed her reading of our popular creative output not as folklore, but as culture. Here, her trip was to "the Northeast." But while it is true that we should salute Lina's "anthropological gaze," it is also true that it should be relativized. That it is correct to point out the limitations of her readings, emphasizing that she incorporated into them ecologically and anthropologically unsustainable myths. And the Northeast was, undoubtedly, chief among these.

Certainly, the definition of "the Northeast" is much more political-administrative than anything else. From a geographical-environmental perspective, for example, this is a definition that lacks criteria; that strives neither for clarity nor rigor. Here, ecosystem configurations can simply be ignored. Eclipsed by political determinations. This becomes clear when we acknowledge these violations of geography and environmental realities. On an ecological, ecosystemic level, the Atlantic Forest does not stop abruptly in the region of Porto Seguro, Ponta de Areia, or Mucuri. It does not teeter at the border of Bahia with Espírito Santo.

On the contrary, it extends down to Rio de Janeiro and further. If from this angle it is difficult to accept the classification of the Recôncavo Baiano in the Northeast, it would be even more complicated to include there the regions of Trancoso and Arraial d'Ajuda. Similarly, the *cerrado* connects western Bahia not with the Recôncavo, but with the country's Planalto Central. This is the same landscape that today covers slices of Goiás and the area currently also known by the acronym Mapito, covering the south of Maranhão, the south of Piauí, and the north of Tocantins, plantations where soy thrives. At the other extreme, the tidal wetlands of Maranhão are much more ecologically linked to the Amazon than they are to the Raso da Catarina or the Pernambucan *agreste*, for example. And while the coast is a kingdom of leafy trees, the *caatinga*, with its cacti, covers a vast expanse of the interior.

But moving on, from the ecological to the anthropological. Well known is the contradiction made by Euclides da Cunha in *Os sertões* (Rebellion in the Backlands, 1902),[2] a book in which we never encounter the expression "the Northeast": on the one hand, the *sertanejo* (countryman) as strong-above-all-else—on the other, the neurasthenic coastal *mestiços* (people of mixed ethnic descent) living parasitically along the Atlantic. Euclides saw authenticity as a kind of trademark of the *sertão* (northern Brazilian scrublands), whereas a false, corrupted Brazil existed nearer to the coast. But it is not Euclides' judgment that interests us here, rather his ecological and ethnocultural bipartition of Bahia and "the Northern States." What he saw in the *sertão* was a tormented landscape. The "martyrdom of the earth" that is immediately evoked: "the accumulation of alluvium in the depressions, the dismantling of the [nearly denuded] hills, the winding of the river beds of intermittent streams, the constriction of the defiles, and the almost convulsive appearance of a deciduous flora lost in a maze of undergrowth."[3] It is the *sertão* of burning summers and torrential rains. Of "smooth, rolling tablelands."[4] Of *jurema* and *mandacaru* trees. From the crudest—and cruelest—light. It is within this framework of the martyrdom of the earth, within the ecological environment, that Euclides situated human martyrdom. "The martyrdom of man is here reflective of a greater torture, more widespread, one embracing the general economy of Life. It arises from the age-old martyrdom of Earth."[5] The human being in question is, of course, the *sertanejo*, the "very core of our nationality, the bedrock of our race."[6] And just as he sees the climatic difference between the lands of the interior and the coast, he observes an anthropological dissimilarity between the coastal dweller and the people of the *sertão*. Ethnically, the Atlantic seaboard is above all the site of the intersection of whites and blacks, generating, as a typical product, *mulatos*. With regard to the strong African presence in the region, he draws our attention to "the great black border [that] hemmed the coast from Bahia to Maranhão."[7] The *sertão*, in turn, appears as the kingdom of the mixture of whites and indigenous, generating *mamelucos*. Take the case of Pernambuco, or that of Bahia. In Bahia, between the Recôncavo and the *sertão*, the anthropological distance is much greater than the physical. In skin color, speech, music, cuisine, religion, sexual morality, etc. *orixás* (Afro-Brazilian gods and goddesses) count for nothing on the banks of the São Francisco River, where Senhor Bom Jesus reigns sovereign, receiving his pilgrims.

From this eco-anthropological reading, with an eye to the environmental context and our "confused intermixture of races,"[8] of course, results a geographical space divided in two. On the one hand, the *mestiço*, humid lands of the *mulato* coast. On the other, the *mestiço*, arid region of the *mameluco* backlands. And this dualistic view, signified as "the Northeast," went on to be continued, explained, nuanced, and enriched, but always ratified, in studies such as *Nordeste* by Gilberto Freyre (1937), and *Brazil, Land of Contrasts* by the French sociologist Roger Bastide (1957). Because, between

2. One of the most recent editions of this classic of Brazilian literature is Euclides da Cunha, *Os Sertões*, ed. Walnice Nogueira Galvão (São Paulo; Sesc Editions, 2018). [Editor's note]

3. Euclides da Cunha, *Rebellion in the Backlands*, trans. Samuel Putnam (Chicago: University of Chicago Press, 1944), 13. [Translator's note]

4. Ibid., 11. [Translator's note]

5. Ibid., 49. [Translator's note]

6. Ibid., 464. [Translator's note]

7. Ibid., 72. [Translator's note]

8. Ibid., 52. [Translator's note]

9. Carlos Sávio Teixeira, "A economia política de transformação do nordeste: de Furtado a Unger," *Caderno CRH* 27 (2014), pp. 201–14. [Editor's note]

da Cunha and the Freyre-Bastide pair, we have the officialization of the question: the governmental creation of this entity called the Northeast. See, incidentally, what Carlos Sávio Teixeira tells us, addressing the issue, in the essay, "The Political Economy of the Transformation of the Northeast: From Furtado to Unger":

The Northeast was officially "invented" as a spatial reality during the Estado Novo dictatorship, when the Brazilian Institute of Geography and Statistics (IBGE) arranged the geographic composition of Brazilian regions into five units, as part of the Vargas government's effort to construct and consolidate the nation's identity.[9]

And so: it was precisely in the field of this new ideological reading of the Brazilian national space that the Northeast Development Superintendence (Sudene)—and, within Sudene, the Artesanato do Nordeste SA (Artene) project—came to be, with Lina under the leadership of Celso Furtado. And Lina would come to tangle things up.

Here is the second part of the anthropological misunderstanding we have pointed out. Lina always insisted not only on the "scientific" character of her research, but repeated ad nauseam that her thinking and practice came from cultural anthropology and not from art. Anthropologically, however, she could never have placed together, as she did at the *Bahia in Ibirapuera* exhibition (5th São Paulo Biennial, 1959), *orixá* garments and items of *vaqueiro* (cowboy) clothing. Lina can be considered "anthropological" only in her general view, for the broad concept of culture she manages and for her refusal of the very suspicious notion of "folklore," but never at a specific, concrete level. Because she was never inclined to undertake a clear and objective reading of the objects she worked with—and which, as a general rule, she uninhibitedly shuffled together, unburdened by the uncomfortable presence of criteria. See the above-cited exhibition. There is no clarification about internal cultural differences in the officially Bahian space. Differences between the coast and the *sertão*, if we want to remain within the dualistic viewpoint, are in themselves reductive. Lina heard about these differences—in passing, she used the phrase "civilizations of the coast and the backlands," or even: "The Museum of Modern Art of Bahia developed so to be linked to the culture of the people of the *sertão* and the coast"—but simply resolved not to concern herself with it. She addressed the Bahia of maps, of official territorial demarcations, not from the cultural mosaic that existed within this denomination. She did not seem to pay attention to (or to give importance to) the fact that Bahia is not an integrated or homogeneous anthropological reality, but a political entity that has been forming over time.

In other words, the current state of Bahia, rather than an anthropologically delimited space, is a unit of Brazilian republican federalism. Its borders are political, not cultural; hence its internal diversity. Political landmarks and politically established territorial boundaries are incapable of setting anthropological boundaries, separating areas of culture. Formations and cultural variants have their internal logics, their determinations and indeterminations, their own movements. They ignore geopolitical limits. Moreover, frontiers between provincial and state units in Brazil have always experimented with changes in configuration—and continue to experiment: for instance, the recent demarcation of Tocantins and the division of Mato Grosso. To offer an example concerning our theme: the entire left bank of the São Francisco River, during the period of the Empire, belonged to Pernambuco. Later Bahian cities such as Remanso, Pilão Arcado, and Barra were found within territory that was then Pernambuco. Pernambuco also belongs to the territory of our present agricultural west, where the city of Barreiras, with its vast soybean plantations and its high rates of population growth, is situated. In fact, the political boundaries of the State of Bahia were not defined until the early decades of the twentieth century, through the boundary treaties signed with Minas Gerais, Piauí, Pernambuco, and Sergipe. But the mere fact that the boundaries between Bahia and Pernambuco have moved—that an imaginary line has come to mark the separation between the stretch from Cachoeira do Sobradinho to the Serra das Marrecas—is not enough to provide any type of cultural transposition. The agreement signed with Pernambuco did not cause the region to migrate automatically from the sphere of Pernambucan culture to that of Bahian culture. It simply passed from one political-administrative orbit to another. Culturally, however, it remained identical to itself, indifferent to the political game of state partitions.

For these and other reasons, to speak of the "northeastern" would be as inaccurate and false as speaking of the "southeastern." And "Bahia" has no less than eight basic areas of culture. It would be impossible to erase the distinctive cultural forms, practices, and elements that distinguish the various Bahian cultural zones. To give just one example, recall that Senhor do Bonfim and the *orixás*, so present in Cidade da Bahia (current-day Salvador), bore no weight in the millenarian *sertão* of Canudos. One is the Bahia of Dorival Caymmi, fruit of the Recôncavo; another is the Bahia of Glauber Rocha, a child of Vitória da Conquista, of the *sertanejo* (rural) culture of the Serra Geral region, strongly influenced by the north of Minas; and yet another is the Bahia of João Gilberto, born in Juazeiro, on the banks of the São Francisco, bordering Pernambuco. And so on. But, looking to Bahia, Lina favored political unity over anthropological configuration. However, there are no *exus* (Afro-Brazilian deities) among pilgrims, there was no Zambiapungo (a Bantu deity) in the Chapada Diamantina, nor were there polytheistic *atabaques* (drums and drumming practices associated with northeastern Afro-Brazilian religions and secular practices) in the *cangaço* (a late nineteenth-century phenomenon of banditry

10. Lina Bo Bardi, "Civilização do Nordeste," in *Tempos de grossura: o design no impasse* (São Paulo: Instituto Lina Bo e P. M. Bardi, 1994), 35. [Editor's note]

11. A play on the name of Minas "Gerais" state, literally translated to "General Mines." [Translator's note]

12. Lina Bo Bardi, "Testemunho Nordeste," in *Tempos de grossura*, 65.

13. Lina Bo Bardi, "Por que o Nordeste," in *Tempos de grossura*, 24.

14. Bo Bardi, "Testemunho Nordeste," 62.

15. Ibid.

16. Lina Bo Bardi and Martim Gonçalves, "Bahia no Ibirapuera," in Marcelo Carvalho Ferraz, ed., *Lina Bo Bardi* (São Paulo: Instituto Lina Bo e P. M. Bardi, 1993), 134.

17. Bo Bardi, "Por que o Nordeste," 21.

18. Lina Bo Bardi, "Um balanço dezesseis anos depois," in *Tempos de grossura*, 12.

19. Lina Bo Bardi, "Repassos," in Ferraz, ed., *Lina Bo Bardi*, 200.

20. Lina Bo Bardi, "Caipiras, capiaus, pau-a-pique," in Ferraz, ed., *Lina Bo Bardi*, 244.

21. Ibid.

in the *sertão* region). In any case, the gods of the Recôncavo are not the gods of the semiarid. And the Caboclo of the popular independence mythology of 1822 meant nothing in Xique-Xique or the region of Brumado. Hence the question: What is the Caboclo of July 2nd doing in the *Civilization of the Northeast* exhibition? Oh, and before anyone hastily buys into trendy facts, it's prudent to mention that our architect had a very idiosyncratic understanding of what *civilization* means: "It is the practical aspect of culture, it is the life of men throughout all periods," she said.[10]

Well. People close to Lina could have helped by clarifying some things. Not Glauber Rocha, certainly. Glauber was never very good at clarity and distinction, whatever the subject matter. And especially remarkable was the anthropological confusion that then reigned in his head. He came to consider "northeastern" territories as distant as the cacao region, in a text written for *Civilization of the Northeast*: "Master Guima [Guimarães Rosa; Glauber referred intimately even to God] is from Minas Gerais (another *sertão*, but I think they are all 'General'[11]—open in Alagoas or closed in the cacao forests of Ilhéus)."[12] However, Jorge Amado, despite all of his optical illusions, performed a socio-anthropology of the region, aesthetically re-creating it in several novels. In the early nineteenth century, Ilhéus was a small village founded by priests of the Society of Jesus. Then came the cacao plantations—and the region entered the twentieth century modernizing, transformed into a center that generated great wealth. Anthropologically, it was difficult to define in schematic terms: an agricultural frontier, a space open to migrations, there lived the most varied population, from the Arab merchant to the *mestiço* of indigenous or African descent. But a northeastern region, no. And Glauber would have known this if he had reflected a little on the difference between his first two feature films—*Barravento* (anti-*candomblé* discourse in the Recôncavo) and *Deus e o diabo na terra do sol* (God and the Devil in the Land of the Sun) ("northeastern" backcountry, the filmings of which Lina accompanied).

In the same beat, Lina mixed *orixás* and *carrancas*, *jangadas*, and *jagunços*. She did not come to an anthropological mapping of their surrounding realities. This is the difference between her gaze and that of Pierre Verger, whose photos were exhibited in Ibirapuera; or between her panoramic view and the ethnographic perspective of Vivaldo da Costa Lima, author of *Família de santo nos candomblés Jejes-Nagôs da Bahia* (Family of Saints in the Jeje-Nagô *Candomblés of Bahia*, 1977), which was also part of the São Paulo Biennial exhibition.

As for the ideological misconception, it forms part of the then prevailing horizon of the idealization of the Northeast as a potentially rebellious region (the *Ligas Camponeses!*, a mid-twentieth century agricultural reform movement) and a space of national authenticity par excellence. Ruralism and artisanal ideologies gripped nearly the entire Brazilian left, who exalted the Northeast, northeasterners, and forms of northeastern popular culture. We see this, sub-Euclidesianly, in the Centro Popular de Cultura (CPC), in Cinema Novo-ism, etc.: faced with northeastern authenticity, the city appeared as a culturally corrupted and alienated organism. Lina then engaged in a regional economic development program. We have mentioned the Artene project, within Sudene. Lina sought to make northeastern artisanal production the basis of a Brazilian industrial design. Let us leave aside the Eurocentric "historicist" definition she gave to "artisanal," linking it back to the realm of the medieval guilds. We consider "artisanal" the set of techno-symbolic products resulting from popular creative praxis on elements manipulated by hand, producing objects from nets to clay bowls. But in that northeastern conjuncture of Brazilian culture, Lina made a point of stressing its differential. She emphasized that her search was not at all romantic, and totally scientific. Nothing to do with art.

This *search* [for the country's roots or cultural foundations] on a strictly scientific basis derides populist romanticism, false traditions, all forms of cultural languishing, as well as the attitudes of ideological technocracy.[13]

Lina strongly believed that she was behaving "strictly scientifically" and was almost childishly proud of it—just as Brecht believed that each of his plays was "scientific" (a sociological experiment, rather) of his "epic theater." And Lina's project—from craftsmanship to design—presented itself as a provisional task: "An intermediate stage that would fall away with development and the increase of incomes. At the 'base' was a survey of the socioeconomic conditions of the rural and semi-rural northeastern people dedicated to 'handicrafts,'" she writes in "Northeast Testimony."[14] From these undertakings, Lina produced exhibitions, enlivening the possibility of transmuting the artisanal into the industrial. In other words, rather than retrospectives, the exhibitions were theoretically prospective. They projected possible futures.

Here the "scientific" is another myth. It leaves Lina imagining that she is immune to romantic and/or populist idealizations, although she operated on conceptually romantic grounds, in the wake of Johann von Herder. This is how she writes about Artene in "Northeast Testimony" (her emphasis): "In 1961, Sudene . . . created Artene, an agency dedicated to helping the 'artisan.' It was not a romantic initiative of the Northeast, it was a dispassionate [*frio*] financing plan with no *aesthetic concerns*."[15] But even here Lina is contradictory. For one thing, she says she acted without aesthetic concerns. On the other hand, a text written in collaboration with Martim Gonçalves presenting the *Bahia in Ibirapuera* exhibition reads: "Outside the 'categories' [of 'superior culture,' of 'great Art'], one no longer fears recognizing the aesthetic value of a paper flower or an object made from a kerosene can."[16] Moreover, let us examine a certain irony of history: Lina created an "intermediate stage" from which she could never free herself. The foundations that supported it crumbled, but she did not abandon the perspective so designed. She was trapped within her own past, backsliding to the romantic ideals she had so despised.

Looking carefully at the cultural foundations of a country . . . does not mean conserving shapes and materials, it means evaluating the possibilities for original creation. Modern materials and modern systems of production will then take the place of primitive means, conserving not the forms but the deep structure of those possibilities,[17]

she proclaimed between the 1950s and 1960s. The situation changed, industrialization did not happen in the direction Lina would have liked, but she persisted along this path. Brazilian modernization pulled the carpet out from under itself. And Lina, protesting against "degenerative television" and "spurious industrial products," held onto the old forms, preserving them. "The return to extinct social bodies is impossible, the creation of artisanal centers, the return to the artisanal as an antidote to an industrialization foreign to the country's cultural principles is wrong," she wrote.[18] But what we'll see is Lina cradling artisanal centers and courting extinct social bodies. She reacted with such vehemence against the defense of folk art precisely because it is soaked in celebratory mystification. And, in despising the glorification of the artisanal in the homes of the wealthy, she forgot to mention that she was among those responsible for it.

Yes: even as she moved away from her original project, bypassing the idea of programmatic metamorphosis of the artisanal in design, Lina couldn't shake off her fantasies and discourse. The tone in the exhibition *A mão do povo brasileiro* (The Hand of the Brazilian People; MASP, 1969) already differed from the projectual-ideological preaching of the "northeastern" exhibitions. In the exhibition *Repassos* (Weaving Patterns; MASP, 1975), with its saints and more saints, there was no shadow left of an industrial design project—and Lina seemed somewhat lost, even speaking about the "counter-artisanal."[19] In the exhibition *O design no Brasil: história e realidade* (Design in Brazil: History and Reality; Sesc Pompeia, 1982), she presented the widest panorama, from indigenous objects to industrial products (including "gadgets," which Lina had previously condemned as spurious, having nothing to do with the country and the Brazilian people), but there is no ideological preaching. However, the projectual-ideological basis, as suggested, was already rooted in her spirit, indelible. See the exhibit *Caipiras, capiaus: pau-a-pique* (Countryfolk, Rustics: Wattle-and-Daub; Sesc Pompeia, 1984). She no longer cultivated that initial projectualism, noting that the exhibition was "mushy" (which, in her terms, was worse than "romantic"). "It is a farewell, and at the same time, an invitation to document the history of Brazil."[20] But she was at once mentally confused and even aimless, writing: "What needs to be made clear is that remaining in the phase of identifying the arts in a community is a means of accessing a tranquilizer for those who can't sleep at naptime."[21] But even so, she didn't intend to create a style of architecture or design from the shapes and practices of the rural world. And here is the difference between Lina and anyone who has taken a road aesthetically and culturally similar to hers. The difference in relation to "Linabobardian" projectualism.

From this perspective, which does not carry a precise project of industrial design and doesn't proselytize around it, Brazilian popular artisanal production comes to mean and have interest for what it is, not for what it should be in the ideal terms of a totalizing proposal of the creation of a new *industrial design* in the country. It gains interest, therefore, as a portrait of and testimony to the past, or in its present reality—and not as a basis or springboard for the dream of an industrializing development with a previously

FIG. 54
From left to right: Martim Gonçalves, Vivaldo Costa Lima, Glauber Rocha, an unidentified person, Lina Bo Bardi, and Luiz Hossaka, at Ibirapuera Park, during the installation of the exhibition *Bahia in Ibirapuera*, 1959

22. Lina Bo Bardi, "A arte popular nunca é kitsch," in *Tempos de grossura*, 33.

23. Lina Bo Bardi, "Nordeste," in Ferraz, ed., *Lina Bo Bardi*, 158.

24. Excerpt from the essay "Inconsciência e inconsequência da atual cultura baiana," published in the *Diário de Notícias de Salvador, Suplemento de Artes e Letras*, 5 February 1961, quoted in Rachel Gerber, ed., *Glauber Rocha* (Rio de Janeiro: Paz e Terra, 1977), 23.

defined direction. Without projectualism, as Lina herself would do one day, achieving all the beauty of Benin House in Bahia, with its stupendous "environments."

I always say that Lina was wonderful, but for this she doesn't deserve our full commitment. She did not always strive for rigor and clarity. She was often ambiguous—often confused. By wavering and letting down her guard on her conceptualizations, she provided alibis for artisanal complacency and was seduced "romantically" by popular creativity. More than sending these shapes and objects off into the future, she was also delighted to be stuck where she was, sampling the symbols of supposed rural wisdom. And so she lost sight, here and there, of the urban horizon on which she lived, delighting, against herself, in a perspective of the countryside and handmade clay pots. Fascination with the people is never due to the total erasure of their knowledge. It is never completely free of folklorism-populism. Of admiration, eruditely surprised and captivated by the use of a color or the manipulation of clay into the shape of a pot. And São Paulo fed this fascination for everything that was preindustrial. As a result of its own "urbanoid" extremisms, it was and is a city seducible by ruralisms, ecologisms, naturisms. And so it favored this misguided journey by Lina, who so often celebrated the supposed means as an end, and seemed to be condemned to not know how to address mass culture.

More. Lina, like the entire avant-garde then linked to industrial design, fed the illusion of the useful or necessary object. We will see this in the concretist theorizations of Décio Pignatari, for example, expounding his functionalist utopia of the poem. Or in Rogério Duarte, criticizing Lygia Clark's *bichos* for their playful nature. Lina, in turn, in "Popular Art Is Never Kitsch," wrote:

Objects of use, utensils of everyday life. *Ex-votos* are presented as necessary objects and not as "sculptures," quilts are quilts, appliqué cloths are "appliqué cloths," colored clothing, colored clothing, made with leftover scraps.[22]

Or even more emphatically, in the *Northeast Civilization* exhibition text:

Each object teeters at the border of the "nothingness" of misery. It is this limit and the continuous, hammered presence of the "useful and necessary" that constitute the value of this production, its poetics of nongratuitous human things, not created by mere fantasy.[23]

Impressive as blind ideology. Because Lina's exhibitions and collections were not formed only by "useful objects." There were, among so many other absolutely useless things, from this dryly pragmatic point of view, 13-centimeter-high bicycles, a parakeet made from a molded can, little oil-painted clay oxen, Lilliputian chairs,

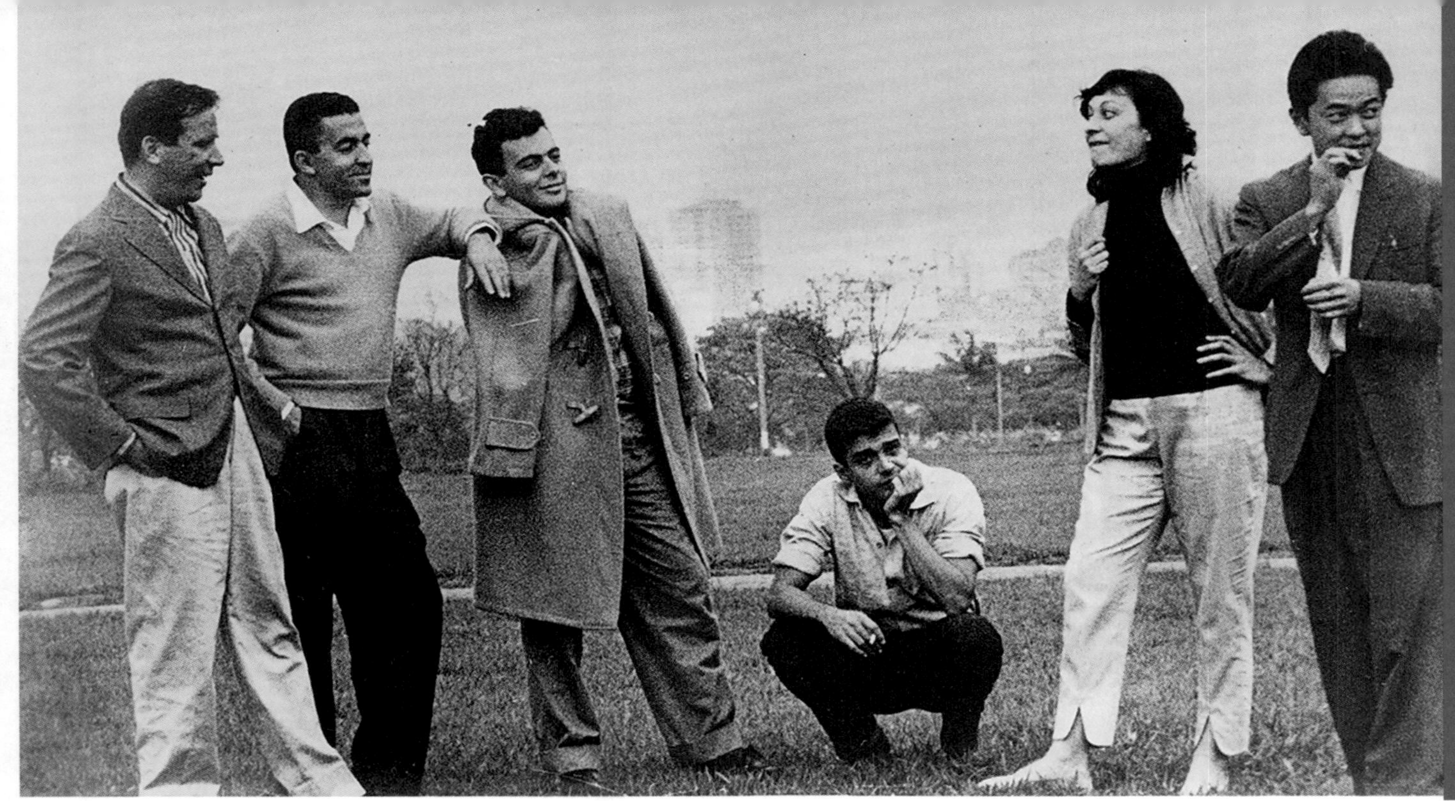

colorful cotton dolls, a radio apparatus with a small bird (in painted raw clay), which Lina found in Santo Amaro da Purificação. Not to mention the exhibition that represents its full reconciliation with the most frankly playful dimension of popular object productions: *Mil brinquedos para a criança brasileira* (A Thousand Toys for the Brazilian Child; Sesc Pompeia, 1982). There, throughout the entire exhibition, the visitor would not find even the slightest shadow of a single useful object.

And so, here, we will finally say something about the language of the exhibitions designed and organized by Lina Bo Bardi. I think her immersion in Bahia was instrumental in clarifying, widening, and deepening a path she had already begun to follow. But of course it was not the only move in that direction. Until the 1970s, at least, we were talking about environments and environmental art, designating environments or ambiences created by visual artists (today, the narrower expression "installation" is instead used). In Allan Kaprow's uncomplicated definition, the term "environment" refers to an art form that fills an entire room (or an extramural space) around the visitor/observer, consisting of any possible materials, including lights, sounds, and colors. And Lina was already out there, putting herself on this track of designing exhibitions as environments (or, should we say, "installations") from work she performed at MASP on Rua 7 de Abril in São Paulo, into the late 1940s. It couldn't be otherwise. After all, although we often forget this fact, architecture is the greatest example of what can be understood as environmental art; especially in the field of so-called "interior architecture." Is preparing a room for a child, designing a kitchen, or setting up a home office not building environments, surroundings? Of course it is. Lina was already technically trained in this sense, however. She also programmatically designed interiors based on store and restaurant layouts.

In addition to carrying forth this "environmentalism" already inscribed in her own architectural practice, Lina knew very well the artistic praxis of the European avant-garde—and she practiced in these fields. In this case, we should not overlook the fact that there was a kind of avant-garde tradition in the field of environmental art. A tradition that, without pretending to historicize, we can trace from at least the famous *Merzbau* by Kurt Schwitters, praised as Hanover's lyrical Dadaist. Following this path, we encounter brilliant creations that must have impressed Lina visually, such as the Surrealist exhibitions in Paris (1938) and New York (1942), assembled by Marcel Duchamp. I think we can say that, in this direction, Lina descended directly from Schwitters and Duchamp. And she moved in the wake of those engaged in the environmental art of the 1960s and 1970s, such as Clarence Schmidt. Or Claes Oldenburg, performing his exhibitions as *environments*: objects independent of one another, but composing an environment. Not to mention Méret Oppenheim, on the Duchampian path, turning the art gallery into an environment in mounting the exhibition. In the Brazilian case, standing out in bold is the presence of Hélio Oiticica in this aesthetic space, creating pieces such as *Eden*, exhibited at the Whitechapel Gallery, London, in 1969, the same year that Lina mounted *The Hand of the Brazilian People*.

Where the influx of Bahia has been felt seems clear to me. It was in the alliance established between Lina (Museum of Modern Art of Bahia) and Martim Gonçalves (the Theater School of the University of Bahia), about which the young Glauber wrote: "The war that the new generations must take up against the province must be immediate: the cultural action of the University and the Museum of Modern Art are two shock tanks."[24] Partnership in the Ibirapuera exhibition and in theatrical montages, with Lina performing the "set architecture" of Brecht's *Threepenny Opera*, directed by Martim. And it is not difficult to see a certain formal affinity between the set design of the *Opera* and the visual structuring of the exhibitions. In the end, what we have is the exhibition viewed as a tensioning or dramatization of space. As dramatic writing. Lina between the theatrical and the anthropological. In *The Hand of the Brazilian People*, for example, we seem to be facing the set design markings of a play. What we can thus say

is that, in her exhibitions, Lina was polishing and deepening this entire repertoire that conceived of exhibitions (and set design) as the creation of environments. And as pioneered by Bahia and the Northeast. Syntactic and semantic influence. Syntactic, in the assimilation of the visual organization of markets and *candomblé* temples. Semantic, at the referential level, with the objects produced in those places. What were visible weren't Surrealistic creations, as in Duchamp's pleasures, but products of the popular creativity of the *sertões* and coastlines in Bahia and the Northeast. Objects displayed in crates, forming shelves, open cabinets, an arrangement inspired directly by the spatial arrangement of objects in northeastern popular open-air markets. And Lina eventually advanced, at least once and even if superfluously, from the sampling of markets to a suggestion of mass culture. On *Design in Brazil: History and Reality*, she speaks about assembly "in the mold of the northeastern *sertão* open-air markets, and São Paulo supermarkets that today flood all the capitals of Brazil."[25]

But let us conclude. As I have said, Lina's exhibitions, in theory, projected futures. And they were very beautiful. They indentified popular creativity with technical precision, cultural respect, and aesthetic sensitivity. But time has passed and those futures did not arrive. The utopia of an industrial design based on artisanal production did not come to fruition. But Lina persisted in that line of exhibitions and began to spin in circles, no longer armed to duel with the present, with no projects for the future. Aesthetic fullness, ideological void. But leaving us a huge lesson. Here, however, we will move away from her position and consider that of Celso Furtado, which she never lost sight of. In a letter to Lina, Furtado wrote:

> I confess that I am not apt to be interested in the ways in which human societies accommodate themselves to misery and exhaust their ingenuity in the simple struggle for survival. By temperament or professional distortion, I am inclined to think that whatever contributes to reconciling man's life with misery must be destroyed, even though by this means we are making the survival of the community unviable.[26]

He's more than right. But what Lina's exhibitions showed us, at the same time, is that even under the harshest living conditions, a community can produce beauty. And remembering Rimbaud, we are obliged to learn how to salute this beauty. As Lina learned. And taught us.

Translated from the Portuguese by Emma Young

FIG. 55
Lina Bo Bardi, Luiz Hossaka, and Carlos Paz during a trip to Ponta Grossa, Paraná, 1958

25. Lina Bo Bardi, "O design no Brasil: história e realidade," in Ferraz, ed., *Lina Bo Bardi*, 236.

26. *Tempos de grossura*, 63.

Antonio Risério was born in Salvador in 1953. A writer (poet, translator, essayist, novelist), he has a master's degree in sociology with a specialization in anthropology. He worked with Lina Bo Bardi in Bahia from 1985 to 1988. Among other books, he has written *Avant-garde na Bahia* (1995) and *A cidade no Brasil* (2012).

WRITINGS BY LINA BO BARDI

FIG. 56
Cover of the book *Tempos de grossura: o design no impasse*, conceived by Lina Bo Bardi and organized posthumously by Marcelo Suzuki (São Paulo: Instituto Lina Bo e P. M. Bardi, 1994)

The São Paulo Museum of Art: The Social Function of Museums

Originally published in *Habitat*, no. 1 (October–December 1950): 17.

To the mind of most people, the idea of the "Museum" is intertwined with a notion of an intellectual mausoleum, understood as the particular result of museum organization based on *conservation* and *specialization*, in which collections, maintained in buildings that architecturally resemble forms from antiquity (classical or Egyptian), suffocate beneath the domes, the monumental staircases, the halls full of columns, thus becoming an embarrassing extravagance . . .

The idea of "conservation," which alone formed the criterion of the museum from the early nineteenth century until almost the present day, is accompanied by "vulgarization" and education, with the associated problems that this new orientation entails. In countries of old culture, where works of art were incorporated into life, the Museum can still retain—particularly when collections are kept in old buildings—the character of selection, providing the visitor with the pleasure of discovery. But in countries still developing their cultures, devoid of a past, the public, aspiring to educate themselves, will prefer elementary and didactic classification.

It is in this new social sense that the São Paulo Museum of Art was established: specifically serving the uninformed, nonintellectual, or *unprepared* general population. The result, in the museum's three years of life, has so far been satisfactory. Founded on 2 October 1947, tens of thousands have visited the museum, today reaching an average of 500 people per day. The Museum's aim is to create an atmosphere, a demeanor capable of evoking for the visitor a state of mind set to understand works of art, and in this sense no distinction is made between an ancient work of art and a work of modern art. To the same end, artworks are not arranged chronologically, but are presented almost intentionally with the aim of eliciting a reaction that arouses curiosity and investigation. Guiding visitors to the permanent collection, created to host a variety of types of work, including paintings, sculptures, and objects, the didactic Exhibition presents, in a synthesis of photographs, color reproductions, and documents, the historical panorama of the development of art throughout the world, or it addresses particular periods or movements. And it was thus, within the same didactic thinking, that the exhibitions of abstractionism and art forms from the most primitive cultures were made; the Exhibition dedicated to the applied arts and the evolution of the chair, in different periods of history of civilization in various countries, exemplified objectively, by historical models more so than by photographic documentation. Didactic shows organized in Europe by Studio Palma de Roma offer their specialized cooperation in every field of art history. The Museum of Art, on the other hand, has nothing to do with external architecture, since it occupies two floors of the Diários Associados building, and the architectural question was thus limited to its internal presentation.

The criterion that informed the Museum's internal architecture was limited to solutions of "flexibility," to the possibilities for transforming the environment, coupled with the strict economy of our time. Evocative refinements and contours have been abandoned, and works of ancient art are not exhibited on velvet or atop fabrics from their time, as still advised by many experts in museology, but are boldly placed against a neutral background. So, too, the modern works, in a standardization, have been situated so that they do not stand out before the observer has them in sight. Thus they do not say, "you must admire this, it's a Rembrandt," instead providing the viewer with pure, unprepared observation, guided only by the caption, descriptive from a point of view that eliminates exaltation in favor of critical rigor. Frames were also eliminated (when they were not authentic to the work's time) and replaced by a neutral band of fabric. In this way, old works of art find new life alongside modern ones, in the sense that they become a part of today's life as much as possible.

In addition to the didactic problem, the Museum faced the question of conservation. The problem of humidity, associated with thermometric instability, is extremely important in the tropics, so that a uniformity between humidity and ambient temperature should be established as much as possible, a basic observation so that the artwork will not come to experience their effects. The problem has been more or less simplified, given the possibility for the Museum to be artificially illuminated during the day, which has removed the dual effects of daylight and night light, and an insulating wall can be raised from the outside by a system of shutters, allowing for continuous ventilation, isolating the environment from sudden contact with the outside and from sudden consequential variations.

The illumination diffuses in solar intensity, cold in the combination of white and pink light bulbs, embedded beneath a metallic cell, removable in sectors; the lamps are fixed against a white cotton background that does not interfere with light refraction. Thus a uniform illumination of uniquely tranquil clarity is obtained, allowing for absolute visibility without color change and completely eliminating "glare."

The Museum features two auditoriums with an intermediate film booth, which operates for conferences, classes, and film showings.

Completing the didactic character of the Museum of Art, the Institute of Contemporary Art was created, which will focus particularly on industrial design and the applied arts, and will have a publication. [It will offer] special courses in natural design, music history, printmaking, and photography, as well as a children's section with painting, music, and dance lessons.

As we have noted, the Museum of Art is dedicated to the general public, and is therefore not dedicated only to collecting "masterpieces," despite the works of importance in its collection. It is neither a Museum of Ancient Art nor a Museum of Modern Art—it is a Museum of Art, and seeks to form a "mentality for understanding art," an atmosphere. And if, with great scandal to some "initiate," they find the "pompiers" exhibited, the explanation is found in the respective description, which defines that this was something that had nothing to do with art. Because we must consider outdated the criterion of ignoring what the general public considers as art; and how can we explain that a thing is worth nothing if this is not made evident, placed next to that which has value?

Beautiful Child

Originally published in *Habitat*, no. 2 (March 1951): 3. Collected in Silvana Rubino and Marina Grinover, eds., *Lina por escrito: textos escolhidos de Lina Bo Bardi, 1943–1991* (São Paulo: Cosac Naify, 2009), 70–73.

How many people know how to distinguish the "authentic" modern from imitations?

The "facade contest" that rewards the Norman and the Baroque is less dangerous than the modern of builders and transformist architects.

We have published a view[1] of the Rio de Janeiro Ministry of Education in order to continue fighting against routine, against the commonplace. Let us be clear,[2] the commonplace is not just the "stylistic"; it is also (and even more dangerously) the so-called "modern." The urge to combat the nascent modernistic "routine"—"the old no longer serves; so, young men, onward with the modern if we don't want to lose the game"—the struggle must be directed against this dangerous generalization, against this demoralization of the spirit of modern architecture, which is a spirit of intransigence and love for man, which has nothing to do with exterior forms and formalist acrobatics.

The new Brazilian architecture has many flaws: it is young, it has not had much time to stop and think, it was born suddenly, as a *beautiful child*; we agree that *brise-soleil* and tilework are "intentional elements," that certain Oscar [Niemeyer] free-forms are visual complacencies, that construction is not always satisfactory, that certain detail solutions are inconsistent with the whole (agreeing here with my European friends), but we do not agree on the fact that Brazilian architecture is already on the road to academicism, as it sometimes appears in certain foreign reviews, as, for example, in the important book by Bruno Zevi;[3] and it will not go [in that direction] as long as its spirit is the spirit of man, his research, the pursuit of the values of his evolving life, as long as he draws his inspiration from the intimate poetry of the Brazilian land; these values exist in contemporary Brazilian architecture. Contemporary Brazilian architecture does not derive from Jesuit architecture, but from the "wattle and daub" of the solitary man, who laboriously cut down branches in the forest; from the rubber tapper's house, with its log floor and thatched roof; it is also alluded to, and resonates, in its furious resolve to create an excellence and a poetry, which are the excellence and the poetry of the backwoodsman, unfamiliar with museums and the great cities of civilization, who does not have a legacy of millennia, but whose achievements—made possible only because of his elusive excellence—are arresting to men from old civilizations.

In order to build itself up, Brazilian architecture chose the style of Le Corbusier, who came to Brazil ([Frank Lloyd] Wright also visited Brazil), [as it seemed to] most correspond to the aspirations of a people of Latin origin: a poetic approach, unrestrained by puritanical presuppositions and prejudices.

This lack of politeness, this rudeness, this taking and transforming without a care, is the force of Brazilian contemporary architecture. It is a continuous possessing of itself, blending consciousness of technique, spontaneity, and the ardor of primitive art. For these reasons, we do not agree with our European friends that Brazilian architecture is on the path to academicism.

This is an attempt to respond to Abelardo [de Souza]'s judgment that "we don't yet know the *why* of this progress of our architecture."[4] Brazilian architecture was born as a beautiful child;

we do not know why it was born beautiful, but we must now educate it, heal it, guide it, and follow its evolution. There was the miracle of birth, but now its direction, the continuation of its life, the achievement of a coherent purpose, will depend on human consciousness, on the possibilities for struggle, conviction, and intransigence. This is what must be affirmed.

1. Referring to a photograph of the ministry building that accompanied the text. [Editor's note]

2. In the original, *entendemos* ("we understand"). [Editor's note]

3. Bruno Zevi, *Storia dell'architettura moderna* (Turin: Einaudi, 1950). [Editor's note]

4. Abelardo de Souza, "Nossa arquitetura," *Habitat*, no. 2 (March 1951): 4–5. [Editor's note]

First: Schools

Originally published in *Habitat*, no. 4 (July–September 1951): 1.

Let's start with schools; if anything is to be done to "reform" men, the first thing is to "form" [educate] them. The argument is nearly exhausted, avalanches of books and pamphlets, the echoes of endless speeches and lectures accompany it; it is natural that one should start with schools, as everyone knows, it is an acquired thing, that, like all acquired things, soon passes into the routine of things that no longer produce effects. Making schools, making schools, making schools, okay, do it, the fact fits into abstract initiatives, resounding ministerial decisions; it lacks the burning interest, the "drama" of the thing. It is necessary to dramatize the problem of schools, to make it alive, present, everyday.

What is a school?

It is a place where one learns to read and write, where we learn to look at a clock and tell the time, where above all one learns to be proud of their country, thanking God every night for bringing us into the world in X instead of Y, whose inhabitants are noticeably less intelligent than us. In schools, many subjects and infinite other things are studied in a progressive order of time, until the day when, upon leaving school, the complex of all these things has formed the baggage, the provisions made to begin one's journey through humanity.

What is school like?
It is SCHOOL; with that special school smell, that school feeling, those school activities, a set of [what defines] school that lifelong will recall SCHOOL, with abandoned attempts [to grow] gardens, narrow windows, hallways, and the Administration; with a teacher urging students on like racehorse trainers, stimulated by arrival [at the finish line], the medals, the ribbons, prizes.

That smell of school remains with us all our lives, along with the knowledge base we continue to practice, without, however, exercising our own ability to examine and form opinions.

We say: "I do such a thing because it is right, I have always done it, I know it is right."

Why is it right?
One day the mind stops and circumscribes and analyzes this thing, returns to the time and origin of that conviction, that belief, and it originated there, long ago, in school, inculcated in school, strongly supported by parents who for their part know that it is right to do this thing, because it is right to do it, without knowing why; and that conviction also originated within a school, even further back in time. The responsibility of school: under acute and penetrating examination, that conviction turns out to be wrong, capable of producing unprecedented consequences. But on whom, then, do schools depend? It is a vicious cycle: they depend on men who, in turn, must be educated in school.

We express our pessimism about the general orientation of schools based on long-considered personal experience. Our greatest struggle lies in what we have done to free ourselves from a crystallized superstructure, a straitjacket formed, in our case, by millennia of commonplaces that, arising from splendid renovations, become, through centuries of routine, acquired, dead places.

Let us state our struggle; the present writer was born in Europe and belongs to the generation of the optimistic-sportive schools par excellence; to a time of heroic presumptions. That entire fortress had been prepared, first and foremost, in schools, word for word, sheet for sheet, nuance for nuance; those beliefs were convenient, firm like rocks, for resolving situations, defending convenient ideas.

The greatest struggle was to find not a solution that evidently was impossible to find, but a clean way of adapting to the facts as we suspected they were in reality—to adapt by searching with one's own strengths. And the biggest struggle was to free ourselves from the crystallized superstructure formed by millennia of commonplaces, acquired during schooldays.

We thought that a possible solution—and it seemed to us the only one—was humility, and we thought that perhaps in perpetuating this attitude we could abolish the recurring birth of "dogmas" that, "true" and brilliant at the moment of inception, periodically plunge men into catastrophe soon after becoming routine and commonplace.

This condition of humility must be continually lived and dramatized so as not to become itself an acquired thing, and the utmost care must be devoted to the formation of the "humble" and extremely civil mentality that "counters nature."

We believe in the possibility of the evolution of men and the possibility of self-improvement of each human being.

At first glance, the premise for buildings constructed as schools appears to supersede the architectural problem, but is, on the contrary, closely linked to it. The schools we present in this issue are all rigorously current, expressed according to the forms of that contemporary architecture that is essentially inspired by man and the "humble" position described above. The [creation of] expanding forms, which connect with the outside, the garden, the wide windows, that air of "nonseverity," is the first step toward the abolition of barriers. The school-fortress,

Gothic, Norman, or lacking any particular style except maintaining the common denominator of a prison building, practically reminding students that learning is a painful obligation—this school has become remote and obsolete. And the very fact that modern architects were called upon to design all these schools seems to us prophetic.

Let's start with schools, and above all, let's start with architecture.

Vitrines

Originally published in *Habitat*, no. 5 (October–December 1951): 60–61. Collected in Silvana Rubino and Marina Grinover, eds., *Lina por escrito: textos escolhidos de Lina Bo Bardi, 1943–1991* (São Paulo: Cosac Naify, 2009), 75–79.

Window displays are an immediate reflection, a quick "tell" of a city's personality, and not just of its outward traits, but its deepest character. The window display is the "medium" for selling a product, it is deeply tied to money, it is a velvet glove that beneath a decorative and indifferent appearance hides the gnarled claws of calculations of "costs," "margins," "profits," columns of dispassionate [*frias*] figures. A veritable theory (called "science" by its interested parties), a special psychology, a calculation of possible probabilities concealed by apparent indifference, the seeming "tribute to the passerby" of a window display, a small mousetrap containing merchandise-cheese for the passerby-mouse. Thus come into being "building cheese-sales," "cheese-liquidations," and all accompanied by posters, writings, arrows. And the window displays shout, "We want to sell, sell, sell, sell by means of X and Y, buy, buy, we want money, MONEY." Money. The wreaths, the chalk vases, the smiles of the mannequins, the velvet draperies shout this word, render transparent the "psychology" of the window-dresser, who in "decoration" was only concerned with the vase-cheese, the velvet-cheese, for the customer-mouse. However, the city is a public space, a great exhibition space, a museum, an open book offering all kinds of subtle readings, and anyone who has a shop, a window display, any hole-in-the-wall closed in with glass, and seeks to exhibit something in that display, who wants to play a "public" role in the city, takes up a moral responsibility, a responsibility which requires that they stop ignoring the fact that "their" window display might help to shape the taste of city-dwellers, help to shape the face of the city and reveal something of its essence.

We have photographed, arbitrarily, window displays: of clothing, sports objects, and even religious objects, in which certain elements that in past centuries were works of art now appear weakened and tragic, depleted of the pure and coherent forms of the time. We photographed stand mixers and electric coffee makers, presented amidst baroque stucco and paper flowers, seeking almost, in this way, to be corrected, to shed their strictly utilitarian forms.

The multitudes of mannequins, their elegance reduced to paper tufts and coats, thus reveal the tastes of the petty, the petit bourgeoisie, the bourgeoisie, and the nouveau riche, nurturing old-fashioned vices and old habits, almost invincible in their violent capacity for immediate contact and public diffusion in the window display, incomparable to the persuasive work of articles, exhibition halls, or books, which must be sought out.

The city's window displays can destroy years of work done to correct and direct taste. We intentionally name the petit bourgeoisie, the bourgeoisie, and the nouveau riche (we can also almost always amplify the small elite), because we exclude popular window displays; as in art, the taste of the people (uncontaminated by false intellectuals) does not err. The windows of the truly popular neighborhoods, the markets, the street fairs, are therefore inspired by spontaneous actions unrelated to any snobbish routine of "art" (in the most common sense attributed to this word since the late nineteenth century) and help to create a pure atmosphere, that atmosphere obtained by the "educated" classes only through very hard discipline and rigorous curation.

With clear controversial intent, we publish the work of a window-dresser who considers window displays to be public tribunes or exhibition halls, who, above all, does not care about the "cheese-mousetrap," but attempts to call attention to their product by following only the dictates of their morals, their sense of collective responsibility.

When asked, the director of a firm confirmed the excellent results of this kind of selected and rigorous publicity; it does not frighten the public; they stop, look, enter, purchase, recognizing in the honesty of that presentation a commercial "cleansing," a nonsale, nonfire, nonliquidation, a nonmousetrap.

Assessments and Museographical Perspectives: A Museum of Art in São Vicente

Originally published in *Habitat*, no. 8 (July–September 1952): 2–5.

Four years ago, with a first and modest group of artworks, and in a location adapted simply, with the most rational of intentions, the São Paulo Museum of Art was inaugurated. Its destiny was characterized by an unparalleled desire to elevate itself to a level of modern, living, coherent, practical, active nature. To elevate it to such an extent that its existence and functioning could gain a reputation as a social and cultural resource for the metropolis—not merely as a jewelry box, a vault of small gems from the past, but an historical decoration. The idea was unprecedented, it seemed fanciful or impossible, as if simply an extravagant idea.

Four years later, it seems that the time has come for a kind of assessment. Especially considering that in the interim certain unforeseen facts came into being, such as requests by administrations of smaller populations to establish similar museums, no doubt on a smaller scale, but certainly with similar intentions and scope. It thus follows that the assessment transforms into greater prospects that now open up to the museum.

In constructing a museum, we must ask ourselves a number of questions, as in the Aristotelian categories:

What, exactly, should we teach here today?
Who should we teach today?
Why must we teach?
How should we teach?
And where will we teach?

All of these questions seem to be more of a rigid list of distinctions of the exclusive competence of scientific disciplines, in the case of pedagogy and education. But history teaches that pedagogy and education have never contributed to educating a single man if not animated by a warmer, more affable, deeper human content, which the mere knowledge of methods and systems would never allow for. There are fundamental laws, or rather a fundamental discipline, in the general orbit of what we commonly describe as "educational." But such laws have a value, a meaning, and an efficacy, that is, a moral and social outcome only when they shift and adapt to environmental conditions, to the complex structure of a given society, with a certain degree of intellectual development and with its typical needs. Education can no longer be conceived of as a manual of amorphous norms, valid everywhere and applicable in any manner. Any education will only be alive when supported by a long effort to adapt to individuals, to whom it applies, with love and with the keen spirit of observation, which allows us to understand the degree of needs and to study the most opportune and suitable means of communication.

Made official and static within the national and political complex, with closed programs, applied with indifference and minimal effort, education is an aspect of modern cultural life. Political bodies themselves, when and where they are open to the influence of the dictates of intelligence, not only do not hinder, but even serve, sometimes request initiative, as it were, private initiative, spontaneous initiative, direct intervention by the people, to shape a culture and to fill the very gaps that no abstract program, no schematic prediction can ever fill.

Thus, we believe it is possible to affirm: only education in movement, understood as "work in progress," conceived as specifically suited to certain local conditions, only an organic and living education can respond quickly to certain popular urgencies, circumscribed and delimited by a number of political conditions. Let us say: only an "organic" education can answer the basic questions of every educational task undertaken. What to teach? What to teach today, here, in this place, in this climate, in this zone, where the people practice such and such things, have such social structure, such sensibilities, such historical formation, such economic conditions, such degree of moral development? First of all, it will be necessary to examine and ask what one wants to know, and secondly, what one needs to know. These are the things that, in an educational program centered at the department of some large capital, drawn up in a council, or according to political or parliamentary requirements, generally go unseen or understood in their essence, in their entirety and details. It has been found that in the present age, when the word seems to have lost in intensive value, and certainly has lost all its power of penetration and persuasion, emphasis and feeling, requirements that it has held for millennia, the word represents, among the multiple instruments of communication, a noble but decadent tool. A less effective tool. What we will discuss is commonplace, but no less true: the greatest communicative force today is given by mechanical instruments that reproduce reality and the word itself. Man's mind today learns visually. Engraving and mechanical reproduction now give human eyes a vast view of the facts of humanity and an anarchic and fragmentary conception of cultural spheres. True culture must, in general, employ the same mechanical means, the same visualization system, to provide a smarter, more disciplined, more humane, and more coherent order than any other, derived from violent and disorderly improvisation of the figurative image.

There is a world of propaganda, of the various advertisements, politics, and trade that violently orient themselves against the human brain, with a bombardment of thousands and thousands of psychologically studied figurations in order to lure, into the orbit of their own interests, all human groups. Well, culture must follow the same methods in order to draw all human groups into the orbit of the higher interests it represents, that is, into the realm of civilization, morality, beauty, utility. For this reason, the typical scholastic education, still commonly imposed on the basis of the word, is no longer able, as a system, to construct on its own a repertoire of beautiful and useful knowledge, for which man often has demonstrated a fundamental and unsurpassed desire. Such needs we seek to address. The world today possesses greater means to disseminate the pornography necessary for the seduction by particular products (for example: certain soft drinks base their preferential advertising on pornography, no doubt simply suggested, but no less morbid), than to attract people to the authentic values of beauty.

For each illustration that reproduces the beauty of a painting by Raphael or Rembrandt, there circle around the world thousands of reproductions of a nude that celebrates a cosmetic with little utility and usually damaging to the epidermis. On the other hand, these illustrations' range of dissemination is vast: they reach everywhere, the highest mountains, the most unknown countries. In the meantime, culture, constrained to work without the means that industry and advertising can skillfully subtract from consumers, must at least work in depth, overcoming obstacles, resistances, hardships, often relying on chance or the goodwill of enlightened people, lovers of their neighbors. Therefore, any modern museum that meets the needs and desires of the people cannot fail to consider such a reality.

These were exactly our purposes in opening the São Paulo Museum of Art. Welcoming a series of masterpieces from the past (which today represent a series worthy of being featured in museums in Europe and North America, and currently the only one of value in all of South America), we were concerned with shining the educational, historical, and civic light on as many people as possible. But we didn't just attend to the visitor, the melancholy scholar, the rushed and tired tourist, the isolated and dispersed, who sees for the first time a famous work and does not understand why it is so important. We didn't just attend, calling over to see, illustrating, clarifying, explaining, answering the many questions asked; on the contrary, we immediately planned and carried out an initiative which in many respects was the first of its kind in the world, that is, elementary, organic, summarized exhibitions, with illustrative materials strategically assembled and arranged in rooms, from all of art history, the arts, culture, thought. First in general, then period by period, gradually improving and widening the range of interest and news, and progressively building a tone. Such exhibitions in part still remain accessible to the public and are objects of continuous examination, as points of reference. Gradually, the original works that the main gallery exhibited took shape as reference to the history and life of man, and emitted a veritable flow of news and notions, consisting of the history of man and his very conscience: his way of being, of proceeding, working, living, dwelling.

Soon after the initial contacts with the first social strata, the Museum of Art suffered its first disappointments, which in many respects constituted the primary material upon which to create its first concrete experiments, worthy of the future. What happened then was in fact the confirmation of previously held convictions, namely, that the social strata most eager to approach the great heritage of past culture and culture in formation are comprised of living, humble, sincere, respectful people. And that is indeed what happened. The Museum considered it its duty to call upon, first and foremost, Brazilian artists, those who should make art not only an ambitious practice or a mundane profession, but, in the first place, a true mission. For this reason, the Museum of Art offered an unconditional welcome to all artists. The result was contrary to any prediction. The so-called old-guard artists, the academics, the *bombeiros*, didn't even show up; and yet what the Museum offered was more directed to them than to any others. They buried themselves further and further in their caves, digging in the dark, like armadillos or moles. Perhaps their blindness doesn't even deserve consideration. The moderns, the so-called moderns, arrived with an air of triumph. Naturally, the Museum, intended for true values, could not encompass everyone. The beginners, the dilettantes, and all those who copy the latest reproductions of European paintings, were at least for some time judged outside the circle of consideration. All of them, then, also ended in their own greatness, in their romantic dream of mastery; and there they remain closed up. Other artists were called upon to collaborate on work that truly required the passionate contribution of all. They considered this a very lowly task, and one by one they disappeared, which is why the Museum of Art was, in turn, isolated, at the center of all responsibilities, and with the obligation to carry out the task alone, working exhaustively. We were only encouraged by the fact that a spontaneous selection had been made: the best, authentic exponents of Brazilian art stayed on with us, giving us their collaboration, their work, their advice, the prestige of their presence: Portinari, Di Cavalcanti, Segall, Burle Marx, and popular artists.

It was then that the Museum could clearly face the situation. It understood its tasks. It elaborated its instruments. It delimited the areas that deserved the most attention, complete dedication.

Thousands of people came to us seeking guidelines, knowledge, practice. They were living people, free of that vanity and sufficiency that characterizes the figures of the artistic world on the scene. [These living people] are usually destined to play the role of the sidekick, often of a second order, who should never utter a word or even a simple reply.

Here are the people to whom we should speak: the people, the young people. What shall we say? Everything that life and school could not say. All that in life is found to be devoid of rational knowledge, rational principles, and practical conscience. Desires and needs were manifold: one wanted to learn about "modern design" that could be useful in life, another wanted to round out their personality, or simply to rhythmically perfect their own body. Thus arose a first school, deeply rationalized, and based on the broad experience of thirty years (the "Bauhaus," European and North American; the recent institutes of North American "industrial design"), of applied design. This is how artists, or at least designers, of modern culture and vitality, are educated. The traditional subjects taught in government academies are entirely outdated, slow, unsuitable for life; at least they can now be rounded out with others capable of scientifically shaping the artist of our day. Special consideration was given to UNESCO's timely advice and suggestions. For their part, children were introduced to music, dance, drawing, painting, modeling, and the visual arts with a pedagogical technique consistent with modern movements in the fields of art and art education.

At first, the problem of children seemed the most difficult, one reason for which was that the application of even the most advanced and intelligent but abstract pedagogical norms could not yield reliable results. It was simply a defect in structure and of educators not yet fully aware of the new educational reality. How to foster the instinct of artistic vitality, to enter the field of children's art education? How can we balance children's tendencies without stunting, but on the contrary, by *provoking* a sense of intellectual and poetic freedom? Thus was born that affectionate and systematic tolerance, designed to help them discover for themselves the means to say and represent ever more clearly what they intend to say and represent.

Then, insisting, tackling new ways and testing new instruments, we finally arrived at the conclusion that, with time and patience, we were progressively achieving more convincing results. What's more, we are studying the possibility of organizing, together with children's art education, and in direct contact with them, a school of children's psychology, which makes a direct contribution to this important sector, in which many scientists in other parts of the world are already working.

In the field, that is, the collective, one of the most striking results (though for us, not the most important) was the founding of a children's and youth orchestra, which in recent times has achieved great success with both critics and audiences, receiving invitations from various concert halls, not only in Brazil, but even from abroad. But the Museum's management was more interested in the social consequences of the event, because the education and instruction of an orchestra of more than seventy people represents a set of individual efforts by very young children, who testify to the absolute possibility of establishing important and ongoing cultural contacts with the people, outside of the spheres of official education, overcoming the difficulties of practical life. What we are trying to do in the orchestral sector, we also do to the same extent in the vocal-choral sector.

Cinema—and here we enter another field—is the cultural activity (we don't use the word "art" so as not to insist on an old polemic, and because it is probably not art) that most strongly engages the people in its exhausting magic. It is the legitimate and most democratically successful successor of the old theater of the last century, the bourgeois theater. Many—the majority—attracted by the halo of cinema lose themselves to its insinuations and are thus content. But others, especially young people, want to go further, to see behind the screen and behind the scenes, to learn how this amazing device is made: cinema, a powerful instrument and vehicle of life, poetry, morality and immorality, passions and melancholy, knowledge and mistakes.

Now, the first thing we proposed, in the foundation of a center of cinematographic studies, was exactly this: unconcerned with establishing elements for a Brazilian cinematography, we intended to spread awareness of an artistic, scientific, technical, and commercial issue, which is inherent to that instrument of modern life. The most useful elements of cinematography provide the Museum of Art's "Cinema Seminar" with this precious function. We cannot claim that we have thus far obtained extraordinary results in this field. However, and in compensation, the results thus far are already tangible, in respect to the Institute of Contemporary Art. A large metropolis such as São Paulo in fact feels the effects of taste and of the precision that this school, first rate in every field, champions and takes as an indispensable model, to the point that large commercial organizations have requested their intervention in the renovation of their display windows. In our experience, it is never too early to introduce children to works of art. However, it is always too late to place adults into contact with the disciplines of art, even the fields in which modern life appears to exclude them. For this reason, the Museum also concerned itself with establishing contact with certain practices of life, in which art can enter as an element of regularity, of precision, of beauty: it concerned itself with fashion, with organizing memorable exhibitions (free of any commercial interest), with publicity, equally preparing exhibitions of top importance, not only for Brazil, but worldwide; it was interested in creating courses on manual weaving, on mannequin styling, gardening, photography, and radio technique, in addition to holding lectures on certain types of music and music history.

In one field among many, our activities have likely produced scarce results or compensations; and, sometimes, have even contradicted our intentions. Our intellectual constitution, subordinated to certain European demands (those which, in Europe, receive the generic name "historicism"), inspired the Museum of Art to institute a cycle of lectures as a basis for work aimed at forming in each area a cultural-historic climate favorable to the life of the entire educational organism. Much of this work led us to the conviction that, in general, everything was obscure, superfluous, or immature. Keeping in mind that European education, founded in two centuries of idealism, historical idealism, historicism, does not find firm grounding in the young mentality of South America, or, at least, doesn't seem destined to provide sufficient stimulus. Perhaps it would be better to seek to develop this original and brilliant mentality and curiosity with respect to the event and the historical fact, rather than explaining the long mechanisms intellectually reconstructed as the base for an analysis whose meaning escapes immediate, normal comprehension. We have decided to always bear in mind that there is no rigid culture to which mentalities must adapt, instead developing a malleable culture, in the face of the spontaneous mentalities of individuals, to whom we provide stimulus for their own deductions and conclusions. Such work of organizing courses (in art history, in music history) leaves furrows and traces that are noticeable, but not incisive. It was, therefore, a mistake; but like all errors, it was useful to our experience. After four years of existence, the São Paulo Museum of Art, whose vicissitudes, whose work, whose results already represent a short but intense chapter in the cultural life of postwar Brazil, has become an example, including for its wealth of artistic material, the possible envy of many North American and European museums. Exemplary and admired to the point of constituting an impetus and model for further spontaneous initiatives of the same or entirely similar genre. In fact, some smaller centers have already approached the Museum, requesting that one be organized in one of these locations. They are locations on the periphery, where the simple desire of having an institution that contributes to raising the cultural level of their respective populations is more strongly expressed.

The fact that small [city] centers hope to establish local museums can be considered exceptional. Indicative of a high civic and intellectual level may be the fact that local authorities, certainly preoccupied with economic problems or those of another nature, are interested in museums. It is a sign that, following our example, they have come to understand a truth à La Palisse, but in which we generally don't enjoy much credit: that the expenses incurred by a population to conquer its own culture are not negative expenses, are not wasteful. What's more, that a modern museum cannot be a place in ruins, where antiques pile up and dust prevails, as in the catacombs.

From the beginning of our activities, we have established that the Museum, emerging from beneath the weight of its authority of safekeeping precious artistic heritage, did not intend to defend or propagate a pure "love of art," whose psychology represents a simple manifestation of European "decadence." As our director wrote some time ago:

All of the normal and exceptional means, known or yet to be discovered, will therefore be employed to transform the Museum into a functional brain of a practical and ideal agreement of all who energetically dedicate themselves to the responsible cause of educators through museums. In this way, and almost suddenly, the Museum changes perspectives, intentions, and orientations, achieving a type of peaceful revolution, changing characteristics or very natures. It is evident that part of the environmental conditions in which museums are still required to maneuver demonstrates itself to be insufficient for the new missions to which they are imperatively assigned.

The Museum is not a set of antiques, not a touristic, aristocratic, mundane, or maniacal spectacle (though of course there are maniacs of the collections). That was what we hoped to demonstrate, and thus, mayors and governors, who before this would never have considered making luxury expenditures, came to us, because we were in a position to place our experience at their disposal. We were very pleased with this, primarily because it corresponded to one of the directives that have guided our activities in the Museum. There is nothing left for us but to give thanks for those invitations that, extended on behalf of the populations they represent, were addressed to us. And we were especially pleased with one result, that such people always declared themselves willing to give way to competence, specialization, and specific experience in the field of museum organization.

For our part, we had decided to wait, even for a hundred years, or to give up everything, if we could not achieve complete and absolute confidence in the results, until our projects were fully recognized and approved, without compromise, without transitions, prevarications, or hybridity between old and new methods. In a city like São Paulo, we would have to endure pressure, often settling for certain compromises. But now anyone who wants to work with us, under our guidelines and for the same good and cultural purposes, can do so. Dilettantes, amateurs, who promote themselves to directors, not knowing exactly what a delicate organism like an art museum means within a social order, should not have a voice active enough to divert us from the right course.

To São Vicente, where, precisely because of this condition, we have decided to establish a new museum, we must first of all answer a question thus far unanswered: Where, or rather, what will the specific building be like, in which the modern museum can provide a steady and continuous lesson? It is logical that, like all typical functions, human activity will also eventually find its architectural aspect, its proper form, which coincides perfectly with the environment in which it comes into being and the purposes for which it is intended: the purposes will be the ones announced by all genuine modern museography, the environment will be that of the natural, of the landscape, the climatic, economic, and social conditions in which it should develop. Thus, architecture itself can acquire educational meaning, expressive meaning. The more attractive the São Vicente Museum's building is, the more important to the interests of the population it will become. [A museum] is born, facing the Atlantic, along a beach, built on the sand. A building blocked on three sides, two smaller and one larger, while the fourth [side] will be fully open to the sea, protected by ninety meters of a single crystal wall. With its reinforced concrete structure, built on four portico beams, the walls covered in "Neve Brasil" marble, polished and lacquered supports, the building will consist of: a gallery for temporary and permanent exhibitions, flanked by an open, cultivated area for outdoor sculpture exhibitions; a 300-seat auditorium, with removable and expandable walls to provide ocean views, even during meetings and events that do not require fully enclosed spaces. The school sector will consist of the necessary number of classrooms, whose walls will be movable, so that the space can be expanded according to the number of students.

We are aware of the difficulties and the whole range of problems that face the establishment of an absolutely new type of museum, in an environment that is not at all prepared for a population to grant itself a museum, that for the first time comes into contact with a cultural organism different from the official culture of the country and the city. On the other hand, however, the difficulties seem to us to be minor compared to those we faced with the creation of a museum in a relatively well-resourced metropolis, but one that was generally less eager to have a disinterested organism superior to the interests, vanities, and ambitions of average and undigested culture.

A museum such as São Vicente will have a lighter, more agile construction that will offer an easier freedom of movement. Or rather, it will not be a true picture gallery in the traditional sense, which would otherwise be useless in a locality that doesn't have superfluous riches, as is the case of metropolises, but it will contain artistic material selected and ordered by content, according to an appropriate theme, on loan from overloaded museums, or those that are, in any case, sympathetic to the initiative. It will present exhibitions organized according to a critical method and a purpose suitable to the intellectual and cultural possibilities of the location. It will alternate exhibitions of pure art, past and present, with exhibitions of the so-called "minor arts" and, above all, the "industrial arts." Moreover, it will be able to, after some time, include in the exhibitions the artisanal, industrial, and artistic work of the population, to inspire emulation, to create values and beautiful, useful, accurate, well-made things. We will bring the world into the city, and then we will bring the people of the city into the world. We think that this consists of spreading civilization, civilization in its finest aesthetic, perfect, and intelligent forms, not abandoned to the anarchy of dilettante improvisations, or to the monotonous current of ethnographic psychology. In fact, in addition to the [museum's] exhibition and educational programs, which will review the most diverse offerings and current applications of the figurative and technical arts, the auditorium will have an informative function regarding other activities: the best films will be screened there, those not normally seen in the area and which are often not screened even in metropolitan centers; informative and explanatory concerts will be held, courses will be given, and, above all, there will be a meeting place and contact with local elements who will closely participate in the museum's everyday life; at the museum, one can seek out what interests them, what they desire.

In a third sector, the same educational subjects that constitute the objective of the São Paulo Museum of Art's activity will be taught, on a smaller but more locally specific and scientific scale, to students that include children as well as adults, fishermen, workers, artisans.

If we know the difficulties inherent in the achievements of an organic museum, we also know its principles dictated by our long experience, which should dictate the rules of action that lead to building, through the museum, an efficient social organization. Entering directly into the spiritual and cultural life of a locality, where to individuals are still accessible the flows of culture they love and respect, the rules of action can be summarized as follows:

1 – bring the region into contact with the world of culture, civilization, comfort, the demands of style and form as factors of public and personal education;

2 – do not separate, in this, the life of the individual from the life of nature, the landscape that is intimate and similar, congenial; but on the contrary, situate them continuously in confrontation with nature, even when work or study demands they enter the atmosphere of other landscapes, of different cultures, of modern or past times;

3 – teach the rational, uniform, and standardized methods that culture generally proposes, without diverting the individual, the spectator, the local pupil from the essential qualities inherent in their own nature (ethnic and ethnographic values, inflows of origins, local traditions, arts and professions); on the contrary, lead individuals to discover in those same elements the foundations of all rationalization, simplicity, adherence to local conditions of the environment (the basis of all the principles of rationalization), and, finally, the improvement of their own artistic sensibilities;

4 – discover and cultivate talents that are rich in relatively exceptional content and expressive ability above the ordinary.

Bringing art to the heart of the people no longer means spreading notions of aesthetics, most often obscure, frequently insignificant, and always distant from the specific interests and intellectual formation of the people in question. On the contrary, it means progressively leading the people, the child, the woman, the worker, to an examination of the material resources of the locale, to working the materials, to reexamining products, to acting rationally in the social and economic sense. It means demonstrating and generating understandings of the modern instruments of observation (optical or mathematical), the clarity, the structure, the utility of forms in nature, to habituate production and technique, to realize the same clarity, structure, and utility in work that must be done. Just as a man who does not know how to speak is not socially complete, neither can a person be considered socially modern if they are unaware of graphic expression, the means of describing objects in two or three dimensions (orthographic, isometric, and perspective projection), methods of drawing, the practical possibilities of art and figurative technique and materials.

Exhibitions, classes, experiences, conversations, exercises, meetings, readings, performances, recitals, concerts—in short, cultural life—will all be included within this scope. And at the same time, the building will constitute rest, recreation, social life.

If the Museum of São Vicente succeeds in its design, that is, if it becomes an organism through which the man of the city can gradually become contemporary with the whole modern world, more and more consciously, we will have created an exemplary way of making culture a truly vital and popular fact.

Culture and Nonculture

Originally published in the Sunday page of *Diário de Notícias*, Salvador, no. 1, September 7, 1958. Collected in Silvana Rubino and Marina Grinover, eds., *Lina por escrito: textos escolhidos de Lina Bo Bardi, 1943–1991* (São Paulo: Cosac Naify, 2009), 87–90.

Culture is relegated to books that few people read; from culture arise rules for living. Opposed to the intellectual, who possesses a sterile and conceited eloquence, who criticizes and justifies everything, is the reader of *Seleções* [Selections], who seeks a norm, a clarification in superficial summaries, or that which is left to chance in life. A superficial cosmopolitan criticism, serving only itself, has taken over the culture useful to man, replacing it with a pseudoculture, which shines through a light reflected only upon the erudite scholar. The solution of the real problems of various countries was replaced by a universal panacea distributed with incredulity and indifference. Specialized philosophical or critical language masks an emptiness or absence of thought, and while the lack of a useful culture is accepted, the problem remains. And science as anticipation, of the capacities for human control over scientific problems, poses the question of the end of humanity.

Why doesn't such a dispassionate diagnosis of the disease of contemporary society correspond with an effective ability to solve the problem? Why is this abstract, metaphysical, cosmopolitan culture not replaced by the various cultures capable of solving the problems of the many countries that together form the great concert of global culture? Why has the lettered class not yet been replaced by the new humanist, with technical bases, capable of solving and understanding human problems? Among the conceited and eloquent scholar, the art critic and the incomprehensible metaphysical poet, the scientist and the isolated technician, is the mass of men who look with dismay at the problems of real existence, abandoned by culture.

Thirteen years after World War II, disabused of the illusion of being able to quickly change, through a violent imposition, the state of affairs that seemed anachronistic in the face of science and lucid critical capacity, we still seek solutions for the majority of men to be provided with the minimum necessary to live, to own a home, to not laugh in the face of a modern painting or sculpture, to not protest against music, poetry, architecture, to not demonstrate incomprehension in the face of the machine, the expression of our time, using it only as an imposed necessity, to not mock the figure of the philosopher, synonymous with isolation and extravagance. We aren't speaking here of a snobbish understanding that accepts problems merely because they are out of the ordinary, the position of the informed class, aware of things that they don't understand, merely because they are "useful to the social record." The part of humanity concerned with economic problems lacks sufficient time for deciphering puzzles, to which they do not have the key; the other part, below average economically, cannot concern itself with problems that fall outside of immediate necessities and whose existence isn't even conceived of. This part of humanity, taken up by the necessity of resolving for themselves the very questions of existence, and lacking this pseudoculture, has the necessary capacity for the development of a new and genuine culture.

This latent force exists to a high degree in Brazil, where a primordial form of primitive civilization (not in the sense of naive, but rather, composed of essential, real, concrete elements) coincides with the most advanced forms of modern thought. Immersion into this deep and vital current of contemporary and historical critical capacities, without which there can be no coherent and modern development of a civilization, is an extremely delicate enterprise. It is important not to violently impose the historical-critical problem, but only to accept existing realities, taking into account all of the currents, including the spurious, modifying and gradually accepting them, conducting effective political action, learning that the failure of preceding efforts was due to vanguard or "small church" positions, which, excluding the existing reality, fought in the abstract, thus obtaining mediocre results.

Maximally safeguarding the country's genuine strengths, seeking at the same time to be in line with international development, will be the base for the new cultural action. Seeking above all to not diminish or debase these problems by presenting them to the public as bland, feeble fare, but not eliminating a language that is specialized and difficult, but that is, interpreting and evaluating these currents. And, above all, it will be useful to remember the words of a philosopher of praxis, "do not bend to speak to the masses, sir intellectuals, straighten your backs."

Industrial Art

Originally published in the Sunday page of *Diário de Notícias*, Salvador, no. 8, October 26, 1958. Collected in Silvana Rubino and Marina Grinover, eds., *Lina por escrito: textos escolhidos de Lina Bo Bardi, 1943–1991* (São Paulo: Cosac Naify, 2009), 107–10.

There exists today a certain confusion between artisanal production, artisans, and popular artists. There is an entire literature (we didn't want to use the word rhetoric) in this regard. What is artisanal production? The expression of a society and of an era, of workers who possess capital (albeit modest) that allows them to work from raw materials and to sell a finished product, with both material profit and spiritual satisfaction, as they designed and created the object themselves. What is an artisan, today? A laborer, an expert lacking capital who lends his services to whomever provides the raw material, be it an owner or a client, receiving a wage in exchange for this labor. The artisan is the so-called proletarian.

What is "true" popular art? It is Art, with a capital A.

What would be a fair question for a valid answer? Evidently: is there adequate reason behind governmental support for this pseudo-artisanship? Clearly not. Because in this manner it takes from the artisan their raison d'être—namely, the satisfaction of being able to artistically create objects and to materially own and sell them. The urgent and very serious problem of knowledge of craftsmanship and the moral satisfaction derived from such labor are confused with artisanal production. Italy, Spain, and Portugal distinguished themselves in this paternalistic protectionism that generated the various Spanish *pueblos* and *instituti d'arte artigianali*, true museums of horrors and catalogues of unspeakable things. This problem is different. It is an urgent issue that derives precisely from the end of the artisanal era: the split between technician and laborer.

The architect who designs a building doesn't interact with the bricklayer, the carpenter, or the blacksmith. Nor the designer of household objects with the potter, the glazier. The furniture designer with the cabinetmaker. Each works independently. The technical designer has an inferiority complex due to a lack of practical competence. The laborer is debased by a lack of ethical satisfaction from his own work. This central problem could be addressed via the immediate gathering of all ancient and modern artisanal production in each country toward the creation of a great living museum, a museum that could be called Artisanal Production and Industrial Art, displaying the roots of that country's popular-historical culture.

This Museum should include an industrial art school (art in the sense of both craft and art) that would allow technicians, designers, and laborers to interact with one another. It would express, in the modern sense, that which was artisanal production, while laying the ground for new generations. Not for future utopias, but for the existing reality we already know: the architect at the drawing board who doesn't understand the reality of the building's physical labor, the worker who doesn't know how to "read" a blueprint, the furniture designer who designs a wooden chair with the characteristics of iron, the typographer who mechanically composes without knowing the elementary laws of typographic composition, and so on. The first, outside of reality and within [the realm of] theory. The latter, embittered by the mechanical work of welding a piece, tightening a nut, without coming to know the end result. We do not aim to devalue the project of governmental support for artisanal groups. This support is a transition, a necessary transition phase, since popular artists are simply artists, and cannot be influenced or directed in rigid ways.

Ours is a collective age. The work of the owner-artisan has been replaced by collective work, and men have to be prepared for such collaboration. Without hierarchical distinctions between designers and laborers. Only in this way can the joy of moral participation in work be recovered. Collective participation, no longer individual; the technical result of today's artisanship: industry.

The New Trianon, 1957–67

Originally published in the Sunday page of *Mirante das Artes*, no. 5 (September–October 1967): 20–23. Collected in Silvana Rubino and Marina Grinover, eds., *Lina por escrito: textos escolhidos de Lina Bo Bardi, 1943–1991* (São Paulo: Cosac Naify, 2009), 122–30.

The "old" Trianon, political center of São Paulo, responsible for the launch of famous candidates, center of meetings and banquets, a sunny terrace (the only or nearly the only in the entire city), still alive in the memory of yesterday's children, was demolished in 1957.

Left over was a bit of bare ground in front of the "Brazilian forest" of Siqueira Campos Park. Passing by during one of those afternoons on Avenida Paulista, I realized that this was the only place where the São Paulo Museum of Art could be built; the only one worthy, by popular opinion, of consideration as the "base" of the first Latin American Museum of Art. The São Paulo City Hall had prepared a decent "public space" project, but one that lacked the sentimental requirements worthy of the old Trianon's inheritance. Time was short, the construction firm had already been chosen, construction would begin. Adhemar de Barros was the mayor, J. Carlos de Figueiredo Ferraz the secretary of public works; I collected necessary data for a modern popular museum, a popular meeting center, oversaw a draft, made a call to Edmundo Monteiro (director of the *Diários Associados*, who created, sustained, and sustains the Museum today), and together we went to the mayor and the secretary of public works. The mayor was enthusiastic (though he wanted a ballroom beneath the belvedere, not a popular theater, as I had designed it), but we met with a cold shower from the secretary of public works: "I have no money, the last of it went to the 'turtle' in Ibirapuera, which is now falling apart; but congratulations on the project and the structural idea." Edmundo did not give up; he thought of how he would gather the money, himself, and build the great complex. "Let's go to the Museum board!" We went. But the board of directors and the Museum's president (Dr. Assis Chateaubriand) had just signed an agreement with Annie Penteado: the Foundation's massive building, a design of the tester's own,[1] reviewed by Perret *in articulo mortis* and badly mistreated by the opinions of nonexperts, would be the headquarters of the future São Paulo Museum of Art, integrated with the incipient Picture Gallery of the same Foundation: the one that would disappear years later. End.

I accepted the invitation of the government of Bahia to found and direct the Museum of Modern Art. In 1960, a telegram: construction on the Trianon Museum would begin. The Museum-Foundation agreement had gone under water (the "agreement" had ended in discussions about who should or shouldn't buy the cleaning soap for the Foundation—which might not want any "cleaning" at all), and the mayor insisted on building a "grand ballroom" with the São Paulo Museum of Art on top. But the belvedere must be "column free," with an 8-meter ceiling height of the building above it, and the building itself could not exceed two floors. And below, the "ballroom." My attempts to maintain the theater were useless: it had to be a ballroom and nothing else. The construction firm had already been chosen: the one that had won the competition.

No columns, 70 meters of light, 8-meter ceiling height. My project could only be done with prestressed concrete. I remembered the former secretary of public works, professor at the Polytechnic and FAU [University of São Paulo Polytechnic School and the College of Architecture and Urbanism], who had praised the project. I went to look for him: "Do you want to work for free on a public project that will be of major cultural importance for São Paulo? I'm working for free, only the designers will be paid." José Carlos de Figueiredo Ferraz accepted. Thus construction began in 1960. I had to face objections from City Hall technicians and the construction firm, who had difficulty accepting, for the pre-stressed concrete, "our own metal," and wanted the Freyssinet patent;[2] but everything was resolved in the end. The new Trianon-Museum is an absolutely national work, from the pre-stressed concrete to the glass in the windows (measuring 5.5 meters high).

Well, I apologize for the long premise, but daily we receive questions and requests for clarification about Trianon, which is a public work, and as we have a commitment to the community, here is our explanation, our attempt to explain that it was, at first (justified, correct, but nevertheless) an "act of violence." Or an act of Faith.

The new Trianon-Museum consists of a foundation (on the Avenida Nove de Julho side), whose cover is the great belvedere. The "ballroom" requested by the 1957 City Hall will be replaced by a large Civic Hall, a center for public and political meetings (the ballroom was designed with the hope of eventual transformation). A large auditorium-theater and a small auditorium–screening room complete this "foundation." Above the belvedere, at the Avenida Paulista level, stands the building of the São Paulo Museum of Art. The building, with 70 meters of light, 5 meters of lateral overhangs, 8-meter ceilings, free of any columns, rests on four pillars, joined by two pre-stressed concrete beams on the roof, and two large beams to support the level that will house the Museum's main gallery. The floor just below the gallery will include offices, temporary exhibition galleries, a library, etc. It is suspended by two large beams by means of steel rods. An open-air stairway and a tempered-glass, steel-mounted elevator allow the museum floors and grand hall to be linked together. All facilities, including air conditioning, will be visible. The finishing is the simplest. Exposed concrete, whitewashing, granite flooring for the great Civic Hall, tempered glass, moveable walls, exposed, whitewashed concrete for the museum building, whose floor is made of industrial-style black rubber. The belvedere will be a "square," surrounded by plants and flowers, paved with natural "pebbles," in accordance with the Ibero-Brazilian tradition. Small reflecting pools with plants are anticipated.

The whole of the Trianon will re-propose, in its monumental simplicity, the now unpopular themes of rationalism. First, it is necessary to distinguish between "monumental" (in the civic-collective sense) and "elephantine."

Monumental is not characterized by "dimensions": the Parthenon is monumental although its scale is the smallest. The Nazifascist construction (Hitler's Germany, Mussolini's Italy) is elephantine but not monumental in its swollen, irrational arrogance. What I describe as monumental is not a matter of size or fussiness, it is simply a fact of collectivity, of collective consciousness. What transcends the "particular," what reaches the collective, can (and perhaps should) be monumental. This is an idea that might be "snubbed" by certain European countries that base their lives and political futures on a false idea of individualism, a falsely democratic individualism of the "civilization of consumption," but which can be "powerful" in a new country whose future democracy will be built on other foundations. Above I mentioned the fact of "re-proposing" rationalism. Rationalism has to be taken up as an important mark in the position against architectural irrationalism and the political reaction that has all to gain from an "irrationalist" position presented as avant-garde and transcendent. But it is necessary to eliminate from rationalism all elements of "perfectionism," a metaphysical and idealistic inheritance, and to face, in reality, the architectural "incident." Due to various causes related to public administration, the museum's construction was delayed; some "incidents" have befallen it. Poorly welded and over-cut iron on the four-pillar frame led to unforeseen vertical bending, and the further addition of the pillars will be an "accepted incident" and not a setback to be disguised, smoothed over, hidden.

Architectural work is a logic of "propositions," which differs from the logic of the "terms" that idealistic culture has presented us with to this day. And as such, demonstrable. And as such, closer to a science. An architecture can be judged linguistically, semantically, syntactically, and pragmatically, that is, according to its "informative transmission," its structure, its historical formation, and its sociological efficiency. But all of these components are those of propositional logic. And these propositions are essentially content.

The grand theater of the Sydney Opera House is today deemed the ultimate in the avant-garde. Structural exhibitionism, the elegance of graphic and formal solutions seem to present something truly new to our eyes. But the meaning of the work, its result, its logical judgment makes it a traditional "theater" in the most common sense of the word; theatrically speaking, a much more "reactionary" work, like the rudimentary farmhouse, the lime-painted garage advocated by Antonin Artaud.

To today's architects, to the architects of the new countries, in particular, who contribute day by day to the creation of their countries' culture, the exciting solution of the problem. I sought, with the São Paulo Museum of Art, to take back certain positions. I sought (and hope it happens) to re-create an "environment" at Trianon. And I hope that the people will be there, viewing outdoor exhibitions and discussing, listening to music, watching films. I hope that children will play in the morning and afternoon sun. And even retreats and everyday bad taste that, faced "coldly," can also serve as [cultural] content.

The Structure

The future site of the São Paulo Museum of Art finds in its structure one of the apexes of current engineering techniques. Obliged to forcibly accompany an entirely simple architecture, the structure—the central point of this architecture—achieves simplicity in pure grandiosity, both for its dimensions and the clarity of the solutions.

The building is basically divided into two parts: the lower, below the Avenida Paulista level, and the upper one above it, separated by the large belvedere. The lower part, which consists mostly of the Civic Hall and the two auditoriums, imposes itself through the roof slab that dominates almost the entire area, 34 x 34 meters in dimension. With a grid structure supported on its periphery by 1.5-meter-high beams in both directions parallel to the edges, each 3.02 meters presents major bending moments of the order of 300 tons/meter.

Here we can also note the two staircases, with 14 meters of overhang each, set into a mold, which in turn works the torsion.

The beams that support the roof of the main theater auditorium are simple reinforced concrete beams with 22 meters of free span.

The building's upper part, which includes two stories and the roof, with an area of 2,100 m^2, with 5 meters of lateral overhang, rests only on four hollow pillars of 4 x 2.5 meters. Force applies to these pillars, which withstand a vertical load of 2,300 tons each, plus a bending moment of 5,000 tons/meter, through four large pre-stressed beams. Two of these beams support only the roof, with a total free span of 74 meters, each receiving a weight corresponding to the width of a 15-meter slab. They are simply supported beams, with freedom of movement in the direction of the beam axis, thanks to their locations on a 6.7-meter-high pendulum. This freedom is essential in light of the effects of temperature and shrinkage. The maximum bending moments in the center of the open space are of the order of 9,000 tons/meter, which makes the concrete work at 250 kg/cm^2. The cast beams have 62 cables, each composed of 36 5-mm wires.

The beams supporting the lower two floors are also hollow and withstand a maximum moment of 20,000 tons at the center of the free space. They have about 122 cables of 40 5-mm wires, which resist 14,000 kg/cm^2. The total pre-stressing per beam is 10,000 tons. In its 64-meter free span, the beams receive a load of 35 tons/meter. The (maximum) stresses on the concrete are 250 kg/cm^2. To support them, concrete with an average rupture stress at compression for 28 days of 580 kg/cm^2 was made.

The force that these lower beams transmit to the supports is 1,200 tons. As the beams must be free to move horizontally—otherwise the bending would deform the pillars rather than the beam—the solution for them was hydraulic support, i.e., support on oil reservoirs, restricted by neoprene. The floor hanging from the two beams is 70 x 30 meters, with ribbed slabs, 50 cm-high reinforced concrete, while the one of the upper floor, supported by the beams, has a 4 cm slab supported by several ribs.

In short, the above is the synthesis of this structure that resists surprising forces, in an attempt to faithfully express what architecture communicates aesthetically and functionally.

1. A reference to the Fundação Armando Álvares Penteado (FAAP) building. [Editor's note]

2. Reference to Eugène Freyssinet, a French structural engineer and proponent of pre-stressed concrete. [Editor's note]

Five Years among the "Whites"

Originally published in *Mirante das Artes*, no. 6 (November–December 1967), 1, leaflet. Collected in Silvana Rubino and Marina Grinover, eds., *Lina por escrito: textos escolhidos de Lina Bo Bardi, 1943–1991* (São Paulo: Cosac Naify, 2009), 130–36.

The worsening of the country's structural tensions that culminated in the events of April 1964 was also reflected in cultural activities. The "democratic" system, in need of basic reforms to survive, challenged the ruling class, and the subsequent crisis marked a *stasi*, a veritable cultural stagnation that, with the progressive demoralization of universities and the interference of foreign elements in national culture, seriously threatens the possibility of Brazil exiting the stage of cultural colonialism. The liberation effort that preceded the April 1964 [coup] clearly demonstrated the country's autonomy in seeking a way out of cultural underdevelopment, and the dismantling of those efforts is assuming calamitous proportions.

In the cultural framework that preceded the events of April 1964, chiefly marked by the anti-intellectualism of the University of Brasília and the action of "dignifying civil service" and the technical position developed by Sudene, are the Museum of Modern Art and the Museum of Popular Art of Bahia. The Museum of Modern Art phenomenon is typical of a new country (the countries of old culture only create museums on the basis of an important collection; there are no museums with small collections or that don't hold collections), where the word Museum has a meaning other than to preserve. The Museum of Modern Art of Bahia was not a "museum" in the traditional sense: given the misery of the state, there is little it could "conserve"; its activities were directed toward the creation of a cultural movement that, embracing the values of a historically "poor" culture (in the sense of "high" culture), could lucidly enter the world of real modern culture, overcoming the "culturalist" and "historicist" phases of the West, by relying on a popular experience (rigorously distinct from that of folklore), with the instruments of technique as a method and the strength of a new humanism (neither humanitarianism nor "humane-ism"). It was not an ambitious program, it was just a path to take. Taking advantage of the "misconception" prevailing in the country (only after April 1964 would the masks come off and positions definitively revealed), it was possible to create a relatively free Museum in its cultural activities, and the fact that it is a state Foundation gave it that "validity" that only public activities provide, distinct (even when "public" does not mean "collective") from private enterprise, whose (disguised) interests are always lucrative or related to advertising.

The Museum of Modern Art of Bahia, founded in January 1960, had to confront, from the very outset, the hostility of a "cultural class" formed in provincial molds, "nationally celebrated" artists gathered around folkloric themes (given the city's touristic character), and the local press. Three factors made it possible to consider the possible development of Bahia as a national cultural center: the existence of an expanding university (whose president, though not progressive, could have been made the most of had the student body not taken intransigent positions truly opposed to the university's and their own political interests); a student body that, albeit confusingly, and at times acting contrary to its own interests, was on the right track to political and cultural awareness; and, above all, the profoundly popular character of Bahia and the entire Northeast. Cultural provincialism was reduced to a ruling class on its way to ruin, and virtually nonexistent when a truly grassroots movement began. This would become evident in the collective peasant literacy experiments in the Bahian Recôncavo and throughout the Northeast.

By assuming, since its founding, the directorship of MAMB, the possibilities of the country's north assured me that the conservative inertia of the south could be overcome in the cultural field via the "restlessness" of the students and the strongly popular character of the Northeast.

I began by eliminating the city's "established culture," seeking the support of the University and the students, opening the Museum free to the people, seeking to develop its didactic programs to the fullest. MAMB functioned provisionally in the *surviving foyer* of the "scorched" Castro Alves Theater, open over Campo Grande, downtown. The collection was small: very few paintings provided by the State Museum, laboriously assembled by José Valladares, director until his death. MAMB's small budget did not allow for large acquisitions, but we obtained loans from the São Paulo Museum of Art, and we were able, with a certain planning of resources, to increase the collection: the Museum came to have an important collection of Brazilian and some international artists. In the theater access ramp we installed a cinema-auditorium for conferences, classes, screenings, and debates; in the large subterranean areas, a beginning arts school for children; the School of Drama and the University's Free Music Seminar collaborated. With Martim Gonçalves, director of the School of Theater, we mounted, on the great semi-destroyed stage, whose nakedness amplified the drama, Brecht and Camus: *The Threepenny Opera* and *Caligula*. Gonçalves had created in the School of Theater a real center of culture. In Bahia, Cinema Novo had emerged: Trigueirinho had just filmed *Bahia de Todos os Santos* on the city streets, and Glauber began *Barravento* on the beaches beyond Itapuã. At Castro Alves, the young filmmakers built the sets with their own hands: *A grande feira* [The Big Market], *Tocaia no asfalto* [Ambush on the Asphalt]. Superintendent of the Castro Alves, I thought to reconstruct it not in the mold of eighteenth-century Italian "court" or nineteenth-century bourgeois theater, but as a modern popular theater without the anachronistic mechanization of the stage and side scenes; without pretentious "decoration." The theater's reconstruction required changing the Museum. I thought of the whole of Unhão, the construction of which dated from the sixteenth century, and which Gonçalves had shown me in 1958 when he was thinking of installing in it an annex of the School of Theater. From the State Government, I was able to obtain the expropriation and the necessary funds for the restoration, and eight months later, March 1963, the set was practically ready; it would house the Museum of Popular Art and the Unhão Workshops, a center for the documentation of popular (nonfolkloric) art and a center for technical studies aiming to flow primitive pre-crafts into industry, in the framework of the country's development. In November of the same year, the Museum inaugurated the first major exhibition of Popular Art in the Northeast and the *Nordeste* [Northeast] exhibition, a collective of fine arts by artists from Bahia, Ceará, Pernambuco, and the Recife Center for Popular Culture. The Museum of Popular Art of Unhão belonged to the Museum of Modern Art of Bahia and programmed a survey of popular artisanal production (pre-artisanal production) from throughout the country.

But grave events came to pass.

The situation was accelerating, ruling-class fear increased day by day: facing the students' aggression, facing the possible explosion of the borders of the old academic culture, whose menacing phantom was the University of Brasília, facing mass literacy, with the Paulo Freire system, mainly by UNE students; in the face of pressure from the entire structure of the country striving to reach the maximum level of self-development within the limits of the old structure, but which needed, in order to survive, those reforms that the privileged class did not want to grant at any price.

In Bahia, with the removal and death of university president Edgar Santos, the University came to a stop; the weekly student page that *A Tarde* newspaper published was suppressed. A violent press campaign forced Martim Gonçalves to leave Bahia; television and newspapers wanted to rebuild Castro Alves in the old way (which took place). The familiar form of cultural reaction, rancid traditions, anger, and fear appeared on the horizon.

Shortly after April 1964, the 6th Military Region occupied MAMB. It presented the exhibition *Didática da subversão* [Didactic of Subversion]. In front of the museum, the cannons from the Amaralina base [army headquarters]. Five years of hard work that revealed attitudes, cowardice, defections, deceit.

Five years, also, of collective hopes that would not be canceled out: Walter da Silveira, Glauber Rocha, Martim Gonçalves, Noêmio Spínola, Geraldo Sarno, Norberto Salles, Rômulo Almeida, Augusto Silvani, Eron de Alencar, Vivaldo Costa Lima, Sobral, Lívio Xavier, Calazans, the Brennand of those days. Five years among the "whites."

An Account Sixteen Years Later

Originally published in Marcelo Suzuki, ed., *Tempos de grossura: o design no impasse* (São Paulo: Instituto Lino Bo e P. M. Bardi, 1994), 12–14.

What is the situation in a country with a dependent capitalist structure, where a bourgeois-democratic national revolution failed to take place, which enters industrialization with the remnants of oligarchic-national structures?

At last Brazil enters the history of Western industrialization, bearer of prehistorical and African elements, rich in popular influences. All the contradictions of the great Western misconception present themselves contemporaneously, or shortly, in its modernization process, with the violent traces of a bankrupt situation. **A process that took centuries in industrialized nations takes only a few years here.**[1] Unplanned, abrupt, structurally imported industrialization leads the country to experience an uncontrollable natural event, not a man-made process. The sinister trappings of real estate speculation, nonplanning for popular housing, the speculative proliferation of industrial design—gadgets, objects, mostly superfluous—weigh on the country's cultural situation, creating serious obstacles, preventing the development of a genuine autochthonous culture. Collective awareness is necessary; at the present moment, any digression is a crime. Deculturation is happening now. If the economist and sociologist can detachedly diagnose, the artist must act, not only in concert with the intellectual, but also actively as part of the people.

A reexamination of the country's recent history is necessary. An account of "popular" Brazilian civilization must be made, even if poor in light of high culture. This account is not one of folklore, always paternalistically supported by high culture; it is the account "seen from the other side," the participating account. It is Aleijadinho and Brazilian culture before the French Mission. It is the Northeasterner of leather and empty cans, the village inhabitant, the Black, and the Indian. A mass that invents, that creates an indigestible, dry, hard-to-swallow contribution.

This urgency, which cannot wait any longer, is the real basis of the work of the Brazilian artist, a reality that needs no artificial stimuli, a cultural abundance at hand, a unique anthropological wealth, with tragic, fundamental historical events. Brazil has industrialized, the new reality must be accepted in order to be studied. A return to extinct social structures is impossible, the creation of artisanal centers, the return to the artisanal as antidote to an industrialization foreign to the country's cultural principles is wrong. Because artisanship as a social structure never flourished in Brazil, what did exist was a sparse immigration of Iberian or Italian craftsmen and, in the nineteenth century, manufactures. What does exist is a sparse domestic pre-artisanship, **never artisanship**.

A cultural survey of Brazilian pre-artisanship could have been done before the country took the path of dependent capitalism, when a bourgeois-democratic revolution was still possible. In this case, the cultural options in the field of Industrial Design could have been different, more in line with the country's real needs (even if poor, much poorer than the cultural options of China and Finland). Brazil had arrived at a crossroads. It opted for *finesse*.

Art is not so innocent: the great attempt to make Industrial Design the regenerative force of an entire society failed and has become the most appalling evidence of the perversity of the entire system. The collective awareness of more than a quarter of the world's population, the one that believed in unlimited progress, has begun. The demystification of design as a **weapon** of a system, the anthropological pursuit of the arts against the aesthetic pursuit that has informed the entire development of Western artistic culture, from antiquity to the avant-garde, is underway in a lucid debate that excludes romantic-artisanal situations in the understandings of Ruskin and Morris: a reexamination of the recent history of "doing" in the arts. Not a blanket refusal, but a careful process of revision. The struggle against technological hegemony, which occurs in the West, and the "technological inferiority complex" in the field of the arts, comes up against the structure of a system: the problem is fundamentally political and economic. Regeneration through art, the Bauhaus creed, has turned out to be mere utopia, a cultural misconception, a tranquilizer of the consciences of those who don't need it. The metastasis of its uncontrollable proliferation brought with it the basic achievements of the Modern Movement, transforming its great fundamental idea—Planning—into the utopian misconception of the technocratic "intelligentsia," which emptied, with its failure, "rationality" set against "emotionality," in a fetishism of abstract models that consider the world of figures and the world of men as equals.

If the problem is ultimately political and economic, the task of "acting" in the field of "design" is, nevertheless, fundamental. This is what Brecht called "the ability to say no." The artist's freedom has always been "individual," but true freedom can only be collective. A freedom aware of social responsibility, which breaks the boundaries of aesthetics, the concentration camp of Western civilization; a freedom linked to the limitations and great achievements of Scientific Practice (Scientific Practice, not technology descended into technocracy). To the romantic suicide of "non-planning," a reaction to technocratic failure, we must urgently counter with the great undertaking of Environmental Planning, from urbanism and architecture, to industrial design and other cultural manifestations. A reintegration, a simplified unification of the factors that comprise culture.

Translated from the Portuguese by Emma Young

1. Bold in the original. [Editor's note]

FIGS. 57–58
Lina Bo Bardi, *Tempos de grossura: o design no impasse*: general layout of the book's images, 1980. Ballpoint pen, marker, and graphite on offset paper, 31.5 x 21.6 cm. Collection of the Instituto Bardi/Casa de Vidro, São Paulo

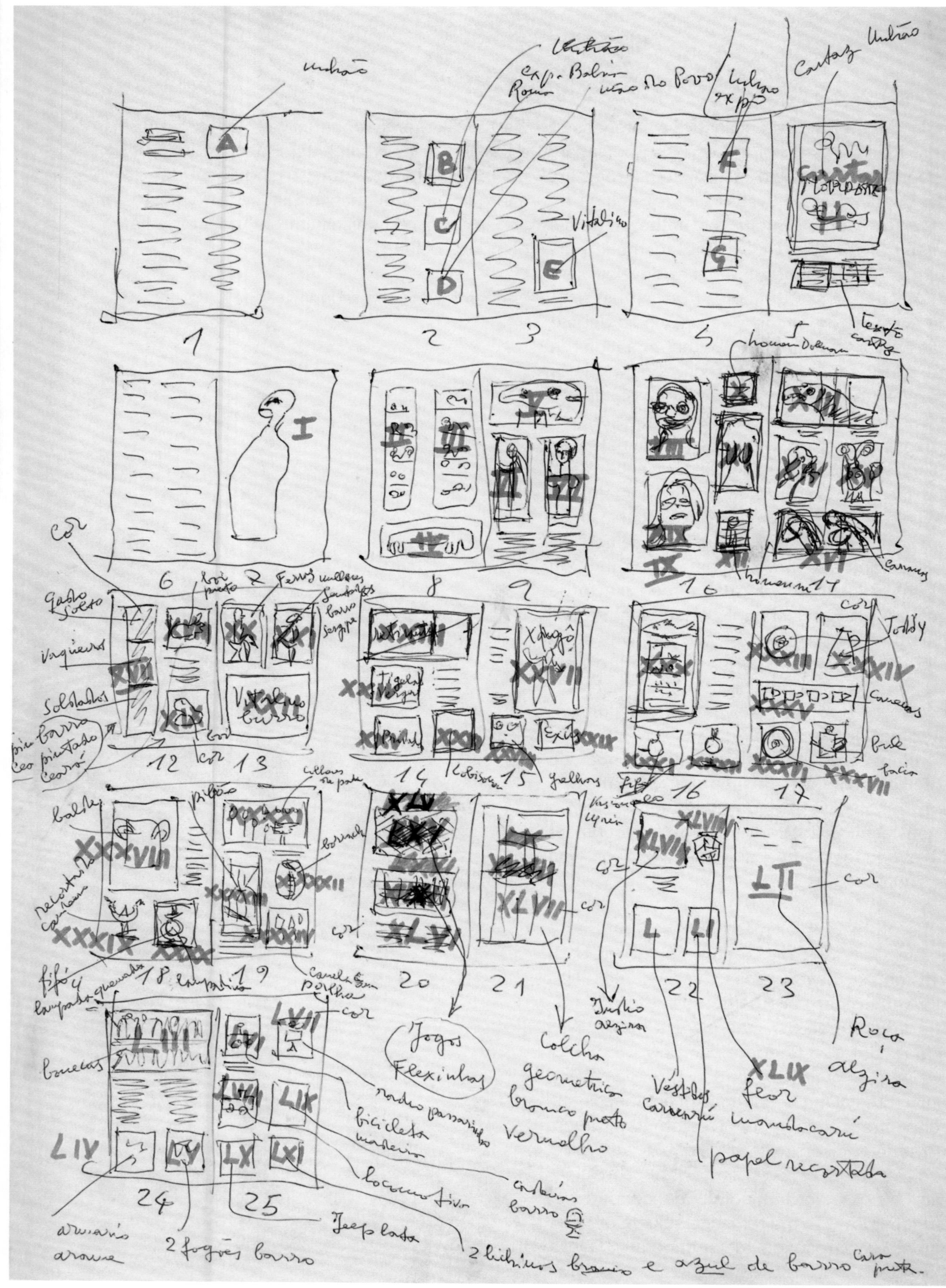

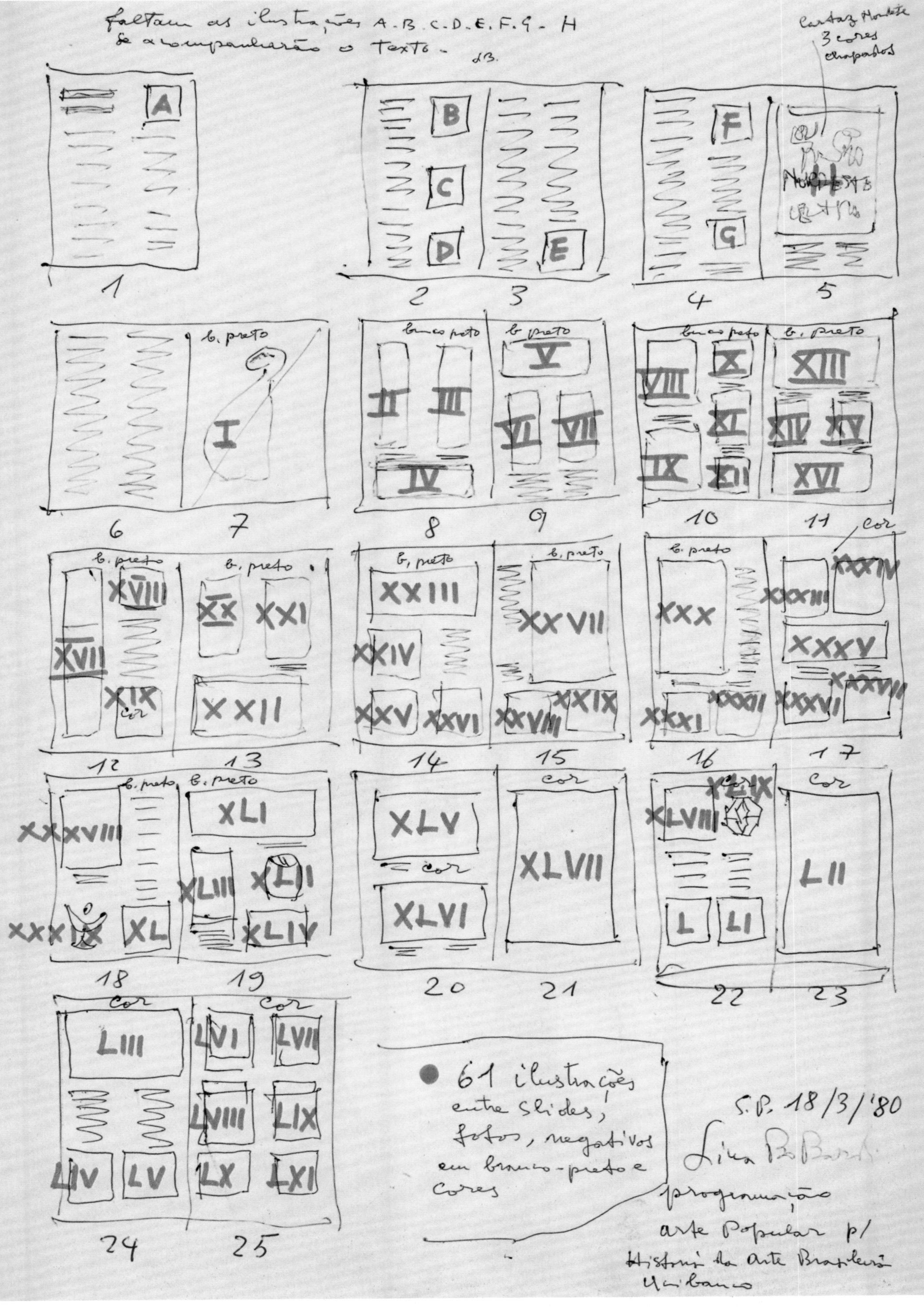

faltam as ilustrações A.B.C.D.E.F.G - H
que acompanharão o Texto - LB.
Cartaz Nordeste
3 cores
chapados
1
2 3
4 5
6 7
8 9
10 11
12 13
14 15
16 17
18 19
20 21
22 23
24 25
61 ilustrações
entre slides,
fotos, negativos
em branco-preto e
cores
S.P. 18/3/'80
Lina Bo Bardi
programação
Arte Popular p/
História da Arte Brasileira
Unibanco

RETHINKING THE MUSEUM

FIG. 59
View of the main gallery at MASP Avenida Paulista, with Lina Bo Bardi's glass easels, 1968

LINA BO BARDI'S POPULAR MUSEUMS

FIG. 60
Kerosene lamp made from an electric light bulb

Introduction

Lina Bo Bardi's career is not limited to her role as an architect. She also worked in the areas of pedagogy, criticism, art, curatorship, museum studies, and publishing, never establishing boundaries between theory and practice.

From the beginning of her career, Bo Bardi had been involved in editorial projects, such as *A* (fig. 40), *Stille*, and *Domus* magazines, in Italy, and *Habitat* magazine in Brazil, which served as a base for her intellectual and aesthetic development. In architecture, both residential and museum projects were of constant interest and engagement. Bo Bardi designed numerous museums and renovations of buildings that would become museums,[1] though few were actually built. The most emblematic are the Museu de Arte São Paulo Assis Chateaubriand (MASP; figs. 116–150), on Avenida Paulista, and the renovation of the Solar do Unhão (figs. 163–169), in Salvador, into the Museum of Popular Art and, later, the Museum of Modern Art of Bahia (MAM-BA). At these institutions, Bo Bardi was involved in the elaboration of the architectural as well as the museological and curatorial programs—in the case of MASP, with Pietro Maria Bardi, her husband and the museum's founding director.

Museum projects are especially representative of Bo Bardi's career path, as they reveal interests, questions, and propositions she developed and worked on throughout her life, such as the relationship between art and education, modern and vernacular architecture, noncanonical perspectives on art history, and new ways of thinking about the idea of the museum. These interests also reflect the period of her academic formation and early career in Italy, in the context of Italian rationalism, when she was in contact and in dialogue with architects such as Carlo Scarpa and Franco Albini. Important names in the renewal of museum architecture and exhibition design, they led the projects of the Castelvecchio Museum in Verona and the Palazzo Bianco Museum in Genoa, respectively.

Parallel to Bo Bardi's museum projects are the curatorial projects and exhibition designs that she developed for various exhibitions from MASP's early years,[2] in whose programming she played a central role. At MASP, already at its new location on Avenida Paulista, in addition to the radical glass easels (fig. 64) she created to display the museum's collection, Bo Bardi curated exhibitions such as *A mão do povo brasileiro* (The Hand of the Brazilian People, 1969; figs. 122–132),[3] *Repassos* (Weaving Patterns, 1975; fig. 146),[4] and *África negra* (Black Africa, 1988; figs. 145–148).[5]

A paradigmatic exhibition by Bo Bardi was *Bahia in Ibirapuera* (figs. 188–201), held in 1959,[6] parallel to the 5th São Paulo Biennial, in a pavilion under the marquee of the park where the São Paulo Museum of Modern Art is today. Various representative objects of Bahian culture were shown, in

1. Bo Bardi's museum or museum renovation projects include: the Museum of Art, Rua do Ouvidor, Rio de Janeiro, 1947; the São Vicente Museum of Art (Oceanfront Museum), 1951; the Marble Museum, Carrara, Italy, 1963; the Butantã Institute Museum, São Paulo, 1965 (projects that were not built); MASP on Rua 7 de Abril, 1947 (renovation project carried out for the museum's exhibition area, installed within a building designed by Jacques Pilon); MASP on Avenida Paulista, 1957–68; the Bahia Museum of Modern Art (Castro Alves Theater), Salvador, 1960 (project designed for the adaptation of the theater foyer); the Museum of Popular Art, Solar do Unhão, Salvador, 1959 (renovation project); the São Paulo Museum of Modern Art, Ibirapuera Park, 1982 (renovation project).

2. MASP was founded in 1947 by Assis Chateaubriand, and was initially located on Rua 7 de Abril in downtown São Paulo, where it operated until 1968, when it was moved to its current headquarters on Avenida Paulista, to the building designed by Lina Bo Bardi.

3. With the collaboration of filmmaker Glauber Rocha and theatrical director Martim Gonçalves.

4. With the collaboration of artist Edmar de Almeida.

5. Curated with photographer and ethnologist Pierre Verger, with the collaboration of Marcelo Carvalho Ferraz and Marcelo Suzuki.

6. Curated with Martim Gonçalves, with the collaboration of Glauber Rocha.

7. In repudiation of this act of censorship, the Italian architect Bruno Zevi published "L'arte dei poveri fa paura ai generali" (The Art of the Poor Frightens the Generals), *L'Espresso* (Rome), March 14, 1965.

8. With the collaboration of André Vainer, Marcelo Carvalho Ferraz, and Marcelo Suzuki.

9. With the collaboration of André Vainer, Dulce Maria, Marcelo Carvalho Ferraz, and Marcelo Suzuki.

10. Curated with Gláucia Amaral, with the collaboration of Marcelo Carvalho Ferraz and Marcelo Suzuki.

11. Only the first fifteen issues of *Habitat* had the direct involvement of the founders—the Bardi couple—in both editing and producing articles. From numbers 1 to 9, the magazine was directed by Bo Bardi; 10 to 13, by Flávio Motta, with the collaboration of Bo Bardi; 14–15, by Bo Bardi and Pietro Maria Bardi.

an innovative exhibition design that merged new configurations of the displays developed for the former MASP building on Rua 7 de Abril (fig. 62) with set-design features such as the use of eucalyptus leaves arranged on the ground. An offshoot of this show was *Nordeste* (Northeast; figs. 203–214), held in 1963 at the Museum of Popular Art at the Solar do Unhão in Salvador and reformulated for a 1964 presentation at the Galleria Nazionale d'Arte Moderna in Rome (figs. 215–221). The show in Italy, however, never opened, as it was dismantled before its inauguration by order of the dictatorial-military Brazilian government.[7]

At the end of her career, Bo Bardi curated a series of exhibitions that resumed, in a sense, the interests of the 1960s and 1970s exhibitions, including *Design no Brasil: história e realidade* (Design in Brazil: History and Reality, 1982);[8] *Mil brinquedos para a criança brasileira* (A Thousand Toys for the Brazilian Child, 1982);[9] *O belo e o direito ao feio* (The Beautiful and the Right to the Ugly, 1982); and *Caipiras, capiaus: pau-a-pique* (Countryfolk, Rustics: Wattle-and-Daub, 1984; figs. 240–244).[10] These were held at Sesc Pompeia (figs. 318–337), a community and cultural center in São Paulo that she also designed.

The issues and themes addressed in these exhibitions, as well as MASP's program and the two museums in Salvador that Bo Bardi designed, can be thought of as unfolding the interests and agenda of the early issues of *Habitat* magazine (figs. 1–30), as we will discuss below.

Founded in 1950 by Pietro Maria Bardi and Lina Bo Bardi[11] four years after the couple's arrival in Brazil, the magazine was a platform for the presentation and elaboration of the architectural, artistic, curatorial, and cultural ideas proposed by both. In the first volume were articles as varied as "Houses of Artigas"—on the Brazilian modern architect Vilanova Artigas—"Ex-Votos from the Northeast," "The Indian Designer," "The Indian Fashion Designer," "Architect of the People, Amazonas," "The Child in the Museum," "Unpublished Documents of Brazilian Art," as well as important texts by Bo Bardi, "The Museum of Art of São Paulo: The Social Function of Museums" (see p. 91 in this volume), and by Pietro Maria Bardi, "Problems with the Baroque: Religion and the Curve," along with several short, anonymous texts, most likely written by the Bardis, presenting MASP's collection and program.

FIG. 61
View of the *Artists from the Northeast* exhibition, realized in conjunction with the *Northeast* exhibition, installation designed by Lina Bo Bardi, composed of a wood structure, Museum of Popular Art, Solar do Unhão, Salvador, 1963

FIG. 62
View of MASP's collection at its former location on Rua 7 de Abril, with installation design by Lina Bo Bardi, composed of a tubular metal structure, 1947

12. "Preface," *Habitat*, no. 1 (October–December 1950): 1.

13. Reprinted in Pietro Maria Bardi, "Um museu fora dos limites," *Boletim do Museu de Arte de São Paulo*, no. 6 (2016): 8.

These themes reverberated in *Habitat*'s editorial proposal, which presented the magazine as a pluralistic vehicle willing to think innovatively and radically about Brazilian arts and architecture, centrally locating education in the construction of society and a critical understanding of Brazilian culture. The magazine's editorial policy was distinctly at odds with the Eurocentric academicism in force in Brazil in the 1950s. The editorial of the first issue, accompanied by a photograph of children in a classroom, is indicative:

> The imaginative beauty of a forest, a wattle and daub hut, a Marajoara vase, a Baroque church, Aleijadinho, the goldsmiths of Bahia, the Manuelino furniture makers of Recife, the epigones of the French Mission, the architects of the Manaus theater and the Rio de Janeiro Ministry of Education and Health, rustic [*caipira*] painters and renowned artists, potters, coastal *gameleiros*, Indians, Africans, descendants of the conquistadores, emigrants, all who contributed, continue to contribute and participate in some way in the arts in Brazil will have their activities featured in *Habitat* through the endeavors of those who know how to appreciate what is most characteristic of the country.[12]

MASP

Bo Bardi's relationship with Brazilian popular culture developed from the early days of her work at MASP. In her elaboration of the museum's conceptual and, above all, architectural program, the notion of the "popular" played a critical role in a proposal that sought to create a more accessible, democratic, and plural museum, as opposed to the traditional museum form: canonical, Eurocentric, and ossified.

MASP, Brazil's first modern museum, was conceived based on a multidisciplinary design that sought to constitute an institution open to all forms of artistic expression, not only focusing on ancient or modern art, but also functioning as a space for education and training. Pietro Maria Bardi, in the article "A Museum Beyond the Limits," published in 1951 in *Habitat*, no. 4, argued that it was

> necessary to design new museums outside of the narrow limits and prescriptions of traditional museum design: organisms in motion, not [built for] the narrow purpose of informing, but of instructing; not a passive collection of things, but a continuous exhibition and interpretation of civilization.[13]

Bardi defended the diversification of the public museumgoer, seeking to establish a more popular institution, "a museum for

14. Ibid., 9.

15. Reprinted in Lina Bo Bardi, "O Museu de Arte de São Paulo—Função social dos museus," *O Museu de Arte de São Paulo [Bulletin]* 6 (2016): 12.

everyone, which interests everyone, not only for scholars and the amusement of tourists."[14]

In dialogue with Bardi's concept, in the article "The Museum of Art of São Paulo: The Social Function of Museums," Bo Bardi critiqued the notion of the museum as an "intellectual mausoleum" and refuted monumental architecture, with its imperial staircases and superfluous adornment.[15] She advocated a simpler and more direct presentation of artistic production, giving the public more freedom by offering less targeted readings of the works displayed.

The MASP on Rua 7 de Abril had a very radical exhibition design for its time. In 1947, in their first configuration, the paintings were suspended from the walls by tubular metal structures (figs. 85–89). In the second configuration, in 1950, the works were displayed on thin panels, suspended by steel cables, which maintained a degree of lightness and transparency in not reaching the floor (fig. 99).

During MASP's early years, Bo Bardi, in addition to designing collection exhibitions, created temporary displays of both key names in Brazilian and international modern art and of design, fashion, and artists outside the canon. The museum's program as a whole received wide pedagogical support, including publications, lectures, and courses. In addition, there was also a sector specifically dedicated to practical courses, the Institute of Contemporary Art (IAC). Created by the Bardi couple in 1951, the IAC was the first school of industrial design in Brazil and an important site for disseminating the ideas of Bauhaus functionalist modernism. It proposed a relationship and collaboration between the artistic and creative fields with industry—which ultimately did not come to pass, during a period in which industrial development in Brazil was still small, leading to the school's closure in 1953.

These propositions, already somewhat radical, become even more potent when applied to MASP's collection, the most important collection of European art in the Southern Hemisphere, whose main nucleus Pietro Maria Bardi assembled from 1940 to 1950. It features works from the medieval and Renaissance periods, through Impressionism and Post-Impressionism to modern art, with a strong representation of Brazilian work, especially by modern artists. However, it was not until 1968, at

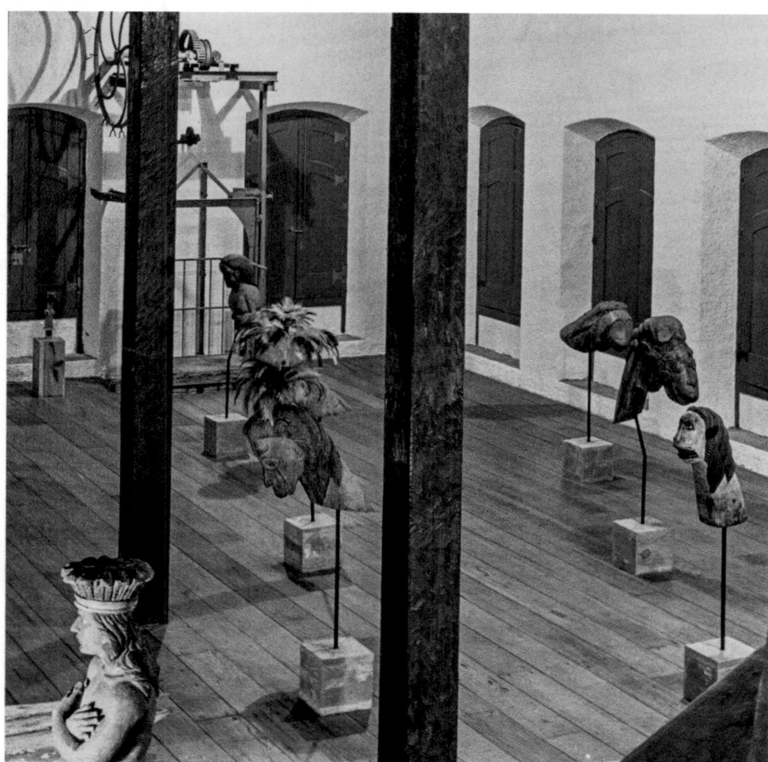

FIG. 63
View of the *Northeast* exhibition, with installation design by Lina Bo Bardi, composed of concrete bases and metal rods, created for the exhibition of figureheads, Museum of Popular Art, Solar do Unhão, Salvador, 1963

FIG. 64
View of MASP's collection on the glass easels, including Vincent van Gogh's paintings *The Arlésienne* (1890) and *Evening Walk* (1889–90), 1960s

the MASP on Avenida Paulista, with the museum's collection exhibited on the glass easels, that the architectural, exhibition design, and urbanistic translation of the concept of the museum that the Bardi couple envisioned could come into being. MASP's architecture, based on the transparency of glass, the permeability of an open plan, and the economy and roughness of concrete, moved away from the museum-as-temple and the white cube, gaining a public dimension, while its suspended concrete volume, a 74-meter slab, creates a large civic square known as the "free span" from which one can see the valley toward the downtown area (figs. 135–136). It can be said that the staircase that links the suspended volume to the ground and underground floors, besides fulfilling its architectural function, contains a political meaning. Initially designed as a spiral, the staircase was ultimately altered by Bo Bardi, who gave it the "hard" shape of an "L," a monumental antistaircase with an intermediate landing that could serve as a stage for public speeches and demonstrations, a naturally political space in its open relationship with the city.

The glass easels materialized the development and radicalization of Bo Bardi's initial projects for MASP. Housed in the second-floor gallery of the new Avenida Paulista building, a large open-plan space enclosed by floor-to-ceiling windows, the easels suspend the paintings on a clear glass slide supported by a concrete block, leaving the backs of the works visible to the public, exposing their constituent structures. As explained in the curatorial statement for *Picture Gallery in Transformation* (fig. 177), which shows MASP's collection on the glass easels since their reinstallment in 2015,[16]

16. The glass easels, present since the inauguration of MASP on Avenida Paulista, were replaced in 1996 by temporary walls, with no relationship to the original architecture, which transformed the open-plan gallery into a segmented space, emulating the ambience of traditional fine arts museums. For the reasoning behind the easels' removal, see the 2003 document, "Parecer sobre a museologia do espaço expositivo do segundo andar do MASP—Inconveniência do tombamento," in Adriano Pedrosa and Luiza Proença, eds. *Concreto e cristal: o acervo do MASP nos cavaletes de Lina Bo Bardi* (Sao Paulo: MASP, 2015), 140–45.

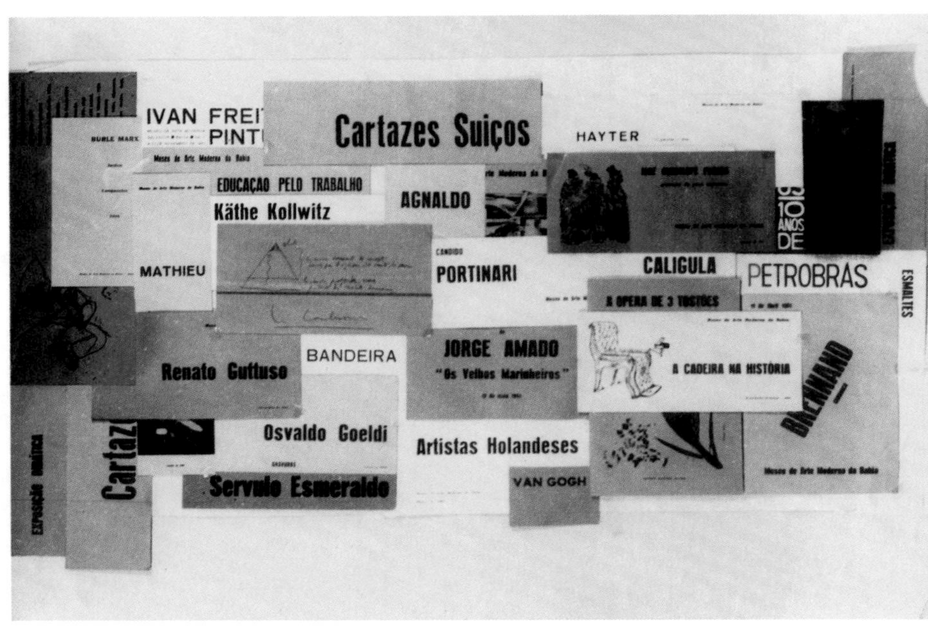

FIG. 65
Selection of invitations, leaflets, and posters for exhibitions held at the Museum of Modern Art of Bahia, from its early years at the Castro Alves Theater, under Lina Bo Bardi's management

The gesture of removing the paintings from the wall and placing them on the easels points to the desacralization of the artworks, rendering them more familiar and accessible to the public. With this perspective, the informative captions placed on the backs of the works allow for a more direct first encounter with them, free of their identification or contextualization in art history. The public is thus led to follow their own paths, allowing for unexpected juxtapositions and dialogues between Asian, African, Brazilian, and European art.[17]

Thus, this desacralization of art,[18] suggested by the removal of paintings from the wall—the traditional exhibition site for this type of artwork—a move that was already sketched out in the exhibition design for MASP's first configuration on Rua 7 de Abril, reveals the political and critical dimension of the traditional approach to art history in Bo Bardi's popular museum.

MASP's commitment to the themes of popular culture extended throughout much of Pietro Maria Bardi's directorship, between 1947 and 1996. The museum organized and presented exhibitions not only of renowned European and Brazilian art, but also devoted space and attention to vernacular productions and self-taught artists, also known as "popular artists," who worked outside of the traditional circuit of the arts and academia. An exemplary case was the pioneering exhibition *Arte popular pernambucana* (Popular Art from Pernambuco, 1949), organized by Augusto Rodrigues with the collaboration of Pietro Maria Bardi, which inaugurated the museum's history of exhibitions on so-called popular art and introduced to the public of São Paulo the sculptures of Vitalino Pereira dos Santos, Mestre Vitalino.[19] The artist was the greatest representative of the Brazilian tradition of small clay sculptures, representing types and scenes of daily life in the *sertão* (hinterlands) of the Brazilian Northeast.

Popular Art from Pernambuco was followed by several other shows by artists working outside the mainstream, such as Emídio de Souza, Cassio M'Boy, Agostinho Batista de Freitas, Maria Auxiliadora da Silva, and Francisco Biquiba dy Lafuente Guarany, Mestre Guarany, as well as exhibitions centered on indigenous and Afro-Brazilian cultures. This vast history, comprising more than thirty exhibitions,[20] indicates the continuing programmatic interest in inserting noncanonical artwork into the museum of art, seeking to inscribe so-called popular art and vernacular manifestations within a context from which they were traditionally rejected.

In conceiving of the MASP project, Bo Bardi chose to dissolve the possible distinctions between art, craft, and artifact, uniting them through shared commonalities—they are all

17. Available at https://masp.org.br/exposicoes/acervo-em-transformacao-tate-no-masp.

18. On these aspects of the glass easels, see Adriano Pedrosa, "Concreto e cristal: aprendendo com Lina," in Pedrosa and Proença, eds., *Concreto e cristal*, 14–21.

19. The MASP exhibition was a development of the *Northeastern Popular Ceramics* exhibition, curated by Augusto Rodrigues at the Castro Alves Library in Rio de Janeiro in 1947, and had a broader scope, as it was not restricted to ceramic sculptures, but also showed other typical northeastern productions, such as wood ex-votos.

20. For more information on this history of exhibitions, see Adriano Pedrosa, "The Hand (and the Names) of the Brazilian People," in this volume.

the *work* of men and women. Paintings or sculptures as much as chairs or pestles are considered "artwork," and therefore enjoy the same status.[21] In an article written for the newspaper *O Estado de São Paulo* in 1970, Bo Bardi elaborated on this proposal:

I want to clarify that in the Museum project it was my intention to destroy the aura that always surrounds a museum, to present the work of art as labor, as a message of labor within everyone's reach.[22]

In the same piece, the architect categorically states: "The São Paulo Museum of Art is popular."

This position afforded the possibilities for dialogue and friction with MASP's collection, and placed into debate the problematic notions of popular and academic, high and low culture. Moreover, it diverged from the prevailing values of the elite and part of the Brazilian cultural establishment of the early postwar period—still extremely conservative, academic, and indifferent to the broader Brazilian reality outside of urban centers such as Rio de Janeiro and São Paulo. Bo Bardi's approach instead called for a recognition of indigenous and African origins, fundamentally constituent elements of the country's society and culture.

Thus, for Bo Bardi, the way in which Brazilian society addressed its history and present was reflected in its cultural interests, highly focused on foreign references—North American and European—and little connected with vernacular expressions, or, in her words:

The history of Brazil is a *white*, Eurocentrist history . . . a white history that ignores Africa's contribution, that ignores the indigenous peoples, a long history of defeats of the vast majority by a minority.[23]

If *Popular Art from Pernambuco* was the founding document of the inclusion of popular culture at MASP while still at its initial location, *The Hand of the Brazilian People* (figs. 222–232), the first temporary exhibition of the newly opened MASP building on Avenida Paulista, can be considered the most eloquent and iconic gesture made in this direction. Organized by Bo Bardi, the exhibition opened to the public in April 1969 and featured in the first-floor gallery[24] a huge selection of objects from the vast Brazilian material culture, from the *sertões* of the northeast to the country's south. The exhibition featured furniture, tools, utensils, machinery, musical instruments, ornaments, toys, fabric, clothing, figureheads, ex-votos, religious objects, paintings, and sculptures. In all, between 1,000 and 1,500 items were displayed (the imprecise number stems from the lack of a consolidated list of works).[25] *The Hand of the Brazilian People* represents a cross between the history of MASP's exhibitions around popular themes and Bo Bardi's own professional trajectory, especially her travels and research in the Northeast and her time spent in Salvador, Bahia. It was also an offshoot of three fundamental exhibitions organized by Bo Bardi, cited here: *Bahia in Ibirapuera* and the two versions of *Northeast.*

A key aspect of Bo Bardi's exhibition design for *The Hand of the Brazilian People*, composed of pine planks arranged on the floor in three rows, the walls covered with the same wood and a checkered lining of pine rafters, is the roughness of the materials used and the quiet and simple nature of the displays. The unpainted, unfinished wood-paneled platforms, niches, and walls, crammed with objects, captured the ambience of a popular market or a wet-and-dry warehouse, and referenced Bo Bardi's pioneering design for the *Northeast* exhibition at the Solar do Unhão.

In both *The Hand of the Brazilian People* and *Northeast*, many of the works presented were products that could be sold at street fairs and popular markets, and in this sense Bo Bardi's display did not create such a sharp break between the original context and the exhibition space, a very common practice in exhibitions of material culture. On this topic, anthropologist Néstor Garcia Canclini critiques the institutions whose aestheticized museographies forge a neutral space that is disconnected from the reality of objects, indicating that,

although they contribute to conceiving of a solidarity of beauty that transcends geographical and cultural differences, they also generate uniformity that hides the social contradictions present in the creation of these works. . . . It would seem that the pots

21. This notion of "work" proposed by Bo Bardi, as well as the desire to interrogate the limits of the history of traditional art and its categories, are topics of discussion within MASP's artistic board and have been developed in exhibitions held by the museum since 2015, including *The Hand of the Brazilian People, 1969/2016* (curatorial statement available at https://masp.org.br/exposicoes/a-mao-do-povo-brasileiro-19692016) and *Thiago Honório: Trabalho* (curatorial statement available at https://masp.org.br/exposicoes/thiago-honorio-trabalho). For more on this topic, see also Pedrosa, "The Hand (and the Names) of the Brazilian People," in this volume.

22. Lina Bo Bardi, "Explicações sobre o Museu de Arte," *O Estado de São Paulo*, April 5, 1970.

23. Excerpt from notes by Bo Bardi for a talk, handwritten and undated, held at the Bardi Institute/Glass House, São Paulo.

24. It is interesting to note that, in the case of *The Hand of the Brazilian People* and *Bahia in Ibirapuera*, there was friction between the vernacular work presented in the exhibitions and the contexts in which they were inserted, more connected with canonical productions—MASP's collection exhibited on the second floor and at the 5th São Paulo Biennial, respectively.

25. In a context of critical revision of its own history and purpose, in 2016 MASP reenacted *The Hand of the Brazilian People* with the aim of relaunching the discussion of the museum's role in society, as well as the status of popular culture and noncanonical artwork in art history. In this sense, *The Hand of the Brazilian People* was taken as an object of study and understood as a radical exhibition that questions territories, hierarchies, and patterns between objects and productions. *The Hand of the Brazilian People, 1969/2016*, a new production of the 1969 exhibition, was held at MASP between September 2, 2016, and January 22, 2017, and was curated by Adriano Pedrosa, MASP's artistic director, Julieta González, adjunct curator of modern and contemporary art, and me. The exhibition did not propose an exact reconstruction of the original, but a reenactment with adaptations, both in the list of works and in its exhibition design, but following the guidelines, typologies, and concepts of 1969.

never served for cooking, the masks never for dancing. Everything is there to be looked at. The fascination with beauty nullifies the wonder at the different. Contemplation is called for, not effort.[26]

The Museum of Modern Art of Bahia and the Museum of Popular Art

The second pivotal moment in Bo Bardi's relationship with museums occurred in Salvador, when she was invited in 1960 by Lavínia Magalhães, the wife of Juracy Magalhães, then governor of Bahia, to found and direct the Museum of Modern Art of Bahia (figs. 151–162). The museum initially occupied the foyer of the Castro Alves Theater, which Bo Bardi adapted, as the building had been partially destroyed by fire. In this first configuration, the exhibitions were held in rooms divided by curtains, which acted as backdrops for the works on display, resuming the use of an element that Bo Bardi had deployed at the MASP on Rua 7 de Abril and at the Glass House, the couple's residence, which she designed. The paintings were displayed on a kind of easel (fig. 157), mixing the bucket-shaped concrete bases used in the panels of *Bahia in Ibirapuera* (figs. 198–199), 1959, with the vertical tubular displays of the first figuration of the gallery at the MASP on Rua 7 de Abril (fig. 62), in 1947. The MAM-BA easel, from 1960, came after the MASP easel, the studies for which date from 1957.

In addition to the connections between MASP and MAM-BA in design solutions, the initial program of the new museum (fig. 65) made reference to the pedagogical proposals, exhibitions, and collection of the São Paulo museum. The museum's inauguration featured individual exhibitions of work by Antonio Bandeira (fig. 157) and Edgar Degas, with the bronze dancers from MASP's collection (fig. 159), a group show titled *Formas naturais* (Natural Forms; fig. 153), and a short presentation of MAM-BA's still incipient collection. Over the next three years, the museum would exhibit the work of Brazilian artists, including Agnaldo Manoel dos Santos (fig. 160), Agostinho Batista de Freitas (fig. 156), Aldemir Martins, Burle Marx, Candido Portinari, Emanoel Araujo, Juarez Paraíso, Lula Cardoso Ayres, Mario Cravo Júnior, and Montez Magno, and international artists such as Käthe Kollwitz, Paul Cézanne, Pierre-Auguste Renoir, and Vincent van Gogh, the last three with paintings from MASP's collection, including iconic works such as Renoir's *Pink and Blue* (1881; fig. 66) and Van Gogh's *Walk at Twilight* (1889–90; fig. 155).[27] The museum also held collective exhibits on industrial design, architecture (with drawings by Le Corbusier; fig. 154), figureheads from the São Francisco River (fig. 161), in addition to educational exhibitions, a clear point of contact with MASP's pedagogical project.[28]

Bo Bardi rejected the term "Museum" for MAM-BA, preferring names such as "Center," "Movement," and "School," because the collection was still small and because of the very notion of a museum she had been formulating since MASP and in texts published in *Habitat*, such as "The Living Museums of the United States," in which she proposed the idea of a museum that does not focus solely on the tasks of collecting, conserving, and exhibiting its collection, but which has an educational mission in the context in which it is inserted.[29] In the article "Houses or Museums," published in Salvador's *Diário de Notícias* newspaper, Bo Bardi states:

In the context of contemporary culture, the museum occupies a dusty and useless position. . . . The modern museum has to be an educational museum, it has to add to conservation the ability to convey the message that the works must be brought to the fore.[30]

At MASP, in São Paulo, these ideas were put into practice with the educational exhibitions, the IAC, and later, at the Avenida Paulista building, with the educational panels designed by Pietro Maria Bardi installed on the back of the glass easels, which historically contextualized the works exhibited and suggested comparisons with others from the same artist, period, or school (figs. 179–180).

The scenario was different in Salvador: a city outside of the Rio–São Paulo axis, removed from Brazil's major economic development, although undergoing a very fruitful period in the realms of culture and education, with the presence of names such as

The reenacted exhibition had 975 works, 44 of which were part of the original show. The new assembly respected, as far as possible, the selection and arrangement of works from the 1969 show. When similar objects were not found, we opted for others of the same type, produced before 1970—with the aim of maintaining the temporal context of the first exhibition. The original exhibition did not have a catalogue, but a book was published for the reenactment that presents historical images and documents from the first. The volume includes texts by curators and essays by Antonio Risério, Durval Muniz, Ricardo Gomes Lima, Guacira Waldeck, Silvana Rubino, and Tício Escobar, as well as republications of texts by Lina Bo Bardi, Bruno Zevi, and Frederico Morais. See Adriano Pedrosa and Tomás Toledo, eds., *A mão do povo brasileiro, 1969/2016* (Sao Paulo: MASP, 2016).

26. Néstor Garcia Canclini, *Culturas híbridas* (São Paulo: Edusp, 2015), 175.

27. Among the featured artists, some had exhibitions previously organized by MASP: Agostinho Batista de Freitas (1952), Burle Marx (1952), Candido Portinari (1954), Lula Cardoso Ayres (1960), Mario Cravo Júnior (1950), and Käthe Kollwitz (1961).

28. On this history of exhibitions at MAM-BA, see Juliano Aparecido Pereira, *Lina Bo Bardi. Bahia. 1958–1964* (Uberlândia: Edufu, 2008).

29. Lina Bo Bardi, "Os museus vivos nos Estados Unidos," *Habitat*, no. 8 (July–September 1952): 12–15.

30. Lina Bo Bardi, "Casas ou museus," in Silvana Rubino and Marina Grinover, eds., *Lina por escrito: textos escolhidos de Lina Bo Bardi, 1943–1991* (São Paulo: Cosac Naify, 2009).

FIG. 66
Arrival in Salvador of Pierre-Auguste Renoir's painting *Pink and Blue (The Cahen d'Anvers Girls)* (1881) from MASP's collection, on loan to the Museum of Modern Art of Bahia, April 2, 1960

the Portuguese philosopher Agostinho da Silva, the Bahian filmmaker Glauber Rocha, the German composer Hans-Joachim Koellreuter, the Pernambucan theater director Martim Gonçalves, and the Swiss musician Walter Smetak, in addition to the general cultural effervescence that only a few years later would lead to the emergence of *tropicalismo*.[31]

In this context, Bo Bardi turned to an educational project that was grounded in popular culture and practice, conceiving of a school of industrial design with popular roots. In the realm of pedagogy, she was close to the thought of the Bahian educator Anísio Teixeira, especially with Escola Parque, a revolutionary proposal for the reorganization of basic education in Brazil with special attention paid to the relationship between architecture and pedagogy, from a multidisciplinary perspective.

In 1963, with the beginning of the Castro Alves Theater renovations, MAM-BA was transferred to the Solar do Unhão, where it occupied the same place as the Museum of Popular Art, founded by Bo Bardi at the same moment. The Solar, an old sugar cane mill erected in Salvador in the seventeenth century that underwent modifications in the eighteenth and nineteenth centuries, was restored by Bo Bardi in 1962. In the renovation project of this seaside building, Bo Bardi preserved the facade's main features, as well as the internal wood structure with the roof trusses and the *muxarabis* on windows and doors (figs. 165–166).

Undoubtedly, the key architectural element added to Bo Bardi's original ensemble was the central staircase linking the two floors of the Solar. Constructed with wood fittings, in direct reference to the ox-carts of rural Brazil, the geometric, spiral stairway brings popular culture and vernacular building techniques to the interior of the museum (figs. 167–170). If the staircase at MASP on Avenida Paulista is permeated with political intentions, the Unhão staircase presents an element of the performative, both in its central and showy location and in the idea of movement implicit in its forms, as in order to climb or descend its stairs the public must travel on an upward or downward circular path, parading through the structure. In fact, in 1977, the Unhão staircase was used as the stage for the dance performance *Vertigem do sagrado* (Vertigo of the Sacred; fig. 68), directed and choreographed by Lia Robatto, a Brazilian dancer who studied with the Polish Yanka Rudzka, a pioneer of modern dance in Brazil and founder of the dance program at the Federal University of Bahia (UFBA), and who came to Brazil at the invitation of Pietro Maria Bardi to teach at MASP.

The inauguration of the Solar do Unhão and the Museum of Popular Art, in 1963,

31. On this, see Antonio Risério, *Avant-garde na Bahia* (São Paulo: Instituto Lina Bo e P. M. Bardi, 1995), and Caetano Veloso, *Verdade tropical* (São Paulo: Companhia das Letras, 1997).

took place alongside the iconic *Northeast* exhibition. The exhibition was organized in two sections, one devoted to a panorama of northeastern artists and another to popular culture, with a large selection of objects, such as ex-votos, figureheads, machinery, fabric, kitchen utensils, and Afro-Brazilian religious objects. Bo Bardi explained her objectives in the curatorial statement:

This exhibition seeks to present a civilization thought out in every detail, technically studied . . . from lighting to kitchen spoons, bedspreads, clothing, teapots, toys, furniture, weapons. It is the desperate and rabidly positive search for men who don't want to be "demoted," who claim their right to life. A struggle of every moment not to sink into despair, an affirmation of the beauty achieved with rigor that only the constant presence of reality can give.[32]

The exhibition of northeastern artists was structured in displays detached from the walls that reinstituted the vertical structures of the MASP on Rua 7 de Abril (fig. 62), but had the metal tubing replaced by wood rafters, in a clear shift in choice of materials, from industrial iron to natural wood (fig. 61). The objects of this section were devoted to popular culture, for the most part presented in the radical exhibition design that emulated the stalls of popular northeastern markets, as mentioned above (figs. 210–211). The other part, especially the figureheads, was exposed on a kind of easel for sculptures composed of the same concrete block as the MASP glass easels, but with the addition of steel rebar to support the objects, giving lightness and a sense of transparency to the exhibition design (fig. 63).

A key aspect of the *Northeast* exhibit and the Museum of Popular Art was not to compromise with the paternalistic, segregationist, and antiquated view of folklore. For Bo Bardi, choosing the name of the museum was quite deliberate, as noted in the inaugural exhibition text:

We call this the Museum of Popular Art and not *Folklore* because *folklore* [represents] a static and regressive heritage, paternalistically supported by those responsible for culture, whereas popular art (we use the word art not only in the artistic sense but also in the technical doing) defines the progressive attitude of popular culture linked to real problems.[33]

And she concluded:

This exhibition is an accusation. An accusation of a world that does not want to renounce the human condition despite oblivion and indifference. It is not a humble accusation [but] shows the desperate effort to produce culture in the face of the degrading conditions imposed by men.[34]

In these passages, Bo Bardi makes direct reference to the economic and social situation of the country in the 1960s, especially to the harsh and extremely impoverished reality of various regions of the Northeast, especially in the *sertão*, which today is still hard hit by drought and state neglect. Bo Bardi also refers to another kind of neglect, not necessarily political, but a product of lack of interest, of prejudice against aesthetics, cultures, and thoughts from social strata other than the ruling white elite that still largely dominates the historical narratives and the means of production and cultural propagation.

Thus, the role of education was central to Bo Bardi's museum program, precisely because of its potential for transformation and social development. At Unhão, she created an area entirely dedicated to workshops and schools (fig. 67) whose educational programs were not only theoretical but also practical and technical, with the aim of laying the foundations for the emergence of industrial design forged in popular culture, thereby empowering the artisan or artist in the system of culture and the production of material goods.

Another critical aim in the conceptualization of the Museum of Popular Art was to seek narratives for the history of Brazil and the history of art beyond dominant Euro-American histories, contemplating other cultural and racial matrixes, fundamental for a country like Brazil, with its colonial past and history of slavery. In this sense, Bo Bardi proposed a series of exhibitions to be held in the museum titled *Program of Brazilian Civilization*, composed of *Civilization of the Northeast*, *The Indian*, *Africa-Bahia* (with the collaboration of Pierre Verger), *Europe*, and *The Iberian Peninsula*. However,

32. Lina Bo Bardi, "Civilização do Nordeste," in Marcelo Suzuki, ed., *Tempos de grossura: o design no impasse* (São Paulo: Instituto Lino Bo e P. M. Bardi, 1994), 35.

33. Ibid., 37.

34. Ibid.

FIG. 67
View of studios at the Museum of Modern Art of Bahia, Solar do Unhão, Salvador, 2008

only the *Northeast* exhibition (which in its final configuration dropped the word "Civilization" from the title) came into being, given the abrupt departure of Bo Bardi from the directorship and the forced closure of the museum by the military coup in 1964, leading to her return to São Paulo.

Lina Bo Bardi's Popular

Among the objects presented in *Bahia in Ibirapuera*, *Northeast*, and *The Hand of the Brazilian People*, Bo Bardi was especially interested in recycled artifacts, usually industrial products, which, after losing their original use or breaking, had their material or morphology taken up for other purposes. This is the case of lamps and funnels fabricated from oil cans, or the emblematic kerosene lamp made from a burnt-out electric light bulb (fig. 60), thus creating a curious metalinguistic object, whose function—that of illuminating—has not been altered, but which was technologically transformed from electric light to kerosene flame. Or, in the words of Flávio Motta:

The light bulb in the lamp did not interest the consumer of the "lamp" as a light bulb. It's there as a glass shell. It has lost its significance as light bulb. The consumers of the light bulb didn't know what to do with it, and they threw it away. The producer who did not know what to do with a light bulb, as a light bulb, knew how to create a new meaning for it.[35]

The transformation—or recycling—of these objects is not fortuitous, but rather pragmatic, as it meets the needs of a resource-poor population and demonstrates the potential for creativity in the face of deprivation. This discussion about the utilitarian aspect of popular material production and the precariousness of Brazil's social and economic conditions was already present in Bo Bardi's curatorial statement for the *Northeast* exhibition at Solar do Unhão:

Raw material: trash. Burnt out light bulbs, scraps of fabric, lubricant cans, old boxes, and newspapers. Each object borders on the "nothingness" of misery. This limit and the continuous and hammered presence of the "useful and necessary" that constitute the value of this production, its poetics of nongratuitous human things, not created by mere fantasy.[36]

Bo Bardi's interest in recycled objects and this "way of doing" of the Brazilian people revealed that her attention was not necessarily focused on the final aesthetic result, but rather on the available means of production and the functionality of these objects. From her writings, it is possible to conclude that her interpretation of the concept of popular art and culture distanced itself from, and was in fact opposed to, the notion of

35. Flávio Motta, "A arte e a vida urbana no Brasil," in Suzuki, ed., *Tempos de grossura*, 59.

36. Lina Bo Bardi, "Civilização do Nordeste," in Suzuki, ed., *Tempos de grossura*, 35.

FIG. 68
View of the dance performance *Vertigem do sagrado* (Vertigo of the Sacred), directed and choreographed by Lia Robatto, which utilized the staircase at Solar do Unhão in its set design, 1977

37. Lina Bo Bardi, "Um balanço dezesseis anos depois," in Suzuki, ed., *Tempos de grossura*, 12.

folklore, considered by the architect to be a paternalistic approach anchored in Eurocentric values. In her view, popular culture could be the basis for the development of an aesthetic, an industrial design, a praxis, and even an ethics, constituted by Brazilian vernacular elements, by the country's own culture and history, and not by foreign models and perspectives. Or, in her words:

A reexamination of the country's recent history is necessary. An account of "popular" Brazilian civilization must be made, even if poor in light of high culture. This account is not one of folklore, always paternalistically supported by high culture; it is the account "seen from the other side," the participating account. It is Aleijadinho and Brazilian culture before the French Mission. It is the Northeasterner of leather and empty cans, the village inhabitant, the Black, and the Indian. A mass that invents, that creates an indigestible, dry, hard-to-swallow contribution.[37]

Both MASP and Bo Bardi's Bahian museums are guided by their very particular notions of "work"—which breaks down the boundaries between art and artifact—and share the desire for the dissolution of a compartmentalized and elitist art history, moving away from the closed-off and austere museum. They are also based on the idea of a museum grounded in education and open to its contexts and to the urgencies that arise in the present, taking popular culture as an important guiding thread in its programming.

Thus, Bo Bardi's vision of the popular, as much in her architectural as her editorial and curatorial work, can be taken as an opportunity to develop other conceptions of museums and histories of art, new ways of doing and thinking about curatorship, not necessarily teleological and linear, but also for rethinking the history of Brazil beyond hegemonic discourses, proposing interpretations built by autonomous and plural voices.

Translated from the Portuguese by Emma Young

Tomás Toledo, Chief Curator, MASP, São Paulo

WHOEVER DOES NOT OWN A DOG HUNTS WITH A CAT

Virtude de urubutinga
De enxergar tudo de longe!
Não carece vestir tanga
Pra penetrar meu caçanje!
Você sabe o francês "singe"
Mas não sabe o que é guariba?
— Pois é macaco, seu mano,
Que só sabe o que é da estranja.
[The hawk's virtue
To see everything from afar!
No need to wear a loincloth
To understand my *caçanje*!
You know the French "singe"
But don't know what *guariba* is?
—Sure, monkey, you man,
Who only knows what is foreign]
MÁRIO DE ANDRADE[1]

At the entrance to the 1969 exhibition *A mão do povo brasileiro* (The Hand of the Brazilian People; fig. 69), a panel dedicated the show to the recently deceased Rodrigo Mello Franco de Andrade, acknowledging his role in the preservation of the diverse manifestations, both material and immaterial, of Brazilian culture, mainly through the Serviço do Patrimônio Histórico e Artístico Nacional (National Historical and Artistic Heritage Service, SPHAN; later IPHAN), which he founded in 1937 and directed until 1967. According to statements by Pietro Maria Bardi and press materials in MASP's archives, *The Hand of the Brazilian People* was part of a long-standing effort to promote Brazilian cultural production, in its manifold expressions, that could be traced back to the establishment of SPHAN by Mello Franco de Andrade and his subsequent endeavors.[2]

Documents from MASP's archives shed light on a lesser-known episode related to the exhibition, particularly concerning its purported "slogan": *quem não tem cão caça com gato*—"whoever does not own a dog hunts with a cat." The vernacular expression appears several times in material related to the exhibition in MASP's archives, mainly described as a "slogan" in a statement signed by Pietro Maria Bardi, and in a letter sent by lawyer Hélio Dias de Moura, where the latter questioned its use, finding it somewhat derogatory, especially given the stature of Mello Franco de Andrade as a public figure and the homage paid to him by the exhibition. Bardi replied that a journalist had made up the story about the "slogan," and that the phrase was in no way connected to the exhibition.

Beyond the anecdote, this incident reveals the tensions within the Brazilian cultural sphere at a time when the intense process of modernization of the previous decades was beginning to lose momentum and its shortcomings were becoming evident. The enduring exclusion of large sectors of society from economic growth, technological advances, and access to education and culture pointed to the unfulfilled promises of developmentalism, as well as to the fact that this process of modernization was seen by many as a form of neocolonialism, as it seemed to revitalize and consolidate the very structures that created these inequities in the first place.[3]

The identification of the exhibition with this folk expression can most probably be attributed to Lina Bo Bardi, for whom it would seem to have been representative of the fact that, despite working under conditions of poverty and lack of material means, a large sector of the Brazilian population produced enormously creative solutions and rich artistic manifestations. The ensuing objection on behalf of a representative of the Brazilian elite, on the other hand, demonstrates the discomfort produced by allusions to situations of material poverty; not only the

1. From Mário de Andrade's poem "Lundu do escritor difícil," quoted in a letter sent by the Associação Brasileira de Folclore to Pietro Maria Bardi on the occasion of the opening of the exhibition *The Hand of the Brazilian People* at MASP in 1969.

2. We could add, among other significant precedents to the exhibition, the Missão de Pesquisas Folclóricas (Mission for Folkloric Research) organized in 1938 by Mario de Andrade, who was also active at SPHAN and IPHAN in different capacities and during different periods.

3. Since the early 1990s, the modernity/coloniality group has promoted this idea, arguing that modernity is the dark side of coloniality. Nevertheless, this kind of thinking was already voiced by artists and cultural practitioners during the 1960s. References to modernization as a form of neocolonialism appear in many films and writings by artists, sociologists, and theorists, for example in Glauber Rocha's texts and in the 1968 film *La hora de los hornos* directed by Fernando Solanas and Octávio Getino, among many others.

FIG. 69
View of the exhibition *The Hand of the Brazilian People*, 1969

FIG. 70
View of the exhibition *Bahia in Ibirapuera*, Ibirapuera Park, São Paulo, 1959

aforementioned "slogan," but perhaps also the actual display of the material culture of a population that had been historically subjected to oppression by an elite minority, and whose cultural production was correspondingly excluded from increasingly Westernized cultural institutions.

Moreover, these conflicting points of view call for a recontextualization of *The Hand of the Brazilian People* within a larger framework, which addresses precisely the paradigm shift that was underway at the time in Brazil, particularly in the cultural milieu, characterized by an effort to break from the narratives of progress and development inscribed in the modernist canon. It is possible to identify an ideological agenda at the root of Bo Bardi's museological practice, one that attempted to decolonize from the hegemonic discourse of Western art-historical traditions, as well as from the modernist canon. Bo Bardi was keenly aware of the situation of dependency and neocolonialism that accompanied the rapid race toward development in Third World countries, and that threatened to destroy local forms of knowledge. To decolonize from the Western canon and from the conventional institutional model meant to rethink the museum from a bottom-up perspective, to "strip the museum of its church atmosphere that excludes the uninitiated," to present art as "work," and to embrace popular forms of culture, inscribing them into but also "contaminating" and hybridizing the grand narratives of Western art history.

This essay aims to identify some of the key ideological coordinates of Lina Bo Bardi's inscription of the popular within a modern museological practice, a process that she initiated with the exhibition *Bahia in Ibirapuera* at MASP in 1959 (fig. 70), and that she continued with the *Nordeste* (Northeast) exhibition organized at the Solar do Unhão in 1963 (fig. 71), *The Hand of the Brazilian People* at MASP in 1969, and the exhibitions that she subsequently organized at Sesc Pompeia in the 1970s and 1980s. On the occasion of the restaging of *The Hand of the Brazilian People*, it seems pertinent to revisit Bo Bardi's ideological terms of engagement with the popular and to contextualize her endeavor within a larger framework. *The Hand of the Brazilian People* was neither the first nor the last of her exhibitions devoted to the cultural production of the Brazilian people; however, it can be considered a point of inflection. In a certain way, it was the culmination of a series of exhibitions that had begun with *Bahia in Ibirapuera* a decade earlier, but also one that marked the intensification of her agenda with the later architectural design and exhibition program at Sesc Pompeia in the 1980s.

Those Who Don't Have [Dogs] (a paradigm shift in the context of the development/dependency dilemma)

In Italy as a young architect, Bo Bardi was active in the resistance movement, and in 1943 she joined the Italian Communist Party. She had also been particularly influenced by the writings of Antonio Gramsci, Benedetto Croce, and in general by the neo-Marxist critical theory of the Frankfurt School. Upon her arrival in Brazil, Bo Bardi's ideological leanings were further informed by her encounter with a new reality—shaped by a colonial past that perpetuated itself through an imposed modernity—into which the critical apparatuses of the West were not as easily translatable or applicable.

It was in this context that Bo Bardi began to question the rapid modernization process that Brazil was undergoing at the time under the influence of *desarrollismo* (developmentalism), and its possible consequences, as well as to subsequently formulate strategies for exiting the double bind imposed by the developmentalist ethos. In undated notes from her personal archive, it is possible to identify her investment in negotiating the complexities of modernity and its conflictive relationship to underdevelopment, as she repeatedly returns to the problem of dependency, specifically addressing the tensions between development and underdevelopment:

Brazil. Situation of a country that enters the history of modern development at a time when highly developed countries denounce, in a display of collective awareness, the perversity of a system. It enters capitalism as a dependent structure of extra-national centers. A process that took centuries to develop in highly industrialized countries only takes years here. These processes thus impose themselves as a destructive avalanche that does away with all values . . . The history of Brazil is a *white*, Eurocentric history . . . a white history that ignores Africa's contribution, that ignores the indigenous peoples, a long history of defeats of the vast majority by a minority.[4]

In *Tempos de grossura* (published posthumously in 1994; fig. 56), she asks a fundamental question in this regard: "What is the situation of a country with a dependent capitalist structure, where a bourgeois-democratic national revolution failed to take place, which enters industrialization with the remnants of oligarchic-national structures?"[5]

During this period, Brazil was not only immersed in a process of rapid industrialization, but was also part of discussions that placed it in the much wider context of

4. Handwritten undated notes in the archives of the Instituto Lina Bo e P. M Bardi, São Paulo, probably for a lecture, as she mentions slides that she would show to illustrate some of her arguments.

5. Lina Bo Bardi, "Um balanço dezesseis anos depois," in Marcelo Suzuki, ed., *Tempos de grossura: o design no impasse* (São Paulo: Instituto Lino Bo e P. M. Bardi, 1994), 11.

FIG. 71
View of the exhibition *Northeast* at the Museum of Popular Art, Solar do Unhão, Salvador, 1963

nonindustrialized, underdeveloped countries, which included the rest of Latin America and the former European colonies of Africa, the Middle East, and Asia. The concurrent decolonization processes in Africa, Asia, and the Middle East generated debates around the legacies of colonialism in the modern world and its effects on what came to be known in the early 1950s as the Third World. The 1955 Non-Aligned conference in Bandung was a key event that aimed to counteract the polarization of Cold War geopolitics and introduced a third factor: a Third World that stood between a violent colonial past and the promise of a modernity that it was not yet prepared to undertake. A new critical framework was needed to address these processes that implied an ideological shift in terms of both discourse and action for many within the fields of political economy, sociology, and culture, and in this sense, it is possible to identify the emergence of decolonial thought during this period of geopolitical transformation throughout the non-Western world.[6]

In Latin America, the complexity and contradictions implicit in the region's "transition to modernity" had been closely monitored and analyzed by sociologists and political economists in the 1960s and 1970s, some of them affiliated with the Comisión Económica para América Latina y el Caribe (CEPAL).[7] One of the analyses that gained currency in that period was that of dependency theory, which emerged in response to the modernization and development theories formulated by CEPAL-affiliated intellectuals and social scientists, identifying the persistence of colonial, archaic, social, and economic forms in the rapid and incomplete modernization process experienced by many countries in the region. Dependency theorists argued that development in such conditions was not only a delusion, but that it essentially guaranteed the flow of

6. The term *decoloniality* is, in fact, more recent and refers specifically to Latin America, in contrast to postcolonial theory, which addressed these processes in Africa and Asia. A group of academics loosely gathered under the Modernity/Coloniality/Decoloniality group have devoted their efforts to the analysis of what Aníbal Quijano defined as "coloniality." The decolonial option, as Walter Mignolo and others affiliated with his group have described it, implies epistemic disobedience and resistance to a modernity that perpetuates the colonial condition.

7. Created in 1948 as a UN commission, CEPAL's aim was to cooperate with governments of the region, providing research and analysis to assist the process of socioeconomic development. The rhetoric of developmentalism was largely articulated and implemented by CEPAL with the economic reforms that were applied throughout Latin America during the 1950s. Among the theoretical

influences guiding developmentalist theories proposed by CEPAL were those of John Maynard Keynes. In the context of the world-systems approach developed by Immanuel Wallerstein, some of CEPAL's affiliates, such as Raúl Prebisch (one of its first executive secretaries), Celso Furtado, Fernando Henrique Cardoso, and Aníbal Pinto, later oriented their analyses toward what theorists associated with André Gunder Frank defined as underdevelopment theory and dependency theory.

8. Mário Pedrosa, "Arte culta e arte popular," *Arte em Revista* (São Paulo), no. 3 (1980).

9. The Neo-Concrete Manifesto was written by Gullar with Amilcar de Castro, Claudio Mello Neto, Franz Weissmann, Lygia Clark, Lygia Pape, Reynaldo Jardim, and Theon Spanudis. Shortly after, Gullar wrote *Teoria do não objeto*, in which he systematically laid the foundation for an avant-garde art based on the rationality of nonobjective forms and perceptual experiences, and deeply anchored in the modernist framework set by the constructivist avant-gardes of the first half of the twentieth century, such as Russian Constructivism and Dutch De Stijl.

10. In the midst of the social reforms carried out by Goulart, which ultimately led to his ouster in the 1964 military coup, various sociocultural organizations emerged that reacted to the developmentalist rhetoric and its translation into the realms of architecture and the visual arts, specifically through the language of geometric abstraction. One of the most notable of these was the controversial Centro Popular de Cultura (CPC), closely linked in its origins to the Teatro de Arena in São Paulo. Many figures were involved with the CPC, including playwright Gianfrancesco Guarnieri, theater director Augusto Boal, filmmakers Leon Hirszman, Carlos Diegues, and Joaquim Pedro de Andrade, who participated in the Cinema Novo movement, among many others, including Gullar, for whom an important aspect of local and popular forms of culture was the fact that they were legible to an otherwise uninstructed population.

11. Pape designed posters and/or credit sequences for films such as the *Mandacaru Rouge* and *Barren Lives* (Nelson Pereira dos Santos, 1961 and 1963); *Ganga Zumba* (Carlos Diegues, 1962–65); *Absolute Majority* (Leon Hirszman,

resources and labor from the impoverished peripheries to the centers, inherently perpetuating colonial dynamics of exploitation and domination.

Echoing the critiques and concerns coming from the field of political economy, intellectuals and artists in Brazil marked a critical distance from the canon and vocabulary of the modern, reclaiming local forms of knowledge and popular and vernacular expressions, recognizing the value of cultural manifestations born out of conditions of material poverty, while acutely aware of the potential effects of the byproducts of rapid and intensive industrialization, namely the burgeoning consumer and mass communications culture. Also aligned to the kind of thought set in motion in 1955 by the Bandung conference and the emergence of the Third World, Brazilian writers and critics who had accompanied the successive modernist avant-gardes of the 1920s and the 1950s, such as Mário Pedrosa and Ferreira Gullar, both involved in the Concrete group of Rio de Janeiro, began to look toward local forms of knowledge and cultural production, identifying another set of epistemologies endemic to the underdeveloped Third World. In this context, Pedrosa stated that:

Ultramodernisms and their progress, usually shaped by the American template, are fundamentally tied to our *favelas* and shantytowns. The paradox is that these don't change, as neither do misery, hunger, poverty, huts, and ruins. But that is where the future passes by. Here is the option of the Third World: an open future or eternal misery.... The creative task of humanity begins to move to other latitudes and advances to the widest and most dispersed areas of the Third World.[8]

Moreover, for Pedrosa, crafts and popular forms of culture held an emancipatory potential for the avant-garde, after what was perceived by some as the exhaustion of the modernist constructive tradition. Similarly, Gullar, who had among other things co-authored the Neo-Concrete Manifesto in 1959, published a book in 1969 titled *Vanguarda e subdesenvolvimento* (Avant-Garde and Underdevelopment).[9] Nevertheless, Gullar, like others in Brazil, had distanced himself from the modernist avant-gardes much earlier, in the early 1960s, during the government of João Goulart.[10]

Also during this period, artists such as Hélio Oiticica and Lygia Pape, formerly major representatives of the brand of geometric abstraction associated with the modernist canon, were also engaged in the structural incorporation of a popular vocabulary into their avant-garde practices. In 1967, Oiticica organized an exhibition at the Rio de Janeiro Museum of Modern Art titled *Nova objetividade brasileira* (New Brazilian Objectivity); his catalogue essay introduced the dilemma of underdevelopment as one of the exhibition's main arguments. For many of these artists, it was important to acknowledge the potential inscribed in the material practices of the poor. Lygia Pape, for instance, repeatedly raised this idea in her master's thesis, "Catiti-Catiti: na terra dos Brasis" (1980), to explain certain directions that her work took in the 1960s, a decade during which she actively collaborated with filmmakers who were invested in showcasing the culture of regions left behind in the rapid transit to modernization, such as the northeastern *sertão* (backlands) of Brazil, in their documentaries and feature films.[11] To work in the context of underdevelopment and dependency also meant to make the most of adverse conditions, an idea compellingly conveyed by Oiticica's 1965 *Parangolé 16 capa 12, Da adversidade vivemos* (1965), a wearable work made of various discarded materials such as jute, plastic, fabric, burlap, and sawdust, which bore the inscription *da adversidade vivemos* (in adversity we live). The phrase expressed a pervasive concern of many Brazilian intellectuals during the 1960s. Moreover, it shared the same message as the purported slogan of *The Hand of the Brazilian People*; both expressions pointed precisely to the resourcefulness of "those who don't have," and to how the avant-garde could learn from their experiences, traditions, and lore.

It is thus possible to situate Lina Bo Bardi within the context of this wave of experimentation of Brazilian culture that sought to embrace and incorporate these other forms of knowledge. It is clear that in her advocacy of popular culture, she was not acting in isolation, albeit independently of the artistic vanguards of Rio de Janeiro and

São Paulo, but rather as part of a significant movement that included the aforementioned intellectuals and many others.

Hunting with Cats (from philosophy to praxis)

One feature that sets Bo Bardi apart from her peers is that her undertaking was not only constant but also spanned four decades, beginning with the intense period of modernization in the 1950s up until her death in 1992. Popular culture was the foremost issue on her agenda, as an architect, designer, writer, exhibition curator, and cultural practitioner, and from that diverse range of fields and practices she set out to construct a framework of representation and enunciation for the popular.

From an ideological standpoint, Bo Bardi had been particularly influenced by Gramsci's notion of the national-popular, which pointed to the emergence of a national-popular collective will achieved only through the participation of the masses in political and cultural life. Working in the cultural field, and with a firm belief in its agency and its potential impact on other spheres of public life, Bo Bardi was interested in promoting a relationship between intellectuals and the popular base. In this sense, it was necessary that she provide a semantic framework for the cultural production of the people (*o povo*) in order to establish a platform for cultural transformation.

Possibly influenced by Gramsci's call for a philosophy of praxis, such a framework was to be a dynamic and also political one, geared toward creating a form of consciousness, rather than a merely anthropological one aimed only at studying the cultural production of a given culture or social group. In one of her undated notes, Bo Bardi writes: "This is the basic and urgent task today—to seize the history of Brazil from true history [*sic*], to seize the instruments necessary to understand it. . . . to document all the cultural activities of the People, even if poor in the eyes of High Culture." To this end, in her notes she makes a chain of associations, referencing Gramsci's distinction between national and nationalist, where the former is "profoundly proper to and characteristic of a country" but also international, whereas the latter is "repressively provincial." For Bo Bardi, in a country such as Brazil, already on the path of irreversible industrialization, "the opening toward internationalism, along with a profound consciousness of the national, is what must be at the base of a country's culture," a responsibility that she placed in the hands of "what Gramsci defined as the national-popular intellectual."[12]

In order to do this, she relied on public space, more specifically those spaces where a collective cultural life could take place; thus her work would mainly be deployed through the design of cultural centers, exhibition spaces, museums, and exhibition-making itself. Having trained and practiced as an architect under the aegis of CIAM, Bo Bardi was not only familiar with but also shared the interests of architects who departed from the precepts of the Athens Charter, such as those affiliated with Team 10, in particular Aldo van Eyck.[13] Like the architects of Team 10, her conception of architecture implied a bottom-up approach that placed human beings and lived experience at the center of architectural practice, and was inextricably bound to ideas of place, the sensorial, and vernacular traditions, rather than to space and the abstraction afforded by the bird's-eye view that dominated modernist architecture and urban planning. In a 1947 article titled "In Europe, the House of Man Collapsed," she states that in the postwar reconstruction effort, for the first time "man thinks of man" and "rebuilds for man," as "the war had destroyed the myths of the monuments."[14] Moreover, she identified the imperatives of a new architecture, which should be at the service of "the 'life,' of man," a statement singularly akin to Alison and Peter Smithson's commitment to the "hierarchy of human associations."[15] We can also find an exceptional affinity between Van Eyck's notion of the "vernacular of the heart," laid out in his *Otterlo Circles* of 1959, and the affective dimension that characterized Bo Bardi's architecture and design practice, as well as her embrace of popular traditions. Nowhere is this more evident than in her dialogical experience of learning from the material culture of her beloved *sertão*, which could also be rethought in terms of a militant and ideological agenda of emancipation from the Western canon inscribed within the decolonial turn.

1964); *God and the Devil in the Land of the Sun* (Glauber Rocha, 1964); and *Memory of the Cangaço* (Paulo Gil Soares, 1965), among many others.

12. See note 4.

13. In a previous essay, I discuss at length the proximity of her approach to that of Team 10 and Aldo van Eyck; see "The Architecture of Playgrounds: From the Logic of Space to the Logic of Place," in *Playgrounds 2016: MASP Mar 18–Jul 24, 2016* (São Paulo: Ministerio da Cultura Itau, 2016). Silvana Rubino also refers to Bo Bardi's proximity to Team 10 architects in her essay, "A escrita de uma arquiteta," in Silvana Rubino and Marina Grinover, eds., *Lina por escrito: textos escolhidos de Lina Bo Bardi, 1943–1991* (São Paulo: Cosac Naify, 2009).

14. Lina Bo Bardi, "Na Europa a casa do homem ruiu," in Rubino and Grinover, eds., *Lina por escrito*, 64–67.

15. Alison and Peter Smithson, in *Team 10 Primer*, ed. Alison Smithson (Cambridge, Mass.: MIT Press, 1962), 78.

16. *Habitat*, no. 1 (October–December 1950): 1.

17. Antonio Risério, *Avant-garde na Bahia* (São Paulo: Instituto Lina Bo e P. M. Bardi, 1995), 54.

It is as an architect and as editor of *Habitat*, the magazine published by MASP, that Bo Bardi began to formalize her engagement with the popular, mapping Brazil's cultural production and architecture to include both modernist and popular manifestations of architecture, design, and culture. The editorial in *Habitat*'s first issue, in 1950, is telling in this regard:

The imaginative beauty of a forest, a wattle and daub hut, a Marajoara vase, a Baroque church, Aleijadinho, the goldsmiths of Bahia, the Manuelino furniture makers of Recife, the epigones of the French Mission, the architects of the Manaus theater and the Rio de Janeiro Ministry of Education and Health, rustic [*caipira*] painters and renowned artists, potters, coastal *gameleiros*, Indians, Africans, descendants of the conquistadores, emigrants, all who contributed, continue to contribute and participate in some way in the arts in Brazil will have their activities featured in *Habitat* through the endeavors of those who know how to appreciate what is most characteristic of the country.[16]

This statement would set the magazine's agenda in the years to come, one that would emphasize the fact that the identification and study of the archaic roots of Brazilian culture were indeed a way to permeate high culture and open up ways to think of a future cultural undertaking that would include both manifestations, and where the former would significantly inform the latter.

During her first decade in Brazil, Bo Bardi traveled extensively throughout the country, especially in the northeastern *sertão*, which extends over a vast territory of the states of Bahia, Pernambuco, Alagoas, Paraíba, Rio Grande do Norte, Ceará, Maranhão, Piauí, and parts of northern Minas Gerais. In Bahia, she came into contact with the flourishing artistic community in Salvador, mostly around the Federal University of Bahia. Its rector, Edgard Santos, had indeed given real impetus to cultural activities in order to generate another cultural hub in Brazil outside the Rio–São Paulo axis, and created departments at the university bringing in important personalities to lead them: Yanka Rudzka, who had originally come to Brazil in 1952 upon the invitation of Pietro Maria Bardi to give a course at MASP, in the dance department; Hans Joachim Koellreutter, who had come from Germany in 1937 to teach in the music department; the theatrical director Martim Gonçalves, in the theater department; Portuguese scholar Agostinho da Silva, who created the university's Center for Afro-Oriental Studies. Foreign artists such as Swiss musician Walter Smetak and French photographer and anthropologist Pierre Verger had been longtime residents of Bahia, adding yet another element to the effervescent scene Bo Bardi encountered during her travels to Bahia in the 1950s.

It is important to note that this cultural landscape differed substantially from that of the Rio–São Paulo axis, dominated in the 1950s by movements linked to the constructive tradition, with an orientation toward Concrete art and poetry in the Noigandres and Ruptura groups of São Paulo, Grupo Frente, and later the Neo-Concrete Group in Rio, all of which came to represent the ideas of progress and modernity associated with developmentalist rhetoric. The Bahia avant-garde was more steeped in popular traditions and had no connections with the language of geometric abstraction. This may be partly due to the fact that some of its major representatives were European expatriates, such as Smetak, Koellreutter, Rudzka, Verger, and da Silva, for whom the modernist project seemed to have reached a point of exhaustion in the aftermath of events such as the tragic foreclosure of the Constructivist movement in Russia at the hands of the Stalinist regime, and World War II. Even if their vision was at times tinged with a fascination for the exotic and mediated by an anthropological gaze, they, like Bo Bardi, saw in Brazil a place where new languages and forms of experimentation were yet to be invented. In his book *Avant-garde na Bahia*, Antonio Risério describes this avant-garde as embedded in a "dialectic between cosmopolitan aesthetic-intellectual information and an anthropological, sociocultural reality," which he abbreviates as "a *dialectic of the cosmopolitan and the anthropological*."[17]

Bahia had a profound impact on Bo Bardi, who appreciated the extraordinary wealth of the region's popular culture, oral traditions, music, architecture, arts, and crafts. Always from the perspective of architect and designer, she had a particular interest in the idea of spontaneous architectural solutions,[18] to which she devoted significant space in *Habitat* in the 1950s. Likewise, from the perspective of industrial design, she was particularly receptive to solutions born out of necessity and material poverty. Artifacts made from recycled refuse (different types of cans, light bulbs, pieces of machinery) were objects of design in their own right for Bo Bardi, who always stressed the utilitarian and functional dimension of these creations born of popular ingenuity. In the posthumously published *Tempos de grossura: o design no impasse*, which summarizes her vision of northeastern material culture in terms of artistic and design production, she states:

> Raw material: trash. Burnt out light bulbs, scraps of fabric, lubricant cans, old boxes, and newspapers. Each object borders on the "nothingness" of misery. This limit and the continuous and hammered presence of the "useful and necessary" that constitute the value of this production, its poetics of nongratuitous human things, not created by mere fantasy.[19]

In 1959, Bo Bardi took the results of her observations and spatialized what had been, for almost a decade, an editorial endeavor mainly in the pages of *Habitat*, shifting to exhibition-making. *Bahia in Ibirapuera*, presented concurrently with the 5th São Paulo Biennial, was the result of her collaboration with theater director Martim Gonçalves. It and the 1963 *Northeast* exhibition constitute the two major precedents of *The Hand of the Brazilian People*. *Bahia in Ibirapuera* aimed to "frame the artistic aspects of Bahia within contemporary art" and to "include in the panorama of the aesthetic activities of modern man the so-called 'lesser arts.'"[20] The exhibition presented the cultural production of the region, a wide range of objects that included the leather garments of the *cangaceiros* ("cowboys") of the *sertão*; the *carrancas* (figureheads) that protected the boats navigating the São Francisco River from evil spirits; Afro-Brazilian art such as *candomblé* ritual objects, *orixás* (Afro-Brazilian deities), and ceremonial clothing; votive figures (ex-votos); Baroque sculptures of saints; and textiles. A series of photographs by Marcel Gautherot, Pierre Verger, Sílvio Robatto, and Ennes Mello accompanied the objects, lending an ethnographic dimension to the exhibition. However, beyond the anthropological inventory of objects that conformed an image of the "civilization of the Northeast," one of the most remarkable features of the exhibition was its display, which merged the respective practices of Gonçalves and Bo Bardi in theatrical *mise-en-scène* and exhibition design. A tree with paper flowers provided a focal point at the center of the exhibition, and the floor was covered in dried eucalyptus leaves, evoking the *candomblé* ritual of spreading pitanga leaves on the ground.[21] Divided into different sections by freestanding walls and set against a backdrop curtain, which emphasized the "theatricality" of the event, the exhibition was more of an environmental installation *avant la lettre*. The theatrical display of the exhibition distanced it from the conventions of ethnographic representation and created a new and original exhibition genre unto itself.

Between 1958 and 1964, Bo Bardi lived in Salvador. After almost a decade of frequent visits and collaborations with artists and intellectuals of Bahia, she made the move following an invitation from Santos to teach at the university. Shortly thereafter, in 1959, she also received an invitation from Governor Juracy Magalhães to direct the Bahia Museum of Modern Art, provisionally installed in the foyer of the Castro Alves Theater, which prompted her definitive relocation to Salvador. During her years in Bahia, Bo Bardi intensified her collaboration with Gonçalves, for whom she designed sets and costumes for his stagings of plays such as Brecht's *Threepenny Opera* (fig. 72) and Camus' *Caligula*. At the museum, her program included a diverse range of exhibitions: Brazilian artists (Candido Portinari, Oswaldo Goeldi, Francisco Brennand, Marcelo Grassmann, Mário Cravo, Argentina-born Carybé, Montez Magno, and Aldemir Martins, among others), European artists (*Three Painters: Renoir, Cézanne, Van Gogh*, featuring works on loan from MASP; Käthe Kollwitz and Stanley William Hayter); exhibitions devoted to architecture and design (*Swiss Posters*, *The Chair in History*, Le Corbusier, Roberto Burle Marx, *Crafts and Industrial Design*), as well as exhibitions of crafts and popular culture.

18. What Van Eyck would describe as the "vernacular of the heart," in reference to the architecture of the indigenous peoples of New Mexico or the Dogon of Mali, or what Bernard Rudofsky would later define as "architecture without architects" in his book and exhibition of the same title at MoMA in 1964.

19. Lina Bo Bardi, "Civilização do Nordeste," in Suzuki, ed., *Tempos de grossura*, 35.

20. Quoted in Juliano Pereira, *Lina Bo Bardi, Bahia, 1958–1964* (Uberlândia: Edufu, 2008).

21. *Candomblé* is a religion that developed as a result of the "creolization" of Yoruba, Fon, and Bantu beliefs, transplanted from West Africa by the slaves who arrived in Salvador de Bahia. The leaves of the pitanga tree (*Eugenia uniflora L.*) hold special significance in *candomblé* rites, as the tree is linked to various *orixás* or divine archetypes.

22. In documentary photographs of the 1959 *Bahia in Ibirapuera* exhibition, Rocha appears with Bo Bardi and Gonçalves outside the exhibition, suggesting that if he was not a contributor to the show, he was at least an interlocutor. Likewise, in press materials in MASP's archives, Rocha is mentioned as one of the co-organizers of *The Hand of the Brazilian People*, although no official museum press release supports this statement. Presumably, as a close friend and collaborator of Bo Bardi and Gonçalves, Glauber was involved in the exhibition's conceptualization.

23. For example, see Glauber Rocha's notion of tricontinental cinema. In his essay "Das sequoias às palmeiras 70" (in *Revolução do Cinema Novo* [São Paulo: Cosac Naify, 2004], 118), he states that: "The Third World filmmaker should not be afraid of being 'primitive.' He would be naïve if he insisted on imitating the dominant culture. He would also be naïve if he becomes a patrioteer! He must be anthropophagic, and operate in such a way that people colonized by the commercial/popular aesthetic (Hollywood), by the populist/demagogic aesthetic (Moscow), by the bourgeois/artistic aesthetic (Europe) can see and understand the revolutionary/popular aesthetic, which is the only objective that justifies tricontinental creation, but it is also necessary to create that aesthetic."

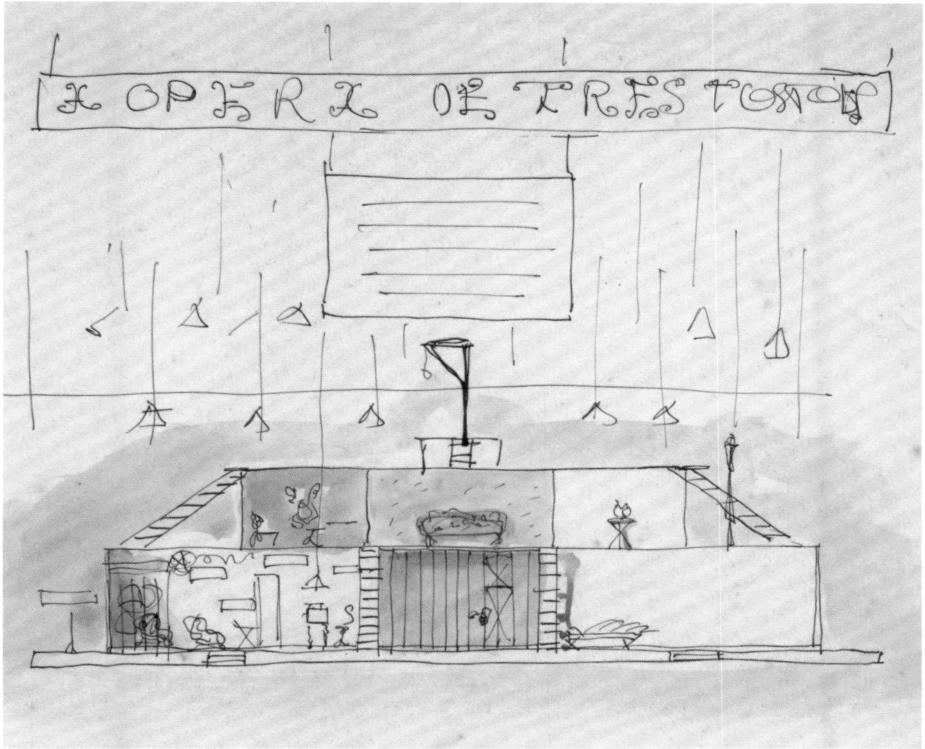

FIG. 72
Lina Bo Bardi, *Sketch for the stage of the Threepenny Opera*, 1960. Watercolor, ballpoint pen, and ink on offset paper. Collection of the Instituto Bardi/Casa de Vidro, São Paulo

In Bahia in the late 1950s, Bo Bardi had met the very young Glauber Rocha, who would become a close friend and interlocutor (fig. 73). They would collaborate formally and informally on his films and her exhibitions, cultivating a mutual fascination with the culture of the *sertão*.[22] Born in 1939, Rocha did not belong to the generation of artists and intellectuals who had revitalized Bahia's cultural landscape in the 1940s and 1950s. Rather, he was part of a younger generation that, experiencing the day-to-day social realities of a region that had been left behind by the train of progress and development, had taken a more radical and militant stance. This was the generation that included Bahians such as Caetano Veloso and Rogério Duarte, who would lead the Tropicália movement in Rio in the late 1960s; it was also the generation that joined the CPCs and supported Third World causes, and later, Tricontinentalism.[23] Unfortunately, according to Antonio Risério, some of the most radical factions were those that, blinded by ideology, eventually drove Santos from the university, ending its period of singular effervescence.[24]

In the early 1960s, we can say that Bo Bardi's practice also took on an increased militant dimension, characterized by her implementation of a systematized and ideological conception of the popular through concrete actions such as her own design and architectural projects, exhibitions, and educational initiatives. An endeavor that involved negotiating and collaborating with ideologically diverse groups, from the Movimento Cultural Popular (founded by a group of intellectuals that included artists Francisco Brennand and Abelardo da Hora, poet Ariano Suassuna, and pedagogue Paulo Freire, among others) to technocratic government agencies such as Sudene and its offshoot, Artene.[25]

Bo Bardi's vision for her most significant undertaking during her years in Salvador, the Museum of Modern Art of Bahia (MAM-BA), placed utmost importance on the study, exhibition, and production of popular culture, and included the creation of the Museum of Popular Art (MAP), the Research Center for Arts and Crafts (CETA), and the School of Industrial Design and Crafts. Bo Bardi conceived a more active role for the institution, as the term "museum" seemed too static in her view; she thought the museum should instead be called a "Center, Movement, School."[26] Since 1962, she had been working on plans to open this school, an unrealized project that nonetheless embodied this enabling and active role that she took on. Popular culture was a strategic endeavor for Bo Bardi, for whom the architect's profession was an "amalgamating factor of different processes, aligned with the intellectuals of the left and with the political actions of

24. Risério, *Avant-garde na Bahia*, 24. Risério states that "Santos was systematically opposed by a schizoleftist student leadership" that resulted in his "defenestration."

25. Sudene (Superintendência de Desenvolvimento do Nordeste / Superintendency for the Development of the Northeast) was created in 1959 by the government of President Juscelino Kubitschek to stimulate economic growth in the northeastern region of Brazil. It was the brainchild of its first director, the economist Celso Furtado, who was affiliated with CEPAL. Despite its alignment with developmentalist rhetoric, during the João Goulart administration Sudene recruited Paulo Freire in 1963 to implement his educational method in the region, through the intervention of then minister of education Darcy Ribeiro. It was in this context that, through the Alliance for Progress, Freire initiated his landmark pedagogic experience at Angicos in the Northeast. Artene was a branch of Sudene established to provide support to craftspeople in the region.

26. Lina Bo Bardi, in Marcelo Carvalho Ferraz, ed., *Lina Bo Bardi* (São Paulo: Instituto Lina Bo e P. M. Bardi, 1993), 139.

FIG. 73
Paulo Gil Soares, Waldemar Lima, Glauber Rocha, Lina Bo Bardi, Walter Lima Jr., and Santi Scaldaferri during the filming of *Deus e o diabo na terra do sol* (God and the Devil in the Land of the Sun, 1964) by Glauber Rocha, Monte Santo, Bahia

different social groups—CPC, Peasant Leagues, the National Student Union."[27]

The project for the museum-school at the Solar do Unhão in Salvador would also comprise a documentation center, Centro de Documentação do Artesanato Popular do Nordeste (Documentary Center for the Popular Crafts of the Northeast).[28] To this end, Bo Bardi had been collecting objects and documenting techniques around the state of Bahia and in the vast and arid area of the *sertão*, also known as the Polígono das Secas (Polygon of Drought). The objects and documentary material served as the basis for the inaugural exhibition of the Museum of Popular Art at the Solar do Unhão in 1963.

Northeast was the title of this exhibition, which presented the "civlization of the Northeast" in all its technical details, "from lighting to kitchen spoons, to quilts, clothing, teapots, toys, furniture, and weapons."[29] For Bo Bardi, to speak of popular culture in terms of civilization was synonymous with removing "the high culture-rhetorical meaning that goes with the word," for "civilization is the practical aspect of culture, it is mankind's life at all times."[30] This technical inflection was probably also indebted to the pedagogic project that Bo Bardi had sought to implement at the Solar do Unhão. While *Bahia in Ibirapuera* had staged a theatrical ethnographic vision of Bahian culture that included its religious manifestations, *Northeast* set forth a design philosophy for the region, one that divested it of nostalgia and placed it in the modern framework of functionalism. Her statement, "we insisted on the craftsmanship-industrial design identity of the object based on technical production connected to the reality of the materials and not on the folklore-choreographic abstraction,"[31] could even be seen as a critique of her earlier exhibition. In the context of the different organizations and government agencies operating in the Northeast at the time, and the region's persistent problems of exploitation, illiteracy, and poverty, a vicious cycle that harked back to the colonial period and the practice of *latifundismo* compellingly described by Darcy Ribeiro in *O povo brasileiro*,[32] the exhibition indeed had a political agenda and a militant dimension; as Bo Bardi stated in an essay on *Northeast* in *Tempos de grossura*, "This exhibition is an accusation. . . . It is not a humble accusation [but] shows the desperate effort to produce culture in the face of the degrading conditions imposed by men."[33]

Frictions in Brazil were growing in 1963, as the social reforms undertaken by the Goulart government did not sit well with the country's elite; agrarian reform, in particular, affected landowners, who for centuries had exploited the population of the Northeast. Similarly, in Bahia, tensions were mounting between the radical student movement and the ruling elite. In 1964, after the coup that ousted Goulart, Bo Bardi was forced to abruptly terminate her activities at MAM-BA and return to São Paulo. In 1967, she wrote a harsh, incisive account of her years in

27. Eduardo Pierrotti Rossetti, "Tensão moderno/popular em Lina Bo Bardi: nexos de arquitetura," Faculdade de Arquitetura e Urbanismo-USP, at https://repositorio.ufba.br/ri/bitstream/ri/12086/1/Tens%C3%A3o%20modernopopular%20em%20Lina%20Bo%20Bardi%20Nexos%20de%20arquitetura.pdf, 60.

28. When the renovation of the Castro Alves Theater began in late 1963, MAM-BA moved to its definitive venue at the Solar do Unhão and was inaugurated as the Museum of Popular Art.

29. Bo Bardi, "Civilização do Nordeste," 35.

30. Ibid.

31. Ibid., 37.

32. See Darcy Ribeiro, *O povo brasileiro* (São Paulo: Companhia das Letras, 2003), 339.

33. Bo Bardi, "Civilização do Nordeste," 37.

Bahia titled "Five Years among the 'Whites,'" published in Pietro Maria Bardi's magazine *Mirante das Artes*. There she described the network of governmental and grassroots alliances that had joined forces to find ways to "exit the stage of cultural colonialism" in the region. Among these efforts she summarized the mission of MAM-BA and MAP as one that, "given the misery of the state," which precluded building or preserving a museum collection, directed its efforts toward "the creation of a cultural movement that, embracing the values of a historically 'poor' culture (in the sense of 'high' culture), could lucidly enter the world of real modern culture, overcoming the 'culturalist' and 'historicist' phases of the West, by relying on a popular experience (rigorously distinct from that of folklore)."[34]

What had begun in the late 1940s as a "cartographic" enterprise guided by anthropological observation revealed itself to be a dialogical experience of learning from the material culture of the *sertão*, not only in terms of Bo Bardi's activities in the arena of culture, museums, and exhibitions, but also for her design practice. Her material and technical approach to architectural and industrial design took a radical turn toward what she would describe as a "poor architecture," one stripped to the bare essentials, that eschewed artifice, revealed structural features, and highlighted the characteristics of the materials employed. This shift becomes evident early on in her furniture designs, such as the Wood Tripod Chair from the late 1940s and early 1950s (figs. 386–387), inspired by fishermen's hammocks on the São Francisco River, and most notably the Roadside Chair in 1967 (figs. 397–400), a unique example of "poor design" (fig. 74). It is also present in her design for the now-demolished Chame-Chame House in Salvador (figs. 277–291), and the Valéria Cirell House in Morumbi, São Paulo (figs. 292–301), the staircase at the Solar do Unhão (figs. 167–169), as well as MASP (figs. 116–150), which was completed in 1968, and Sesc Pompeia (figs. 318–337), among many other examples. This learning experience enabled her to acquire a new set of critical and formal tools, as Bo Bardi identified in the visual, formal, and material vocabulary of the popular another epistemology, other ways of knowing the world through the circumstances of hardship and material poverty, which were translated into the clean lines and austere forms of the objects produced by craftspeople in the Northeast. This epistemology was as valid for Bo Bardi as that of the modern, and inextricably bound to it if approached from a programmatic, functionalist, industrial, and design perspective.

The Hand of Those Who, Not Having Dogs, Hunt with Cats (the hand of the people)

Upon her return to São Paulo, Bo Bardi focused on completing MASP's building on Avenida Paulista and developing its future program. The museum opened briefly in July 1968 for its official inauguration, with the permanent display of its collection installed on the glass easels she had designed for this purpose. The museum closed soon after for final construction work and reopened in April 1969 with two exhibitions in addition to the permanent collection display on the third floor. An outdoor show of works by Nelson Leirner, *Playgrounds*, was installed in the building's "free span" at street level (fig. 143), and the first-floor gallery featured *The Hand of the Brazilian People*, which, as the glass-easel display had already opened a few months back, could be considered the main inaugural exhibition.

Conceived and organized by Bo Bardi, with the collaboration of Gonçalves and Rocha (according to press materials in MASP's archives), the exhibition sought to inscribe popular art and culture within the domain of the art museum, and presented a panorama of Brazil's rich material culture, from the backland regions of the northeast to the country's south. It featured hundreds of objects, including figureheads, ex-votos, textiles, clothing, furniture, tools, kitchen utensils, musical instruments, ornaments, toys, sculptures of saints and religious figures, as well as paintings and sculptures. The scope of *The Hand of the Brazilian People* was broader than Bo Bardi's former exhibitions, incorporating objects from across the country and from various cultural traditions, such as the production of Amerindian and Afro-Brazilian peoples. It also encompassed a wider temporality, as it included works and artifacts ranging from the colonial period to the 1960s.

34. Lina Bo Bardi, "Cinco anos entre os 'brancos,'" in Rubino and Grinover, eds., *Lina por escrito*, 130–31.

In a sense, *The Hand of the Brazilian People* resumed what the *Northeast* exhibition at Solar do Unhão in 1963 had initiated. It shared traits with both of its predecessors: its theatricality with *Bahia in Ibirapuera*; with *Northeast*, its presentation of objects from the perspective of a "craftsmanship-industrial design identity" based upon a "technical production connected to the reality of the materials."[35] The setting, however, could not have been more different; the exhibition took place in South America's largest and most industrialized city, at its most important museum, with the largest collection of European art in the region. All of this in the midst of a dictatorship that in 1968 had tightened its grip with the promulgation of Institutional Act No. 5 (AI-5), which suspended constitutional guarantees, including freedom of speech. If *Northeast* had been an accusation, *The Hand of the Brazilian People* was an act of outright provocation.

In this context, it is pertinent to return to the problematization and simultaneous reformulation of the modern inherent in Bo Bardi's practice, particularly in relation to the development-dependency dilemma. For Bo Bardi, a modern practice of architecture, design, and museum practice would necessarily include the epistemology of the popular. Her numerous activities in Bahia in the fields of journalism, culture, art, and architecture showed that the modern was for her "the scale of concern and the social reach of projects, the relation between project and city . . . the desire for democratic participation and a collective public life."[36] She was simultaneously modern and popular, what in the words of Néstor García Canclini could be described as "constantly thinking up strategies for entering and leaving modernity." In his book *Hybrid Cultures*, Canclini states that "in popular ceramics, textiles, and altarpieces one can find as much formal creativity, generation of original meanings, and occasional autonomy with respect to practical functions as in high art."[37] This perspective is shared by Bo Bardi and evidenced in her exhibitions, writings, and the gesture of inscribing the popular within the framework of a fine arts museum the way she did with *The Hand of the Brazilian People*. Moreover, for Canclini,

> Knowledge of culture and of the popular would be advanced more if the sanitary preoccupation with distinguishing the pure and the uncontaminated in arts and crafts were abandoned and if we were to study them starting from the uncertainties that provoke their crossings.[38]

It is thus possible to read Bo Bardi's exhibitions devoted to popular culture as ones that enabled these crossings, provoking zones of disturbance and uncertainty that still elicit important questions today.

To frame Bo Bardi's multidimensional practice within the paradigm shift that took place in Brazil in the context of the development/dependency dilemma also makes it possible to consider her writings, exhibitions, furniture and building designs during this period as early manifestations of an epistemic break from the visual and formal vocabularies of Western culture and from the developmentalist rhetoric that guided the modernization process in Brazil and Latin America. The more recent concept of *coloniality*, as well as the earlier formulations of dependency theory during the 1960s and 1970s, have become tools for rethinking the world beyond the East–West divisions of the Cold War, beyond Marxism and critical theory; positing what is now called the Global South as an active agent in the articulation of new forms of knowledge and agency.

To rethink the conceptual, contextual, and ideological coordinates of an exhibition such as *The Hand of the Brazilian People* today is to offer an exceptional opportunity not only to revisit Bo Bardi's museological vision, but also to understand her incorporation of the vocabulary of the popular within a fine arts museum model as part of an ideological agenda that sought to break from the Western canon. A highly radical gesture and an early instance of decolonial museum practice, *The Hand of the Brazilian People*, much like the artworks and objects included in it, remains at the margins of histories of canonical exhibitions, therefore virtually unknown, especially outside of Brazil. As an exemplary precedent of a decolonial approach to exhibitions, it deserves critical reappraisal and inscription within the framework of groundbreaking exhibitions of the twentieth century.[39]

35. Bo Bardi, "Civilização do Nordeste," 37.

36. Rossetti, "Tensão moderno/popular em Lina Bo Bardi," 37.

37. Néstor García Canclini, *Culturas híbridas: estrategias para entrar y salir de la modernidad* (Mexico City: Grijalbo, 1990), translated as *Hybrid Cultures: Strategies for Entering and Leaving Modernity* (Minneapolis: University of Minnesota Press, 2005), 175.

38. Ibid.

39. This text is a revised and expanded version of the essay published in Adriano Pedrosa and Tomás Toledo, eds., *A mão do povo brasileiro, 1969/2016* (São Paulo: MASP, 2016).

FIG. 74
"Móveis novos" (New Furniture), *Habitat*, no. 1 (October–December 1950): 54

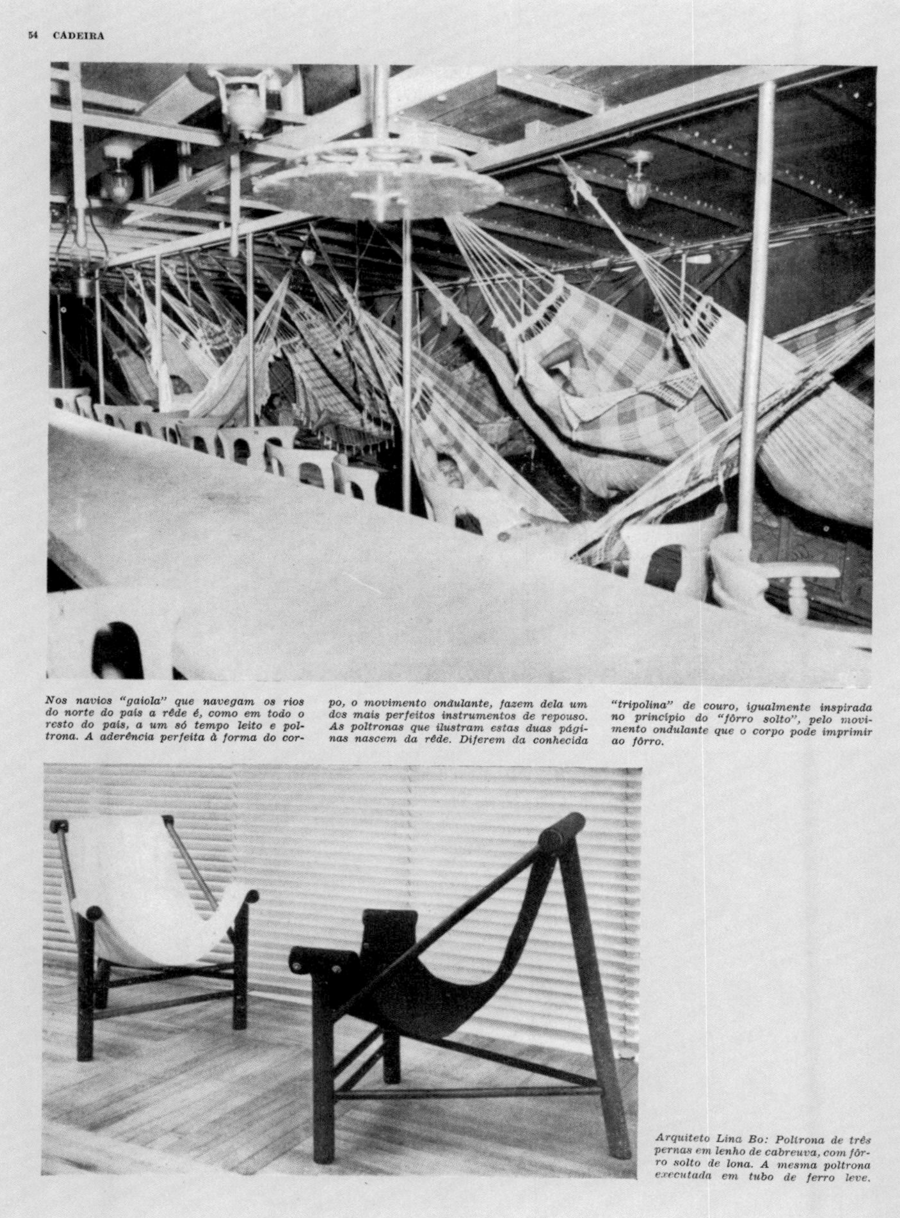

54 CADEIRA

Nos navios "gaiola" que navegam os rios do norte do país a rêde é, como em todo o resto do país, a um só tempo leito e poltrona. A aderência perfeita à forma do corpo, o movimento ondulante, fazem dela um dos mais perfeitos instrumentos de repouso. As poltronas que ilustram estas duas páginas nascem da rêde. Diferem da conhecida "tripolina" de couro, igualmente inspirada no princípio do "fôrro solto", pelo movimento ondulante que o corpo pode imprimir ao fôrro.

Arquiteto Lina Bo: Poltrona de três pernas em lenho de cabreuva, com fôrro solto de lona. A mesma poltrona executada em tubo de ferro leve.

During the conception and organization of this exhibition, **Julieta González** was artistic director at Fundación Jumex Arte Contemporáneo.

THE HAND (AND THE NAMES) OF THE BRAZILIAN PEOPLE

FIG. 75
View of the exhibition
The Hand of the Brazilian People,
MASP, São Paulo, 1969

The art of the poor frightens the generals.
BRUNO ZEVI[1]

A mão do povo brasileiro (The Hand of the Brazilian People; fig. 75) was the temporary exhibition that inaugurated Museu de Arte de São Paulo's new building on Avenida Paulista on April 7, 1969,[2] presenting a vast panorama of Brazil's rich material culture: some 1,000 objects, including figureheads, ex-votos, fabric, clothing, furniture, tools, utensils, machinery, musical instruments, decorations, toys, religious objects, paintings, and sculptures. One of the most striking features of the exhibition was that it established dialogues and frictions, through juxtapositions and contrasts, between a great variety and quantity of objects and *typologies* traditionally kept outside of the museum—from art to artifact—questioning and blurring hierarchical, territorial divisions between these two concepts.

The exhibition was designed by Lina Bo Bardi in collaboration with filmmaker Glauber Rocha, theater director Martim Gonçalves, and museum director Pietro Maria Bardi, who provided its title. It forms part of two histories of exhibitions: those organized by Bo Bardi, on the one hand, and those by MASP, on the other, constituting an overlap or emblematic intersection between the two. It is the museum's most important temporary exhibition (alongside its picture gallery, with the crystal easel displays (fig. 150), understood as a long-term exhibition of the collection) and constitutes a landmark in the history of exhibitions in the 1960s.

In 1969, *The Hand of the Brazilian People*, on the museum's first-floor gallery, found itself in dialogue, on the one hand, with the museum's rich collection of European and Brazilian art on the second floor, the territory of canonical, so-called erudite art, exhibited on the radical crystal easels designed by Bo Bardi; on the other, with *Playgrounds* (fig. 144), a show of a playful and interactive nature by the young artist Nelson Leirner, located in the museum's free span, an extramural space in open and frank confrontation with the city and its passersby. We find here, at the museum's inaugural moment on Avenida Paulista, the configuration of a popular–*playgrounds*–picture gallery triad that points to a program and a project, a concept and configuration of an inclusive, diverse, and pluralistic museum, which articulates works from different times, fields, typologies, and territories—from ancient to contemporary, from art to artifact, from the object within the museum to the one outside it.[3]

Intersecting Histories: Bo Bardi and MASP[4]

In the history of the exhibitions organized by Bo Bardi, *The Hand of the Brazilian People* was the result of years of experience, travels, and research the architect undertook in Salvador and other cities in the Brazilian Northeast,[5] as well as the further development of three other exhibitions also organized with

1. *L'Espresso* (Rome), March 14, 1965. The artist Ivan Grilo created an artwork consisting of a bronze plaque with the Italian expression written in relief, although the title of the work is in Portuguese: *A arte dos pobres assusta os generais*, 2015, bronze plate, 30 x 45 cm.

2. MASP was inaugurated by Queen Elizabeth II of England on November 7, 1968, but opened to the public five months later, on April 7, 1969.

3. See Adriano Pedrosa, "Concrete and Crystal: Learning with Lina," in Adriano Pedrosa and Luiza Proença, eds. *Concreto e cristal: o acervo do MASP nos cavaletes de Lina Bo Bardi* (São Paulo: MASP, 2015), 22–27.

4. Thanks to Tomás Toledo for his research on Bo Bardi and MASP's popular art exhibitions.

5. Bo Bardi spent a first season in Salvador in 1958, when she taught at Bahia's School of Fine Arts, and later lived there between 1960 and 1964, when she directed the Museum of Modern Art of Bahia and the Museum of Popular Art.

FIG. 76
View of the reconstruction of the exhibition *The Hand of the Brazilian People*, MASP, 2016

Rocha and Gonçalves. In 1959, *Bahia in Ibirapuera* (figs. 188–201) was a parallel exhibition to the 5th São Paulo Biennial, located in a temporary pavilion under the marquee of Ibirapuera Park, where the Museum of Modern Art (MAM) is today located (figs. 175–176). In 1963, Bo Bardi organized *Northeast* (figs. 202–209), on the occasion of the inauguration of the Museum of Popular Art at the Solar do Unhão, in Salvador.[6] In 1965, the same *Northeast* exhibition from Salvador was redesigned for the Galleria Nazionale d'Arte Moderna in Rome (figs. 215–221). The Rome exhibition represents a trauma in this history: although it was mounted by the architect, in her hometown, it was dismantled shortly before the opening by order of the Brazilian embassy in the city. The next day, in a now famous article in Rome's *L'Espresso*, architect Bruno Zevi criticized the action under the title "L'arte dei poveri fa paura ai generali" (the art of the poor frightens the generals). It was supposed that objects made by the hand of the (poor) Brazilian people would not represent, to the European gaze, the image of a modern, developing, "forward"[7] country to which the nascent military regime aspired. It is in this sense that a subversive element can be identified in *The Hand of the Brazilian People*, which, if it previously frightened generals under the military dictatorship, still today seems to frighten the generals of taste, of so-called high or erudite culture. A central question that arises from the exhibition, in a museum known to have the most important collection of European art in the Southern Hemisphere, in the heart of a major Latin American financial center, is: How can histories of art and culture in Brazil be reconstructed, remembered, and reconfigured beyond the modes, tastes, and professions of the ruling classes?

With regard to the history of Bo Bardi's exhibitions, we can identify three exhibitions organized at Sesc Pompeia as developments of *The Hand of the Brazilian People*: *Design no Brasil: história e realidade* (Design in Brazil: History and Reality, 1982), *Mil brinquedos para a criança brasileira* (A Thousand Toys for the Brazilian Child, 1982), and *Caipiras, capiaus: pau-a-pique* (Countryfolk, Rustics: Wattle-and-Daub, 1984; figs. 240–244), in addition to the 1978 Popular Art Crates project (figs. 237–239). Each, in its own way, represented continuities of Bo Bardi's thought and research over the years. However, in contexts outside of an art museum, the exhibitions lose the potential for friction found in *The Hand of the Brazilian People* at MASP, which is crucial for grasping its decolonizing potential.

In the history of exhibitions at MASP, by its third year, in a truly pioneering way, the museum held *Arte popular pernambucana* (Popular Art of Pernambuco, 1949), which in turn was an offshoot of the 1947 *Cerâmica popular nordestina* (Popular Northeastern Ceramics), curated by

6. The Museum of Popular Art was inaugurated in 1963 at the Solar do Unhão, in Salvador, next to the Museum of Modern Art of Bahia, which had existed since 1959 at the Castro Alves Theater. In 1964, with the military coup, Bo Bardi was dismissed from the direction of both institutions, and the Museum of Popular Art was terminated, only the Museum of Modern Art of Bahia surviving.

7. The reference here is to Miguel Gustavo's patriotic song "Pra frente Brasil," composed to publicize the Brazilian team during the 1970 World Cup in Mexico, which Brazil won, at the height of the military dictatorship.

Augusto Rodrigues at the Castro Alves Library in Rio de Janeiro. The original show introduced the work of Vitalino Pereira dos Santos, Mestre Vitalino, to the art and exhibition circuit, formerly dominated by academic, modernist, and elitist precepts, and it can be said that the exhibition represents a foundational milestone in the dissemination of popular art in Rio de Janeiro and São Paulo.[8] In a letter from P. M. Bardi to Renato de Almeida, secretary general of the National Folklore Commission under Itamaraty (Brazil's Ministry of Foreign Affairs), dated January 19, 1949, the founding director discusses MASP's *Popular Art of Pernambuco* exhibition, elaborating his wish to dedicate space to popular art in the museum:

> We are very aware of the importance of preserving national folklore and have various manifestations in this regard in our program of activities, including the desire to organize a permanent section of popular art in our exhibition halls.[9]

At that time, the term "folklore" was still used uncritically, which Bo Bardi, among others, would later reject for its paternalistic character, "supported by high culture."[10] Ironically, the *popular desire of* P. M. Bardi, who acquired so many extraordinary works of European art for the museum in such a short time, remained unfulfilled—the permanent section devoted to popular, vernacular, or folk art was never implemented. However, we can recall that three works by artists associated with so-called popular art were donated to MASP's collection by its founding director: Gilvan Samico's 1965 *O barco do destino e as três garças do rio* (The Boat of Destiny and the Three River Herons), donated in 1976; Maria Auxiliadora's 1970 *Capoeira*, donated in 1981; and Hélio Mello's 1983 *O serrador* (The Sawyer), donated in 1983.

If MASP never came to have a permanent gallery of *popular* art, the museum organized and hosted a long list of exhibitions around so-called popular art, including self-taught artists from humble origins, operating outside the traditional art circuit and the academy,[11] including Mestre Vitalino himself, as well as Afro-Brazilian and indigenous art: *Emídio Souza* (1949); *Exposição de arte indígena* (Exhibition of Indigenous Art, 1949); *Diógenes Duarte Paes e desenhos sobre assuntos folclóricos* (Diógenes Duarte Paes and Drawings from Folklore, 1951); *Cássio M'Boy* (1951); *Agostinho Batista de Freitas* (1952); *Amazônia* (1972); *Exposição afro-brasileira de artes plásticas* (Exhibition of Afro-Brazilian Visual Arts, 1973); *I ação arte no vale do Paraíba* (Artistic Production from the Paraíba Valley, 1975); *Festa de cores* (Feast of Colors, 1975); *O rio: carrancas do São Francisco* (The River: Figureheads from São Francisco, 1975); *Repassos: exposição documento* (Weaving Patterns: Documentary Exhibition, 1975; fig. 146); *José Antonio da Silva* (1976); *Dito Pituba (1848–1923): um*

8. Guacira Waldeck, *Mestre Vitalino e artistas pernambucanos* (Rio de Janeiro: Iphan, 2009).

9. Document archived in a folder on the 1949 *Popular Art of Pernambuco* exhibition, at the MASP Research Center.

10. Lina Bo Bardi, "Um balanço dezesseis anos depois," in Marcelo Suzuki, ed., *Tempos de grossura: o design no impasse* (São Paulo: Instituto Lino Bo e P. M. Bardi, 1994), 12.

11. We have avoided the terms *folk*, *primitive*, *naïf*, or *naïve* to label such artists.

santeiro paulista (Dito Pituba: A São Paulo Maker of Saints, 1977); *Da senzala ao sobrado: arquitetura brasileira na Nigéria e Benin* (From the Senzala to the Sobrado: Brazilian Architecture in Nigeria and Benin, 1978); *Tropa, tropeiro, tropeirismo* (1978); *A cidade de Goiás e o escultor goiano Veiga Valle* (The City of Goiás and the Goianian Sculptor Veiga Valle, 1978); *Arte no Brasil: uma história de cinco séculos* (Art in Brazil: A History of Five Centuries, 1979); *Guarany: 80 anos de carrancas* (Guarany: 80 Years of Figureheads, 1981); *A arte popular do Brasil* (Brazilian Popular Art, 1981); *Maria Auxiliadora da Silva* (1981); *Cerâmicas de Apiaí* (Ceramics from Apiaí, 1981); *Tecelagem artesanal de Minas Gerais* (Artisanal Weaving from Minas Gerais, 1982); *O presépio no artesanato* (The Nativity in Artisanal Work, 1982); *Bordados da caatinga do Piauí* (Embroidery from the Piauí Caatinga, 1983); *Arte Kayapó* (Kayapó Art, 1983); *A visão estereotipada do índio do Brasil* (The Stereotyped Image of the Indian in Brazil, 1983); *Projeto Zumbi* (Zumbi Project, 1983); *39a Exposição do presépio artesanal paulista* (39th Exhibition of Nativities in São Paulo Artisanal Production, 1984); *Semana do índio Karajá* (Week of the Karajá Indian, 1984); *Bonecos de pano* (Rag Dolls, 1984); *Artesanato em madeira* (Artisanal Woodwork, 1984); *Joias artesanais* (Artisanal Jewelry, 1984); *Brinquedos artesanais* (Artisanal Toys, 1984); *4a Exposição de presépios artesanais: presépio—nasce o menino de mãos artesãs* (The 4th Exhibition of Artisanal Nativity Scenes: Nativity—Born Is the Boy of Artisan Hands, 1985); *Trançado brasileiro* (Brazilian Weaving, 1985); *A arte do povo brasileiro* (The Art of the Brazilian People, 1986); *Máscaras brasileiras* (Brazilian Masks, 1986); *Arte indígena Kaxinawá* (Kaxinawá Indigenous Art, 1987); *Mês da pintura ingênua brasileira* (The Month of Naïf Brazilian Painting, 1988); *A maloca Marubo* (1988). More recently, two monographic exhibitions were organized: one centering around the work of Agostinho Batista de Freitas, in 2017, curated by Fernando Oliva and Rodrigo Moura, and the other, on Maria Auxiliadora, 2018, curated by Oliva and myself, both accompanied by extensive catalogues.

Artifacts and Art in the Museum

On the international scene, two major exhibitions sought to juxtapose different typologies of objects, between art and artifact: traditional African art and modern art, in the case of *"Primitivism" in 20th Century Art: Affinity of the Tribal and the Modern* (Museum of Modern Art, New York, 1984), curated by William Rubin and Kirk Varnedoe; and art and artifact, in *ART/artifact: African Art in Anthropology Collections* (Center for African Art, New York, 1988), curated by Susan Vogel. Both received harsh criticism,[12] especially for falling into the trap of maintaining a hierarchy (albeit offering friction and dialogue) in which Western art is above artifact (indicated in the very title of Vogel's exposition, where ART takes precedence over artifact, the first in capital letters, the second in lower case). In her catalogue preface, Vogel pointed to the fact that,

> During the four or five decades that art museums have been dealing with ethnographic art . . . the separation between the anthropological and the art historical approaches has narrowed. Anthropologists are increasingly sensitive to the aesthetic dimension of the objects in their care, as art historians have become alive to the vast amount of anthropological information that they can use to understand art. This has tended to make their respective museums' installations resemble each other more than ever before.[13]

Sally Price also writes about the different museological contexts and the distinction between *objets d'art* and ethnographic artifacts. Traditionally, on the one hand, the art museum favored minimalist montages in neutral spaces, white cubes, isolating the artwork from its context and history and providing only bare-bones information about the object (author, title, date, technique). On the other hand, museums of anthropology and ethnography provided captions with extensive information on the technical, religious, cultural, social, and political functions and contexts, often with data on the people or culture, without naming creators, thereby rendering the work anonymous. Sometimes the museum would even name the "collector"[14] (usually a European anthropologist), the research mission, and the year

12. See, for example, James Clifford, "Histories of the Tribal and the Modern," in *The Predicament of Culture: Twentieth-Century Ethnography, Literature, and Art* (Cambridge, Mass.: Harvard University Press, 1994), 189–214; Thomas McEvilley, "Doctor, Lawyer, Indian Chief," in *Art & Otherness: Crisis in Cultural Identity* (New York: McPherson, 1992), 27–56; Hal Foster, "The 'Primitive' Unconscious of Modern Art," *October*, no. 34 (Fall 1985): 58–70; Rasheed Araeen, "From Primitivism to Ethnic Arts," *Third Text* 1 (Fall 1987): 6–25; Alfred Gell, "Vogel's Net: Traps as Artworks and Artworks as Traps," in *The Art of Anthropology: Essays and Diagrams* (London: Athlone Press, 1999), 187–214.

13. Susan Vogel, "Introduction," in *ART/artifact: African Art in Anthropology Collections* (New York: Center for African Art, 1988), 13.

14. A Brazilian example is the catalogue *O museu paraense Emílio Goeldi* (São Paulo: Banco Safra, 1986), in which many of the reproduced Amerindian works are presented with data about the collector—such as German ethnologists Theodor Koch-Grünberg and Curt Nimuendajú—and the year of collection, but without informed individual authorship of the piece.

FIG. 77
View of MASP's main gallery with the works *Vista do MASP* (View of MASP, 1978), *Circo Piolin no vão do MASP* (Piolin Circus in the MASP Free Span, 1972), and *MASP* (1971) by Agostinho Batista de Freitas, 2017

of the object's "collection."[15] In 2001, in a postscript to her book, originally published in 1989, Price states that, today,

> The most visible evidence has been an explosion, over the past couple of decades, of exhibitions integrating anthropological issues and art historical issues and scholarship, juxtaposing arts from previously segregated categories, and calling attention to the defining (and redefining) power of display context.[16]

Much of the juxtaposition and friction between art and artifact seems to suggest that the artifact, in extraordinary or exceptional cases, may be raised to the category of Art—as if, from a perspective of traditional art history, there was an "elevation" or "progress" from status as artifact to that of art. However, this supposed elevation ends up implying a paternalistic, Eurocentric, and, as Marianna Torgovnick demonstrates, colonialist attitude, even though one based on aesthetic criteria.[17] Donald Preziosi writes about the violent colonizing operation of museums and art history, which establishes a hierarchy between typologies of objects, their cultures and peoples:

> To each people and place its own true art, and to each true art its proper position on a ladder of evolution leading toward the modernity and presentness of Europe. . . . All different objects are ranked as primitive, exotic, charming, or fascinating distortions of a central classical (European) canon or standard.[18]

The configuration of MASP exhibitions during the inauguration of the building on Avenida Paulista in 1969—with the gallery of crystal easels in friction with *The Hand of the Brazilian People*—somewhat anticipated issues raised by the *Primitivism* and *ART/artifact* exhibitions two decades later, but without falling into the same exoticizing ethnocentric pitfalls. The Eurocentric, formalist, and modernist perspective of New York exhibitions is not seen in *The Hand of the Brazilian People.*

Primitivism at MoMA provoked strong reactions and fueled debate in the context of multiculturalism in the United States regarding the practices of exhibiting, collecting, and contextualizing the art of the Other—the non-European and non–North American—traditionally excluded from the canonical history of art. Virulent criticism provided an opportunity to articulate discourses and foster debate about the relationships between productions (from art to artifact) of different cultures, between "us" and "them," the West and its Other, in that context identified as "primitive." One should bear in mind that Brazil and Latin America in this debate are considered "others," "them," alongside Africa and Asia; both the so-called popular artist and the modern or contemporary art-

15. The notion of "collecting" is enclosed in quotes because it is the term used by anthropological and ethnographic museums, but which often masks more violent acts—war, theft, pillaging, conquest—common to the colonizing enterprise.

16. See Sally Price, *Primitive Art in Civilized Places*, 2nd ed. (Chicago: University of Chicago Press, 2001), 128.

17. Marianna Torgovnick, *Gone Primitive: Savage Intellects, Modern Lives* (Chicago: University of Chicago Press, 1990), 82.

18. Donald Preziosi, "The Art of Art History," in *The Art of Art History: A Critical Anthology* (New York: Oxford University Press, 2009), 493, 499.

FIG. 78
View of MASP's main galley with the works *Vélorio da noiva* (Funeral of the Bride, 1974), *Candomblé* (1968), and *Capoeira* (1970) by Maria Auxiliadora, 2019

ist from these continents are othered in the Eurocentric perspective of that time.[19] This is how, in 1987, London-based Pakistani artist Rasheed Araeen responded to that othering in the first issue of *Third Text* (the title of the magazine he edited, which immediately points to the interest in themes and perspectives of the so-called Third World):

> The "primitive" has now indeed learned how to draw, how to paint and how to sculpt; also how to read and how to write and how to think consciously and rationally, and has in fact read all those magical texts that gave the white man the power to rule the world. . . . I'm no longer your bloody objects in the British Museum. I'm here right in front of you, in the flesh and blood of a modern artist. If you want to talk about me, let us talk. BUT NO MORE OF YOUR PRIMITIVIST RUBBISH.[20]

The MoMA exhibition, for all its problems, had in some ways opened the possibility for another show that is today considered a watershed in the history of exhibitions: *Magiciens de la terre*, curated by Jean-Hubert Martin at the Musée National d'Art Moderne and at the Grand Halle de la Villete in Paris in 1989. The purpose was to show Western and non-Western artists side by side; in the latter group, next to Araeen himself, were three Brazilians: Cildo Meireles, perhaps today the living Brazilian contemporary artist who has received the most international recognition, and two artists who employ strong African references in their work: Mestre Didi and Ronaldo Pereira Rego.

One can think of *Magiciens de la terre*, with all of its limitations and problems that cannot be fully addressed here, as an inaugural exhibition for bringing the art of the Other into dialogue with and into the Center, something that, in another perspective of otherness, is also sought with so-called popular art in *The Hand of the Brazilian People*.

During the last decade, certain exhibitions organized on the contemporary art circuit have included the production of popular, self-taught, or outsider artists, pointing to a desire to incorporate other narratives and practices within the framework of contemporary culture: *Glossolalia: Languages of Drawing* (Museum of Modern Art, New York, 2008), curated by Connie Butler; *Alternative Guide to the Universe* (Hayward Gallery, London, 2013), curated by Ralph Rugoff; and *Il Palazzo Enciclopedico* (55th Venice Biennale, 2013), curated by Massimiliano Gioni. Thomas Lax reviews some of these exhibitions and texts in the catalogue for his *When the Stars Begin to Fall: Imagination and the American South* (Studio Museum in Harlem, New York, 2014). In the wake of other American authors and curators, Lax draws attention to the intersections of this practice with issues of race, which deserves further reflection that space does not permit here. However, I recall

19. Since then, modern or contemporary Latin American artists have had access to European and North American spaces, mainly through museum exhibitions, but also through art history books, bringing their art closer to them, which is not the case of the so-called popular artist, who remains remote and marginalized.

20. Araeen, "From Primitivism to Ethnic Arts."

that, not by chance, one of the greatest researchers and disseminators of popular art in Brazil, author of several texts and exhibitions, is the artist, curator, and director of the Museu Afro Brasil in São Paulo, Emanoel Araujo, who organized the sections *Popular Art* and *Black Body and Soul* in the context of the *Rediscovery Exhibition* in São Paulo in 2000, both accompanied by catalogues. On the other hand, it is worth reproducing a passage quoted by Lax from the catalogue of another anthology exhibition, this time in the United States, curated by Jane Livingstone and John Beardsley, *Black Folk Art in America, 1930–1980* (Corcoran Gallery, Washington, D.C., 1982). In Livingstone's words:

It cannot be coincidental that perhaps fully half of the truly great artists in the recent American folk genre, from the early 1920s to the present, are blacks and predominantly Southern blacks.[21]

Names

The denominations associated with so-called popular practice remain quite contentious, and the very term "popular art," widely used in Brazil, is diffuse, inaccurate, and insufficient. It is worth remembering that both P. M. Bardi, in the title of the MASP exhibition in 1969, and Lélia Coelho Frota, anthropologist, art critic, and curator, in her fundamental *Pequeno dicionário da arte do povo brasileiro*,[22] avoid the denomination "popular art," preferring "art of the people." Frota, a major researcher and disseminator of this production in Brazil, attempts to define the "polysemic designation of 'popular,'" which

encapsulates the working classes that maintain a network of experienced and shared relations in their territory, in the countryside and in the city, as well as a heterogeneous universe of strata, as described by Gilberto Velho, consisting of small landowners, migrant farmworkers, fishermen, the unemployed, the semi-employed, people on the margins of the labor market or otherwise marginalized, domestic workers, civil servants, middle-level technicians, traders, bankers, various middle-class sectors, slum dwellers, groups, people in the suburbs, on the periphery, etc.[23]

However, "so-called popular art" or "art of the people" are surely more appropriate than other extremely perverse, biased, ethnocentric, and paternalistic terms—"primitive," "naïf," or "naïve," for identifying paintings, prints, drawings, and sculptures; "artisanal" and "folkloric," for objects with some useful though now abandoned function.[24] "Primitive," "naïf," and "naïve" translate an elitist, classist, bourgeois perception that there is a simplicity of solutions, premises, and thinking involved in the intellectual or manual elaboration of the work in question. Even more perversely: if "naïf" suggests that the creator does not understand the complexity of his or her own work, "primitive" underscores that the creator *and* the work are in a developmental stage prior to the erudite, in the infancy of civilization, indicating a retrograde progressivist perspective.

In Brazil in 1981, another term was introduced at the 16th São Paulo Biennial: "unusual art" ("arte incomun") as a translation of *outsider art*, employed by the curator of a special section of the exhibition, the English poet, collector, and art dealer Victor Musgrave.[25] In the catalogue, Walter Zanini, another curator at the Biennial, writes of "a highly creative production on the fringes of the system of cultural art," distinct from "naïve or semicultural art" and associated with "mentally ill or individuals unmoored from the normal contexts of visuality."[26] Musgrave, for his part, writes rather poetically about

a secret race of creative giants, inhabitants of a land we always knew existed but of which we had only glimmers or intimations. . . . Outsiders cannot be labeled, because each one of them is one. In fact, it would be better to call them Insiders if we had to name them. One feels that they are not on the fringes of art, but at its center.[27]

The question of names is the subject of much discussion,[28] particularly with regard to the term "primitivism," and revisiting the debate allows us to address the pitfalls of naming. As a reflection of the transformation of the use of the term "primitivism," Jack Flam recounts how the collection of the Museum of Primitive Art, founded by Nelson Rockefeller in New York in 1954, was absorbed into the Metropolitan Museum of Art's Department of Primitive Art in 1969, which in

21. Thomas Lax, *When the Stars Begin to Fall* (New York: Studio Museum in Harlem, 2014), 13.

22. Lélia Coelho Frota, *Pequeno dicionário da arte do povo brasileiro* (Rio de Janeiro: Aeropolano, 2005).

23. Ibid., 16, citing Gilberto Velho, "Memória, identidade e projeto," in *Projeto e metamorfose* (Rio de Janeiro: Jorge Zahar, 1994).

24. In this production in Brazil, the classic examples of objects whose original functions were abandoned to gain status as collectible objects and an artistic or sculptural dimension are ex-votos and figureheads, both represented with significant groupings in *The Hand of the Brazilian People*.

25. The Musgrave collection, built with his partner Monica Kinley, herself an art dealer, collector, and curator, is now housed at the Whitworth Art Gallery, University of Manchester, named the Musgrave Kinley Outsider Art Collection. See http://www.whitworth.manchester.ac.uk/collection/ourcollection/musgravekinleyoutsiderart/.

26. Walter Zanini, "A Bienal e os artistas incomuns," in *XVI Bienal de São Paulo*, vol. 3, *Catálogo de arte incomum* (São Paulo: Fundação Bienal, 1977), 7. Zanini returns to this theme in "A visão ingênua e popular," in *História geral da arte no Brasil* (São Paulo: Instituto Walther Moreira Salles/Fundação Djalma Guimarães, 1983), vol. 2, 810.

27. Victor Musgrave, "Apresentação," in *XVI Bienal de São Paulo*, vol. 3, *Catálogo de arte incomum*, 11.

28. Another name could be mentioned, though I will not address it here because of its more historical nature, one that is particularly connected to the French context: *art brut*. Coined by French artist Jean Dubuffet in 1945, it denoted "drawings, paintings, works of art of all kinds emanating from dark, maniacal, impulsive, spontaneous, fantasy-driven, even delusional [personalities], and unaware of the paths tread by art catalogues." Dubuffet quoted in Lucienne Peiry, *L'art brut* (Paris: Flammarion, 2016), 13.

1991 was renamed the Department of the Arts of Africa, Oceania, and the Americas.[29] In Paris, the Musée du Quai Branly, dedicated to the art of Africa, the Americas, and Asia, opened in 2006, having inherited the collections of the Musée National des Arts d'Afrique et d'Océanie and the Musée de l'Homme, and avoided selecting a name for itself that would identify the vast typologies of objects it maintains by simply opting for the name of its location, at the Branly quay in the 7th arrondissement.[30]

In the late 1980s, American art critic, curator, and activist Lucy Lippard harshly criticized the term "primitivism," pointing to the need to challenge it:

> The most pervasive and arguably most insidious term artists of color must challenge is "primitivism." It has been used historically to separate the supposedly sophisticated civilized "high" art of the West from the equally sophisticated civilized art it has pillaged from other cultures. The term locates the latter in the past—usually the distant past—and in an early stage of "development," implying simplicity on the positive side and crudity or barbarism on the negative. . . . The term "primitive" is also used to separate by class, as in "minor," "low," "folk," or "amateur" art—distinguished from the "fine," "high," or "professional" art that may in fact be imitating it. There is an inference that such work is "crude" or "uncooked," the product of "outsiders." "Primitives" are those who "naively" disregard the dictates of the market and make art for the pure joy of doing so. In fact, much "primitive" art is either religious or political, whether it is from Africa or from today's rural or urban ghettos. It is not always the quaint and harmless genre, the ideological captive, pictured in the artworld.[31]

More recently, Australian art curator and historian Lynne Cooke, in her anthology exhibition *Outliers and American Vanguard Art* at the National Gallery of Art, Washington, D.C., in 2018, proposed another term for identifying these artists: outliers. The denomination evokes the title of Canadian author Malcolm Gladwell's book *Outliers: The Story of Success*,[32] which attempts to explain how individuals achieve extraordinary success in their respective fields. Gladwell begins the book with a definition of "outlier": "1: Something that is situated far away from or classed differently from a main or related body. 2: A statistical observation that is markedly different in value from the others of the sample."[33] Cooke, in turn, argues that, in the field of artistic production, the novelty of the term avoids the contradictions and problematizations of the previous terms and brings some advantages over the others:

> typically, today's outlier is a mobile individual who has gained recognition by means at variance with expected channels and protocols. Having no past usage in the field, and so not freighted with negative associations that cling to so many earlier terms, "outlier" is also unmistakably of our era; it situates this project in the present. And, not least, it sidesteps questions of "inside" versus "outside" in favor of distances nearer and farther from an aggregate so that being at variance with the norm can be a position of strength: a place negotiated or sought out rather than predetermined and fixed.[34]

If "outlier" in English, as Cooke argues, is a term "unmistakably of our time," the Portuguese translation, "fora de série" (outstanding), seems somewhat outdated and does not evoke the extraordinary character of the original in English, or can sometimes be associated with a luxury good produced in a special series that does not conform to the artistic production in question. In any case, it is important to note that Cooke's definition of the "outlier" or "outstanding"[35] artist refers mainly to the production of paintings and sculptures and even textiles, but is restricted to the universe of art and generally with identified authorship, thus excluding objects with a present or past function, such as figureheads and ex-votos, but also the fabric, clothing, furniture, tools, utensils, machinery, musical instruments, adornments, toys, and religious objects included in *The Hand of the Brazilian People.*

Perhaps the best way to categorize this production is simply to call it art or work. However, the act of naming can erase differences and end up marginalizing a practice that, if difficult to label properly, is also possibly difficult to research, catalogue, disseminate, exhibit, or publish if one cannot associate a name with it. In this sense, our choice has been to use the denomination

29. "The Museum of Primitive Art proudly bore that name until it was absorbed in 1969 by the Metropolitan Museum of Art. The Metropolitan then founded a Department of Primitive Art that retained that name until 1991, when it was changed to Department of the Arts of Africa, Oceania, and the Americas. . . . During the 1970s there was an increasing feeling that 'Primitive' implied deficiency or lack and was inherently critical—even insulting—to the peoples who created the art." Jack Flam, *Primitivism and Twentieth-Century Art: A Documentary History* (Berkeley: University of California Press, 2003), xiii.

30. For a critique of the museum shortly after its opening, see Michael Kimmelman, "A Heart of Darkness in the City of Light," *The New York Times*, July 2, 2006. See also Sally Price, *Paris Primitive: Jacques Chirac's Museum on the Quai Branly* (Chicago: University of Chicago Press, 2007). In 2016, the museum added the name of the French president who sponsored the project: Musée du Quai Branly–Jacques Chirac.

31. Lucy Lippard, "Naming," in *Mixed Blessings: New Art in a Multicultural America* (New York: New Press, 1990).

32. Malcolm Gladwell, *Outliers: The Story of Success* (New York: Little, Brown, 2008).

33. Ibid., p. 3.

34. Lynne Cooke, *Outliers and American Vanguard Art* (Washington, D.C.: National Gallery of Art, 2018), 4.

35. *XVI Bienal de São Paulo*, vol. 3, *Catálogo de arte incomum*, 7.

FIG. 79
View of MASP's main gallery with the works *Lindo Lindo Lindo* (Beautiful Beautiful Beautiful, 1976) and *Colheita de algodão* (Cotton Harvest, 1948) by José Antônio da Silva, 2018

"so-called popular art" or the phrase "self-taught artists operating outside the traditional circuit of art and academia."

Works in the Popular–*Playgrounds*–Picture Gallery Triad

To remove from the Museum the air of a church that excludes newcomers, to remove from paintings their "aura" in order to present the work of art as a "work," highly qualified, but work; to present it so that it can be understood by the uninitiated, by the *senhores* from Guarulhos, so different from the elegant visitors of the great traditional museums, whose "auras" persist, even in modern arrangements. Seeing thousands of people walk among the paintings with an almost familiar, nonauratic air . . . is frightening, like a prophecy of fundamental changes. The São Paulo Museum of Art is popular.[36]

The notion of "work," in the sense of every object produced by humans, is instrumental in overcoming the old hierarchies and territories established by the museum and the history of art with respect to the typologies of objects, which underlie the distinctions between art and artifact, between erudite and popular culture, as well as between the art museum, on the one hand, and the anthropological or ethnographic museum on the other. A painting by the Brazilian modernist Candido Portinari is as much a work as a hoe; a painting by Paul Gauguin is as much a work as a piece of correspondence about its price or acquisition—all are products of human labor.[37] The notion of work therefore includes art and artifact, and to read a work we may use any possible theoretical or methodological framework—anthropological or artistic, political or poetic, aesthetic or sociological, material or procedural, semiotic or psychoanalytic, biographical or personal, etc.

In this sense, it's worth recalling a very revealing passage by Bo Bardi, published in 1994, likely written in the 1980s:

A reexamination of the country's recent history is necessary. An account of "popular" Brazilian civilization must be made, even if poor in light of high culture. This account is not one of folklore, always paternalistically supported by high culture; it is the account "seen from the other side," the participating account. It is Aleijadinho and Brazilian culture before the French Mission. It is the Northeasterner of leather and empty cans, the village inhabitant, the Black, and the Indian. A mass that invents, that creates an indigestible, dry, hard-to-swallow contribution.[38]

Here we see Bo Bardi sketching a critique of Eurocentrism, folklore, high culture, which today we can interpret as a decolonizing gesture—even if we do not find the

36. Lina Bo Bardi, "Explicações sobre o Museu de Arte," *O Estado de São Paulo*, April 5, 1970, in Pedrosa and Proença, eds., *Concreto e cristal*, 136.

37. The reference here is, on one hand, to the hoe that the man holds in Candido Portinari's famous 1934 painting, *O lavrador de café* (The Coffee Farmer), which was exhibited in dialogue with Thiago Honório's 2013–16 *Trabalho* (Work), an installation made up of various working tools, including hoes, both in parallel to *The Hand of the Brazilian People 1969/2016* at MASP in 2016. On the other hand, Paul Gauguin's two paintings in MASP's collection, *The Poor Fisherman* and *Self-Portrait (near Golgotha)*, both from 1896, were exhibited next to documentation about their acquisitions in *Arte da França: De Delacroix a Cézanne* at MASP in 2015.

38. Bo Bardi, "Um balanço dezesseis anos depois," 12.

term used in the architect's writings. This is the potential of *The Hand of the Brazilian People* that we are interested in developing, exploring, and further advancing.[39]

Limits

We must, however, be mindful of the exhibition's limits—both the original of 1969 (fig. 75) and its reenactment by MASP in 2016 (fig. 76). The first concerns a spatial segregation that existed in 1969 and persists between the permanent collection on the second floor and the work made by the hand of the people, located in the temporary exhibition gallery on the first floor. The challenge that remains is to merge the so-called popular with the main gallery, elevating works from the first floor to the second, so that they can effectively live side-by-side in the long term. Some works have already been rearranged in such a way for the exhibition *Picture Gallery in Transformation* (fig. 177), at MASP since December 2015, when the crystal easels were reinstalled in the museum's collection exhibit, coexisting with works by artists from throughout history, from Raphael and Vincent van Gogh to Marcelo Cidade and the Guerrilla Girls collective: a painting by Amadeo Luciano Lorenzato, four by Agostinho Batista de Freitas (fig. 77), one by Elza O.S., two by Heitor dos Prazeres, two by José Antônio da Silva (fig. 79), four by Maria Auxiliadora (fig. 78), two by Rafael Borjes de Oliveira, and one sculpture by Agnaldo Manoel dos Santos. In the program of exchange with foreign institutions for *Picture Gallery in Transformation*, through which MASP has received a selection of works from other museums on loan for nine months, special attention has been given to this practice. For *Picture Gallery in Transformation: Tate at MASP* in 2018–19, we received a painting by the English artist L. S. Lowry from the Tate's collection; in *Picture Gallery in Transformation: Museum of Contemporary Art Chicago at MASP*, in 2019–20, a painting by the American artist Forrest Bess was on display on a crystal easel. There remains a desire to integrate a figurehead and a set of ex-votos on the second floor of the museum.

The second limit concerns a certain fantasy or idealization of what *the hand of the Brazilian people* would be, something eloquently critiqued by Antonio Risério in an essay published in this volume. Every exhibition is a construction, and is in fact limited by the experiences, readings, and knowledge of its curator(s), and this is also the case with *The Hand of the Brazilian People* and Bo Bardi—a European looking at the production of the Brazilian Other. Today, we would like to understand the exhibition not so much as an anthropological gaze, but as a poetic, political, and creative exercise, both with regard to the works of the various creators included in the exhibition and the curator/architect herself.

A third limit, this one specific to the reconstruction of the show, titled *The Hand of the Brazilian People, 1969/2016* (fig. 76), refers to the decision not to update the exhibition. All of the assembled objects were made, as far as we know, before 1970. Why not add more recent works? Many exhibitions in recent decades have done so—*Puras misturas*, *Arte popular*, *Mostra do redescobrimento*, among others[40]—but our aim was to understand what in fact *The Hand of the Brazilian People* was, and from there to develop new possibilities for the future, both in relation to temporary exhibitions and to the policies of the collection. We continue to draw lessons from the museum's historical and inaugural moment, to *encounter* new directions and reinforce the presence of the people's hand at MASP.

Translated from the Portuguese by Emma Young

Adriano Pedrosa, Artistic Director, MASP, São Paulo

39. The reenactment of *The Hand of the Brazilian People* is part of a set of other decolonizing strategies of MASP's exhibitions since 2015. First, the shows *Arte do Brasil até 1900* (Brazilian Art before 1900), *Arte do Brasil no século 20* (Brazilian Art after 1900), *Arte da França: De Delacroix a Cézanne*, and *Arte da Itália: De Rafael a Ticiano* juxtaposed works of art with documentary work on them, transforming the two typologies of objects into works exhibited on the same wall, side by side. The main gallery itself, with crystal easels in an open, permeable space, mixes objects from different schools and origins, and though organized chronologically in sets, lays out a meandering pattern rarely followed by viewers, who are free to find their own paths in *Picture Gallery in Transformation*, the show's title. (See Pedrosa and Proença, eds., *Concreto e cristal*). Most of the works on display, particularly until the nineteenth century, are European; after 1950, they are mostly Brazilian. Our challenge, therefore, is to establish frictions on both ends. In this sense, the Landmann Collection long-term loan allowed us to frame our Raphael, *The Resurrection of Christ* (1499–1502), with two Marajoara vases. Moreover, the series of exhibitions, seminars, and publications—*Histories of Sexuality*, in 2017; *Afro-Atlantic Histories*, 2018; *Women's Histories, Feminist Histories*, 2019, and *Indigenous Histories*, scheduled for 2021—deliberately move away from themes, movements, and schools in art history to propose other histories closer to lived experience and the contemporary, drawing from the strategy of merging collections and typologies, placing them into contact, dialogue, and friction with one another. Finally, noteworthy as well is the Art and Decolonization seminar and publishing project, a partnership between MASP and Afterall, a research and publishing center at the University of the Arts in London dedicated to contemporary art and its histories. See https://masp.org.br/seminarios/arte-e-descolonizacao.

40. See Adélia Borges and Cristina Barreto, eds., *Pavilhão das Culturas Brasileiras: puras misturas* (São Paulo: Terceiro Nome, 2010); and Emanoel Araujo, ed., *Mostra de redescobrimento: arte popular* (São Paulo: Fundação Bienal, 2000).

MUSEUMS

Museum of Art (Rua do Ouvidor)

FIG. 81
Lina Bo Bardi, *Perspective of the main entrance, Museum of Art, Rua do Ouvidor*, 1947. Ink and collage on parchment paper, 50 x 52 cm. Collection of the Instituto Bardi/Casa de Vidro, São Paulo

Rio de Janeiro
1947
(Unrealized project)

In 1946, Lina Bo married Pietro Maria Bardi and, in the same year, the couple visited Rio de Janeiro for the installation of three exhibitions of Italian art in the city. On the occasion, Assis Chateaubriand reextended his invitation to create a "museum of art" in the country. Initially intended for Rio, the museum later came into being in São Paulo as MASP. Bo Bardi proposed the renovation of an eclectic four-story building. A new facade would provide a veil of sunshades interspersed with openings for artwork and vegetation. The ground floor would open out to the city, with gardens invading the building's projection. A large gallery ramp would invite passersby into the mezzanine. With the exception of this ramp, all vertical circulation and the bathrooms were positioned at the back of the building, freeing the street facade for large halls on the upper three floors. This first draft already contains features characteristic of the architect's museological projects, in particular the permeability between building and city based on the pedagogical character of the museum as an institution in constant flux.—DJ

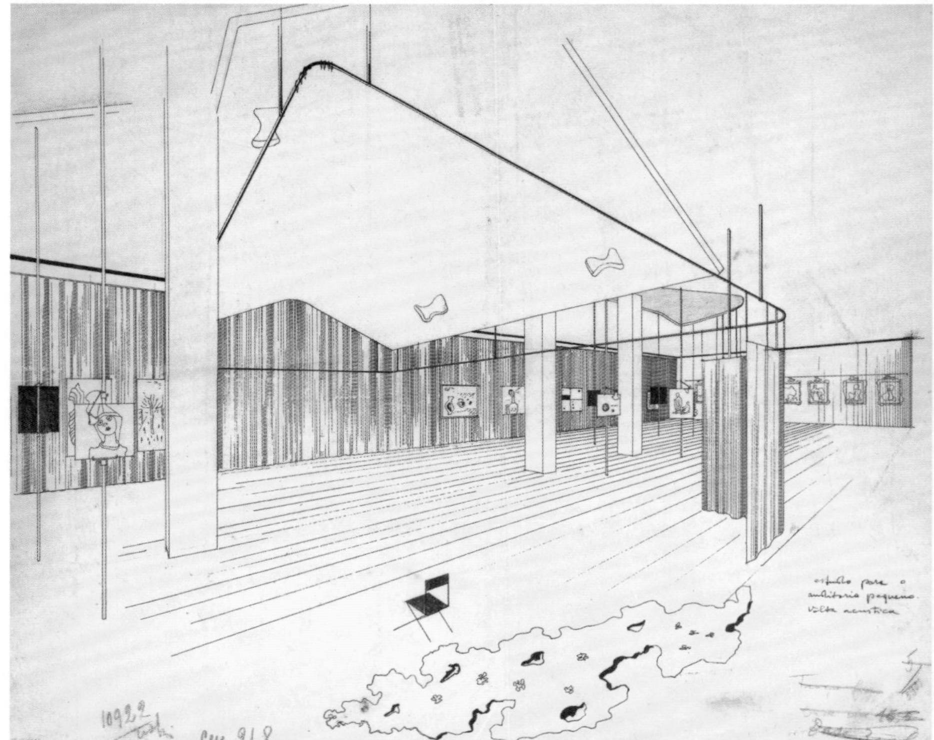

FIG. 80
Lina Bo Bardi, *Study for a small auditorium, acoustic return*, undated. Ink and pencil on paper, 43 x 54.5 cm. MASP, MASP.03721

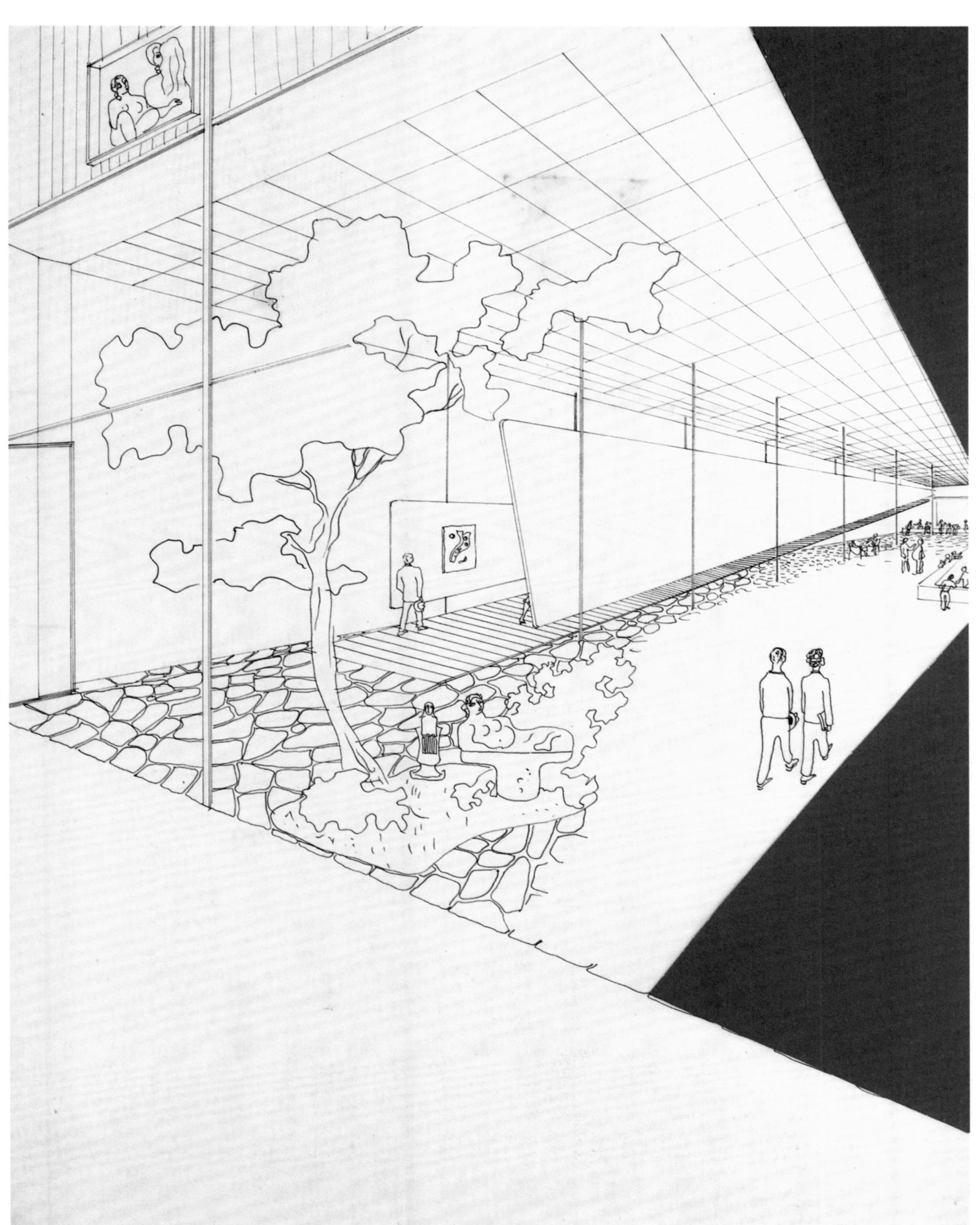

MASP, Rua 7 de Abril

São Paulo
1947
(Renovation project and exhibition design)

FIG. 82
Lina Bo Bardi, *Design for the entrance, MASP, Rua 7 de Abril*, 1947. Watercolor, graphite, and ink on offset paper, 31.5 x 47.5 cm. Collection of the Instituto Bardi/Casa de Vidro, São Paulo

MASP, the first modern museum in Brazil, was designed as a multidimensional institution open to all kinds of artistic manifestations, not only the display of art but also education and training. Founded by Brazilian businessman Assis Chateaubriand, the museum was first housed at the headquarters of his major media conglomerate, Diários Associados, on Rua 7 de Abril in downtown São Paulo. At Chateaubriand's invitation, Italian art critic and dealer Pietro Maria Bardi moved to Brazil to run the museum and acquire its collection, which was to be composed of works from the Renaissance to the Paris School, constituting the most important assemblage of European art in the Southern Hemisphere, and also featuring foundational names in Brazilian modern art. Lina Bo Bardi, Pietro's wife, was charged with adapting the two floors of the building designed by Jacques Pilon for the museum. The space had a large room for the exhibition of the collection, a gallery dedicated to educational exhibitions, and another for temporary shows, as well as an auditorium and activity rooms. Bo Bardi designed a very radical installation for its time, which presented, in its first configuration, the collection's paintings suspended from the ceiling and attached to the ground by tubular metal structures. After a second renovation, in 1950, the works began to be displayed on thin wood panels suspended over the floor on steel cables, thereby creating even greater lightness and transparency in the gallery space. In addition to designing the collection installations, Bo Bardi created displays for temporary exhibitions—with works by key names in Brazilian and international modern art as well as artists outside the canon—and actively participated in the design of the museum's program as a whole, which received significant pedagogical support in the form of publications, lectures, and courses.—TT

FIG. 83
Roberto Sambonet at the entrance to MASP, Rua 7 de Abril, 1947

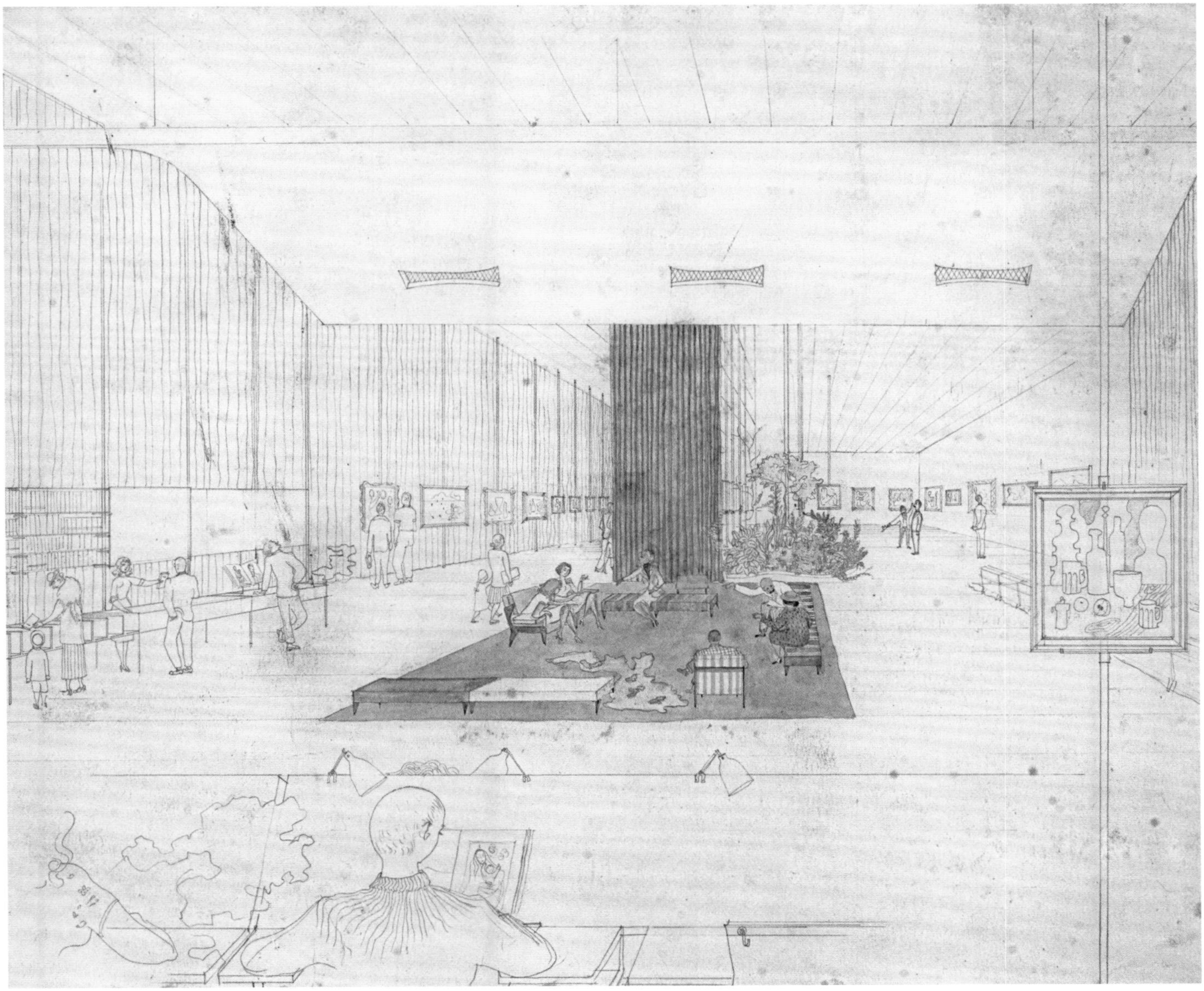

FIG. 84
Lina Bo Bardi, *Perspective drawing: layout of the exhibition room, Museum of Art, Rua 7 de Abril*, 1947. Watercolor, graphite, and ink on card stock, 34.5 x 51 cm. Collection of the Instituto Bardi/Casa de Vidro, São Paulo

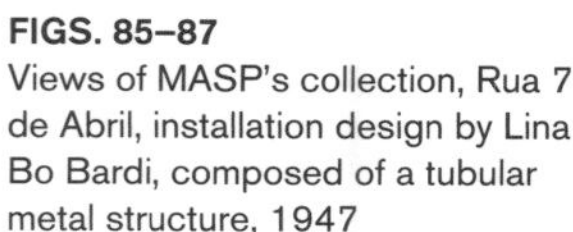

FIGS. 85–87
Views of MASP's collection, Rua 7 de Abril, installation design by Lina Bo Bardi, composed of a tubular metal structure, 1947

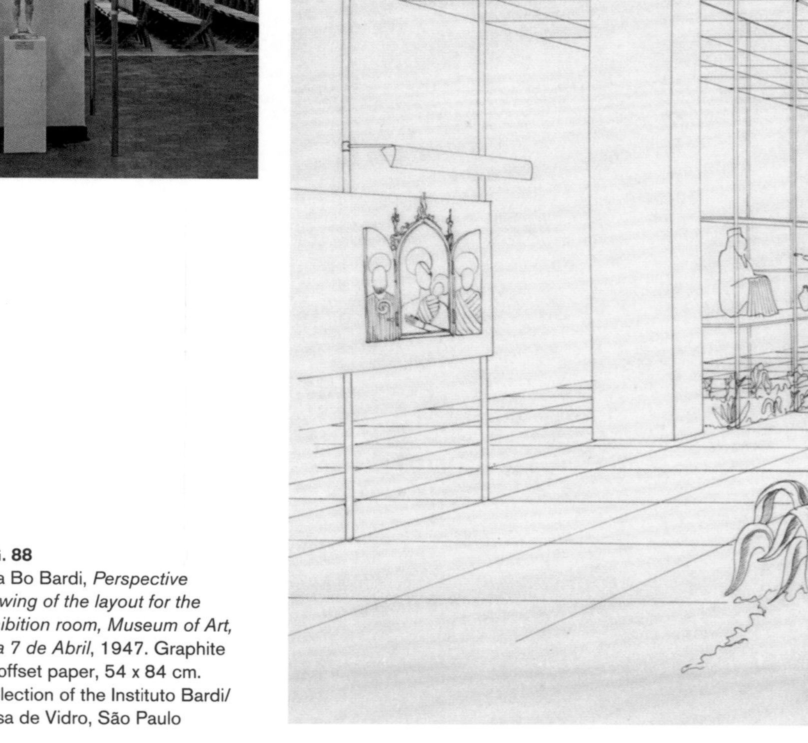

FIG. 88
Lina Bo Bardi, *Perspective drawing of the layout for the exhibition room, Museum of Art, Rua 7 de Abril*, 1947. Graphite on offset paper, 54 x 84 cm. Collection of the Instituto Bardi/ Casa de Vidro, São Paulo

FIG. 89
View of MASP's collection, Rua 7 de Abril, installation design by Lina Bo Bardi, composed of a tubular metal structure, 1947

FIG. 90 ↓
Installation component used for MASP's educational exhibitions, Rua 7 de Abril, 1947

FIG. 92 ↓↓
Lina Bo Bardi, *MASP 7 de Abril, Perspective: exhibition layout and installation support components*, 1947. Marker, graphite, colored pencil, and ink on parchment paper, 36.6 x 50.5 cm. Collection of the Instituto Bardi/Casa de Vidro, São Paulo

FIG. 91 ↓
Lina Bo Bardi, *MASP 7 de Abril, three lighting components fixed to supports of the artworks*, 1947. Blueprint and dry pastel on offset paper, 31 x 38 cm. Collection of the Instituto Bardi/Casa de Vidro, São Paulo

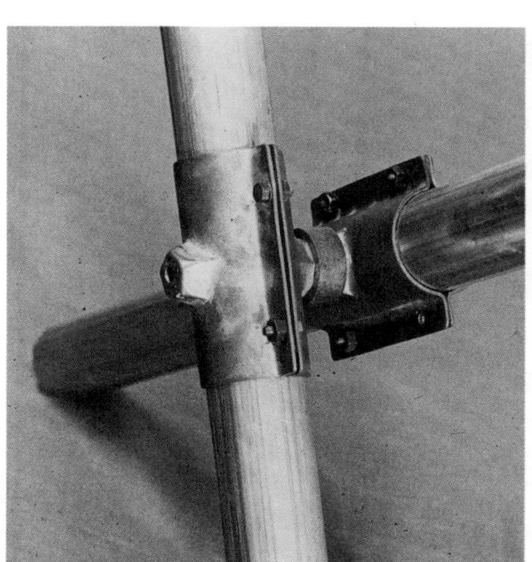

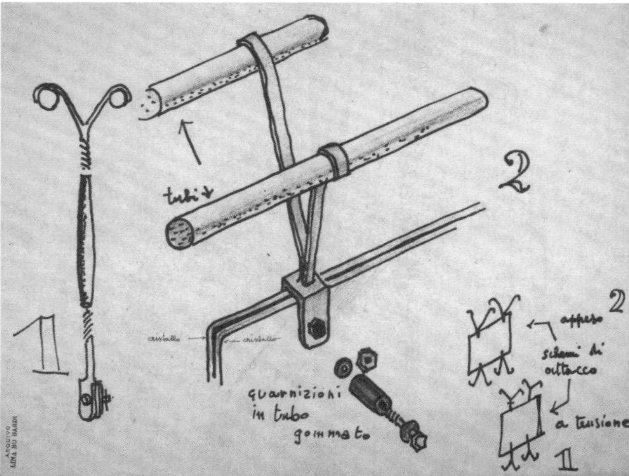

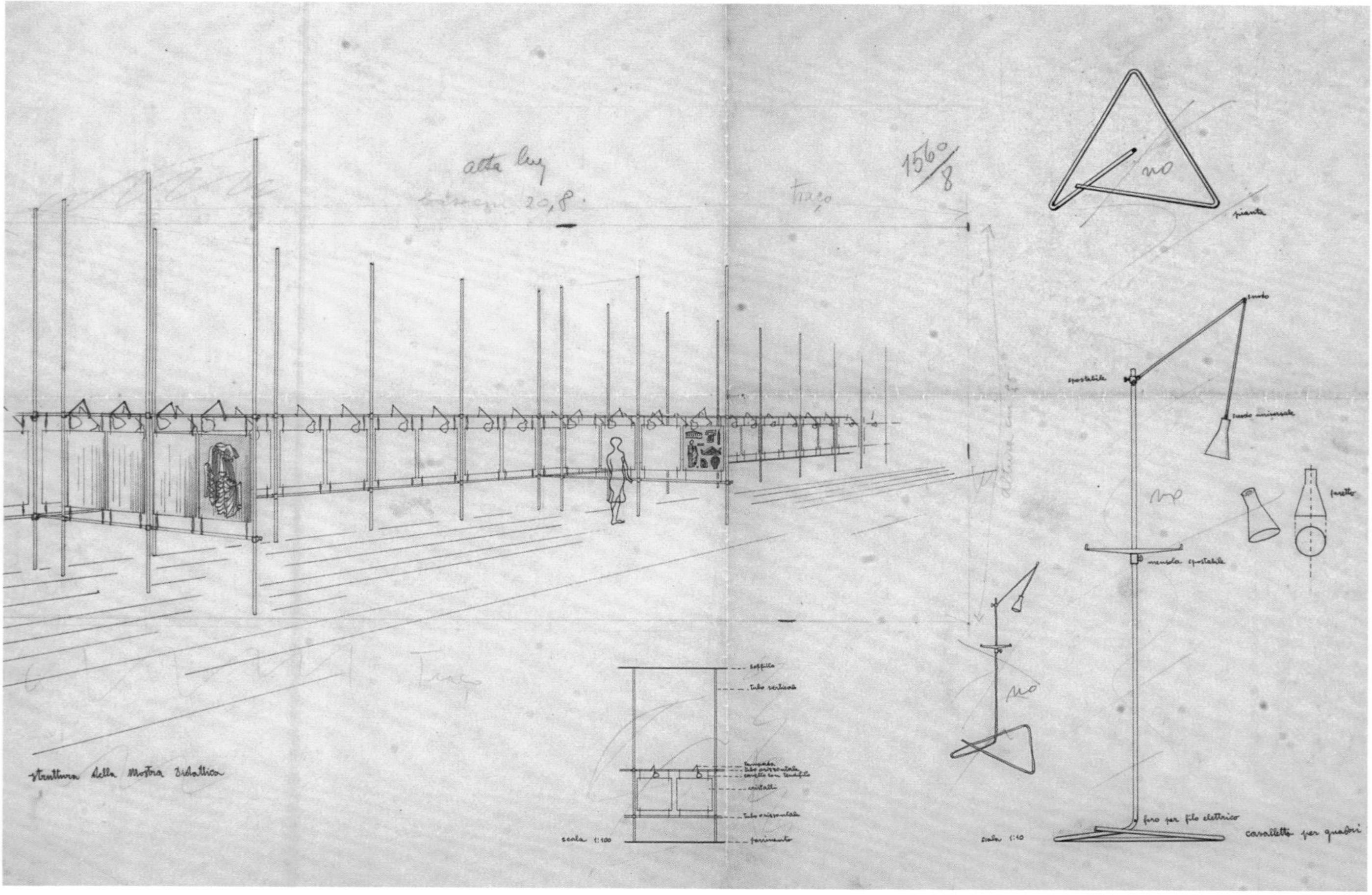

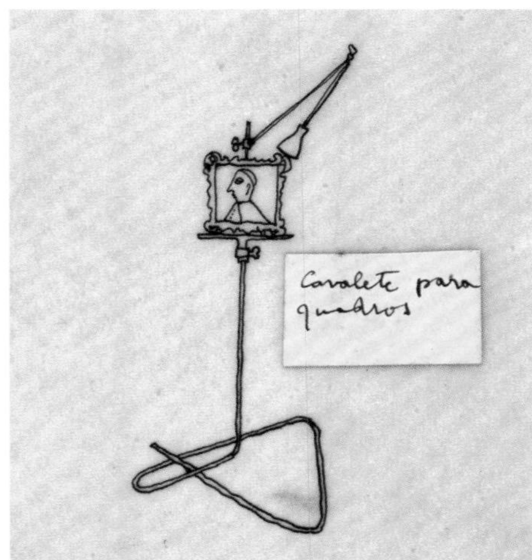

FIGS. 93–94
Lina Bo Bardi, *Artwork supports, Museum of Art, Rua 7 de Abril*, 1947. Graphite and ink on parchment paper, 14 x 11 cm. Collection of the Instituto Bardi/ Casa de Vidro, São Paulo

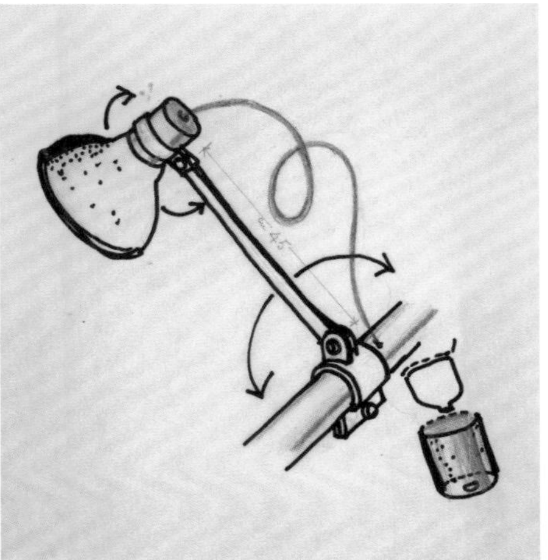

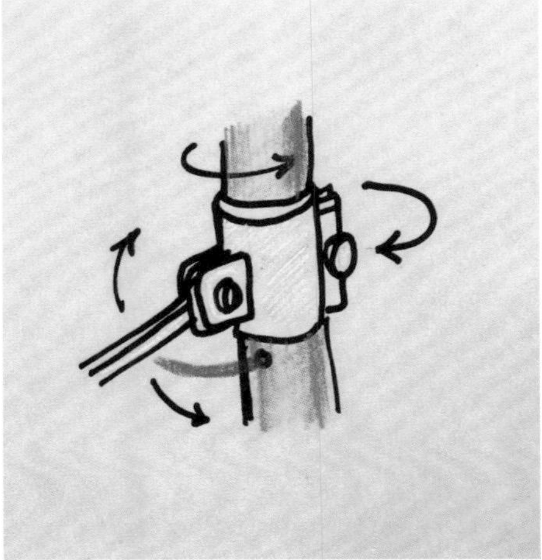

FIGS. 95–96
Lina Bo Bardi, *MASP 7 de Abril, two lighting components*, 1947. Blueprint, graphite, colored pencil, and oil pastel on parchment paper, 24 x 41.5 cm. Collection of the Instituto Bardi/ Casa de Vidro, São Paulo

FIG. 97
View of the gallery dedicated to educational exhibitions, MASP, Rua 7 de Abril, installation design by Lina Bo Bardi, 1947

FIG. 98 →
View of the exhibition *Homage to Le Corbusier*, MASP, Rua 7 de Abril, installation design by Lina Bo Bardi, 1950

FIG. 99 →→
View of MASP's collection, Rua 7 de Abril, after the second renovation, with installation design by Lina Bo Bardi, composed of suspended panels, 1950

FIG. 100 →
View of the Roberto Burle Marx exhibition at MASP, Rua 7 de Abril, installation design by Lina Bo Bardi, 1952

FIG. 101 →→
Lina Bo Bardi, *Perspective of the exhibition room with layout of the closing panels, Museum of Art, Rua 7 de Abril*, 1947. Ink on card stock, 70 x 100 cm. Collection of the Instituto Bardi/Casa de Vidro, São Paulo

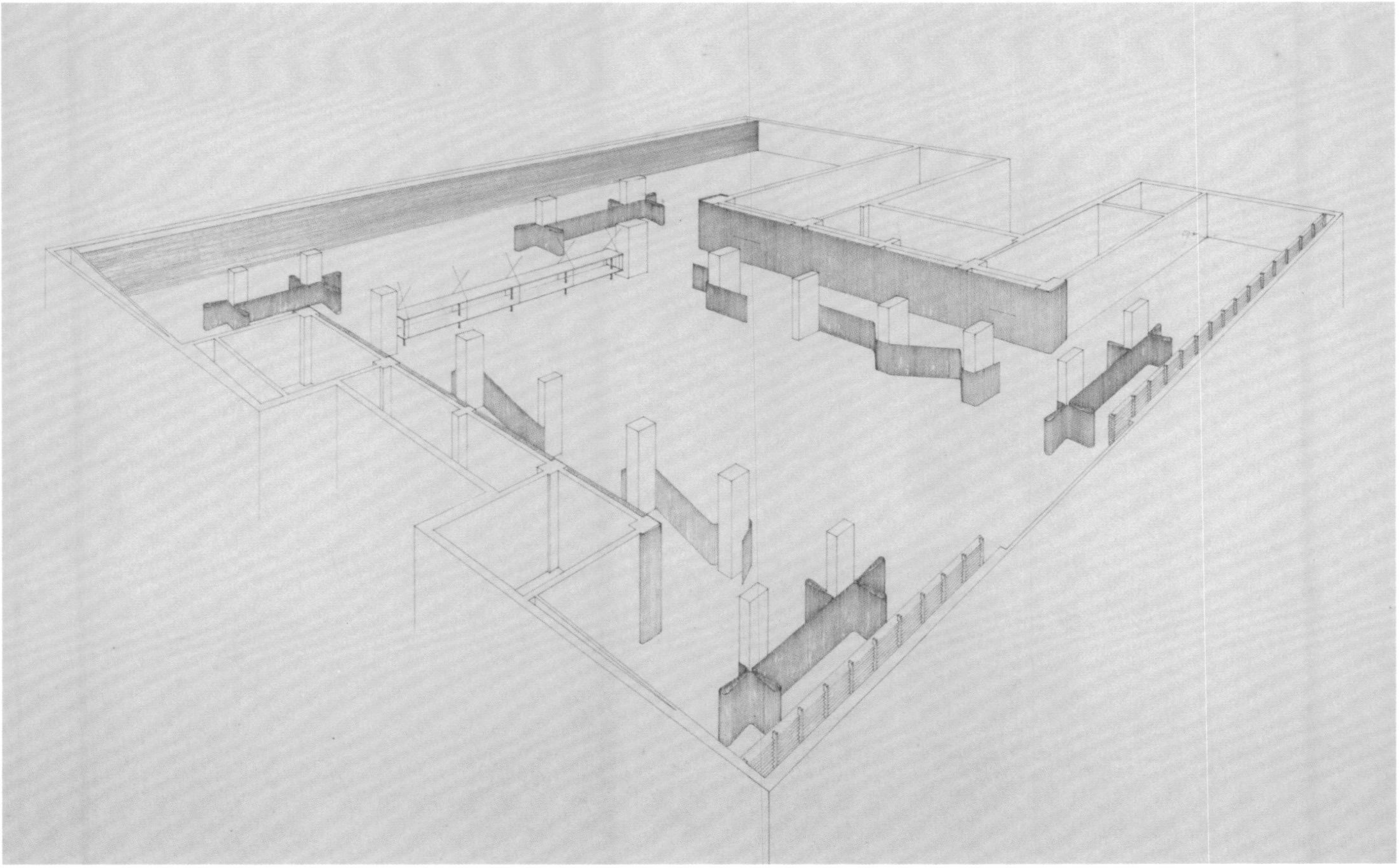

FIG. 103 ↓
View of MASP's collection, Rua 7 de Abril, with Édouard Manet's painting *The Amazon (Portrait of Marie Lefébure)* (1870–75), ca. 1960

FIG. 104 ↓↓
View of MASP's collection, Rua 7 de Abril; in the foreground, next to Amedeo Modigliani's painting *Madame G. van Muyden* (1916–17), the model Gloria presents the "Balaio" dress, created by Clara Hartoch in MASP's textile workshops in conjunction with a Brazilian fashion show at the museum, 1952

FIG. 102 ↓
View of MASP's collection, Rua 7 de Abril, with Paul Cézanne's paintings *O negro Cipião* (Cipião the Black Man, 1866–68) and *Madame Cézanne in Red* (1890–94), 1950s

FIG. 105
Lina Bo Bardi, *Study for the installation of a group show*, undated. Ink and watercolor on paper, 10.5 x 24.5 cm. MASP, MASP.03722

FIG. 106
View of MASP, Rua 7 de Abril, with the Vitrine of Forms, designed by Lina Bo Bardi, which presented objects from different times, places, cultures, materials, and contexts within the same environment, combining, for example, a mobile by Alexander Calder with an Agnaldo Manoel dos Santos sculpture, and an Olivetti typewriter with a fragment of old wood, 1950

FIG. 107
View of MASP, Rua 7 de Abril, with installation design by Lina Bo Bardi; in the foreground, the exhibition *Homage to Le Corbusier*; at the center, the Vitrine of Forms; in the background, the collection, 1950

São Vicente Museum of Art (Oceanfront Museum)

São Vicente, São Paulo
1951
(Unrealized project)

← FIG. 108
Lina Bo Bardi, *Oceanfront Museum: perspective drawing of the lot*, 1951. Graphite and ink on parchment paper, 50 x 70 cm. Collection of the Instituto Bardi/ Casa de Vidro, São Paulo

FIG. 109 →
Lina Bo Bardi, *Oceanfront Museum: photomontage of the model and beach site*, 1951. Impression on photographic paper, 18 x 20.5 cm. Collection of the Instituto Bardi/Casa de Vidro, São Paulo

Proposed to be sited directly on the beach, the building would be elevated on five reinforced concrete frames positioned at 20-meter intervals.
In Bo Bardi's work, this project reveals the closest approximation to Ludwig Mies van der Rohe, both in its spatial formulation—the arrangement of the entire structure in a sequence of porticos external to the volume—and in the unusual graphic treatment of the presentation, which overlaps drawings, collages, and photomontages, recurrent devices in the German architect's practice. With three blind facades and the front oriented to the ocean, the building would have received little direct sunlight. The suspended prism would have two incisions: a large balcony for outdoor exhibitions and hanging gardens, and a patio that would accommodate classrooms, a library, administration and maintenance rooms, and an auditorium. Drawings published in the second issue of the French magazine *Architecture d'Aujourd'hui* show the proposed auditorium with a rotating circular stage. On the stage, rotating axes would support prisms with paintings affixed to them. Original works from the collection could be placed on this carousel for use in classes and conferences. Although the final proposal settled on exposed concrete for the porticoes, a photomontage reveals that the color red was under consideration—an embryonic version of MASP on Avenida Paulista.—DJ

FIG. 110 →
Lina Bo Bardi, *Oceanfront Museum: photomontage of the model with color study of the structure*, 1951. Impression on photographic paper, 17 x 24 cm. Collection of the Instituto Bardi/ Casa de Vidro, São Paulo

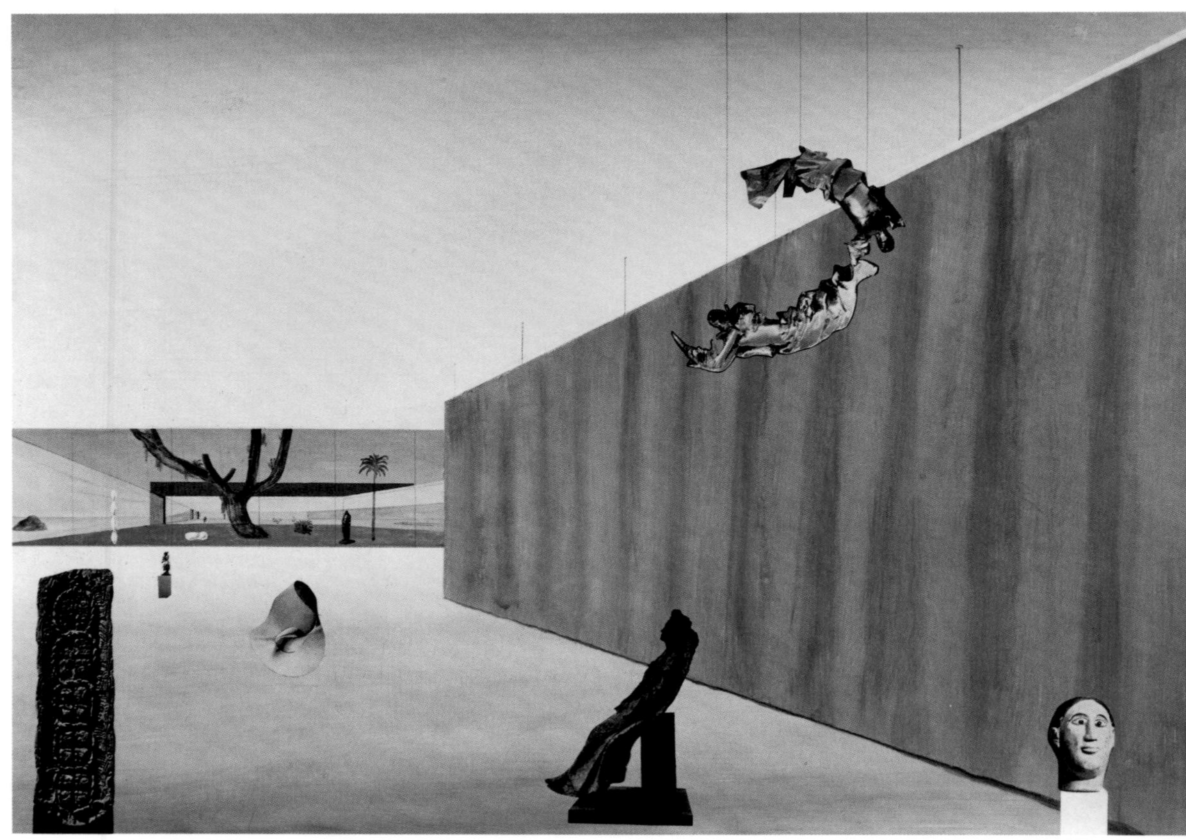

FIG. 111
Lina Bo Bardi, *Study for museum exhibition area*, 1951. Photographic collage, 18 x 24 cm. Collection of the Instituto Bardi/ Casa de Vidro, São Paulo

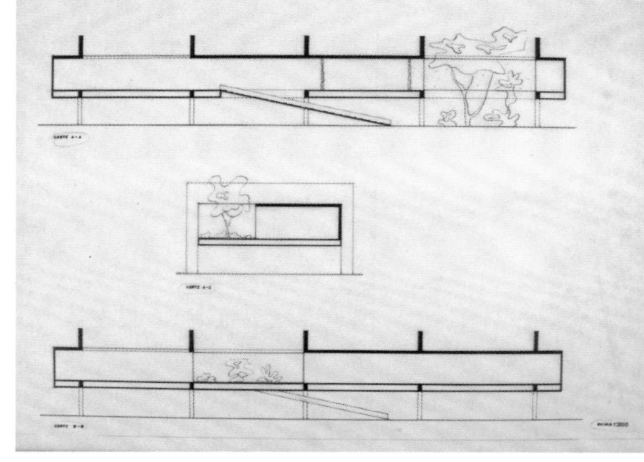

FIG. 112
Lina Bo Bardi, *Longitudinal section, cross section, Oceanfront Museum*, 1951. Graphite and ink on parchment paper, 45 x 62.5 cm. Collection of the Instituto Bardi/Casa de Vidro, São Paulo

FIG. 113
Lina Bo Bardi, *Elevations, Oceanfront Museum*, 1951. Ink on parchment paper, 45 x 62 cm. Collection of the Instituto Bardi/ Casa de Vidro, São Paulo

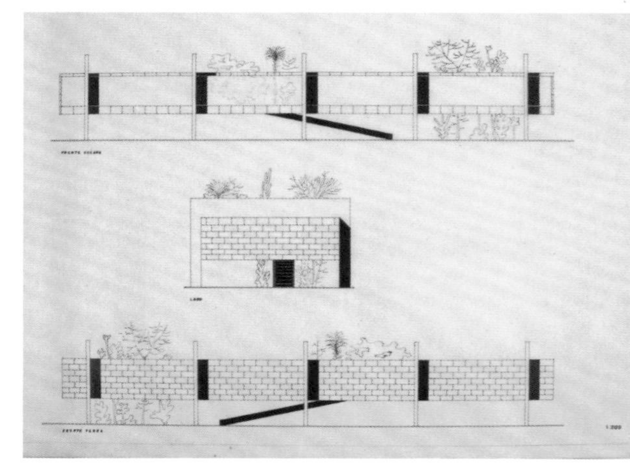

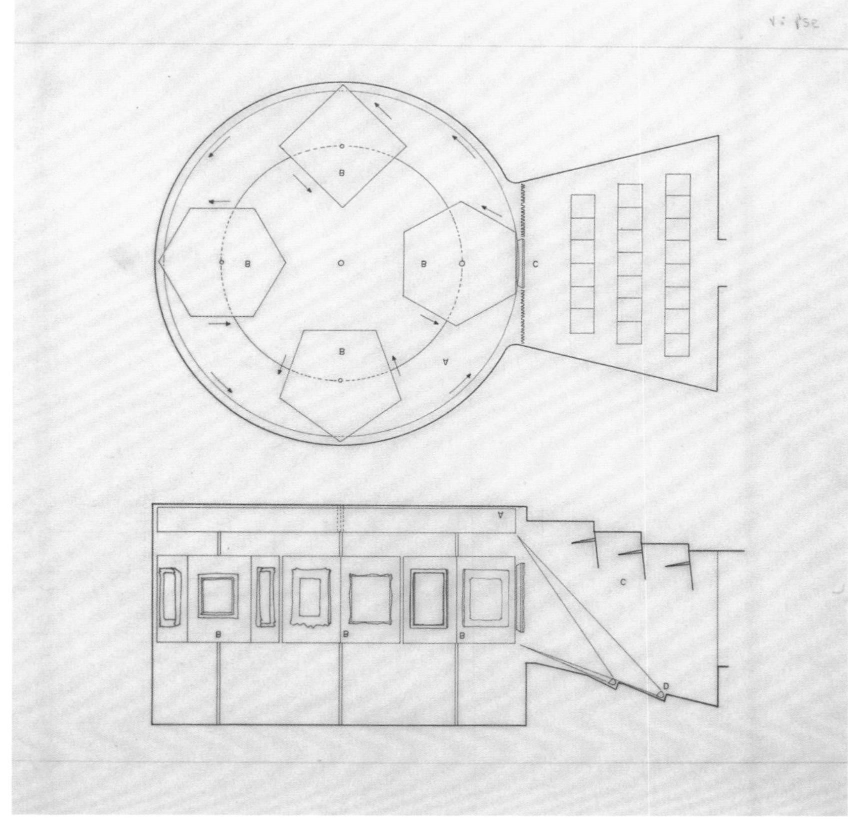

FIG. 114
Lina Bo Bardi, *Plan and elevation, Giratório Museum*, 1951. Graphite and ink on offset paper, 32.5 x 50 cm. Collection of the Instituto Bardi/Casa de Vidro, São Paulo

FIG. 115
Lina Bo Bardi, *Study for museum exhibition area*, 1951. Photographic collage, 18 x 24 cm. Collection of the Instituto Bardi/Casa de Vidro, São Paulo

MASP, Avenida Paulista

São Paulo
1957–68
(Architectural and exhibition design)

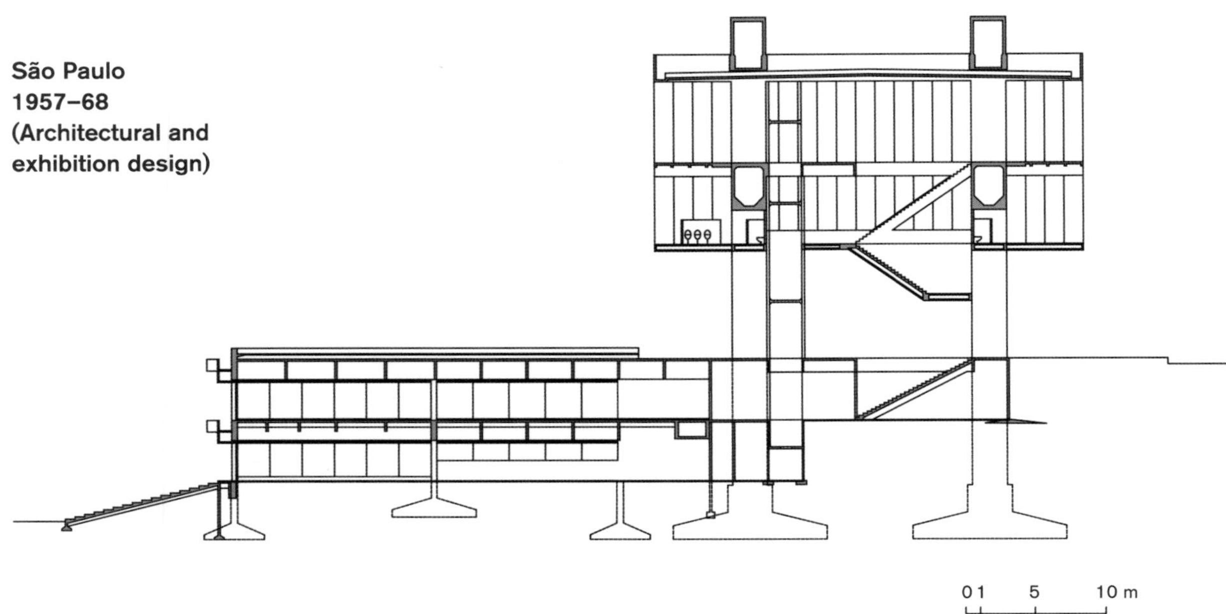

FIG. 116
Cross section of MASP, Avenida Paulista, showing the two upper floors, the free span, and the two lower floors

Over the years, MASP's ambitions outgrew its headquarters on Rua 7 de Abril. Before its definitive transfer to Avenida Paulista, it occupied, between 1957 and 1959, the galleries of the current Museum of Brazilian Art, at the Armando Alvares Penteado Foundation (FAAP). MASP's ultimate location, designed by Lina Bo Bardi, is a landmark in São Paulo's modern architecture and retains its iconic status in the urban landscape today. The building is structured on two levels. On the upper level, facing Avenida Paulista, the structure is encased in vertical panes of glass and suspended by thick reinforced concrete pillars—painted red only in 1991 to solve a persistent infiltration problem. On the level below the Avenida Paulista, or "basement" level, the building's windows open out to hanging gardens. The museum has a large open-plan gallery on the second floor dedicated to the collection, displayed on crystal easels; three temporary exhibition galleries on the first floor and second basement level; plus a research center, restaurant, and two auditoriums. MASP's architecture, based on the transparency of glass, the permeability of free arrangements, and the economy and roughness of concrete, moves away from the sequestered museum-as-temple and the white cube, gaining a public dimension, while its suspended concrete volume, a 74-meter-long slab, creates a large civic plaza known as the free span from which to view the city looking down Avenida 9 de Julho. To arrive at MASP's current configuration, Bo Bardi elaborated several preliminary designs, among them, one with a theater in the second basement and access to the upper floor by a central column, and another with a spiral staircase and a facade consisting of precast concrete panels that would eventually be covered by a vertical garden.—TT

FIG. 117
Lina Bo Bardi, *São Paulo Museum of Art: perspective*, 1957–68. Graphite, ink, and collage on parchment paper, 50 x 70 cm. Collection of the Instituto Bardi/Casa de Vidro, São Paulo

FIG. 118
Lina Bo Bardi, *São Paulo Museum of Art: perspective showing the Belvedere occupied by sculptures*, 1957–68. Graphite and ink on paper, 47 x 70 cm. Collection of the Instituto Bardi/Casa de Vidro, São Paulo

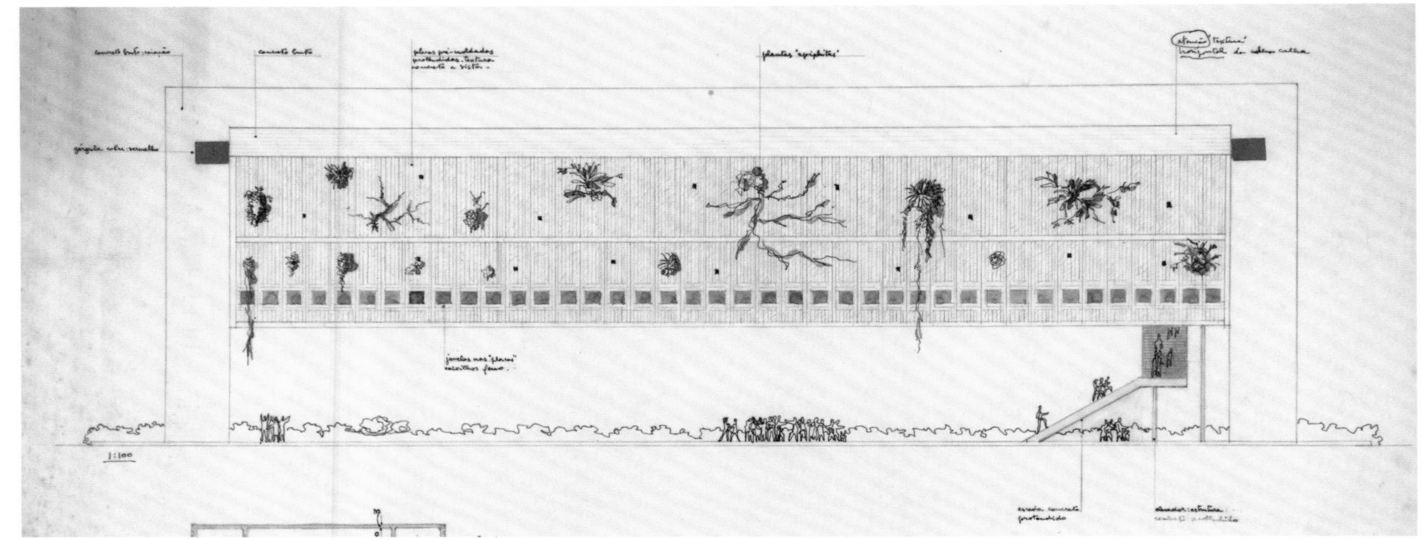

FIG. 119
Lina Bo Bardi, *Front elevation with precast panels and vegetation, São Paulo Museum of Art*, 1957–68. Graphite, ink, and collage on vegetable paper, 57 x 99.5 cm. Collection of the Instituto Bardi/Casa de Vidro, São Paulo

FIG. 120
Lina Bo Bardi, *Facade study, MASP*, 1961. Gouache and graphite on paper, 100 x 190.5 cm. MASP, MASP.03724

FIGS. 121–122
Models, MASP Avenida Paulista project; preliminary design with a spiral staircase and solid concrete facade, 1960

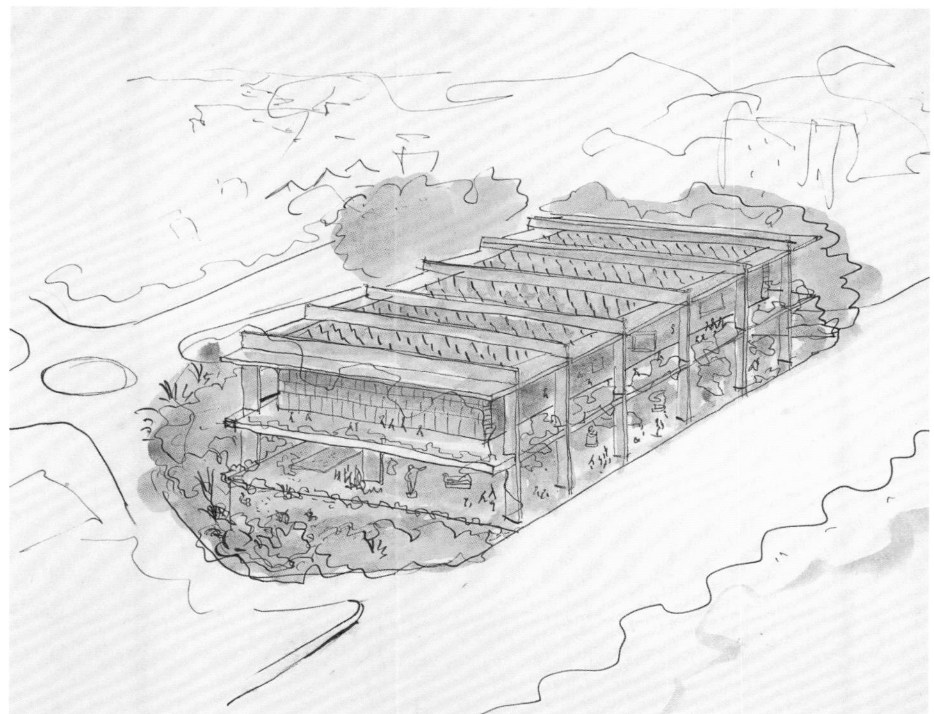

FIG. 123
Lina Bo Bardi, *Perspective, São Paulo Museum of Art*, 1957–68. Watercolor and ink on card stock, 32 x 90.5 cm. Collection of the Instituto Bardi/Casa de Vidro, São Paulo

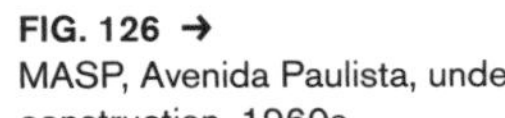

FIG. 126 →
MASP, Avenida Paulista, under construction, 1960s

FIG. 127 ↘
Lina Bo Bardi at the MASP construction site; in the foreground, the pre-stressing system for the museum's reinforced concrete structure, 1963–64

FIG. 124 ↓
Lina Bo Bardi, *MASP: perspective*, undated. Watercolor on paper, 49.5 x 70 cm. Collection of the Faculdade de Arquitetura e Urbanismo, Universidade de São Paulo

FIG. 125 ↓↓
Lina Bo Bardi, *Plan: MASP, Avenida Paulista*, undated. Watercolor on paper, 50 x 50.5 cm. Collection of the Faculdade de Arquitetura e Urbanismo, Universidade de São Paulo

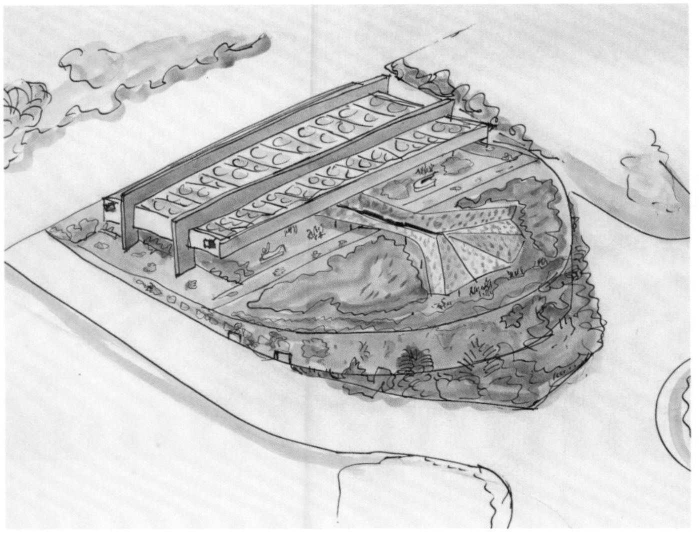

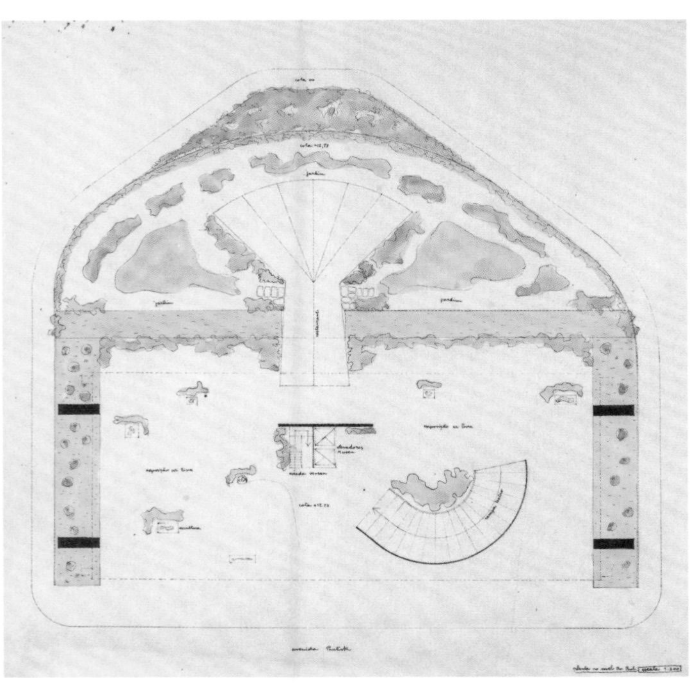

FIG. 128 ↗
MASP, Avenida Paulista, 1968

FIG. 129 →
Lina Bo Bardi, *MASP: longitudinal section and details of the museum and restaurant roof*, undated. Watercolor on paper, 53.5 x 50 cm. Collection of the Faculdade de Arquitetura e Urbanismo, Universidade de São Paulo

FIG. 130 →→
Lina Bo Bardi, *MASP: lateral and main facades and cross section*, undated. Watercolor on paper, 50 x 53 cm. Collection of the Faculdade de Arquitetura e Urbanismo, Universidade de São Paulo

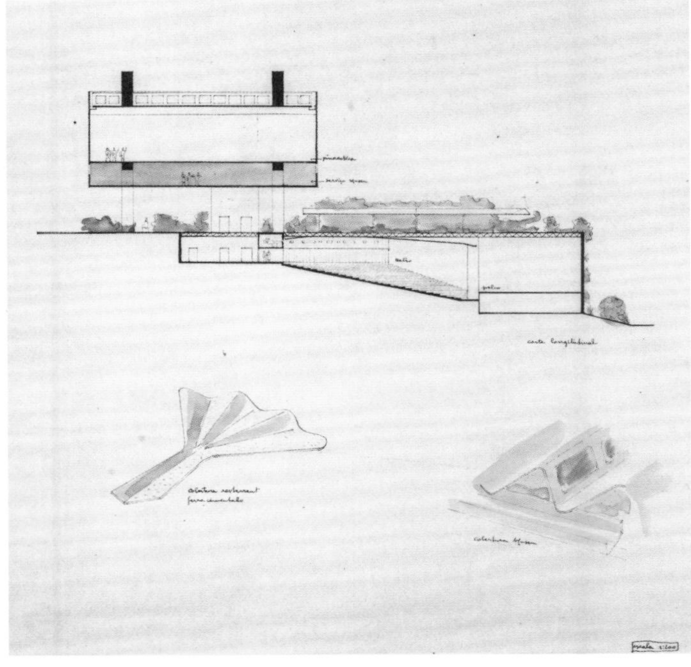

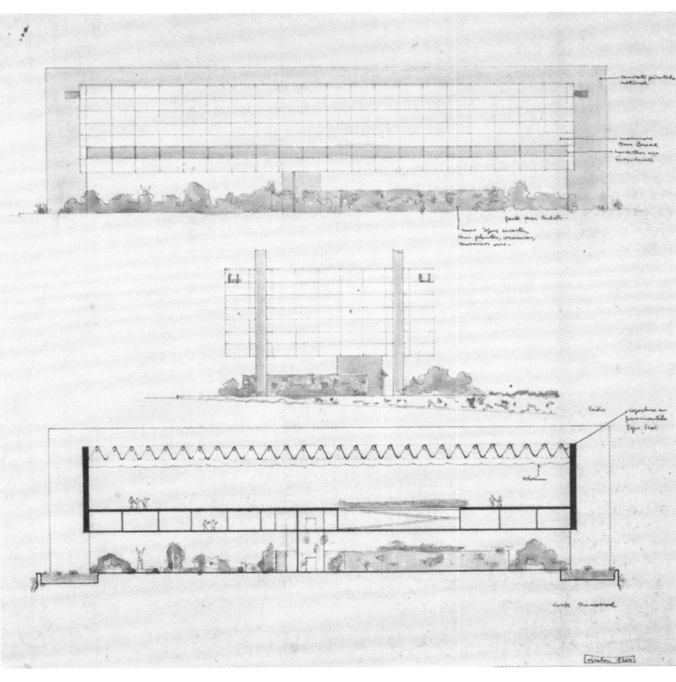

FIG. 131
Lina Bo Bardi, *MASP*, undated. Ink on paper, 47.5 x 28.5 cm. MASP, MASP.03720

FIG. 132
MASP, Avenida Paulista, 1969

FIG. 133
MASP, Avenida Paulista, 2002

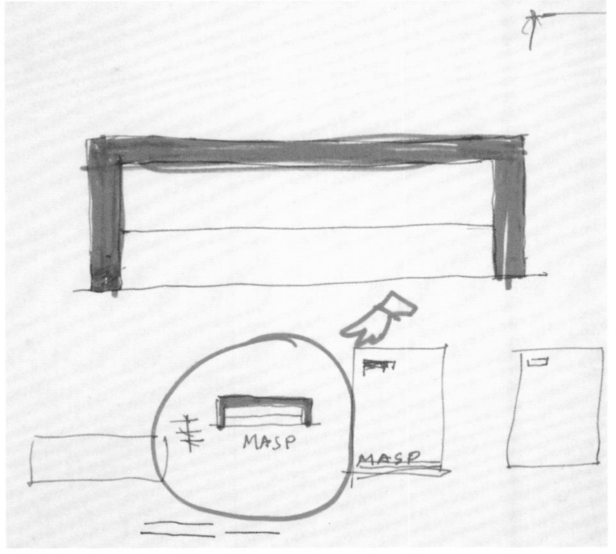

FIG. 134
Lina Bo Bardi, *São Paulo Museum of Art: logo and stationery design*, 1957–68. Marker, graphite, and ink on offset paper, 16 x 21.6 cm. Collection of the Instituto Bardi/Casa de Vidro, São Paulo

FIG. 135
Lina Bo Bardi, *São Paulo Museum of Art: perspective drawing of the Belvedere*, 1957–68. Ink and dry pastel on parchment paper, 50 x 69.5 cm. Collection of the Instituto Bardi/Casa de Vidro, São Paulo

FIG. 136
MASP's free span, 1970

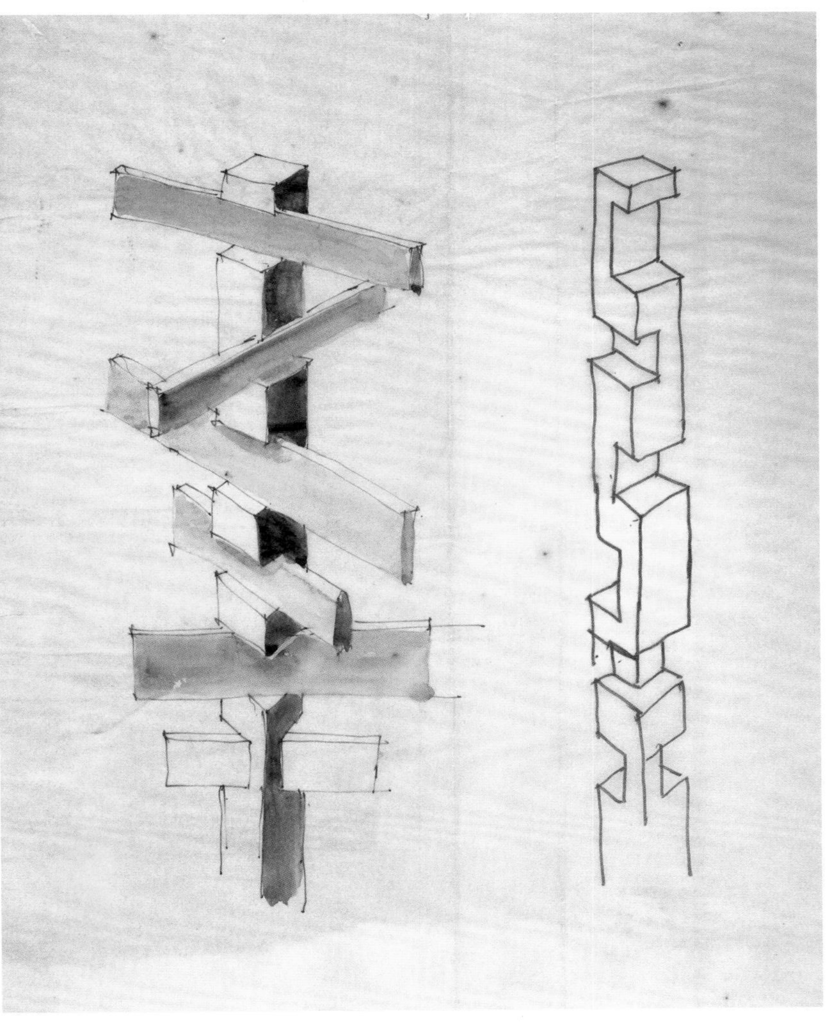

FIG. 137
Lina Bo Bardi, *São Paulo Museum of Art: perspective drawing*, 1957–68. Watercolor and marker on parchment paper, 43 x 34 cm. Collection of the Instituto Bardi/ Casa de Vidro, São Paulo

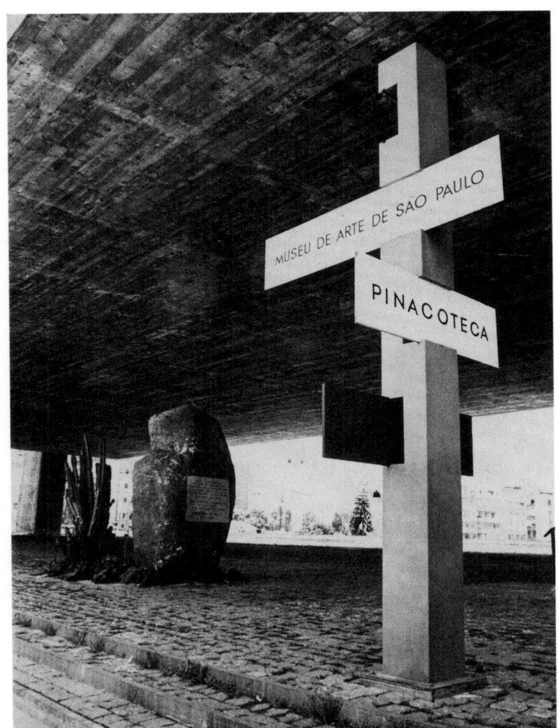

FIG. 138
MASP's free span with the directional totem, 1970

FIG. 139
MASP, Avenida Paulista, with the Piolin Circus in the free span, 1972

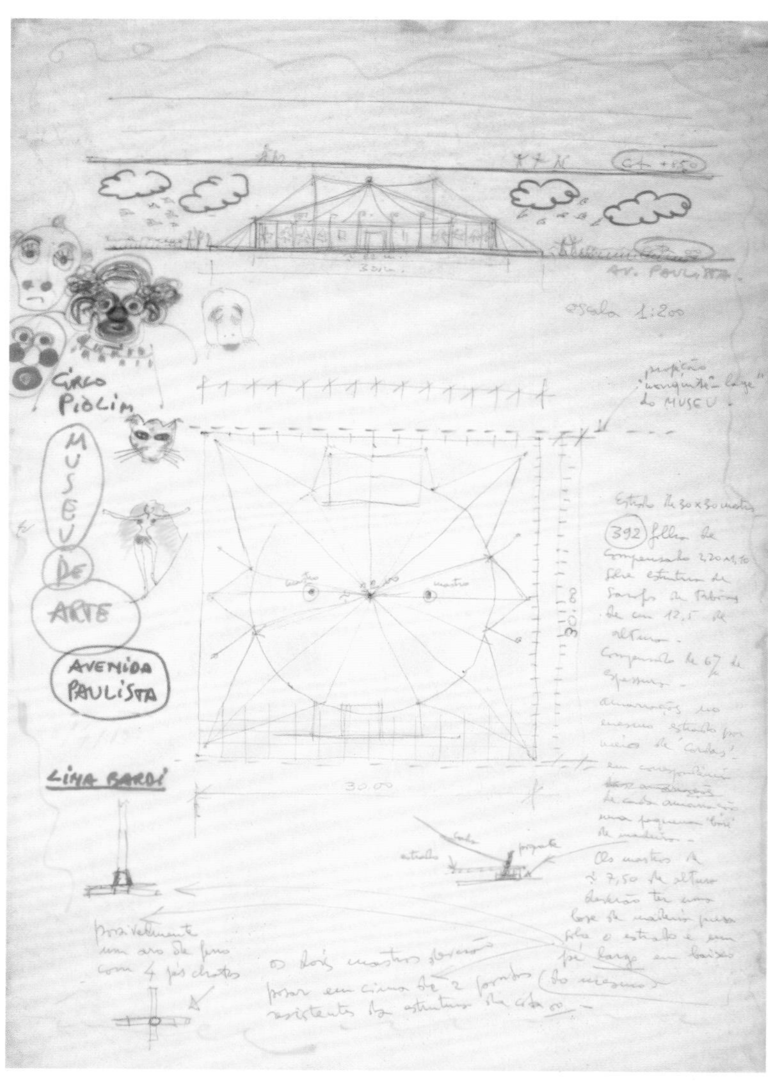

FIG. 140 ↑↑
Lina Bo Bardi, *Perspective drawing of the Belvedere showing the installation of the Piolin Circus, São Paulo Museum of Art*, 1957–68. Watercolor, ballpoint pen, and marker on card stock, 32 x 47 cm. Collection of the Instituto Bardi/Casa de Vidro, São Paulo

FIG. 141 ↑
Lina Bo Bardi, *Elevation of the circus tent indicating the installation of the museum's Belvedere/Circus tent plans and annotations, São Paulo Museum of Art*, 1957–68. Ballpoint pen, marker, and graphite on parchment paper, 50 x 35 cm. Collection of the Instituto Bardi/Casa de Vidro, São Paulo

FIG. 142 ↓
The carrousel by Carlos Blanc and Maria Helena Chartuni in MASP's free span, 1970

FIG. 144 ↓↓
Lina Bo Bardi, *Preliminary study: feasible sculptures for the Trianon Art Museum Belvedere*, 1968. Ink and watercolor on paper, 56.6 x 76.5 cm. MASP, donation by the Instituto Lina Bo e P. M. Bardi, 2006, MASP.04442

FIG. 143 ↓
View of the *Playgrounds* exhibition organized by Nelson Leirner in MASP's free span, 1969

FIG. 145
Second basement level of MASP, Avenida Paulista, with stands designed by Lina Bo Bardi for the 5th International Congress of Psychodrama and Sociodrama, 1970

FIG. 146
View of the exhibition *Weaving Patterns: Documentary Exhibition*, organized by Lina Bo Bardi and Edmar José de Almeida, on the first floor of MASP, Avenida Paulista, 1975

FIG. 147
View of the Augusto Gerlinger exhibition on the first floor of MASP, Avenida Paulista, installation design by Lina Bo Bardi, 1970

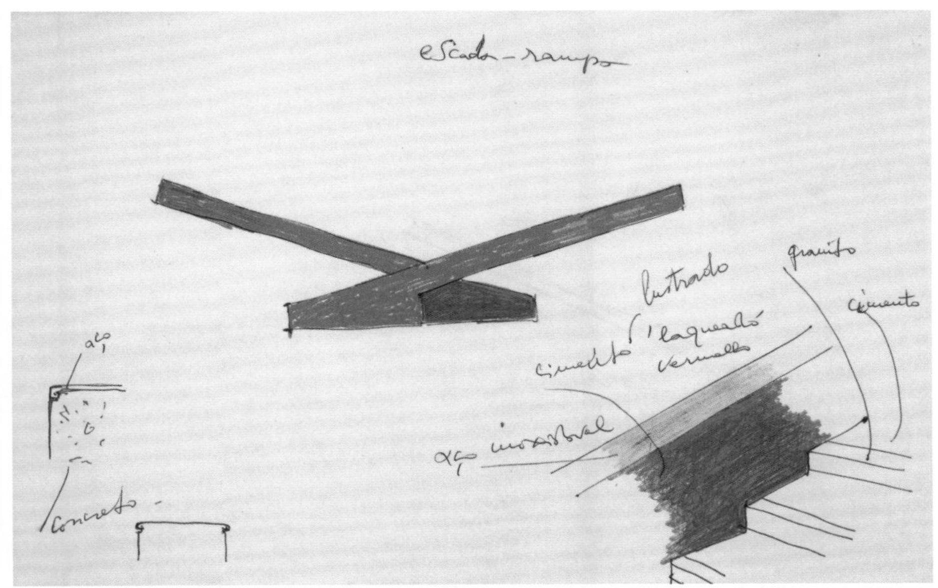

FIG. 148
Lina Bo Bardi, *São Paulo Museum of Art: detail of handrail, elevation, and perspective drawing indicating finishes*, 1957–68. Ballpoint pen, marker, graphite, and colored pencil on offset paper, 15.5 x 24.5 cm. Collection of the Instituto Bardi/ Casa de Vidro, São Paulo

FIG. 149
View of the Rubens Gerchman exhibition on the second basement level of MASP, Avenida Paulista, 1974

FIG. 150
View of the main gallery at MASP, Avenida Paulista, with Lina Bo Bardi's glass easels, 1968

Museum of Modern Art of Bahia (Castro Alves Theater)

Salvador
1960
(Foundation and direction of the museum, renovation project, curatorial project, and exhibition design)

In 1960, Lina Bo Bardi was invited by Lavínia Magalhães, the wife of Juracy Magalhães, then governor of Bahia, to found and direct the Museum of Modern Art of Bahia (MAM-BA). The museum initially occupied the foyer of the Castro Alves Theater, adapted by Bo Bardi, as the building had been partially destroyed by fire. The exhibitions took place in curtained environments, which served as a backdrop for the works presented, recalling an installation technique that Bo Bardi had employed at MASP on Rua 7 de Abril and at the Glass House. The paintings were displayed on easels that merged the conical-shaped concrete bases used in *Bahia in Ibirapuera* (1959) with the vertical tubular displays of the initial configuration of MASP's main gallery. Bo Bardi refuted the designation "Museum" for MAM-BA, preferring terms such as "Center," "Movement," and "School," because the collection was still incipient and because of the very idea of "museum" that she had been developing since MASP's founding and in texts published in *Habitat* magazine. She proposed the notion of a museum that focuses not only on the tasks of collecting, conserving, and exhibiting its collection, but that also has an educational mission and is grounded in its social context. The inauguration of MAM-BA featured exhibitions of work by Antonio Bandeira and Edgar Degas, the group show *Natural Forms*, and a small presentation of the permanent collection. Over the next three years, until the museum's transfer to the Solar do Unhão, exhibitions were held of Brazilian and international artists, including Agnaldo Manoel dos Santos, Agostinho Batista de Freitas, Burle Marx, Emanoel Araujo, Käthe Kollwitz, Paul Cézanne, Pierre-Auguste Renoir, and Vincent van Gogh.—TT

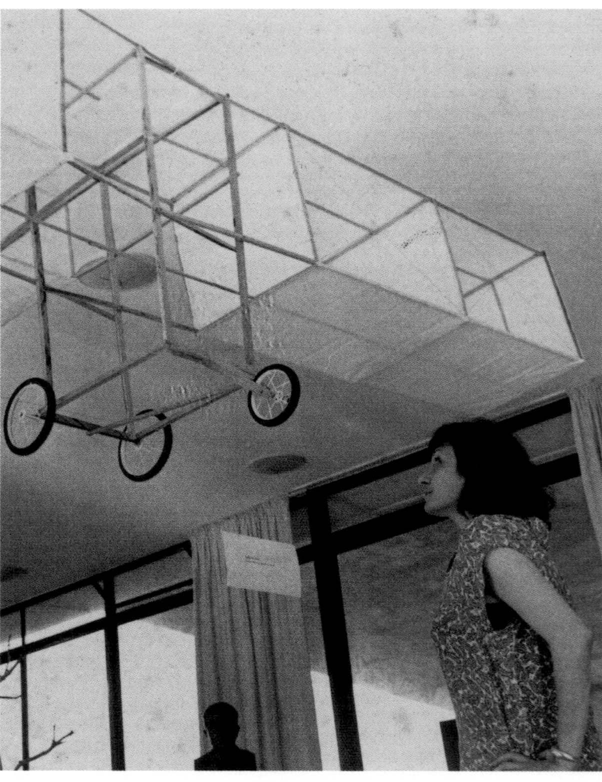

FIG. 151
Lina Bo Bardi looking at an airplane model at the exhibition *Week of the Wings,* Museum of Modern Art of Bahia, Castro Alves Theater, 1960

FIG. 152
Temporary installations at the Museum of Modern Art of Bahia, Castro Alves Theater, 1960

FIG. 153
View of the *Natural Forms* exhibition, Museum of Modern Art of Bahia, 1960

FIG. 154
View of the Le Corbusier exhibition at the Museum of Modern Art of Bahia, installation design by Lina Bo Bardi, composed of a metal tubular structure, 1963

FIG. 155
Vincent Van Gogh's painting *Evening Walk* (1889–90) from MASP's collection at the Museum of Modern Art of Bahia, installation design by Lina Bo Bardi, 1960

FIG. 156
View of the Agostinho Batista de Freitas exhibition at the Museum of Modern Art of Bahia, 1961

FIG. 157
View of the Antonio Bandeira exhibition at the Museum of Modern Art of Bahia, installation design by Lina Bo Bardi, composed of a metal tubular structure and a conical concrete base, 1960

FIG. 158
Pierre-Auguste Renoir's painting *Pink and Blue (The Cahen d'Anvers Girls)* (1881) from MASP's collection at the Museum of Modern Art of Bahia, installation design by Lina Bo Bardi, 1960

FIG. 159 ↓
Selection of twenty bronze ballerinas by Edgar Degas from MASP's collection at the Museum of Modern Art of Bahia, installation design by Lina Bo Bardi, 1960

FIG. 160 ↓↓
View of the Agnaldo Manoel dos Santos exhibition at the Museum of Modern Art of Bahia, 1961

FIG. 161 ↓
View of the São Francisco figureheads exhibition at the Museum of Modern Art of Bahia, installation design by Lina Bo Bardi, 1961

FIG. 162 →
Article by Lina Bo Bardi on the Museum of Modern Art of Bahia, *Mirante das Artes*, no. 6 (1967): 17

A miséria de cada dia beira o genocídio.

Seu destino se esgota em uma vida rudimentar.

A redentora piedade colonial.

Lançados aos centros metropolitanos os homens do atrasado Nordeste não conseguem situar-se no sistema de trabalho.

Os Sofrimento de CRISTO

A mendicância, tradição da piedade colonialista, alterna-se ao trabalho braçal e ao biscate.

BAHIA

MUSEU DE ARTE MODERNA

por

Lina Bo

Apresentando o Museu de Arte Moderna da Bahia tentamos situá-lo em sua concretização histórica. Assumindo a direção em 1960, ano de sua fundação, procuramos, por cinco anos uma 'necessidade' que tornasse justificavel sua atividade, numa terra cujas 'prioridades' poderiam não ser as da Arte.

A manifestação 'cultural' da fome é a violência.

O ex-voto-caveira: obsessão da morte por doenças curáveis.

A 'sêca' não é o verdadeiro 'grande inimigo'.

Só a alienação do misticismo os tira da passividade.

Nas Universidades, grandes 'latifúndios do saber' a sombra de Coimbra domina.

A Máquina-política: contrôle das posições de mando.

'O petrolio é nosso' é uma lembrança.

O mundo oficial da arte, gerador de exposições, festivais e bienais.

Gente rica, casas bonitas. Andando em automóveis de luxo.

Museum of Popular Art (Solar do Unhão)

Salvador
1963
(Foundation and museum direction, renovation project, curatorial project, and exhibition design)

In 1963, as the Castro Alves Theater underwent renovation, the Museum of Modern Art of Bahia moved to the Solar do Unhão in Salvador, its current location. At that time, MAM-BA shared the site with Bo Bardi's newly founded Museum of Popular Art. She restored the Solar, a seventeenth-century mill, in 1962, preserving the main features of the facade and the internal wood structure, with the roof beams and the *muxurabis* on the windows and doors, which she then painted red. Bo Bardi added a central staircase that links the Solar's two floors. Built with wood fittings, a reference to the ox-carts used in rural Brazil, the stairway, with its geometricized spiral shape, brings popular culture and vernacular building techniques into the museum. Education, with its potential for social transformation, was central to the Museum of Popular Art's program. At Unhão, the architect created areas dedicated to classes and workshops in order to lay the foundation for the emergence of an industrial design forged in popular culture. Another key aspect of the museum's program was the articulation of narratives of Brazilian and art history that countered dominant Euro-American approaches, contemplating other cultural and racial matrices with an exhibition series titled *Program of Brazilian Civilization.* Of the five proposed exhibitions—*Northeast*, *The Indian*, *Africa-Bahia*, *Europe*, and *The Iberian Peninsula*—only the first was realized. The military coup in 1964 forced the Museum of Popular Art's closure and Bo Bardi's abrupt return to São Paulo.—TT

FIG. 163
Solar do Unhão after Lina Bo Bardi's renovations, 1963

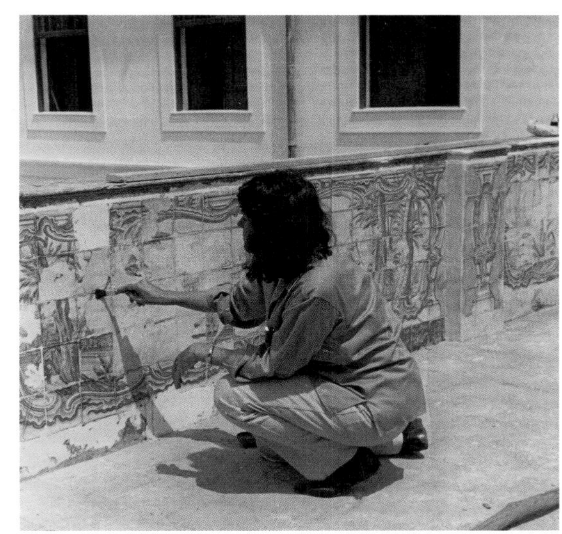

FIG. 164
Lina Bo Bardi on the Solar do Unhão access walkway, restoring seventeenth-century Dutch tiles, 1962

FIGS. 165–166
Interior and facade of the Solar do Unhão after renovation, 1963

FIG. 170 →
Interior view of the Solar do Unhão with wood ladder fittings designed by Lina Bo Bardi, 1963

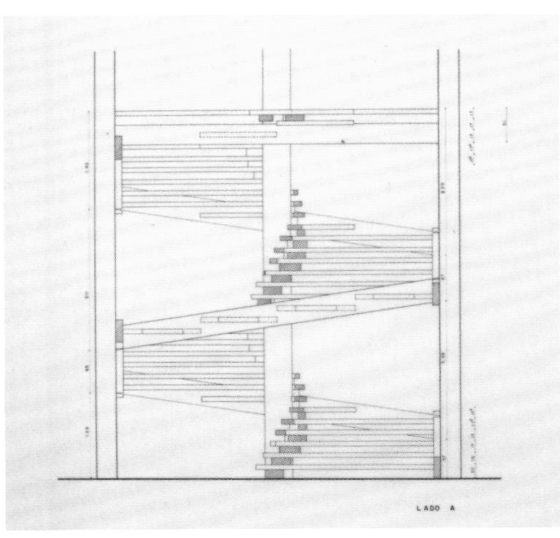

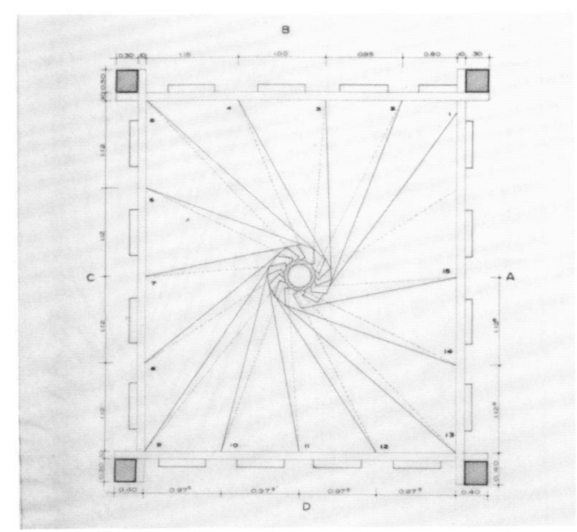

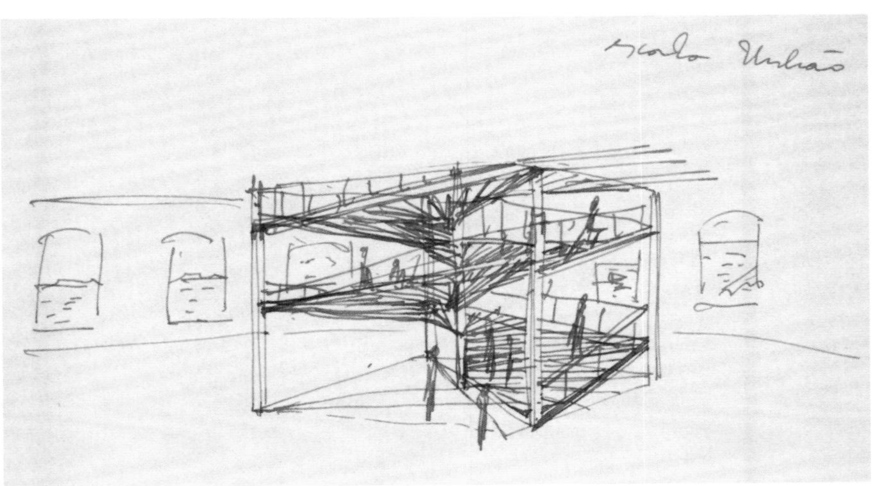

FIG. 167 ↑
Lina Bo Bardi, *Lateral elevation (side A), Solar do Unhão, Museum of Popular Art*, 1959. Marker and ink on parchment paper, 52 x 89.5 cm. Collection of the Instituto Bardi/Casa de Vidro, São Paulo

FIG. 168 ↗
Lina Bo Bardi, *Plans of steps 1 to 15, Solar do Unhão, Museum of Popular Art*, 1959. Ink on parchment paper, 54.5 x 101 cm. Collection of the Instituto Bardi/Casa de Vidro, São Paulo

FIG. 169 →
Lina Bo Bardi, *Perspective drawing of the staircase, Solar do Unhão, Museum of Popular Art*, 1959. Marker on offset paper, 33 x 22 cm. Collection of the Instituto Bardi/Casa de Vidro, São Paulo

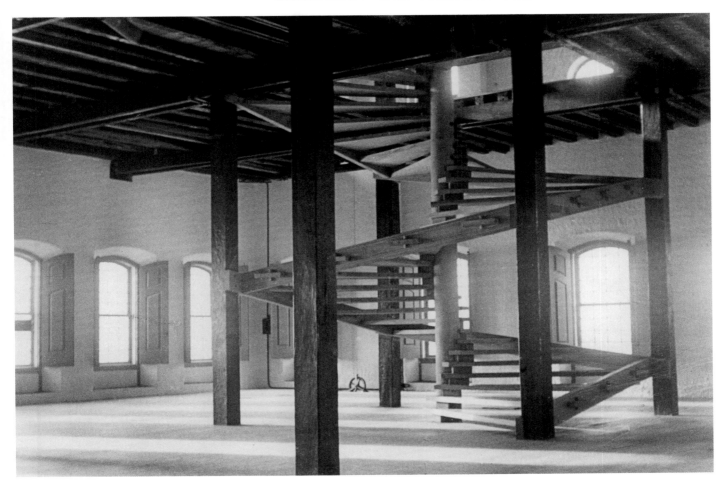

Marble Museum

Carrara, Italy
1963
(Unrealized project)

FIG. 172
Site where the Marble Museum would have been constructed, Monte Altissimo, Carrara, Italy, 1960s

Occupying a defunct quarry in Carrara, Italy, the proposed building for the Marble Museum was conceptualized as a counterpoint to the sublime landscape of Monte Altissimo. Bo Bardi envisioned three horizontal prisms of equal dimensions in a staggered alignment. Two of the buildings would feature roofs made entirely of a glass skylight; the third building would be covered by a garden, opening out to a view of the valley through a single glass facade. A small walkway crossing the valley would lead to square terraces on stilts, suggesting the precise cuts of cubic marble blocks. In Bo Bardi's words, this orthogonal rigidity conveyed a "message of human endeavor."—DJ

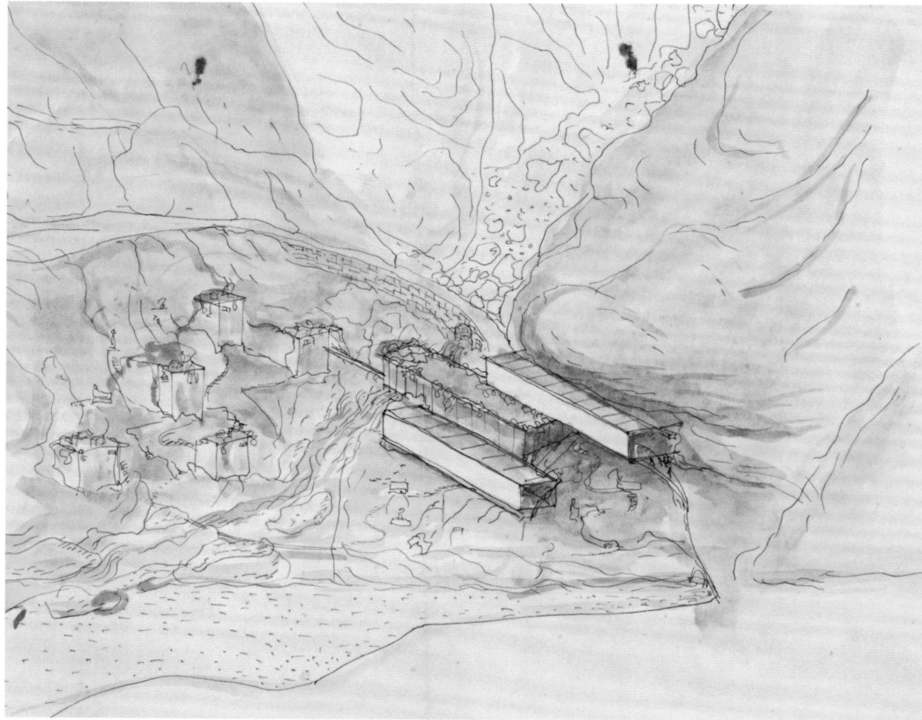

FIG. 171
Lina Bo Bardi, *Perspective of the lot*, 1963. Watercolor, ballpoint pen, and ink on offset paper, 33 x 46 cm. Collection of the Instituto Bardi/Casa de Vidro, São Paulo

Museum of the Butantã Institute

São Paulo
1965
(Unrealized project)

FIG. 173
Lina Bo Bardi, *Exhibition perspective*, 1964. Gouache, graphite, and ink on card stock, 28.5 x 46 cm. Collection of the Instituto Bardi/Casa de Vidro, São Paulo

The museum would have featured the work and collections of the Butantã Institute, a leading research center for the medical and biological sciences and a pioneer in the production of antivenom vaccines. Research on insects, spiders, and snakes would be didactically presented in a popular museum within an Art Nouveau pavilion amidst the institute's gardens. Wood walkways would traverse the existing building's patio and interior spaces, staged as dioramas—three-dimensional scenes representing different environments through lighting and background images—displaying different Brazilian biomes. The vegetation and the walkway would link inside and outside in a continuum reflecting the subject on exhibition: Brazilian nature.—DJ

FIG. 174
Lina Bo Bardi, *Perspective of the inner courtyard*, 1964. Gouache, graphite, and ink on card stock, 28.5 x 46 cm. Collection of the Instituto Bardi/Casa de Vidro, São Paulo

São Paulo Museum of Modern Art

Ibirapuera Park,
São Paulo
1982
With André Vainer and Marcelo Carvalho Ferraz (Renovation project)

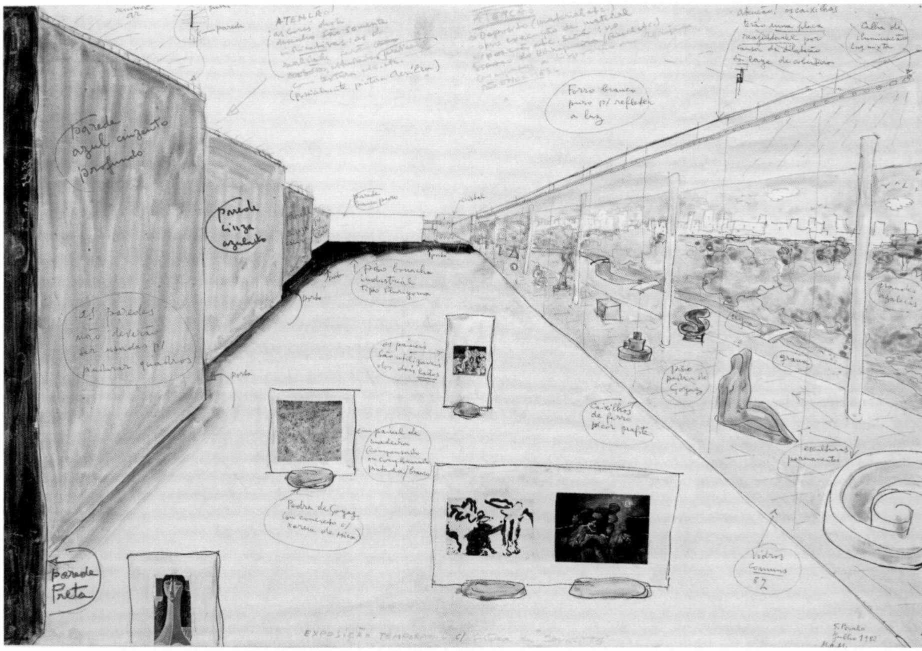

The São Paulo Museum of Modern Art (MAM) is a private institution founded by Ciccillo Matarazzo in 1948. Located in Ibirapuera Park, it maintains a collection of chiefly Brazilian modern and contemporary art. Lina Bo Bardi had worked in the same building where MAM is located today when, in 1959, she organized the *Bahia in Ibirapuera* exhibition in the pavilion built beneath the park's marquee (part of an architectural ensemble designed by Oscar Niemeyer in 1951–54). For MAM's 1982 renovation, Bo Bardi concentrated the administrative areas on the south side of the exhibition room behind staggered walls, which she had intended to be painted in gradient shades of blue and gray, though this was never executed. The exhibition room, in turn, is separated from the park by a floor-to-ceiling glass curtain, permitting visual communication between interior and exterior, a design Bo Bardi had previously proposed for the second-floor gallery at MASP on Avenida Paulista. In a preliminary proposal, the museum also had a small technical area and an auditorium. The entrance was originally designed to face the Biennial Foundation building, opposite of its current location. In the project's design, Bo Bardi implemented versions of MASP's glass easel throughout the gallery, with some modifications: the concrete block became a stone fragment, and the crystal easel was replaced by a wood plate, thereby losing its transparency.—TT

FIG. 175
Lina Bo Bardi, *Museum of Modern Art: perspective drawing of the interior*, 1982. Watercolor, ballpoint pen, marker, gouache, colored pencil, ink, and collage on card stock, 49.5 x 69.5 cm. Collection of the Instituto Bardi/ Casa de Vidro, São Paulo

FIG. 176
View of the main exhibition hall of the São Paulo Museum of Modern Art after renovation, 1980s

CURATORIAL PROJECTS AND EXHIBITION DESIGN

Crystal Easel Picture Gallery

MASP, São Paulo
1957–68
(Exhibition design)

FIG. 177
View of MASP's main gallery after the reinstallation of Lina Bo Bardi's glass easels, 2015

MASP's crystal easel picture gallery was designed to be in intimate dialogue with the building and its collection. The easel consists of a glass plate inserted into a concrete cube with a wood wedge and a rubber (or neoprene) blade, forming a self-supporting transparent panel of varying widths. The work's caption is affixed to the back, freeing the visitor's initial encounter with it from any historical contextualization. Bo Bardi sought to present artworks as the product of labor, desacrilizing them and expelling any churchlike ambience from the museum. Rough, raw, or industrial materials were employed in both the building's construction and the easels, without the use of scenographic devices, in a Brechtian strategy and in friction with the works of the European art collection, many of which featured elaborate frames. Nearly 200 easels can be installed in this space of 2,000 square meters, distributed in more or less organically organized rows, as if in a parade, or a forest of artworks. The result is an open gallery, fluid and transparent. While monumental, the space does not dominate the visitor, nor does the installation design impose a path to be traveled through a succession of rooms or a curatorial narrative. Removed from walls, the works become more accessible, and the visitor can establish a closer and more direct relationship with them. The glass easels were introduced at MASP during the inauguration of its building on Avenida Paulista in 1968. They were removed in 1996 and reinstated in 2015. Bo Bardi's system was influenced by Franco Albini's exhibitions at the Pinacoteca de Brera in Milan in the 1940s, and most recently inspired the Galerie du Temps at the Louvre-Lens, designed by Kazuyo Sejima and Ryue Nishizawa, which opened in 2012.—AP

FIG. 178
Lina Bo Bardi during the construction of MASP on Avenida Paulista next to a prototype of the glass easel with a reproduction of Vincent van Gogh's *The Schoolboy (The Postman's Son, Gamin au Képi)* (1888), 1960s

FIG. 181
Prototype of the glass easel with a reproduction of Vincent Van Gogh's *The Schoolboy (The Postman's Son, Gamin au Képi)* (1888) at MASP, Rua 7 de Abril, 1968

FIGS. 179–180
Views of the MASP collection including the front and back of the glass easel with Frans Hals' *Portrait of Andries van Hoorn* (1638), 1970s

FIG. 182
Lina Bo Bardi, *Installation perspective, São Paulo Museum of Art*, 1963. Watercolor, graphite, and collage on offset paper, 33 x 24 cm. Collection of the Instituto Bardi/Casa de Vidro, São Paulo

FIG. 183
View of the main gallery at MASP, Avenida Paulista, with Amedeo Modigliani's painting *Renée* (1917) displayed on the glass easel, 1970s

FIG. 184 ↑↑
Concrete base of an original glass easel, 2015

FIG. 185 ↑
Lina Bo Bardi, *Perspective*, 1957–68. Ballpoint pen and graphite on parchment paper, 23 x 30 cm. Collection of the Instituto Bardi/Casa de Vidro, São Paulo

FIG. 186 ↗
Lina Bo Bardi, *Cross section and front elevation*, 1957–68. Ballpoint pen and graphite on parchment paper, 33.5 x 59 cm. Collection of the Instituto Bardi/Casa de Vidro, São Paulo

FIG. 187 →
View of the main gallery at MASP, Avenida Paulista, 1970s

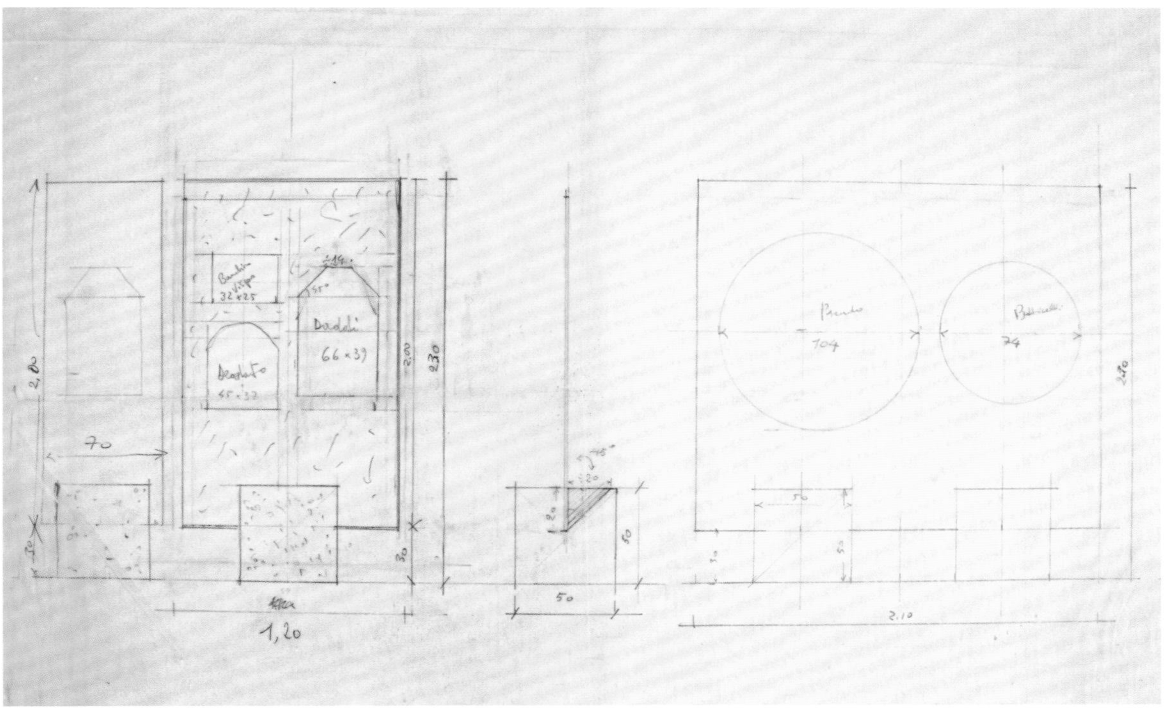
Daddi
66 × 39
70
1,20
50
104
74
2,10

Bahia in Ibirapuera

Ibirapuera Park,
São Paulo
1959
With Martim Gonçalves and the collaboration of Glauber Rocha
(Curatorial project and exhibition design)

The *Bahia in Ibirapuera* exhibition brought Lina Bo Bardi's travel, research, and teaching experience in Salvador into the center of the São Paulo art scene. Presented in the context of the 5th São Paulo Biennial, under the marquee of Ibirapuera Park, the exhibition pushed the boundaries between the popular and the erudite, calling into question the elitism and austerity of art spaces. On display were photographs of the architecture and customs of Bahia by Pierre Verger and Marcel Gautherot; everyday objects such as cages, nets, baskets, and weathervanes; religious items such as church embroidery, ex-votos, *terreiro* flags, and musical instruments used in *candomblé* and *capoeira* performances; eighteenth-century Baroque works; and woodcuts, paper and tin flowers, figureheads from boats on the São Francisco River, and other works by local artists, in fabric, ceramic, and wood. In addition, typical *vaqueiro* (cowboy), Bahian, and *orixá* costumes were presented on straw mannequins. Bo Bardi's installation design consisted of panels suspended over conical-shaped concrete bases adorned with shells (as if encrusted at sea), cube supports with iron rods, clothesline-type structures, siding, curtains, and walls with various cladding—in gold color or exposed brickwork, for example, depending on the object displayed. In this way, she developed modern exhibition design solutions while arranging items according to the principles of stage-set design. The exhibition featured Afro-Brazilian songs and percussion performances, as well as leaves scattered on the floor (in reference to *candomblé terreiros*), which also produced sound as visitors moved through the space, complementing the overall synesthetic, immersive, and ritualistic experience.—GG

FIG. 188
View of the exhibition *Bahia in Ibirapuera*, 1959

FIG. 189
Arrival in São Paulo of the crates containing the works to be exhibited in *Bahia in Ibirapuera*, 1959

FIG. 190
Lina Bo Bardi, *Presentation drawing: general and partial perspectives of the installations, Bahia in Ibirapuera*, 1959. Watercolor, ballpoint pen, graphite, ink, and metallic paint on card stock, 50.5 x 70.5 cm. Collection of the Instituto Bardi/ Casa de Vidro, São Paulo

FIG. 191
View of *Bahia in Ibirapuera*, 1959

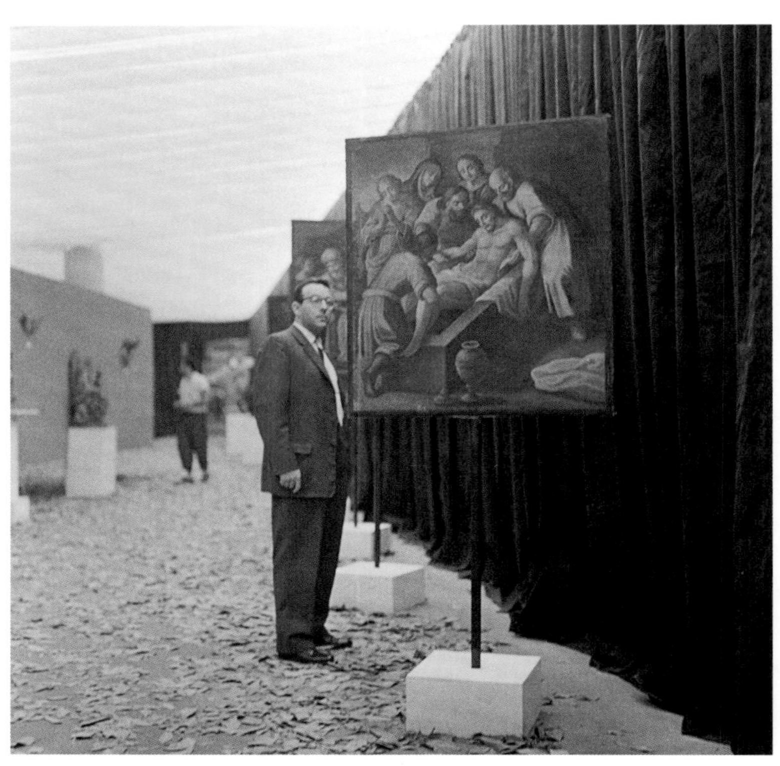

FIGS. 192–193
Views of *Bahia in Ibirapuera*, 1959

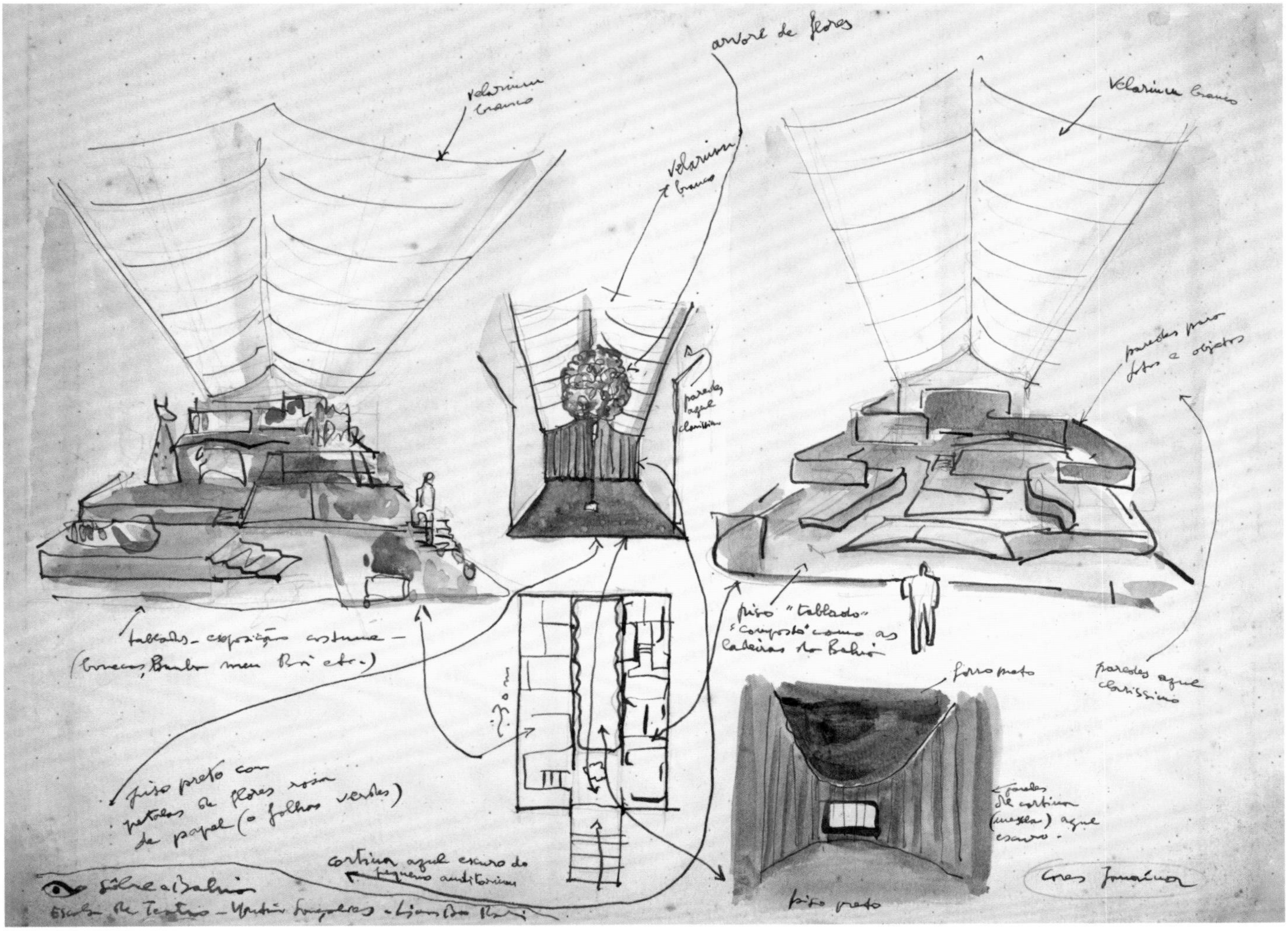

FIG. 194
Lina Bo Bardi, *Presentation drawing of the plan and partial perspectives of installations, Bahia in Ibirapuera*, 1959. Watercolor, graphite, and ink on canson paper, 24.5 x 32 cm. Collection of the Instituto Bardi/ Casa de Vidro, São Paulo

FIG. 195
Lina Bo Bardi cleaning a figurehead during the installation of the exhibition *Bahia in Ibirapuera*, 1959

FIG. 196
Poster for *Bahia in Ibirapuera*, 1959

FIGS. 197–198
Views of *Bahia in Ibirapuera*, 1959

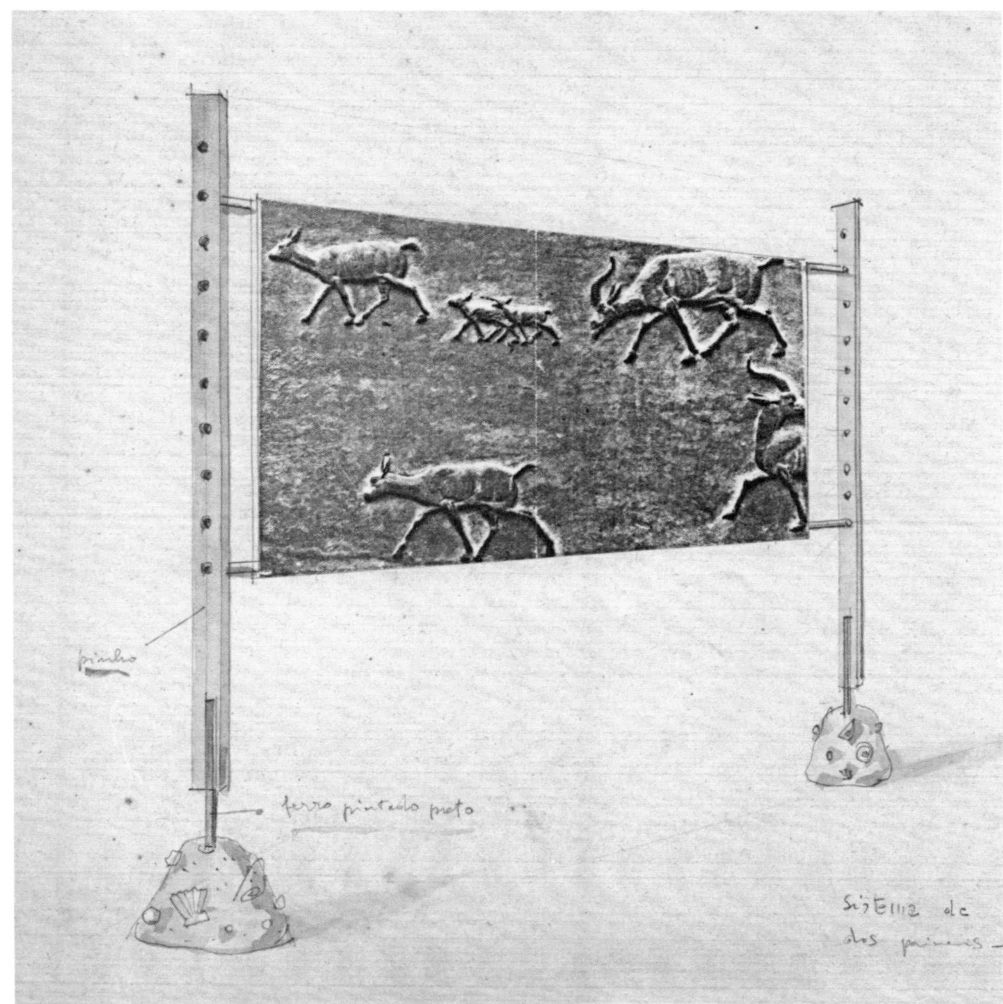

FIG. 199
Lina Bo Bardi, *Bahia in Ibirapuera: perspective*, 1959. Watercolor, graphite, collage, and print on card stock and offset paper, 28 x 37.5 cm. Collection of the Instituto Bardi/ Casa de Vidro, São Paulo

FIGS. 200–201
Views of *Bahia in Ibirapuera*, 1959

Northeast

Museum of Popular Art, Solar do Unhão, Salvador
1963
(Curatorial project and exhibition design)

The inauguration of the Museum of Popular Art at Solar do Unhão in 1963 coincided with the iconic exhibition *Northeast.* The show was divided into two sections, one dedicated to a panorama of northeastern artists, and the other to popular culture, with a large selection of objects including ex-votos, figureheads, machinery, fabrics, kitchen appliances, and Afro-Brazilian religious items, the result of Lina Bo Bardi's research in the Northeast of Brazil as well as her exhibition *Bahia in Ibirapuera* (1959). The northeastern artists' exhibition was arranged on detached wall displays, employing the vertical structures of MASP on Rua 7 de Abril, but replacing the metal tubing with wood rafters, in a clear shift from industrial to vernacular materials. The objects in the popular culture section were presented in a radical format, emulating the displays of street markets in the Northeast, with shelves and boards of raw wood. The figureheads received their own specific display, a kind of easel for sculptures, made up of the same concrete block as the MASP glass easels, but with an added steel rebar to support the pieces, providing a certain lightness to the exhibition. A fundamental aspect of *Northeast* was that it did not compromise with the paternalistic, segregationist, and antiquated view of popular art that permeated traditional approaches to Brazilian popular culture. Bo Bardi sought to make visible and to highlight the value of noncanonical productions from regions beyond the urban centers dominated by European cultural taste, as pointed out in her essay in the show's brochure: "This exhibition is an accusation. An accusation of a world that does not want to renounce the human condition despite oblivion and indifference. It is not a humble accusation [but] shows the desperate effort to produce culture in the face of the degrading conditions imposed by men."—TT

FIG. 202
Poster for the exhibition *Northeast*, 1963

FIGS. 203–204
Views of *Northeast*, 1963

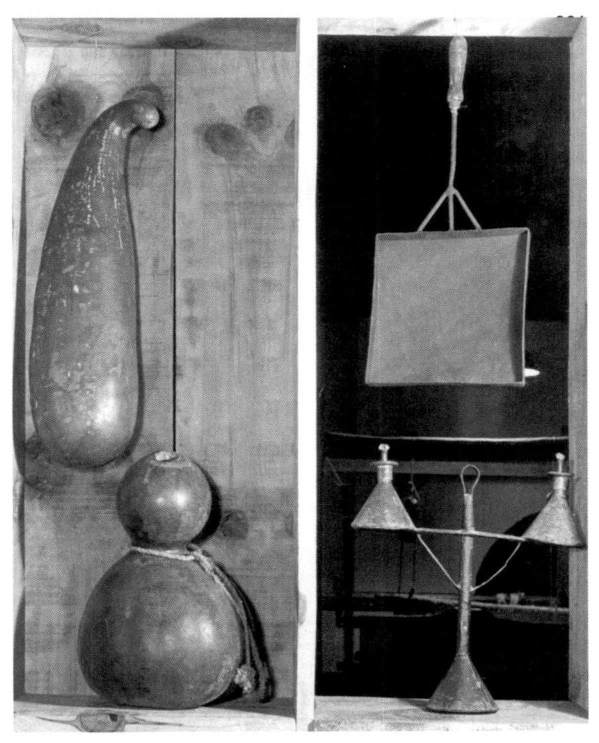

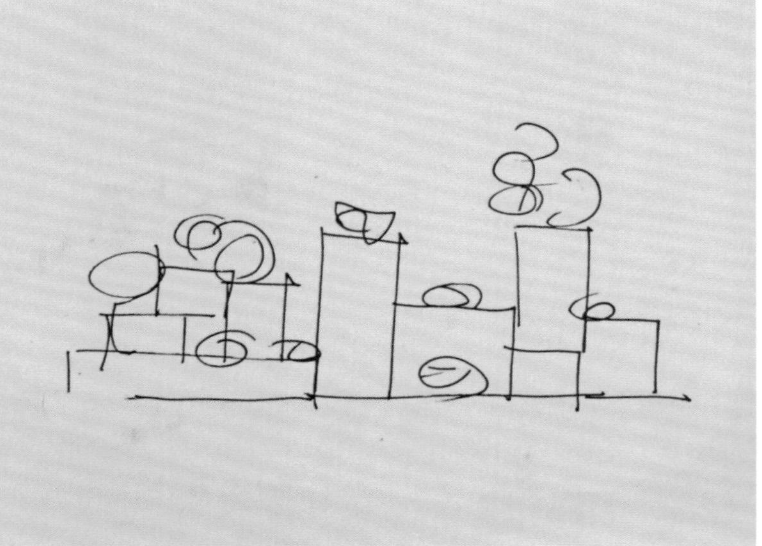

FIGS. 205–206
Lina Bo Bardi, *Northeast: layout of objects*, 1963. Ballpoint pen and collage on offset paper, 31.5 x 21.5 cm. Collection of the Instituto Bardi/Casa de Vidro, São Paulo

FIGS. 207–209
Views of *Northeast*, 1963

FIGS. 210–211
Views of *Northeast*,
1963

FIGS. 212–213
Lina Bo Bardi, *Northeast: layout of objects*, 1963. Ballpoint pen and collage on offset paper, 31.5 x 21.5 cm. Collection of the Instituto Bardi/Casa de Vidro, São Paulo

FIG. 214
View of *Northeast*, 1963

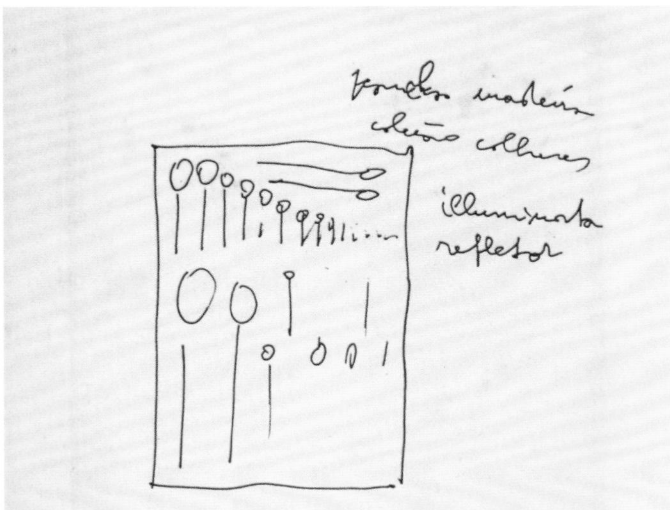

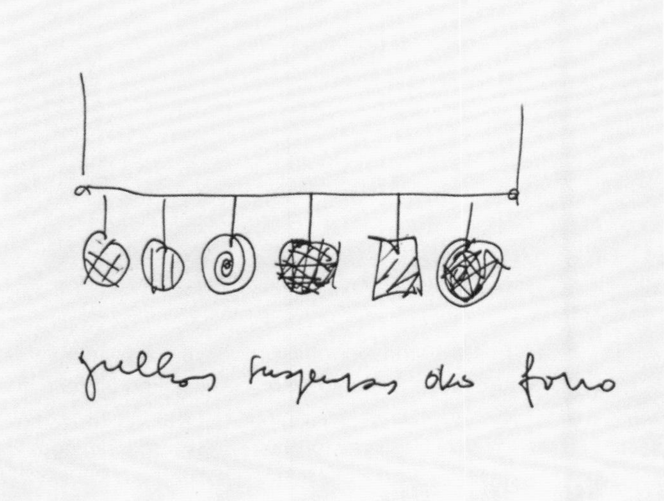

Northeast

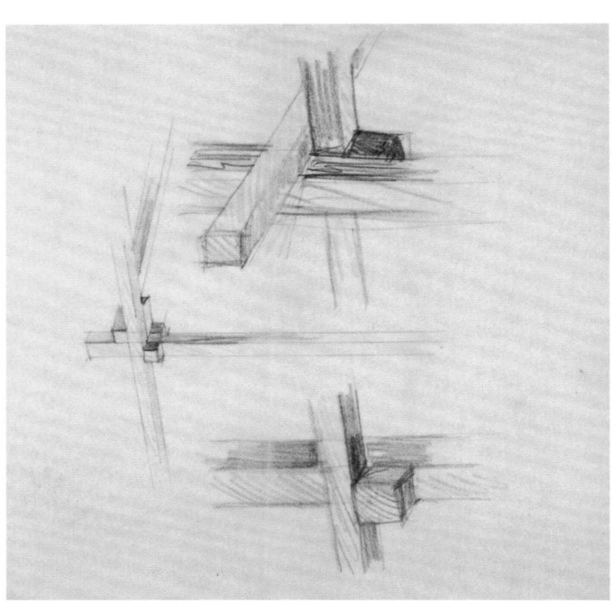

Galleria Nazionale d'Arte Moderna, Rome
1965
(Curatorial project and exhibition design)

In 1965, the *Northeast* exhibition, first shown in Salvador, was redesigned by Lina Bo Bardi for the Galleria Nazionale d'Arte Moderna in Rome. The show in Italy represents a traumatic episode, because although the architect organized it specifically for a museum in her hometown, it was dismantled shortly before opening on the orders of the Brazilian embassy in the city. The following day, architect Bruno Zevi penned a biting response to the arrogant action in a now-legendary article in *L'Espresso* titled "L'arte dei poveri fa paura ai generali" (The Art of the Poor Frightens the Generals). It was supposed that objects made by the hand of the (poor) Brazilian people would not properly convey, to European eyes, the image of a modern, developing, "forward" country, to which the nascent military regime aspired. In photographs of the exhibition being assembled, we can see various objects included in the Salvador version, such as figureheads, fabrics, and ex-votos, that four years later would reappear in *The Hand of the Brazilian People* at MASP. The installation frame of wood slats with openings at the top departs from the original exhibition design at the Solar do Unhão, in which the objects were presented on displays that dialogued with the aesthetics and functionality of popular street markets. In Rome, the assemblage of objects was less dense and seems to have been composed for a more traditional museum setting, but the display carries something of the popular in its wood fittings, a reference to Brazilian vernacular construction techniques.—AP/TT

FIG. 215
Lina Bo Bardi, *Elevation of installation component*, 1965. Graphite and colored pencil on parchment paper, 32.5 x 24 cm. Collection of the Instituto Bardi/Casa de Vidro, São Paulo

FIG. 216
View of the installation of *Northeast* in Rome, 1965

FIG. 217
Lina Bo Bardi, *Elevation: layout of objects*, 1965. Graphite and colored pencil on parchment paper, 24 x 32.5 cm. Collection of the Instituto Bardi/Casa de Vidro, São Paulo

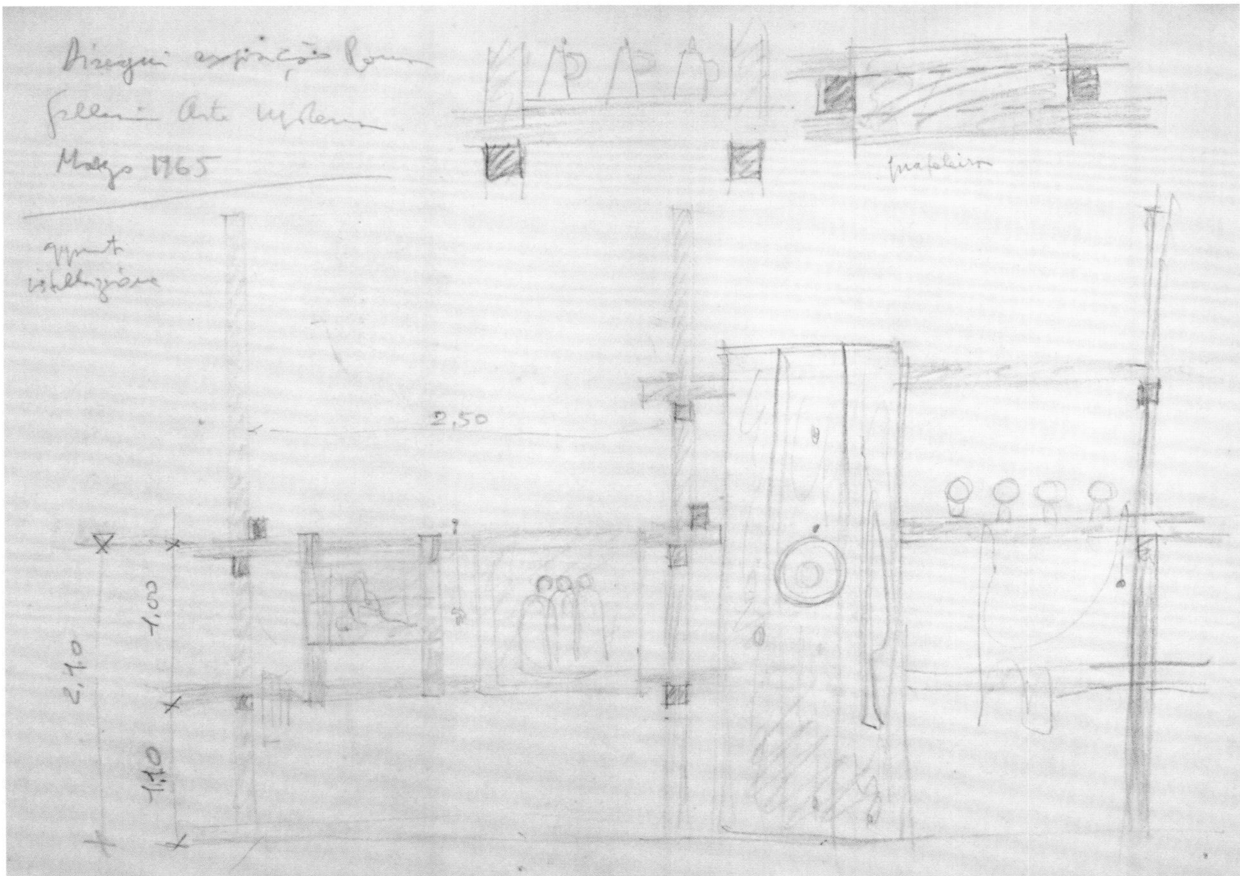

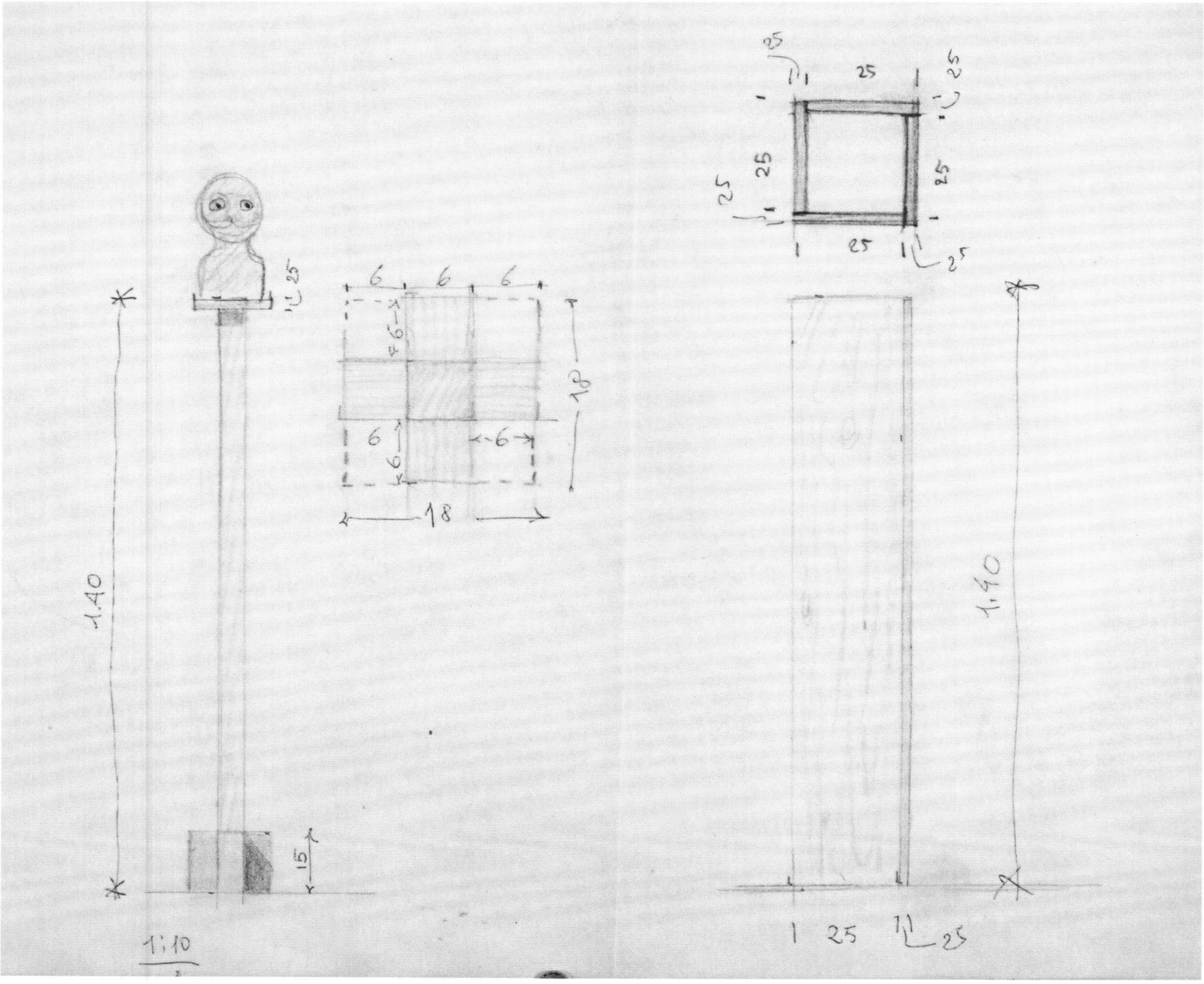

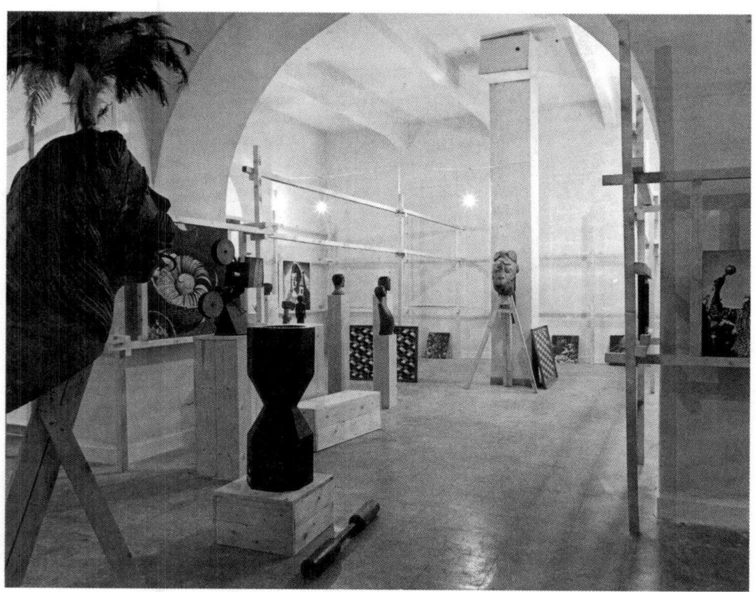

FIG. 218
Lina Bo Bardi, *Elevation: layout of objects*, 1965. Graphite and colored pencil on parchment paper, 24 x 32.5 cm. Collection of the Instituto Bardi/Casa de Vidro, São Paulo

FIG. 219
View of the installation of *Northeast* in Rome, 1965

FIGS. 220–221
Views of the installation of *Northeast* in Rome, 1965

The Hand of the Brazilian People

MASP, São Paulo
1969
With the collaboration of Glauber Rocha, Martim Gonçalves, and Pietro Maria Bardi
(Curatorial project and exhibition design)

The Hand of the Brazilian People, the temporary exhibition that inaugurated MASP's new building on Avenida Paulista on April 7, 1969, presented a vast panorama of Brazil's rich material culture—nearly 1,000 objects, including figureheads, ex-votos, fabric, clothing, furniture, tools, utensils, machinery, musical instruments, ornaments, toys, religious items, paintings, and sculptures. One of the most striking features of the exhibition was that it established dialogues and frictions, through juxtapositions and contrasts, between a great variety and quantity of objects and typologies that traditionally remained outside the museum's purview, questioning and clouding hierarchical and territorial demarcations between art and artifact. Bo Bardi conceived of the show in conjunction with filmmaker Glauber Rocha, theater director Martim Gonçalves, and museum director Pietro Maria Bardi, who provided it with its title. It forms part of two exhibition histories: those organized by Bo Bardi, on the one hand, and those at MASP, on the other, constituting an emblematic intersection of the two. It is the museum's most important temporary exhibition (next to its easel-based picture gallery) and is effectively a landmark in the history of exhibitions in the 1960s.—AP

FIG. 222
View of *The Hand of the Brazilian People*, 1969

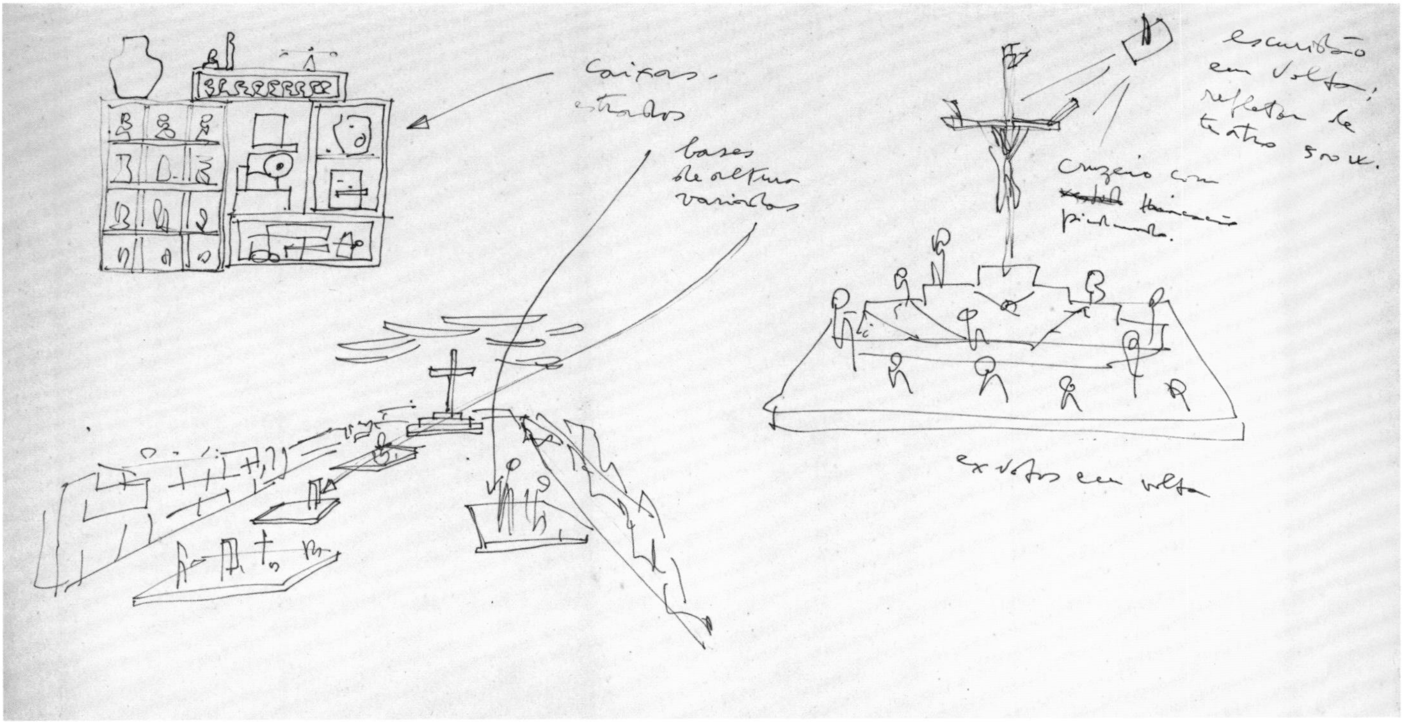

FIG. 223
Lina Bo Bardi, *Perspectives of bases with objects, The Hand of the Brazilian People*, 1969. Marker and collage on card stock, 21 x 37.5 cm. Collection of the Instituto Bardi/Casa de Vidro, São Paulo

FIG. 224
View of *The Hand of the Brazilian People*, 1969

FIGS. 225–228
Views of *The Hand of the Brazilian People*, 1969

FIGS. 229–232
Views of *The Hand of the Brazilian People*, 1969

One Hundred Portinari Masterpieces

MASP, São Paulo
1970
(Exhibition design)

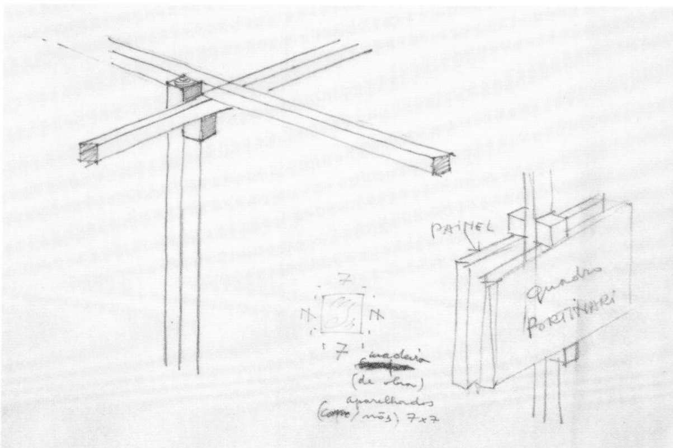

The exhibition *One Hundred Portinari Masterpieces*, organized by Pietro Maria Bardi, with Lina Bo Bardi's exhibition design, was the third by Candido Portinari to be held at MASP since the museum's inauguration in 1947. The retrospective brought together paintings and poems by the artist, a foundational figure in Brazilian modernism, with portraits and compositions representing types and themes of the popular world, labor, and the countryside. Installing Portinari's canvases in MASP's main gallery atop the crystal easels, Bo Bardi opted for a wood-paneled display system that incorporated vernacular construction techniques. The works, affixed to the pillars of the structure, were dispersed throughout the gallery between open spaces, similar to Bo Bardi's arrangement of the crystal easels, reproducing the lightness and transparency of the exhibition space on the museum's second floor. Her scheme for public circulation around the exhibition was an open course threading through the overall checkerboard layout, creating a maze through the phases and periods of the artist's work. Coffee branches were placed at the top of the pillars, above each painting; this recurring motif in Portinari's work thus moved from the canvas into the observer's immediate environment. The self-supporting wood system designed by the architect was rebuilt with some adjustments for MASP's *Popular Portinari* exhibition in 2016.—VM

FIG. 233
View of the exhibition *One Hundred Portinari Masterpieces* on MASP's first floor, 1970

FIG. 234
Lina Bo Bardi, *Installation component: artwork support panel*, 1970. Marker and graphite on parchment paper, 33 x 48 cm. Collection of the Instituto Bardi/Casa de Vidro, São Paulo

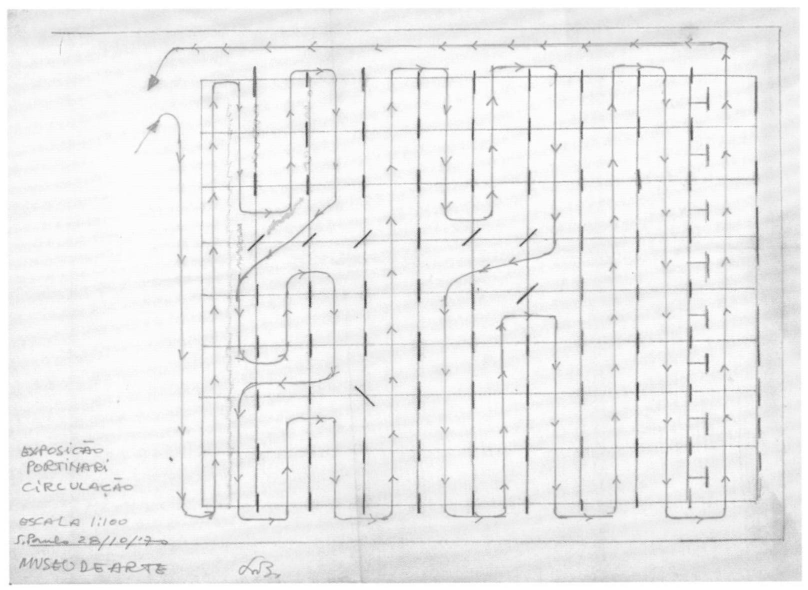

FIG. 235
Lina Bo Bardi, *Plan of the circulation scheme*, 1970. Marker, graphite, and colored pencil on parchment paper, 32.5 x 48 cm. Collection of the Instituto Bardi/Casa de Vidro, São Paulo

FIG. 236
View of *One Hundred Portinari Masterpieces* on MASP's first floor, 1970

Popular Art Crates

Sesc, São Paulo
1978
(Curatorial project and exhibition design)

Formulated during the construction of Sesc Pompeia, and designed to be replicated in other Sesc units, the Caixotes de Arte Popular—Popular Art Crates—are small galleries for the exhibition and sale of objects. The cube structure, which resembles a container, is made of polished wood slats and is slightly raised from the floor. An external column with a pyramidal base of rough wood, counterweighted with cobblestones, suspends a lamp that illuminates the interior space, which is arranged in shelves for objects of different sizes. These included baskets, fabrics, ceramics, toys, and musical instruments—utilitarian and decorative pieces reflecting popular uses and customs and acquired in various regions of Brazil. The selection of materials derived from Bo Bardi's research in Bahia in the 1950s and 1960s, as well as her other exhibition projects, namely *Northeast* (Museum of Popular Art, Salvador, 1963) and *The Hand of the Brazilian People* (MASP, São Paulo, 1969), and was augmented by the additional expeditions of Sesc employees. Merging the functions of exhibition and sale, the crates allow for the creation of sustainable networks of financing for artisanal production, as well as for the circulation of these objects in urban centers, fulfilling Bo Bardi's desire to promote Brazilian modern and industrial design developed and inspired by popular methods. The project also represents a specific genre in Bo Bardi's career: miniature, moveable, and itinerant exhibition design prototypes, reminiscent of Marcel Duchamp's *Boîte-en-valise* (1935–41), for example—in this case, a microcosm combining the spatial layout of open-air street markets and the shelves of a supermarket.—GG

FIG. 237
Interior view of a Popular Art Crate, 1978

FIG. 238
Exterior view of a Popular Art Crate, 1978

FIG. 239
Interior view of a Popular Art Crate, 1978

Countryfolk, Rustics: Wattle-and-Daub

Sesc Pompeia,
São Paulo
1984
With Gláucia Amaral and the collaboration of Marcelo Carvalho Ferraz and Marcelo Suzuki (Curatorial project and exhibition design)

Countryfolk, Rustics: Wattle-and-Daub was among the exhibitions Lina Bo Bardi organized at Sesc Pompeia, a cultural center she also designed, in addition to *Design in Brazil: History and Reality* (1982), *A Thousand Toys for the Brazilian Child* (1982), and *Entr'acte for Children* (1985). The show's title refers to countryfolk (*caipiras*) and rustics (*capiaus*), popular names for peasants who live in wattle-and-daub housing, a traditional building system that utilizes overlapping slats covered with clay. The exhibition documented rural cultures from a critical perspective, denouncing the disappearance of their ways of life and means of production. Bo Bardi's drawing, which illustrated the poster and served as the basis for the exhibition catalogue's cover, can be read simultaneously as the eye of a chicken, a dartboard, and a straw hat. A "grove of wood masts" was installed at the entrance to the exhibition shed. Each mast—a common element in popular festivities in the interior of Brazil—was hand-painted with symbols alluding to the exhibition's critical narratives, such as "Above and Below the Equator," "Caramuru," and "Homage to Marshal Rondon." In the background, rural architectural structures were crafted in wood, presented together with working tools, creating an integrated environment that referred to their original contexts. As in the exhibitions *Bahia in Ibirapuera* (1959), *Northeast* (1965), and *The Hand of the Brazilian People* (1969), Bo Bardi avoided the paternalistic perspective of folklore. One of the drawings for the exhibition reads: "Attention! The objects gathered here integrate with their environments and are not exhibited as folkloric pieces!"—VM

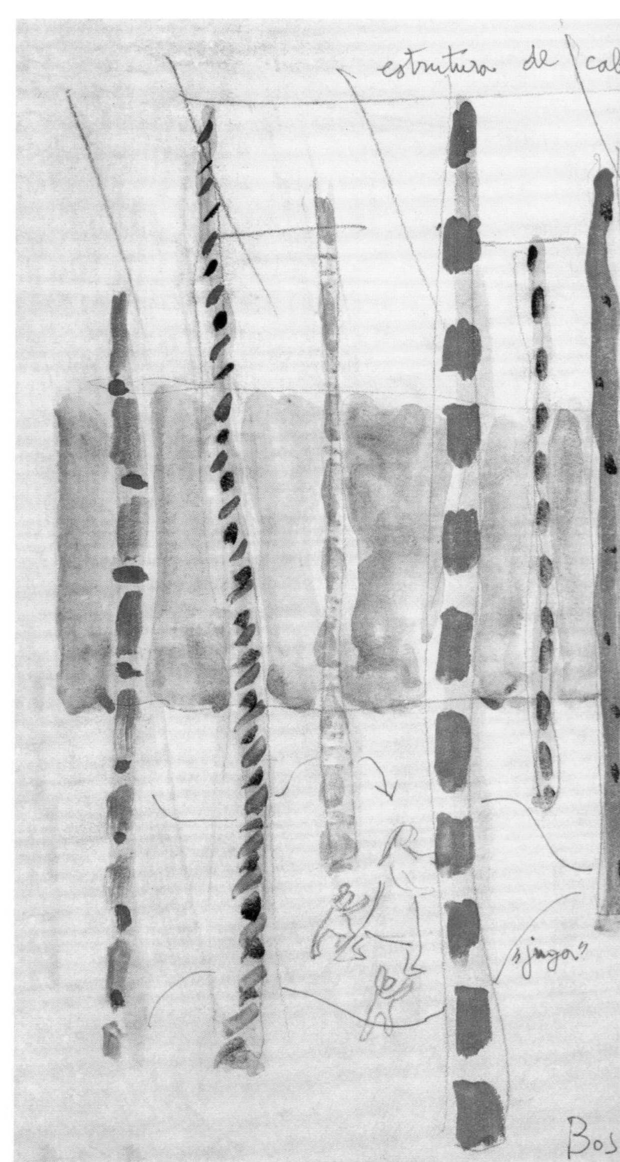

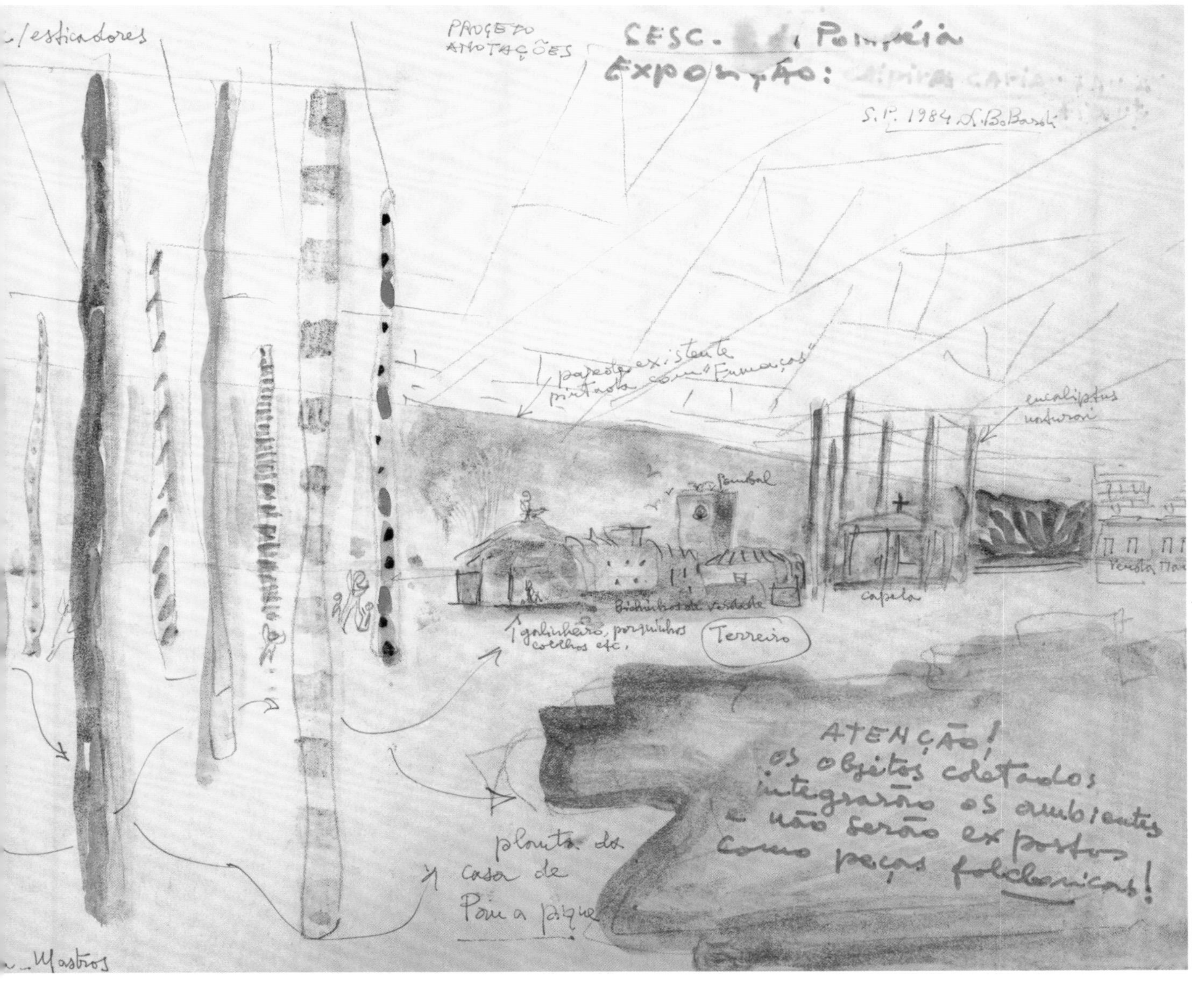

FIG. 240
Lina Bo Bardi, *Perspective drawing: mastwood forest and large wall*, 1984. Watercolor, marker, gouache, and graphite on eggshell finished paper, 33 x 59 cm. Collection of the Instituto Bardi/Casa de Vidro, São Paulo

FIG. 241
Brochure for the exhibition *Country-folk, Rustics: Wattle-and-Daub*, 1984

FIG. 242
Lina Bo Bardi, *Elevation*, 1984. Ballpoint pen, marker, and graphite on offset paper, 21.5 x 31.5 cm. Collection of the Instituto Bardi/Casa de Vidro, São Paulo

FIG. 243
Lina Bo Bardi, *Illustration for poster: chicken eye*, 1984. Ballpoint pen, gouache, and graphite on card stock, 35 x 25 cm. Collection of the Instituto Bardi/Casa de Vidro, São Paulo

FIG. 244
View of *Countryfolk, Rustics: Wattle-and-Daub*, 1984

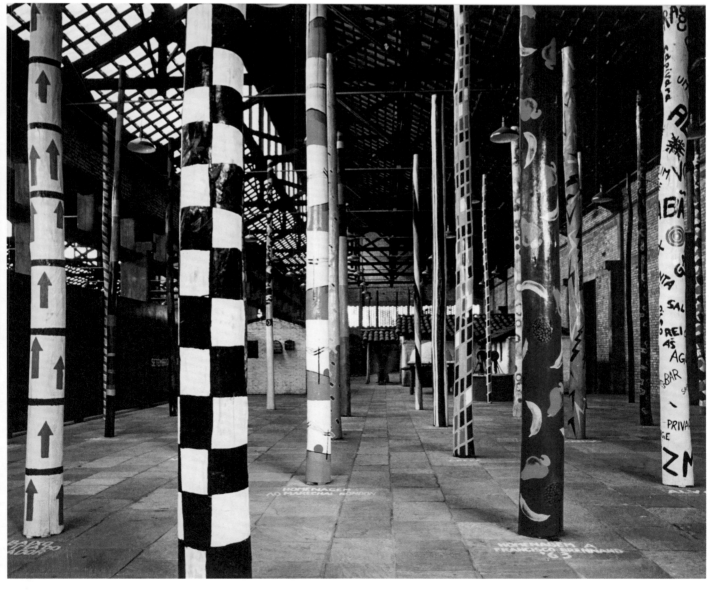

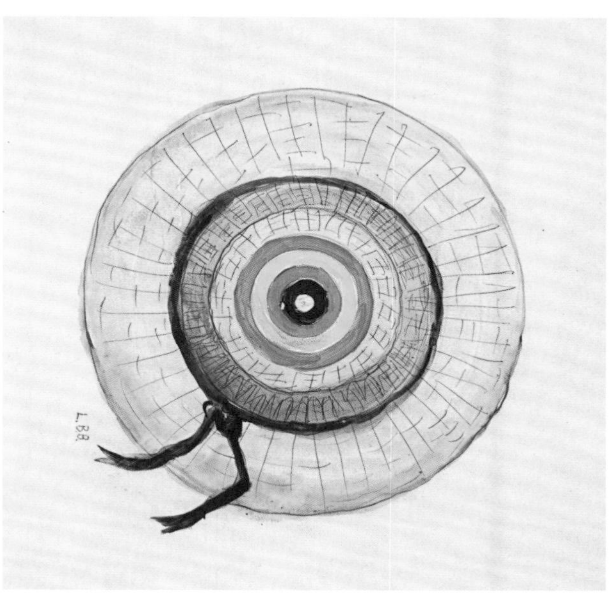

Black Africa

MASP, São Paulo
1988
With Pierre Verger
(Curatorial project and exhibition design)

Black Africa, a project conceived by Lina Bo Bardi and Pierre Verger beginning in 1959, rolled out in two stages: the first in Salvador, inaugurating the Benin House in Bahia, and the second in São Paulo, at MASP, to commemorate the centenary of Lei Áurea (the "Golden Law," which abolished slavery in Brazil). The exhibition focused on reciprocal influences between Africa and Brazil and featured objects of African art on loan from the Musée de l'Homme and the Musée National des Arts d'Afrique et d'Océanie, in Paris, among other collections. The works included statuettes, masks, games, and other objects of black communities in Sub-Saharan Africa. The catalogue cover, with graphic design by Bo Bardi, reproduces a *nyi-kar-yi*, a "ring of silence" produced by the Senufo of northwestern Côte d'Ivoire. Bo Bardi structured the exhibition space in MASP's second basement gallery with a modular system of display cases that formed two concentric circles, thus creating a circular route around the objects that emulates African spaces of worship. The exhibition also included interlaced palm fronds from Salvador and long strips of African fabrics attached to the railing of the mezzanine. Thus Bo Bardi brought to the museum space elements that pointed up the works' contexts, a technique she had previously utilized, for example, in *Bahia in Ibirapuera* (1959), with eucalyptus leaves covering the floor, and in *One Hundred Portinari Masterpieces* (1970), with coffee plants arranged at the top of the displays.—VM

FIG. 245
Lina Bo Bardi and Pierre Verger at the Glass House, 1987

FIG. 248 →
View of the *Black Africa* exhibition at MASP, second basement level, 1988

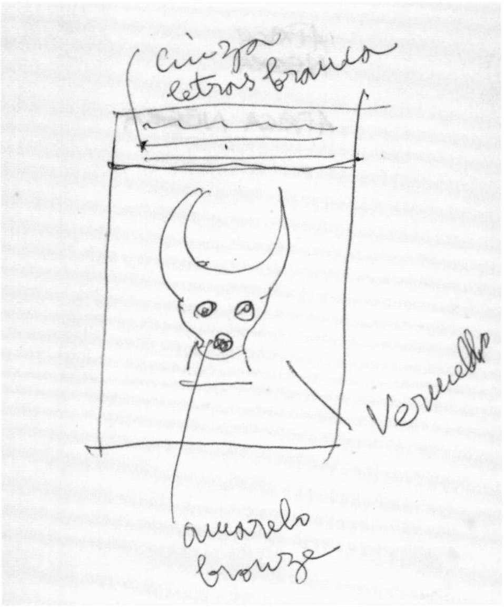

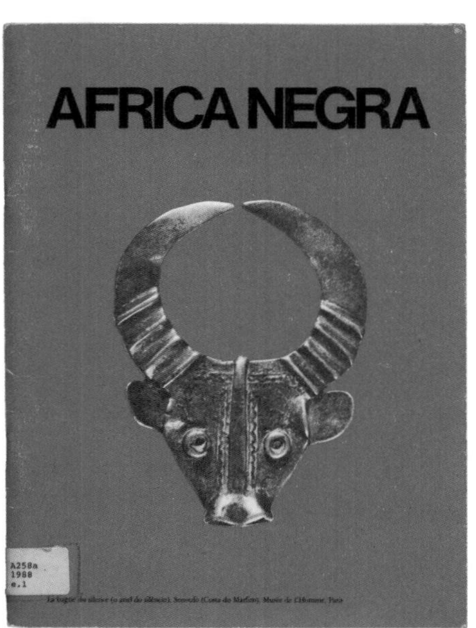

FIG. 246
Lina Bo Bardi, *Study for the catalogue layout of the Black Africa exhibition*, 1988. Ballpoint pen on parchment paper, 15 x 12 cm. MASP

FIG. 247
Cover of the *Black Africa* catalogue, 1988

FROM GLASS HOUSE TO HUT

FIG. 249
Lina Bo Bardi on the staircase of the Glass House, 1952

INSIDE OUT

FIG. 250
View of the Glass House, 1951

FIG. 251
View of the "Casinha" (Little House), Lina Bo Bardi's studio constructed on the grounds of the Glass House, 1986

Only two years after her departure from Italy to Brazil in 1946, the intrepid journalist, editor, designer, and architect Lina Bo Bardi was already fleshing out ideas and experiences through projects that would require a merging of her multiple interests and skills. She was by now working for Assis Chateaubriand, a major businessman and politician with a very public life, on exhibitions and interior renovation projects in the museum he created—Museu de Arte de São Paulo (MASP) on Rua 7 de Abril—alongside her husband Pietro Maria Bardi, who was the museum's founding director. Hosted inside the headquarters of Diários Associados, a media company owned by Chateaubriand, this nascent museum with big ambitions presented exhibitions from a growing collection of European art among other shows with a focus on modernist production, such as those of Le Corbusier and Max Bill (fig. 98), both in 1951.

At the museum on Rua 7 de Abril (figs. 82–107), Bo Bardi worked primarily indoors at an almost domestic scale in rooms with wood floors that were not designed to display art. Here she created simple yet innovative display systems for mostly European paintings to be seen by a growing audience of museumgoers. During this time, her practice as an architect was mainly channeled through the design of creative structural mechanisms of display that revealed how they were assembled. Modular walls with inbuilt hanging systems allowed the art to be easily placed at any desired height, and chalkboard-like panels held not only artworks but also their provenance. These innovations demonstrate the architect's interest in creating a unique space that was almost custom-made for the new visitor. Her practice as an editor and journalist also took a different turn now that it was spatialized through exhibitions that were meant to cultivate a new audience; for example, Bo Bardi's strategy of inserting extended informative labels within a space that also used domestic tropes such as curtains and plants sought to be both educational and welcoming.

Other interior design projects kept Bo Bardi busy during her first years in Brazil, and while the scope and scale of her work was mostly for interior spaces, she quickly became well-versed in the broader design language and social dynamics of São Paulo. Only five years after her arrival, she was naturalized as a Brazilian citizen and moved into a new residence with her husband, where they would live until the end of their lives. Designed by Bo Bardi and called the Glass House (figs. 264–281), this home was the first major project she would oversee from early stages as initial sketches into a self-standing building. The Glass House was sited on the top of a hill in what was then the periphery of São Paulo (fig. 250), but which quickly developed into the high-end neighborhood of Morumbi.

This house looked perhaps more like an exhibition space than the museum on which she had been working in the years prior. Floating above the hilltop of Morumbi over slim pilotis, the Maison Dom-Ino–style Glass House followed the lines of the so-called International Style architecture that was predominant in Europe prior to Bo Bardi's arrival in Brazil. It was here that she turned into real form many of the ideas she had been developing over the course of her years as an architect and editor in Italy. The house is now almost invisible from a distance because of its luscious surrounding vegetation, of which much was planted by Bo Bardi herself. In its early years, however, it appeared prominently as a viewing platform cantilevered off the hill with a glass filter presenting the city as an object of study. But of course, the inverse also happened: the house became a space of exhibition—its large glass panes resembled a vitrine, where modern domesticity could be performed for a viewing audience. It could be argued that this unlikely display box followed the pedagogical principle that Bo Bardi aimed to achieve in her museum practices, where new audiences would learn through observation and interaction.

Shortly after the Bardis moved into the house—and unlike many of the other glass houses of its time, from the Farnsworth House by Mies van der Rohe (1945–51) to the Glass House by Philip Johnson (1945–49)—it soon began to fill up with colorful objects representative of Brazil's rich cultural diversity, from small-scale ex-votos to full-size saints. It was no longer just a space where the couple would perform their modern domesticity alongside exclusively designed objects, but also a space in which Bo Bardi would experiment with form, meaning, and diverse cultural histories—all from the inside of what was tantamount to a living vitrine.

In 1950, while working on the house, Bo Bardi also designed the Vitrine of Forms (fig. 106) for MASP. This long horizontal glass case created two distinct spaces in the museum's gallery and was used to display a wide range of objects. Conceptualized as a sort of laboratory or evidence room, it imposed no logic or hierarchy on the objects, which ranged from designed industrial pieces such as an Olivetti typewriter to found organic wood pieces and crafted objects from across Brazil. This radical *dispositif* stripped down the meaning of the objects on display to heighten their formal qualities while simultaneously highlighting their diverse cultural meanings. Although it was meant as an apparatus that would allow the viewer to objectively see a work, in its process it also achieved something quite the opposite, much like the Glass House.

The alignment, therefore, between the way Bo Bardi was thinking of her practice within the space of a museum and the domestic setting in which she lived—one often associated aesthetically with the International Style—reveals a house that operated and performed as much (if not more) like a museological vitrine as a home.

In 1951, the year she became Brazilian and moved into her new home, Bo Bardi published an article titled "Vitrines" in her magazine *Habitat*, which was produced as an extension of MASP and was a major conceptual outlet for the exploration and development of many of her ideas. In this brief piece, she writes that "Window displays are an immediate reflection, a quick 'tell' of a city's personality, and not just of its outward traits, but its deepest character."[1] She also connects vitrines to the market and to theories of consumption in which demand is created through desire. But she continues by saying:

> However, the city is a public space, a great exhibition space, a museum, an open book offering all kinds of subtle readings, and anyone who has a shop, a window display, or any hole-in-the-wall closed in with glass, and seeks to exhibit something in that display, who wants to play a "public" role in the city, takes up a moral responsibility, a responsibility which requires that they stop ignoring the fact that "their" window display might help to shape the taste of city-dwellers, help to shape the face of the city and reveal something of its essence.[2]

There is something quite telling about the way that Bo Bardi frames the meaning and social role of vitrines and the use of glass in her architectural practice. While glass is understood by many as a clinical modern material—one that is somehow devoid of meaning, perhaps, or associated with

1. Lina Bo Bardi, "Vitrinas," *Habitat*, no. 5 (October–December 1951): 60–61.

2. Ibid.

transparency—she used it instead as a screen on which her larger pedagogical ambitions were enacted. Rather than bringing the city or nature indoors, glass for Bo Bardi was used to share the inside out. Her glass boxes, whether at the scale of a museum vitrine or a house, became a monitor through which a new type of life was imagined, performed, and broadcast—one where multiple cultures coexisted and learned from each other.

Bo Bardi began design work for the new premises of MASP in 1957 (figs. 116–150), although construction didn't start until 1966 and concluded in 1968. One of her most prominent and ambitious architectural projects, the site was a huge piece of land alongside Avenida Paulista, an important cultural and commercial street of São Paulo. Like the Glass House, this major building also follows the Dom-Ino model and suspends a glass box contained within concrete slabs. In this case, however, what had been a slick and refined look for the white house in Morumbi was now raw and radically out of proportion. While the structure of the project might be inspired by the Corbusian model, the dimensions, use of materials, and programmatic ambitions defy this analogy. At the MASP on Avenida Paulista, Bo Bardi not only created a massive vitrine with a span of 74 meters, but also a public plaza of the same length that connected street life with the museum.

The architecture of Bo Bardi's first built house and her first built museum suspends vitrines on columns and exposes an interior to be seen through a clear glass screen from the outside. Floating above the city, they are both like large TV screens where a new lifestyle is performed. They are vitrines in which an assemblage of the referents of daily life are on display—learning spaces, that is, for all to observe. And while these two career-defining architectural projects share the spirit of showcasing their interior activity with the public, the treatment of materials and the raw nature of MASP on Avenida Paulista speaks to the architect's new experiences in the years that elapsed between the 1951 house and the 1968 museum.

As her garden in Morumbi grew taller and slowly masked the activities of the Glass House, Bo Bardi's personal interests in pedagogy took her to Salvador in the northeastern state of Bahia, where she was confronted with a radically different culture from that of urban São Paulo. An invitation to teach at the Federal University of Bahia in Salvador in 1958 led to an appointment as director of the Museum of Modern Art of Bahia (MAM-BA) a year later. Her time in Salvador exposed Bo Bardi to a different Brazil, one that was not only more politically engaged, but also more diverse and connected to the crafts and traditions of the many cultures that intersect in Brazil's Northeast. Bo Bardi's contemporaneous involvement with and proximity to a multidisciplinary group of prominent cultural figures—from theater director Martim Gonçalves to the young and radical filmmaker Glauber Rocha—impacted her development as a creative individual. From 1958 to 1964, she worked on exhibitions and on establishing the MAM-BA, first inside the premises of the Castro Alves Theater (figs. 151–162), and then in the Solar do Unhão (figs. 163–166), a large seventeenth-century colonial complex by the sea. The vision and restoration plan for the Solar do Unhão showcases a different approach to design and museum practices for Bo Bardi, one more connected and engaged with local references than with Europe's idea of modernism.

A dematerialization process happened in Bo Bardi's architecture during this period, and her writing became increasingly critical of the bourgeoisie. There is also a noticeable shift in both her style and approach to exhibitions and building projects. In her architecture, the glass panels of the early Glass House were soon replaced by walls made with local, raw, and easy-to-access materials, as seen in the 1958 Chame-Chame House (figs. 288–291). Economical architecture, or "poor architecture," as she called it, became Bo Bardi's new approach to the practice. Simple materials were given use through simple assembly, by which Bo Bardi aimed to surface latent histories of place (fig. 252). This can be seen in the prominent stairs inside the Solar do Unhão, where she stacked and assembled wood pieces without screws to create a spiral staircase inspired by the popular crates used on the backs of oxen (figs. 167–170).

FIG. 252
Lina Bo Bardi, *Beach House: front elevation and perspective drawing of the exterior*, 1958. Graphite on parchment paper, 48 x 50.5 cm. Collection of the Instituto Bardi/ Casa de Vidro, São Paulo

Years before Glauber Rocha's 1965 manifesto "The Aesthetic of Hunger," Bo Bardi was already no longer communicating to the "civilized man," as Rocha would declare, but rather to the local context of Brazil.[3] She intrinsically understood Rocha's claim that "only a culture of hunger can qualitatively surpass its own structures by undermining and destroying them."[4] Bo Bardi was creating a new language of spatial relations through material culture in her architecture, one in which European modernist references were no longer present. This is visible in the cultural center of Sesc Pompeia (figs. 318–337), her next major project, which began eleven years after concluding MASP's new building and working on multiple exhibitions for it.

Beginning in 1977 and concluding in 1986, Bo Bardi worked on Sesc Pompeia, an architectural renovation that reprogrammed a former factory into a social space for leisure, sports, theater, and learning. Here, her renewed approach to an architectural project learned over the course of her time in Brazil came to life in ways that no other had been able to accomplish, and revelations from each of her past projects are visible in Sesc Pompeia's realization. It grounds the program and ambitions expected of the teaching floating vitrine at MASP, merging it with the street life of its open plaza. The unexpected relationships that unfold within its unprogrammed areas are the focus of this new cultural complex, rather than a space that broadcasts a specific modernity. Through simple materials and mere insertions of pathways and areas for gathering, Bo Bardi created an architecture that is built almost entirely by the social dynamics of the people who use it.

Bo Bardi was not only an architect of buildings, but one of relationships. Toward the end of her career especially, her practice became more about the human interactions that happen within a given space rather than the forms and shapes that constitute that space. Each of the architectural projects she engaged was meant to be understood as a pedagogical spatial experience—one that connected the materials, the process, and the history of its site with the individuals who took part in it. Sesc Pompeia performs this interest by simply exposing the didactic experience of living as part of a broader community.

The Sesc Pompeia complex opened in 1986, and by this time the Glass House was filled with objects that presented a portrait of Bo Bardi's four decades in Brazil. That same year, she also designed and

3. Glauber Rocha, "The Aesthetics of Hunger" (1965), in Scott MacKenzie, ed., *Film Manifestos and Global Cinema Cultures* (Berkeley: University of California Press, 2014), 218.

4. Ibid., 219.

built a small, simple log cabin as her studio, on the lower grounds of the Morumbi site (fig. 251). With barn doors that open the space to nature, this is a structure seemingly without design and all but the opposite of the architecture of the suspended glass vitrine above it. Here, the ambition of communicating publicly through the performance of living is subdued but nonetheless present; there is something about the way one learns by spending time in nature that is both intuitive and organic. The architecture of Bo Bardi's pedagogical turn in Brazil is now experienced at once outdoors and as a kind of intimacy. Moreover, the routine procession down the slanted, narrow hillside steps from the glass vitrine above to the wood hut below marks an almost ceremonial event. It is as if a process of unlearning happens during this walk.

Brazilian scholar Esther da Costa Meyer has this to say about the wood cabin:

> New materials call for new codes of representation. The short, stocky pilotis that prop up the little house make no reference to Le Corbusier. Earthbound and empirical, architecture is here reinterpreted by a practitioner who no longer professes the puritanical and renunciatory ethos of high modernism, nor the adversarial relation between high and low on which it is predicated. An almost totemic respect for nature overrides the cerebral geometries of the avant-garde. Nevertheless, this is no "primitive hut," haunted by the myth of the noble savage, but a research institute for urban sophisticates in which the architect opted for a new formal idiom, soft-spoken rather than declarative, low- rather than high-tech.[5]

The glass vitrine with which Bo Bardi engaged during her early years in Brazil eventually morphed into the Glass House and MASP. New approaches to a poor architecture and its connection to life on the ground, learned in Salvador, then gave way to the raw social spaces of Sesc Pompeia. With time, the openness of the social programs seen at the multi-use space of Sesc translated into a simple wood hut exposed to an open habitat. Bo Bardi's unlearning during her life in Brazil demonstrates an evolution that acknowledges the world we inhabit has somehow already been designed by larger systems that are always present, but which are not always visible to the eye of the architect. Over the course of her life, she gave in to this predesigned world by allowing it to take over. She performed the role of the architect as one who conceives spaces by inhabiting them from within, rather than creating them from the outside.

5. Esther da Costa Meyer, "After the Flood," *Harvard Design Magazine*, no. 16 (Spring–Summer 2002), at harvarddesignmagazine.org/issues/16/after-the-flood.

José Esparza Chong Cuy was previously an associate curator at the Museum of Contemporary Art Chicago and is currently the executive director and chief curator at the Storefront for Art and Architecture in New York.

LINA'S HISTORY LESSON

1. Irene Small, *Hélio Oiticica: Folding the Frame* (Chicago: University of Chicago Press, 2016).

2. Zeuler R. M. de A. Lima, *Lina Bo Bardi* (New Haven: Yale University Press, 2013).

FIG. 253
Lina Bo Bardi at the Glass House, 1952

Even the most cursory look at the historiography of twentieth-century Latin American architecture reveals the narrowness of its scope. In the case of the architecture of twentieth-century Brazil, the relationship between modern architecture and official culture has exerted a particularly powerful influence on this panorama. State-sponsored works have historically received the bulk of attention, most of it laudatory, so much so that "official" and "modern" architecture are largely indistinguishable from one another.

Not all modernisms in Brazil were official or state-sponsored, of course, although it must have often seemed that way to the artists and architects of the time. As Irene Small demonstrates in her analysis of the mid-twentieth-century artistic landscape of Brazil, the alignment between the state apparatus and the architectural circles of its largest cities, particularly Rio de Janeiro, created more than just a restrictive institutional landscape for the profession. The understanding of modern architecture's cultural promise as a whole evolved alongside a narrowly defined conception of what state-sponsored modernization could offer the developing country. This confluence of factors eventually came to represent an ideological frontier against the grain in which many architects and artists chose to operate.[1]

As an émigré and a woman practitioner in a male-dominated field who operated far—geographically and institutionally—from these clientelist circles, Lina Bo Bardi completed work that often rubbed against these institutional and ideological limits, too. In recent years, critics have pointed out the multiple ways—formal, ideological, curatorial—in which Bo Bardi's work calls into question the assumptions of more than one dominant tradition within modern architecture, not just the predominant one in Brazil. As architect Zeuler R. M. de A. Lima points out, the relatively recent attention that Bo Bardi's work has received, particularly outside of Brazil, should compel us to take more than a superficial look at a career that, captivating even at face value, has much more to teach us if we look beyond the surface.[2]

In this essay, I attempt to sketch out historiographic lessons from Bo Bardi's interventions. I propose that, as we strive to afford Bo Bardi's work a place of greater prominence within the existing canon of modern architecture in Brazil, Latin America, and the world, we should clarify the points of incision where her practice calls into question the canon's structure and assumptions. More specifically, I highlight the ways in which her curatorial and architectural work sought to give architectural form to the traumatic dimension of Brazil's modernization. This element, elided by the majority of the better-known modern architecture of Brazil, should in turn compel us to reevaluate the underlying assumptions of the canon itself. Because Bo Bardi crafted an architectural practice out of a largely adversarial environment, I've taken care that my historiographic attempts to negotiate her position within the field do not lose sight of that ethical position.

Not-so-humane Modernism

Writing on the occasion of Oscar Niemeyer's death a few years ago, US-based critic Sarah Goldhagen provided a reductive account of his career. Precisely because of its methodological limitations, Goldhagen's interpretation offers a compelling point of entry into a broader discussion of how we memorialize modernism in Brazil and elsewhere. Goldhagen accused the patriarch of the Brazilian modern tradition of having cultivated an overly formalist approach, one that, contrary to the claims of the celebratory literature about him, did not actually exert a transformative influence over the international tradition of modern architecture during the last century. Niemeyer, she argues, failed to take "the chill off modernist design with his flamboyantly curving, white thin-shell concrete buildings." In her view, claims made by Niemeyer apologists about the innovative dimensions of his oeuvre are the kind of "nonsense" that "gets peddled in obituaries and hagiographies, particularly when a charismatic charmer distorts the historical record to inflate his own contribution, takes credit for the innovations of others, and outlives—by decades!—his competitors."[3]

Goldhagen takes issue with the claim that Niemeyer's architecture introduced a "humane" dimension into modernism. She argues that a "humane" tradition did take shape in the twentieth century, but that many architects before Niemeyer's time contributed to this creation. What is this "humane" tradition? Goldhagen describes it somewhat cryptically as a marked formal departure from the presumably *less humane* architecture represented by the early, machine-aesthetic-influenced works of Le Corbusier.

Leading the pack of architects whom Goldhagen does credit with having created a "humane" modernism before Niemeyer is Frank Lloyd Wright. Wright's work, she writes, was much more "in thrall to materials, nature, and the peculiarities of triangular and circular geometries" than Niemeyer's. Further, she claims that Berthold Lubetkin, László Moholy-Nagy, and Alvar Aalto also produced "humane" work earlier in the century.

Not only is Niemeyer's work not truly "humane," Goldhagen concludes, it is ultimately derivative. For Goldhagen, the iconic design and construction of the Ministry of Education and Health in Rio de Janeiro does not represent a moment of triumph for Niemeyer and his generation.[4] Ignoring the context of its production, Goldhagen declares that the ministry is only embellished by "a couple of Niemeyeresque touches" but remains fundamentally the work of Le Corbusier himself. Throughout the modern canon, she writes, there exist other examples of "humane" modernism that predate Niemeyer's. Lubetkin's Penguin Pool at the London Zoo, "an elegantly intertwined composition of sinuous thin-shelled concrete ramps," is basically "Niemeyer before Niemeyer." Having benefitted from more institutional support than almost any of his twentieth-century peers, Niemeyer, Goldhagen argues, eventually cemented his status in the history of modernism not on account of his real innovations but as a result of the elaborate apparatus that constructed his reputation.

Humane Modernism

Exemplifying dominant trends within much of the historiography of modern architecture, Goldhagen not only takes a markedly defensive and Eurocentric position vis-à-vis the history of modernism, but she also limits her scope to questions of biography, authorship, and architectural form. Even at that level, her case against Niemeyer's influence is debatable. Nonetheless, in paying such close attention to architectural form and in pointing out that Niemeyer indeed controlled his own mythology, Goldhagen is not far off the mark. It was, after all, through a critique of his own generation's formalism, written in his own architectural journal, *Módulo*, that Niemeyer attempted to articulate a turn toward more socially aware work in the mid-1950s.[5] Up to that point, he and his close associates had not only produced the bulk of private and state-sponsored works that constituted the country's sanctioned

3. Sarah Williams Goldhagen, "The Beauty and Inhumanity of Oscar Niemeyer's Architecture," *The New Republic* (December 2012).

4. This exceedingly well-documented commision was famously produced by a team of architects that included Niemeyer, Lúcio Costa, and Affonso Eduardo Reidy, among others. At one critical, early point of the commission that served as a genesis for a subsequent debate about its authorship, Le Corbusier was a consultant for the project. Roberto Segre, *Ministério da Educação e Saúde: Ícone urbano da modernidade brasileira, 1935–1945* (São Paulo: Romano Guerra, 2013).

5. Oscar Niemeyer, "Depoimento = Testimony," *Módulo*, no. 9 (February 1958): 3–6.

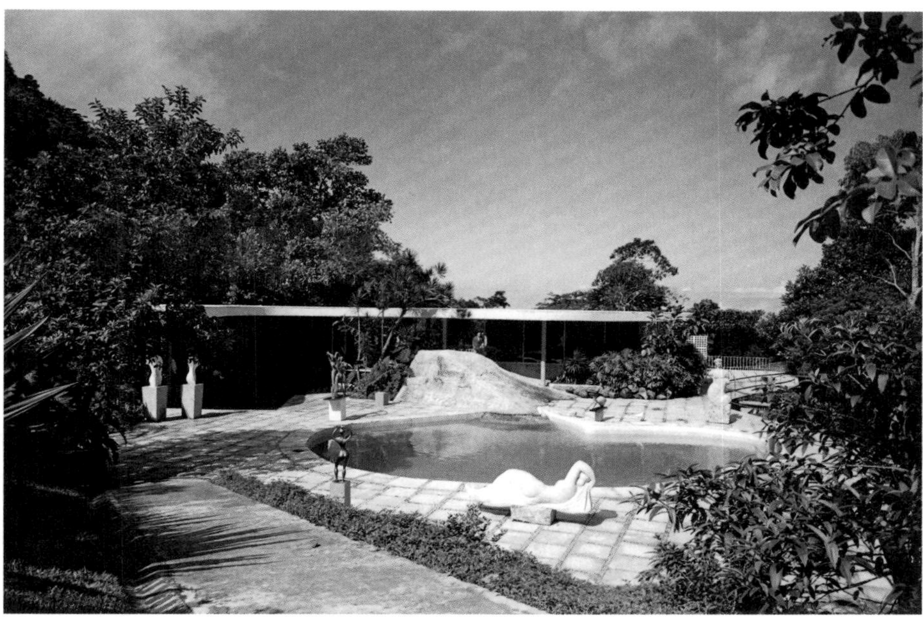

FIG. 254
Canoas House by Oscar Niemeyer, Rio de Janeiro, 1956. Ó Niemeyer, Oscar/AUTVIS, Brazil, 2019

modernist tradition, but they had also managed to control its discourse.

Years before that debate unfolded in and around *Módulo*, architects working in Brazil at the time, including Bo Bardi, had heeded Niemeyer's self-criticism more insightfully than he himself ever would. If the "humane" modernism to which Niemeyer did not contribute takes "the chill off modernist design," one would be hard-pressed to find a better representative of the trend than Bo Bardi. Her Glass House (1951; figs. 264–281) inscribes itself within a contested and crowded lineage of similar projects in Brazil and elsewhere, including Niemeyer's Canoas House (fig. 254), but it goes further than most in negotiating its relationship to the specificity of its site, its landscape, and the carefully selected objects in its interior. Unlike other houses in the same vein, the residence famously invites inhabitation and was intended to cede protagonism, over time and harmoniously, to the rich flora and fauna of its semi-tropical environment.

If a tradition of "humane" modernism could encompass more than just form to approximate Bo Bardi's understanding of a "poor architecture," her relevance vis-à-vis Brazil's canon and the broader canon of modernism can be looked upon more ambitiously. In her nondomestic architecture, particularly her work in the Brazilian Northeast, Bo Bardi sought to bring back into focus precisely what the dominant tradition of state-sponsored modernism had excluded, and not precisely through a methodology that was wedded to the profession's traditional standards. Bo Bardi's "poor architecture" was partly defined by a formal distillation of modern architecture's propositions to some of their basic tenets, including a stringent belief in the purity of materials and the abstraction she believed was inherent in well-articulated structures. The rest of the formulation included more than one predetermined formal program, however, taking on multiple architectural manifestations over time.

Unlike Bo Bardi's work, which lacks the kind of formal or programmatic homogeneity one would want in order to neatly create an architectural tradition out of it, the state-sponsored architecture of Niemeyer's cohort indeed had a predefined stylistic profile exported beyond Brazil's borders that its own authors explicitly and successfully sought to elevate to a national tradition. The mid-twentieth-century body of work of the most prolific architects of the time provides multiple examples of formally homogenous architecture that not only looks similar but carries with it much the same promise of social progress. Hence, the Jorge Machado

6. Elizabeth Campos Rodrigues Martins, "A Realistic Vision of Utopian University City of Rio De Janeiro," in Carlos Garciavelez Alfaro, *Form and Pedagogy: The Design of the University City in Latin America* (San Francisco: Applied Research + Design, 2014), 246–49.

Moreira–led effort to create a major public university in Rio de Janeiro's Fundão Island (1957; fig. 255) attempts to articulate a similar understanding of state-sponsored social progress through mass education as Reidy's public housing works or the kind of public education experience that his experimental school built in Paraguay (1953) wanted to export (fig. 257).[6]

Like similar works produced in other developmentalist contexts, these buildings aim to provide a largely universal experience of modernization for their inhabitants regardless of their site-specificity. Excluded from the vision of progress that these works aimed to articulate across time and space is an explicit representation of the multiple social tensions that modernization itself engenders. As such, the ecologies that the Fundão reinvention disrupted or the displacement of the island's inhabitants as a result of its construction are only marginally accounted for within the still-scant historiography of the project. Also excluded from this architecture's form or discourse is any allusion to the geographical limitations of modernization's reach, which was essentially confined to a few focal points of state attention and failed to affect the experience of the majority of the country while expressing much more totalizing aims.

Architecture Is Not Enough

Despite Bo Bardi's own primitivist limitations, expressed most obviously in her idealization of rural life in Brazil, the architect remained acutely aware of both the

FIG. 255
Aerial view of the Federal University of Rio de Janeiro, chief architect Jorge Machado Moreira, 1957

FIG. 256
MASP, Avenida Paulista, São Paulo, 1960s

site-specificity of her interventions and the limitations of architecture to represent, or much less affect, its immediate social context. Indeed, in more ways than one, Bo Bardi operated specifically by taking the blindspots of the normative practice of architecture around her as her programmatic starting points. Writing in 1963 to Lomanto Júnior, then governor of the state of Bahia, about the Museum of Modern Art of Bahia, Bo Bardi makes explicit her awareness of her own architecture's inadequacy to marshall social change. Embedded within a broader initiative of historic preservation that was nothing if not site-specific, Bo Bardi called into question her own work's ability to provide the underrepresented region with cultural representation by expressing everything else the museum needed aside from a work of architecture to succeed.[7] Because the presentation of objects in a museum was not enough to exert socially tangible effects on its own, she articulated the need for other parallel activities, including sponsorship for contemporary artistic production, an engine for economic development that she saw as inseparable from her museographic aims.

Museums were, not by coincidence, a primary battleground for the representation of modernization's effects and futures in mid-twentieth-century Brazil. The canonical modern museum is embodied by Reidy's Museum of Modern Art in Rio de Janeiro (1955; fig. 258). A monumental insertion in the fabric of the city's waterfront, the conception of the project associates together the developmentalist idea of providing public education through a school for the urban masses and the embrace of modernist culture. As in the case of multiple other modern art museums built during the mid-twentieth century, there were limitations regarding just how much the institution actually embraced the culture that the building represented. As Small points out, the museum itself was one of the poignant terrains of contention for many artists who sought to expand what this culture encompassed at the time.[8]

The first curatorial program developed at MASP (fig. 256) represented a radical departure from these assumptions. Born out of São Paulo's more specific tradition of a socially engaged avant-garde and shaped by Lina Bo and Pietro Maria Bardi's transnational experiences, the museum aspired to destabilize rather than create clear taxonomies for cultural interpretation, including the interpretation of artistic production in the present tense. Because of its adversarial disposition toward the limited tradition of mid-twentieth-century museums and its approximation of what Bo Bardi once described as a "living museum," understanding the museum's architectural and structural innovations (its most commonly analyzed features) only partially accounts for its importance in the broader landscape of Brazil's architectural production.[9]

7. Lina Bo Bardi to Lomanto Júnior, Governo do Estado da Bahia, Salvador, Bahia, May 1, 1963. Instituto Lina Bo e P. M. Bardi, São Paulo.

8. Small, *Hélio Oiticica*, 71–81.

9. Lina Bo Bardi, "Os museus vivos nos Estados Unidos," *Habitat*, no. 8 (July–September 1952): 12–15.

FIG. 257
Colégio Experimental Paraguai Brasil (Paraguay-Brazil Experimental College, CEPB) by Affonso Eduardo Reidy, Asunción, Paraguay, 1953

Discussing Bo Bardi's museum in Bahia, Glauber Rocha famously defined it as "not a museum."[10] As a figure embedded within the context of radical innovations from which many of Bo Bardi's museographic and pedagogical ideas emerged, Rocha was only talking about architecture peripherally. Indeed, what he celebrated was the space's participatory and performative conception, which seemed to declare that architectural production, as understood by a previous generation of prolific and powerful practitioners, was simply not enough to advance the project's larger agenda. In a much broader sense, the museum's interactive aims were inscribed within the more ambitious goals that Bo Bardi understood as the task of cultural preservation. If Lúcio Costa's preservation work, long the established modality for architects to interact with Brazil's patrimony, aimed to emphasize the Luso-Brazilian formal legacies of the country's historic buildings, Bo Bardi sought to openly display the history behind the structures. A central element, for instance, was the history and multiple legacies of slavery in Brazil, which she sought to inscribe within the purview of historic preservation not only in a fixed memorialization of the phenomenon but as an opportunity to intervene critically in the present.[11]

One would be exaggerating only slightly if Rocha's pronouncement were expanded to claim that—by the standards of the canon of architectural history, and even by the standards of Bo Bardi's own professional landscape—much of her architectural work was "not architecture." As our understanding of her work continues to evolve, the formulation should come full circle: we should not only admit that Bo Bardi gave us much more than just architecture to work with, but also we should hope that our own disciplinary and institutional landscapes are flexible enough to give this body of work the space it needs to continue disrupting their limitations.

10. Glauber Rocha, "MAMB não é museu: é escola em 'movimento' por uma arte que não seja desligada do homem," *Jornal da Bahia* (September 1960).

11. Zeuler R. M. de A. Lima, "Preservation as Confrontation: The Work of Lina Bo Bardi," *Future Anterior* 2, no. 2 (Winter 2005): 25.

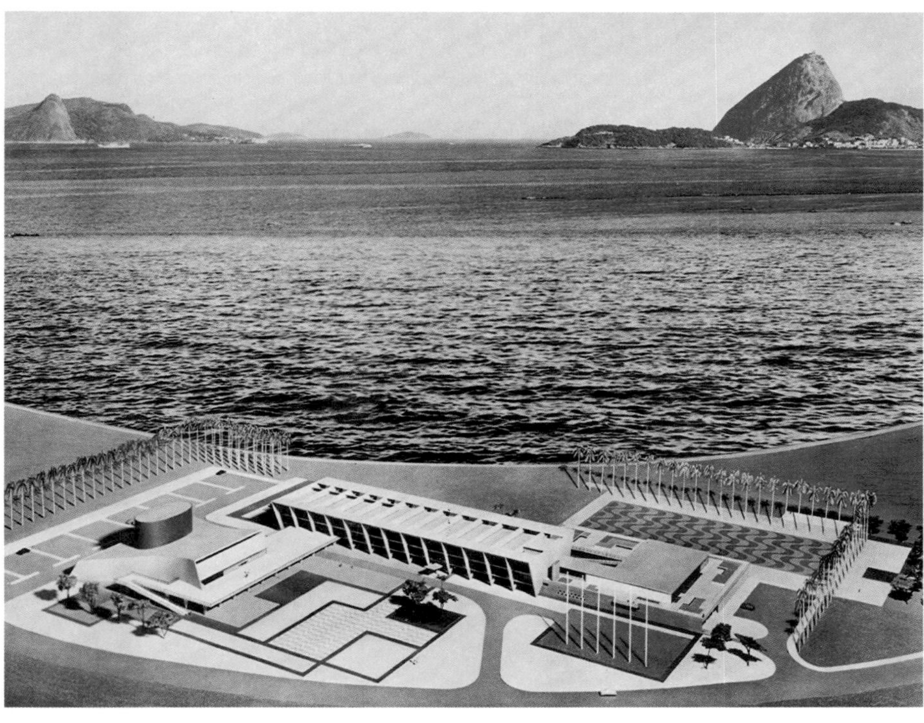

FIG. 258
Photomontage by Affonso Eduardo Reidy for the Museum of Modern Art, Rio de Janeiro, 1955

Luis M. Castañeda is a design historian and software engineer based in New York City. He is the author of essays on the relationship between design, culture, and politics, and the book *Spectacular Mexico: Design, Propaganda, and the 1968 Olympics* (2014).

LINA BO BARDI AT TEATRO OFICINA: THE CONSTRUCTIVE AND THE SACRIFICIAL

FIG. 259
Exterior view of Teatro Oficina, São Paulo, by Lina Bo Bardi, 2015

Although not yet completely finished, the new Teatro Oficina (Theater Workshop, fig. 259) was finally opened on October 3, 1993, presenting William Shakespeare's *Hamlet* (*Ham-let*, in the Oficina's adaptation; fig. 381). This brought to a close a period of more than twenty years of hibernation, since 1972, when the theater company, directed by José Celso Martinez Corrêa, performed Anton Chekhov's *Three Sisters.*[1]

Located at 520 Jaceguai Street, in the Bexiga neighborhood of São Paulo, Teatro Oficina occupies a narrow, long, sloping lot, 9 x 50 meters with a 3-meter grade. If the spatial organization of the previous theater, designed by Flávio Império and Rodrigo Lefèvre, had a revolving Italian stage at the bottom of a single set of seating on the natural slope, the space of the new theater, designed by Lina Bo Bardi and Edson Elito, abolished the entire scenic area, transforming the stage into a continuous track that features two segments, one flat, the other a ramp, like a street or a sambadrome, down which the actors parade like members of a carnivalesque-Dionysian choir.

Innovative, the building opens to its surroundings through both the large glass side facade, which is traversed by a large tree, and the retractable roof, which opens during performances, revealing the open sky. In this unusual space, the audience sits on metal scaffolds parallel to the central track (the "stage"), vertically overlapped on two and three levels (fig. 262).

Lina Bo Bardi and Zé Celso had been engaged in powerfully explosive artistic partnerships since 1969, when the Italian-Brazilian conceived of the scenic architecture for *In the Jungle of Cities* (figs. 260, 363–371) by Bertolt Brecht, staged by the Oficina group. It was this cathartic experience, in which Lina constructed a stage shaped like a boxing ring with rubble from the demolition of neighborhood residences around the theater, that spawned the later-matured idea of destroying the Oficina building to construct a new home. As Zé Celso has noted:

> *In the Jungle of Cities* is one of the most beautiful stagings I've ever done, and is the origin of this space, the Teatro Oficina, as it is today. It was very important because it put me in touch with Lina Bo Bardi, and Lina had already started in the theater with the boxing ring and the demolition. The play has eleven rounds. In each round, it destroys an institution, until it destroys its own ring. In the end, the actors are taking apart the theater's floor and reaching dirt.[2]

Lina's most finished sketches for the new theater date from 1984 (fig. 380), but the first studies began four years earlier. As it turns out, the spatial area of a stage/street that stretches across the lot, even removing the brick arches from the building's outside walls, opening to an open-air stadium theater, had already been introduced by her to the group in 1980 during a slideshow presentation.[3] A year earlier, upon returning

1. After the 1972 season of *Three Sisters*, the group eventually disbanded as a result of a combination of artistic entropy and repression by the military state. In direct exchange with the American group Living Theater, founded in 1947, the Oficina transformed into a community and traveled throughout the *sertões* of Brazil, performing and improvising. In 1974, Zé Celso and other members of the group—now renamed the Oficina Samba Coletivo Multimídia—were arrested and tortured. Released shortly thereafter, they went into voluntary exile in Portugal and Mozambique, countries where they performed collectively, creating street shows as well as video and radio experiments.

2. Zé Celso Martinez Corrêa, "O decano do gozo: Entrevista a Otávio Frias Filho e Nelson de Sá," in Karina Lopes and Sérgio Cohn, eds., *Encontros: Zé Celso Martinez Corrêa* (Rio de Janeiro: Azougue, 2008), 206–7.

3. "On August 24 [1980], Lina Bo Bardi and fellow architect Marcelo Suzuki made a slideshow presentation at the Teat(r)o Oficina on the primary risk of a street that crossed through the Roman arches of the Oficina and set up the stadium-style theater [Teat(r)o de Estádio] around it." Mariano Mattos Martins, "Currículo," in *Oficina 50+ Labirinto da criação* (São Paulo: Pancron Indústria Gráfica, 2013), 240.

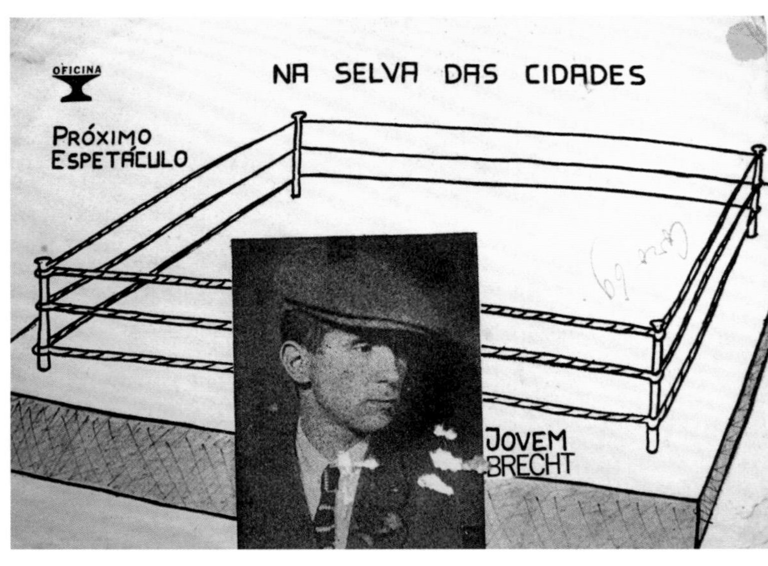

FIG. 260
Invitation to the play *In the Jungle of Cities* (1969), designed by Lina Bo Bardi

from exile in Portugal and Mozambique, the theater company—renewed and renamed as the Oficina Samba Coletivo Multimídia—had begun to drill holes in the back wall, unveiling a large open space, used as a parking lot by the Silvio Santos Group (GSS), owner of several properties around the theater. It was, according to an expression created by the group, an Epidaurus Theater in the Baú da Felicidade (a type of lottery company owned by Silvio Santos). In Lina's sketches, these holes in the walls are referred to as the "Spanish Civil War," alluding to a resistance struggle that assumes violence—in this case, the holes—as a weapon of regeneration. Indeed, this is the tone of the small descriptive tribute accompanying the project in its monographic book, which describes the new Oficina as an embodiment of the modern principle of creative destruction: "The storm destroys. We need to reformulate and rebuild. . . . In terms of architecture, *the storm* has destroyed everything, and the Oficina will act again."[4] In a manifestation of this idea, between 1980 and 1981, over a series of cathartic and carnivalesque rehearsals, the actors destroyed the theater, turning it into ruins.

Locating, thus, the origin of the current Teatro Oficina in the staging of *In the Jungle of Cities*, which took place in 1969, we can understand in depth its nonunivocal, anthropophagic, urban, and essentially sacrificial artistic condition. In January 1971, the military government inaugurated the work that would become its great ideological landmark in the capital of São Paulo: the set of highways formed by the President Costa e Silva elevated freeway (currently renamed for President João Goulart), the Júlio de Mesquita Filho Viaduct, and the Jaceguai Viaduct, known as the "Minhocão" (the "Big Worm").[5] It was the jingoist height of Brazil's so-called "economic miracle" of hydroelectric power plants and highways in the Amazon, extending with a more technocratic and grandiloquent intonation Juscelino Kubitschek's "developmentalism," which saw the construction of the city of Brasília and encouraged the growth of a national automobile industry. Approximately seven kilometers long, this elevated highway system sliced through central areas of the city, including some of its historic, popular, and culturally rich neighborhoods, such as Bexiga (or Bixiga), literally, "Bladder," the nickname given to the neighborhood of Bela Vista.

Formed by a significant immigration from southern Italy,[6] and after the internal migration from the Brazilian Northeast, Bexiga

4. Lina Bo Bardi, "Teatro Oficina," in Marcelo Carvalho Ferraz, ed., *Lina Bo Bardi* (São Paulo: Instituto Lina Bo e P. M. Bardi, 1993), 258.

5. These constitute the so-called East-West São Paulo Link (Ligação Leste-Oeste de São Paulo), which connects Radial Leste Avenue, in Brás/Mooca, to Francisco Matarazzo Avenue, in Água Branca.

6. Especially from Campania, Basilicata, and Calabria. See Ana L. D. Lanna, "O Bexiga e os italianos em São Paulo, 1890/1920," in *São Paulo, os estrangeiros e a construção das cidades* (São Paulo: Alameda, 2011), 119.

had been an epicenter of São Paulo's bohemian life from the 1950s, with cantinas and theaters that were among the most important in the city, such as the Teatro Brasileiro de Comédia (TBC, 1948), the Maria della Costa Theater (1954), the Oficina Theater (1958), the Ruth Escobar Theater (1963), and later the Sérgio Cardoso Theater (1980). However, the Oficina is the only theater that remains active as the headquarters of its own company. With irregular topography, formed by hills and grottoes and swampy areas, subject to floods and landslides, the neighborhood was formed by small plots resulting from the subdivision of the Chacara do Bexiga (Bexiga Farmstead), in the late nineteenth century, where there was a *quilombo* (colonial-era maroon settlement of formerly enslaved or free people of African descent). This resulted in an occupation of the area by buildings, with modest townhouses, many of them over time transformed into tenements and generally inhabited by domestic workers, informal workers, and small traders. The neighborhood also houses one of the most popular samba schools in São Paulo, Vai-Vai, which emerged as a "cordão carnavalesco" (a recreational samba club) in 1928, raising its status to that of a school in 1972.

Bexiga is therefore considered the quintessential site of São Paulo samba, frequented by figures such as singer and songwriter Adoniran Barbosa, the son of Italian immigrants, and author of classics such as "Trem das onze" and "Saudosa maloca." The greatest chronicler of daily life in the city of São Paulo in the 1940s and 1950s, and especially in bohemian and immigrant neighborhoods such as Bexiga, Brás, and Centro, Adoniran added a mix of popular accents to his songs, enriching the normative cult of poetry with the orality of popular culture and dialects from the streets. The song "Saudosa maloca" takes as its theme the process of transformation of the urban landscape, with the verticalization of its buildings, describing the feeling of helplessness in the face of this process. So does "Despejo na Favela" (Eviction in the Favela), in which a police officer is forced to warn residents being evicted: "It's of a higher order." "Saudosa maloca" tells of the expulsion of three poor men who illegally occupy an old mansion that will be demolished for the construction of a tall building in its place. Originally in reference to indigenous communal houses, the word *maloca* has come to designate, in the urban context, a makeshift, precarious collective dwelling, such as tenements and slums. Adoniran invokes the term again in "Abrigo de vagabundos" (Vagabond Shelter): "My *maloca*, the most beautiful in this world / I offer to vagabonds / who have nowhere to sleep."

From the 1960s to the 1970s, Bexiga was violently fractured by the brutal scar this road complex carved, disrupting streets, demolishing countless houses and blocks, and dividing the neighborhood in two. Traditionally characterized by intense street life, Bexiga was suddenly exposed to the traumatic experience of express road traffic—the Oficina is only twenty meters from the Viaduct—similar to what took place in the New York neighborhood of the Bronx with the construction of the Cross Bronx Expressway in the 1950s, as described by Marshall Berman.[7]

Beacon of avant-garde theatrical production, led by director Zé Celso Martinez Corrêa, the Oficina group staged plays that entered not only the history of dramaturgy, but of São Paulo and Brazilian cultural life, such as in Oswald de Andrade's 1967 *O Rei da Vela* and the 1968 *Roda Viva* by Chico Buarque de Hollanda, in which actors threw objects—including raw meat—at the public in order to stir them from a position of contemplative passivity. And such was the provocation created at the time by the group's aesthetic radicality that a paramilitary group beat the cast of *Roda Viva* after a performance, burning the nipples of actresses with cigarettes.

In 1969, with the recent promulgation of Institutional Act No. 5 (AI-5) and the

7. See Marshall Berman, *All That Is Solid Melts Into Air: The Experience of Modernity* (New York: Simon & Schuster, 1982). An immigrant neighborhood, characterized by an intense street life, the Bronx was largely razed by the great highway project, becoming a desertified area, conducive to various forms of social delinquency.

FIG. 261
"Uma cidade mais humana" (A More Human City), report in *Manchete* magazine, special edition, January 25, 1971

escalation of political and social tensions in the country, the engineer Paulo Maluf became the mayor of São Paulo, setting into motion his great urban project, the Minhocão. It was in this context, when entire blocks began to be demolished in Bexiga, opening clearings taken over by debris and rubble in its urban fabric, as if bombed out, that the Oficina decided to stage *In the Jungle of Cities*, inviting Lina Bo Bardi to design the play's set and costumes. The scenery was disposable and the raw material for its production was found by Lina in the neighborhood's wreckage—in the indistinct mix of demolition and construction remains that had accumulated on the streets during the building of the highways that year. As Zé Celso noted:

> [Bexiga] was a fantastic, marginal neighborhood. It had millions of mouths, an incredible marginalia! A world of tenements, suddenly torn by this Minhocão, this viaduct that split the streets in half and devastated everything . . . It gave me the sensation that what happened to the world, to us, was happening in that neighborhood there, too. It was being littered with trash. . . . Then there was that garbage there in Bexiga being removed, and indeed being replaced by other [rubbish]: the Minhocão, which passes today in front of the theater door. And there was the garbage inside the theater, too: Lina Bardi, who did *Jungle*'s set design, took Bexiga's garbage and brought it on stage. So much so that we paid almost nothing for the set construction. She was going crazy in the middle of the street: "How beautiful! How wonderful!" The drivers thought the woman was crazy; she would pick out the filthiest things, sort them, and put them on the stage.[8]

Not only was *Jungle*'s boxing ring (fig. 263) built with wood planks collected in the streets—recalling that some of the houses destroyed had been shacks made of wood—but also with trees torn from the ground brought in complete, fastened inside the theater with steel cables until they fell, as well as the personal objects found in the piles of rubble, such as mirrors, family portraits, and various pieces of furniture, attesting to the presence/absence of former residents and the violence of their removal. After all, the issue is exactly the emergence of violence in its multiple forms, that is, the experience of violence contained both in

8. Zé Celso Martinez Corrêa, "Don José de la Mancha," interview with Hamilton Almeida Filho, in *Primeiro ato: cadernos, depoimentos, entrevistas, 1958–1974*, ed. Ana Helena Camargo de Staal (São Paulo: Editora 34, 1998), 168.

the physical destruction of the blocks and houses and in the removal of people, in the divvying up of the neighborhood, in the construction of a concrete structure, robust and aggressive at its core, and at the same time the aesthetic decision not to retreat from these violent acts, but to replicate them with renewed aesthetic violence, metabolizing the city's ruins in the theater space, daily destroying it anew, so that this destruction would become an operation of denudation.

This operation, of course, is distinctly anthropophagic: transforming the taboo into a totem, erecting the trauma of the neighborhood into new construction, continually destroying it until nothing remains, except for the original land of the Bexiga neighborhood that lies beneath the theater's floor. Akin to the "beach" that the May '68 students and Situationist artists spotted beneath the cobblestone pavement of the streets of Paris during those weeks of guerrillas at the barricades ("Sous les pavés, la plage")—in reference to the sand beneath the city's urban floor. Or the revelation of the *sertão* (backlands) hidden beneath the theater, the *sertão* of 520 Jaceguai Street, as Lina liked to say.

In *Jungle*, in addition to incorporating urban ruin as raw scenic material, a series of phrases were carved into the walls around the stage, including the paradoxical slogan of Paulo Maluf's administration at that time: "São Paulo, the city that humanizes" (fig. 261). The parodic effect of this incorporation into a play that constituted a real battlefield is evident. After all, we were at an important historical turning point of the city, because in the short period between 1969 and 1972 its major express arteries were

FIG. 262
View of the interior of Teatro Oficina, São Paulo, by Lina Bo Bardi, 2002

FIG. 263
Scene from the play *In the Jungle of Cities*, set design by Lina Bo Bardi, 1969

built and inaugurated, including the Marginal Tietê and the Avenues 23 de Maio and the Radial Leste, in addition to the Minhocão. And, crowning the connection between the elevated highway and the Radial Leste are the numerous constructions (loops, viaducts, and avenues) that turned Dom Pedro II Park into a wasteland. It is therefore necessary to ask where the notion of humanity lies for this city, whose public spaces were voraciously sacrificed in the name of roadways. A city which, borrowing the concept of the French writer Charles Baudelaire on the subject of Paris during the Haussmann reforms, experienced its "spleen."[9] Once again, the Oficina and Lina Bo Bardi's response to this situation was not defensive or nostalgic, but anthropophagic, parodic, and affirmative. And in this, the sacrificial rite gained a truly constructive dimension.

Translated from the Portuguese by Emma Young

9. Of Greek origin, the term *spleen* designates melancholy, decay, foreboding of destruction. In his 1867 book of prose poems titled *Paris Spleen*, Baudelaire baptizes this expression as a sign of modernity—modernity that can be read, in the case of São Paulo, as the inverted mirror of its jingoistic ideology of progress.

Guilherme Wisnik is a professor of architecture and urbanism at the Universidade de São Paulo. His most recent publications include *Espaço em obra: cidade, arte, arquitetura*, with Julio Mariutti, and *Dentro do nevoeiro: arte, arquitetura e tecnologia contemporâneas* (both 2018). He was the lead curator of the 10th São Paulo Architecture Biennial (2013), and the exhibition *Infinito vão: 90 anos de arquitetura brasileira* (Casa da Arquitectura de Portugal, 2018), with Fernando Serapião.

HOUSES

Glass House

São Paulo
1950–51
(Architectural project)

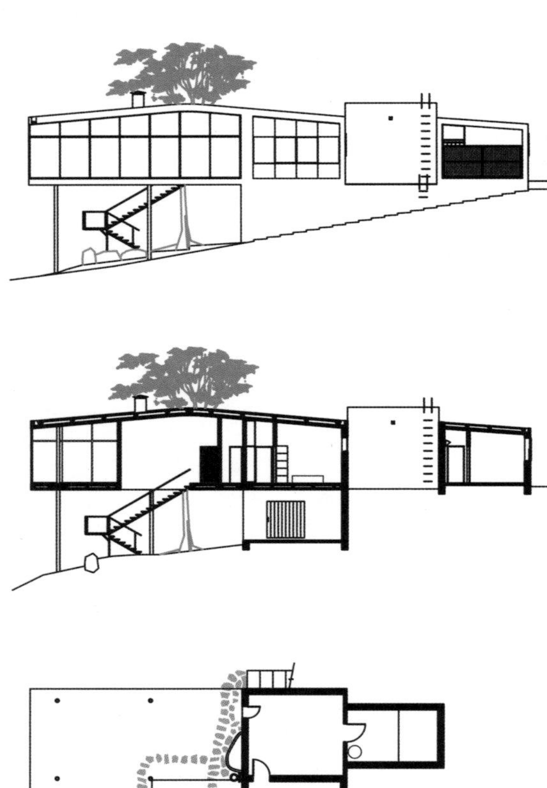

The Glass House, the Bardi couple's residence, was inaugural on two counts: for Bo Bardi's career, as it was her first work completed in its entirety, and for the neighborhood of Jardim Morumbi, as the initial settlement of its lots, until then occupied only by the Atlantic Forest. Located on a sloping site, the house sits peculiarly on its topography. The glassed-in living room hovers over slender steel pylons, accommodating the garage and entrance beneath it. The bedrooms and utility rooms are arranged directly atop a mound, shaped by the walls that delimit the parking area and contain the land that supports the open patio and the utility module. Public, daytime areas are structurally separated from private, evening areas. The house is effectively divided into three modules: living, sleeping, and utility. Two courtyards create the intermediary spaces between them. In the living room, there is a contrast between the lightness of the metal pillars—only 17 centimeters in diameter—and the weight of the concrete slabs. This effect is reinforced in the chromatic treatment: the frames and pillars are a grayish blue, blending them with the surrounding vegetation, while the slabs are white. The sloped roof defies a direct lineage from Mies' glass houses, and water flows along gutters in the slabs to an artificial pond on the ground—a solution that Lina would later repeat in the MASP building on Avenida Paulista.—DJ

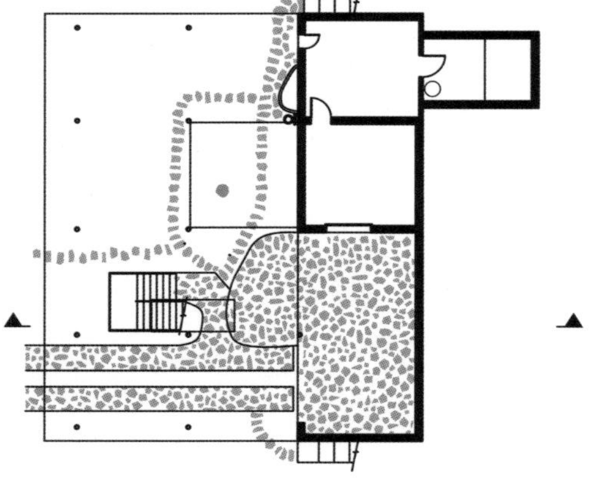

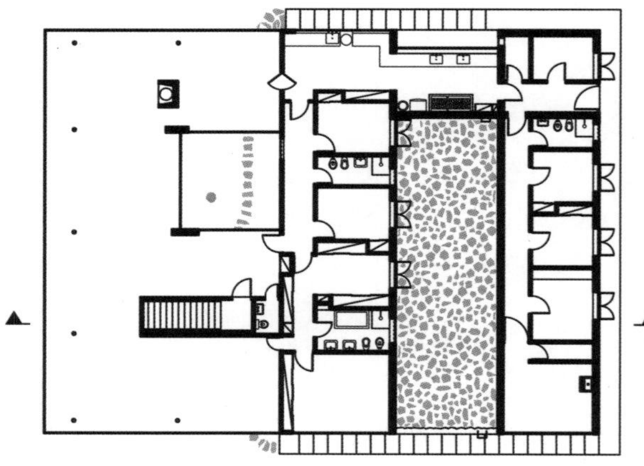

FIGS. 264–267
Northeastern elevation, section, and plans for the ground floor and rooftop paving of the Glass House

FIGS. 268–269
Exterior views of the Glass House, 1951 and 2008

FIG. 270
Exterior view of the Glass House, 1951

FIG. 271
Lina Bo Bardi, *Interior perspective*, 1951. Ink on offset paper, 11 x 12 cm. Collection of the Instituto Bardi/Casa de Vidro, São Paulo

FIGS. 272–273
Lina Bo Bardi, *Interior perspectives*, 1951. Ink on offset paper, 11 x 12 cm. Collection of the Instituto Bardi/Casa de Vidro, São Paulo

FIGS. 274–275
Interior views of the Glass House, 1951

FIG. 276
Exterior view of the Glass House, 2002

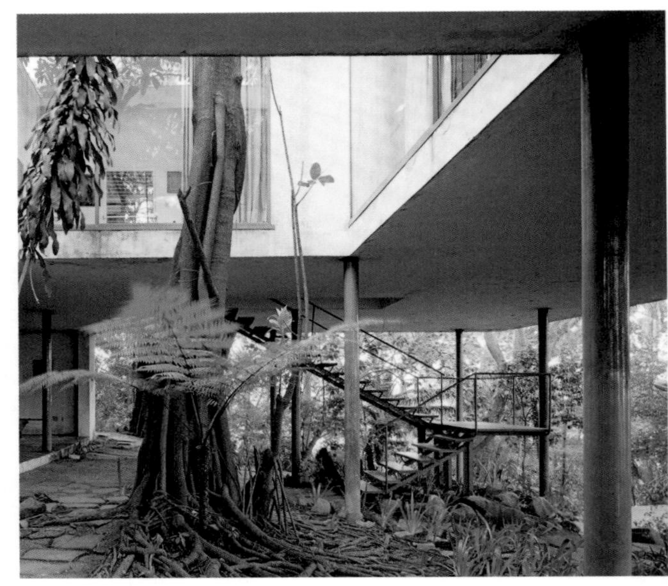

FIGS. 277–278
Interior views of the Glass House, 2002

FIG. 279
Exterior view of the Glass House, 2002

FIG. 280
Interior view of the Glass House, 2002

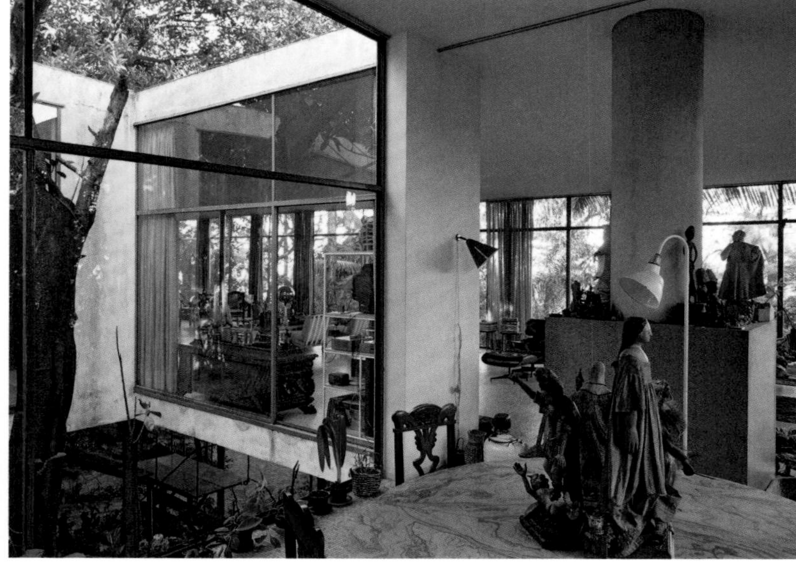

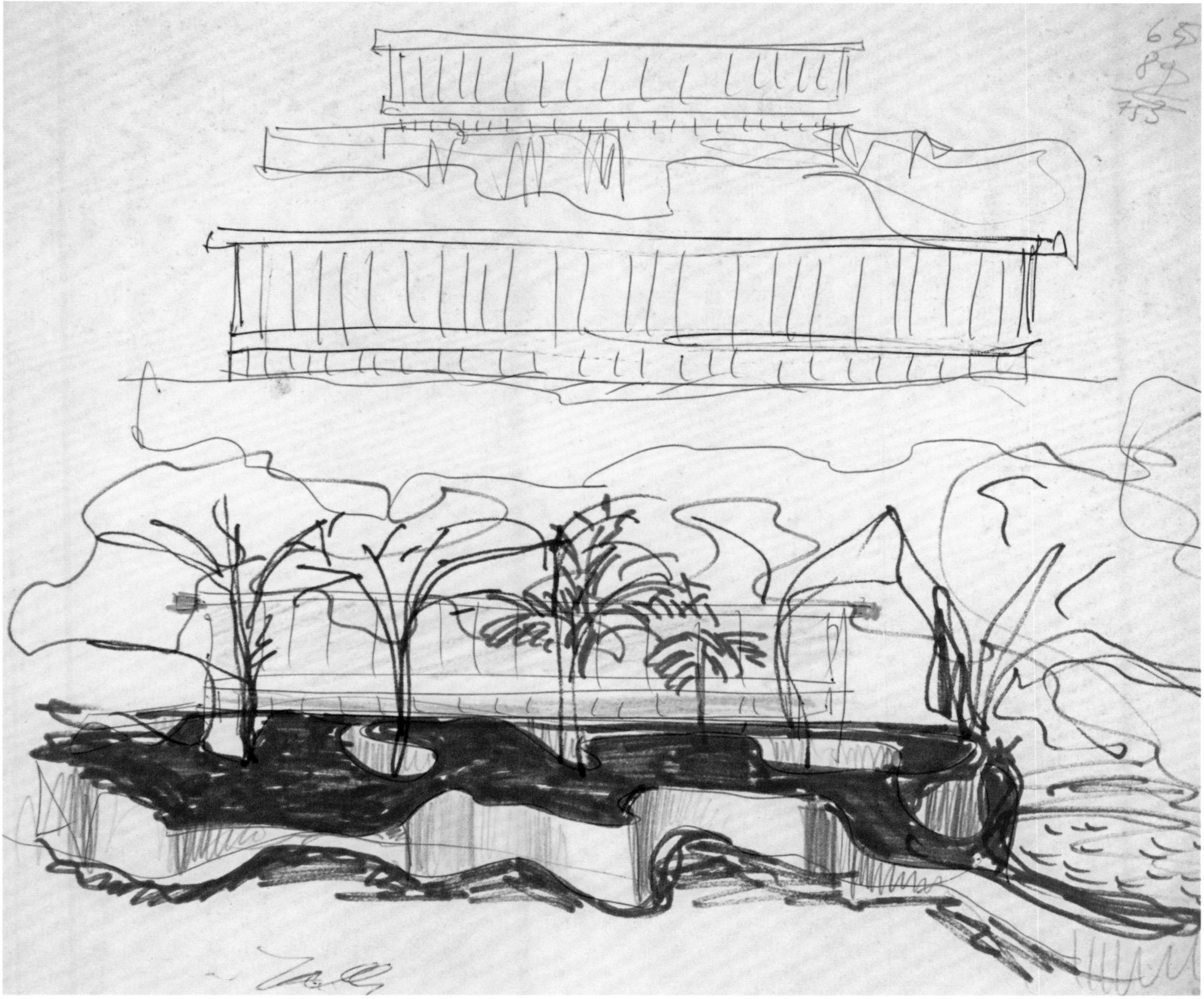

FIG. 281
Lina Bo Bardi, *Elevation, perspective*, 1951. Ballpoint pen, marker, and graphite on offset paper, 22 x 31.5 cm. Collection of the Instituto Bardi/Casa de Vidro, São Paulo

Economic Houses

1951
(Unrealized project)

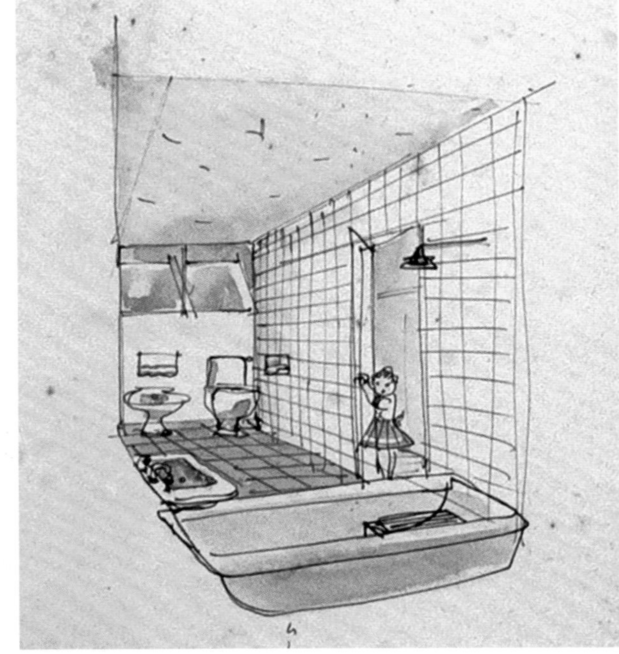

These prototype studies coincide with the design and construction of Bo Bardi's Glass House and the publication of her article in *Habitat*, no. 3, "7,000 cruzeiros homes" (the cruzeiro was the Brazilian currency at the time). Here Bo Bardi described a residence built by a woman in the south of São Paulo, highlighting her creative and economic use of materials, and the beauty and intelligence of the house itself. The studies for the Economic Houses, which do not refer to a specific site or program, investigate design possibilities for small homes based on different materials and building solutions. One proposal refers to the Glass House: a rectangular volume resting on pilings and covered by transparent planes. This prototype becomes a unit in a study for a housing development, replicated among green areas and other service buildings—conforming to the logic of modern architecture and urban development.—VM

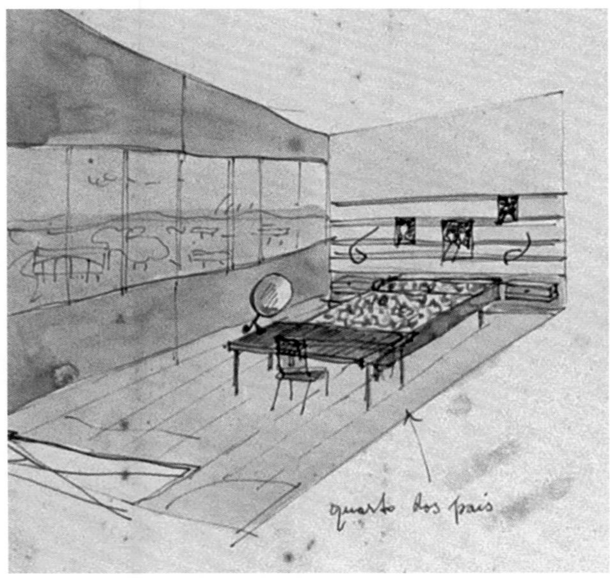

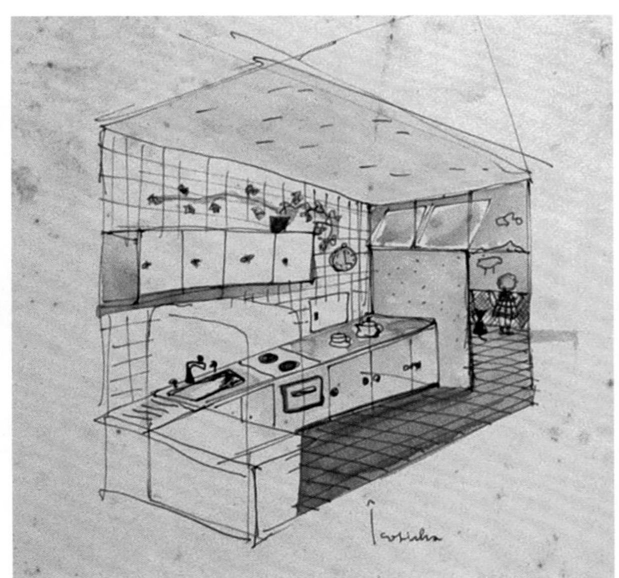

FIGS. 282–287
Lina Bo Bardi, *Perspectives: Economic Houses*, 1951.
Watercolor, marker, and ink on card stock, 70 x 100 cm.
Collection of the Instituto Bardi/ Casa de Vidro, São Paulo

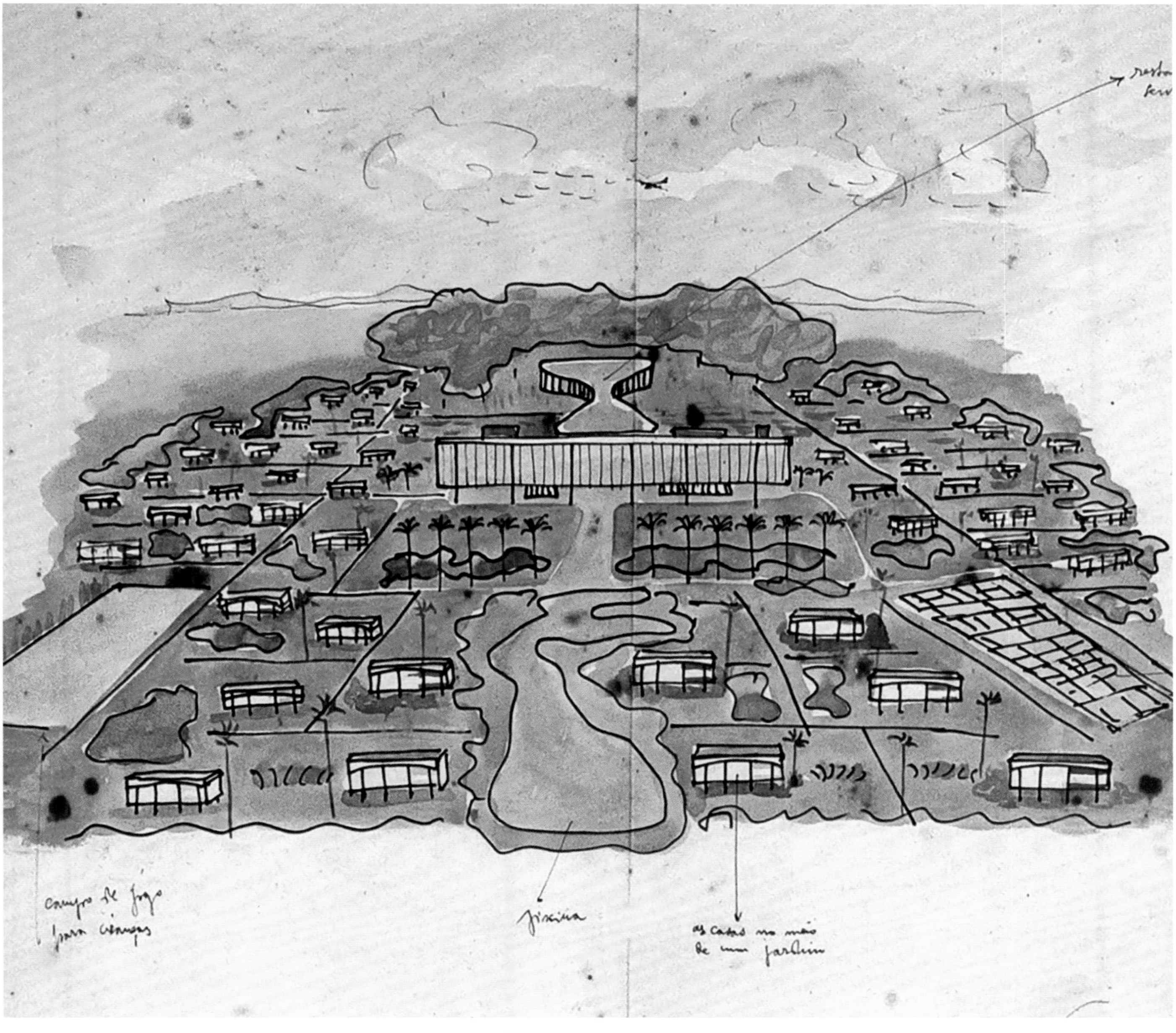

Chame-Chame House

Salvador
1958
(Architectural project)

FIG. 290 →
Exterior view of the Chame-Chame House, undated

FIG. 291 ↘
Lina Bo Bardi, *Cross section, lateral elevation*, 1958. Graphite and ink on parchment paper, 50.5 x 60 cm. Collection of the Instituto Bardi/Casa de Vidro, São Paulo

FIG. 288 ↓
Lina Bo Bardi, *Implementation plan and ground floor*, 1958. Watercolor, graphite, and ink on parchment paper, 60.5 x 85.5 cm. Collection of the Instituto Bardi/ Casa de Vidro, São Paulo

FIG. 289 ↓↓
Lina Bo Bardi, *Implementation plan and upper floor*, 1958. Watercolor, graphite, and ink on parchment paper, 60.5 x 85.5 cm. Collection of the Instituto Bardi/ Casa de Vidro, São Paulo

Concurrent with the installation of *Bahia in Ibirapuera*, this project demonstrates Bo Bardi's radical move away from the modernist architectural canon to an idiosyncratic relationship with place and Afro-Bahian culture. The design for the Chame-Chame House was developed around a large preexisting jackfruit tree—a powerful symbol in Afro-Brazilian religions—and fuses vegetation, topography, and architecture. Its pebbled surfaces were incised with shells, fragments of dolls, and other elements that evoke the ancestry of indigenous *sambaquis* (shell mounds). The curves marking the border between landscape and street were created with walls that form the garage access ramp and unfolded from the volume of the house itself. The spiral ascent continued from the garage, level with the public and utility areas of the house, up the curved staircase to the first floor, which contained the bedrooms. From bottom to top, the whole narrowed in width, like a ziggurat. The roof over the living area served as a hanging garden and provided the rooms with access to the jackfruit. The house was demolished in 1984 to make way for a residential building.—DJ

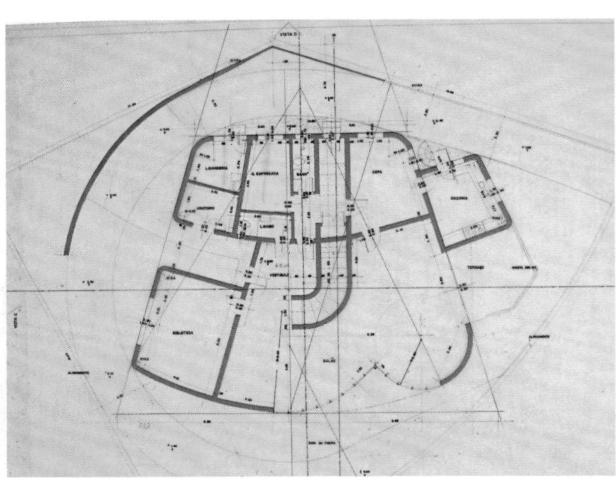

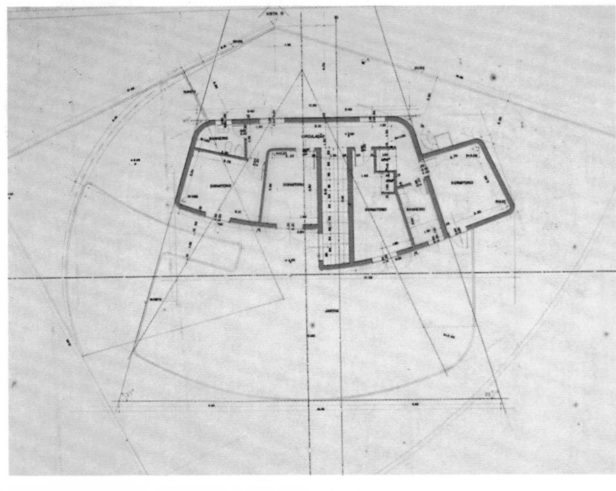

Valéria Cirell House

São Paulo
1958
(Architectural project)

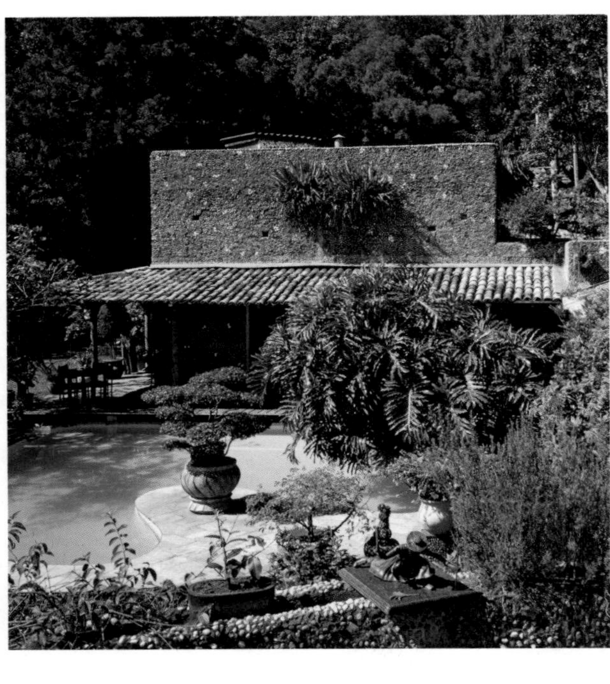

FIG. 292
Exterior view of the Valéria Cirell House, 2002

Bo Bardi built this simple villa for Valéria Cirell around 100 meters from the Glass House. The project dates from the same year as the Chame-Chame House, in Salvador, and although the surface treatment is similar in both cases, the spatial organization of the Cirell House more closely approximates that of the Glass House. The residence is a cubic volume divided by a diagonally oriented mezzanine that accommodates the single bedroom; a smaller block contains the utility rooms. As in the Glass House, a patio between them provides structural definition. If the thin metal pillars of the Bardi residence express a certain developmental optimism about technology, the rough logs that support Cirell's porch signify a rethinking of this idea. Simplicity in construction, self-supporting masonry, and a traditional wood mezzanine combine with a radical spatial concision: there is no physical separation between environments. All spaces orbit around the fireplace, as in huts and primitive houses organized around a hearth. The surrounding veranda was originally covered with thatch, alluding to Brazilian vernacular architecture. This house exemplifies the poetic economy of what Bo Bardi called "poor architecture," in line with both the *arte povera* phenomenon in Italy and the "aesthetic of hunger" manifesto by Bahian filmmaker Glauber Rocha.—DJ

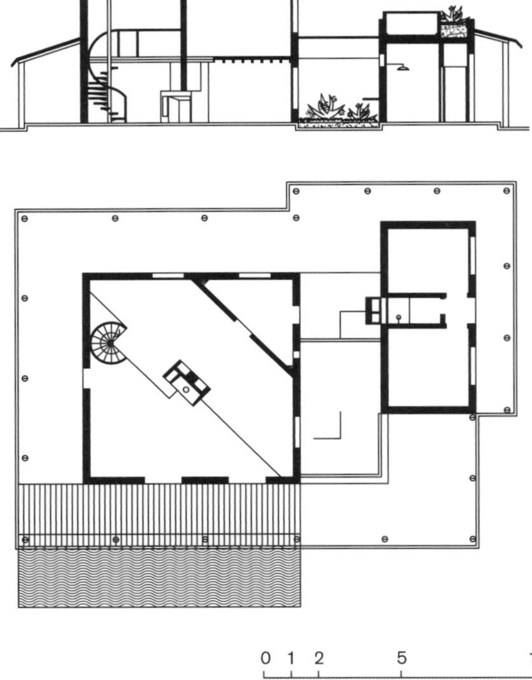

FIGS. 293–294 ↑
Section and plan of the Valéria Cirell House

FIG. 295 ↗
Lina Bo Bardi, *Front elevation with treatment of the roof, doors, and wall*, 1958. Watercolor, ballpoint pen, and colored pencil on offset paper, 54.5 x 64 cm. Collection of the Instituto Bardi/Casa de Vidro, São Paulo

FIG. 296 →
Exterior view of the Valéria Cirell House, 1958

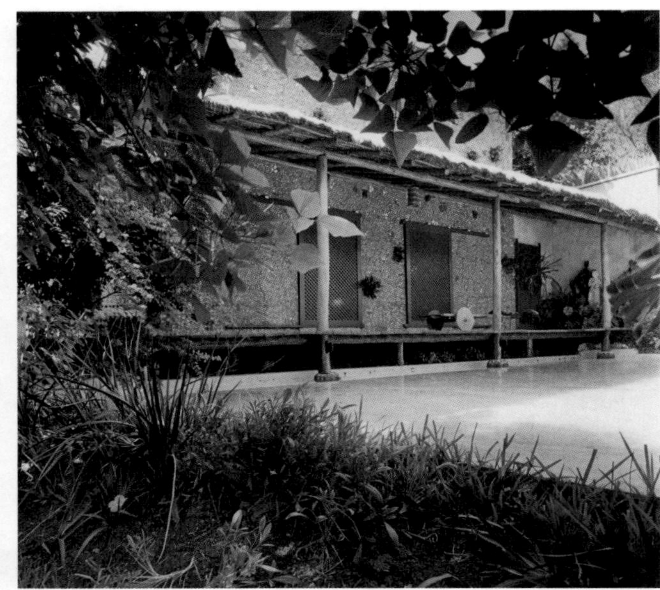

FIGS. 297–298
Exterior views of the Valéria Cirell House, 1958

FIG. 299
Lina Bo Bardi, *Lateral elevation*, 1958. Graphite and ink on parchment paper, 20 x 40.5 cm. Collection of the Instituto Bardi/ Casa de Vidro, São Paulo

FIG. 300
Interior view of the Valéria Cirell House, 1958

FIG. 301
Exterior view of the Valéria Cirell House, 2002

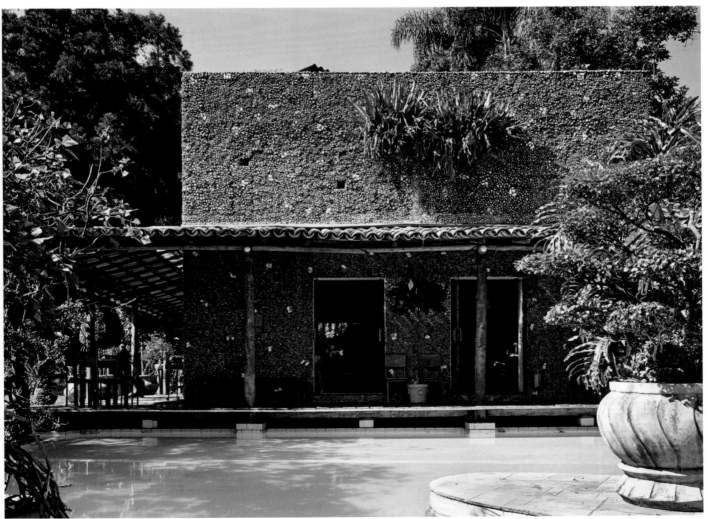

Circular House

1962 (Unrealized project)

FIG. 302
Lina Bo Bardi, *Elevation*, 1962. Watercolor, graphite, and ink on parchment paper, 27.5 x 42.5 cm. Collection of the Instituto Bardi/Casa de Vidro, São Paulo

The Circular House was created by Bo Bardi for Figueiredo Ferraz, the engineer responsible for MASP's construction. The design of the house evolves from a spiral form surrounding a central space that articulates the circulation between rooms and floors. In the perspective drawings that illustrate the relationship between interior and exterior, she sketched a volume that references an ancient housing typology: the hut. Here it is updated with a glassed-in structure that provides direct visual interaction between the central internal space, the garden/roof, and the sky. As in other Bo Bardi projects, for instance the sketches for MASP and the Cirell House (1958), the drawings for the Circular House highlight its vegetation, which seems to spread freely onto the building facade. Thus, Bo Bardi's visual presentation takes into account the action of time upon the landscape and emphasizes the organic nature of the construction.—VM

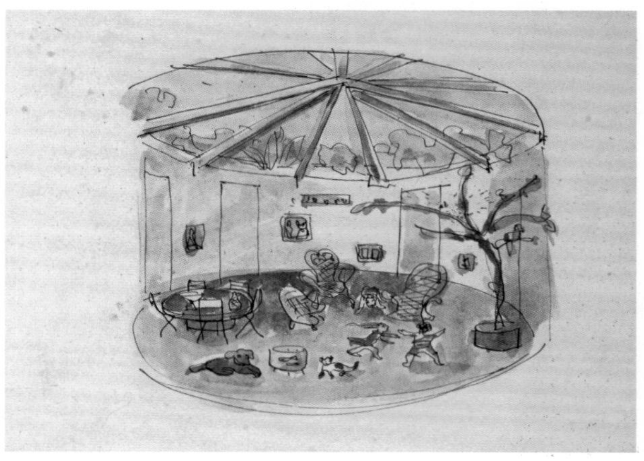

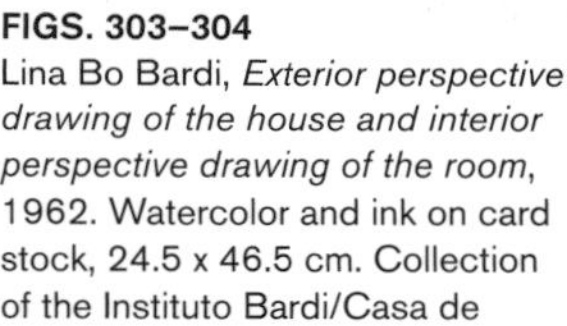

FIGS. 303–304
Lina Bo Bardi, *Exterior perspective drawing of the house and interior perspective drawing of the room*, 1962. Watercolor and ink on card stock, 24.5 x 46.5 cm. Collection of the Instituto Bardi/Casa de Vidro, São Paulo

CONVIVIAL SPACES

Pavilion at Lage Park

Rio de Janeiro
1965
(Unrealized project)

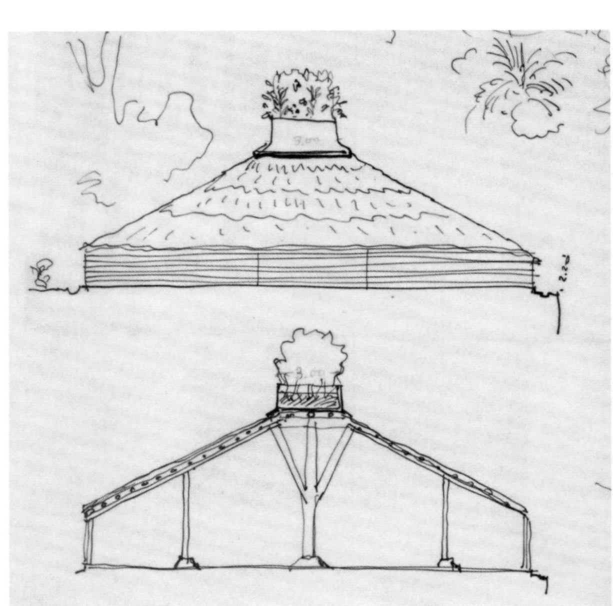

FIG. 305
Lina Bo Bardi, *Pavilion at Lage Park: section and elevation*, 1965. Ballpoint pen, graphite, and ink on parchment paper, 40 x 71 cm. Collection of the Instituto Bardi/Casa de Vidro, São Paulo

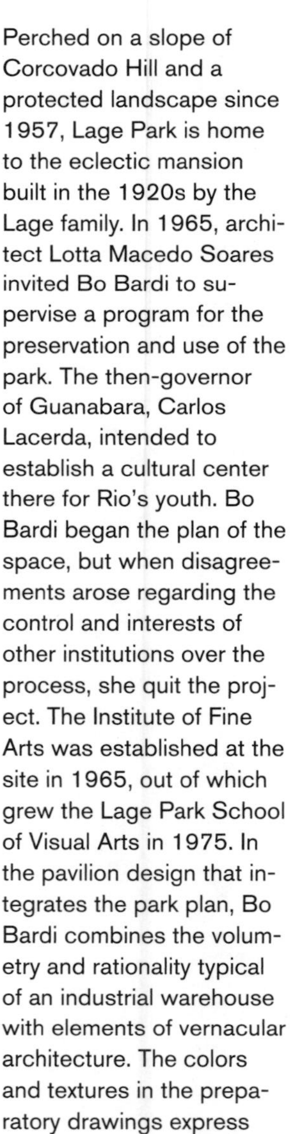

Perched on a slope of Corcovado Hill and a protected landscape since 1957, Lage Park is home to the eclectic mansion built in the 1920s by the Lage family. In 1965, architect Lotta Macedo Soares invited Bo Bardi to supervise a program for the preservation and use of the park. The then-governor of Guanabara, Carlos Lacerda, intended to establish a cultural center there for Rio's youth. Bo Bardi began the plan of the space, but when disagreements arose regarding the control and interests of other institutions over the process, she quit the project. The Institute of Fine Arts was established at the site in 1965, out of which grew the Lage Park School of Visual Arts in 1975. In the pavilion design that integrates the park plan, Bo Bardi combines the volumetry and rationality typical of an industrial warehouse with elements of vernacular architecture. The colors and textures in the preparatory drawings express the structure's materiality and its relationship to the surroundings. The stone floor and the "dead trees" form the transition between the building and the park's vegetation. The thatched roof ridge, highlighted in red in the perspective drawing, sprouts like a plant bed between the two roof gables.—VM

FIG. 307
Lina Bo Bardi, *Pavilion at Lage Park: perspective drawing*, 1965. Watercolor and ink on offset paper, 24.5 x 46.5 cm. Collection of the Instituto Bardi/Casa de Vidro, São Paulo

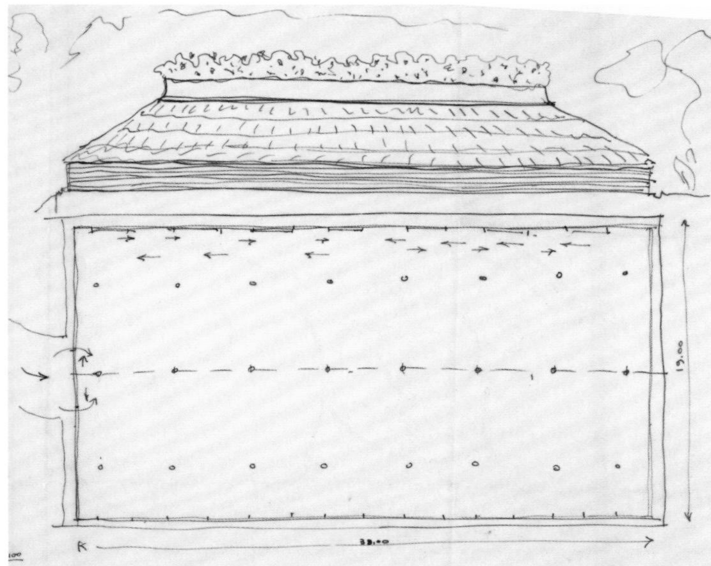

FIG. 306
Lina Bo Bardi, *Pavilion at Lage Park: section and elevation*, 1965. Ballpoint pen, graphite, and ink on parchment paper, 40 x 71 cm. Collection of the Instituto Bardi/ Casa de Vidro, São Paulo

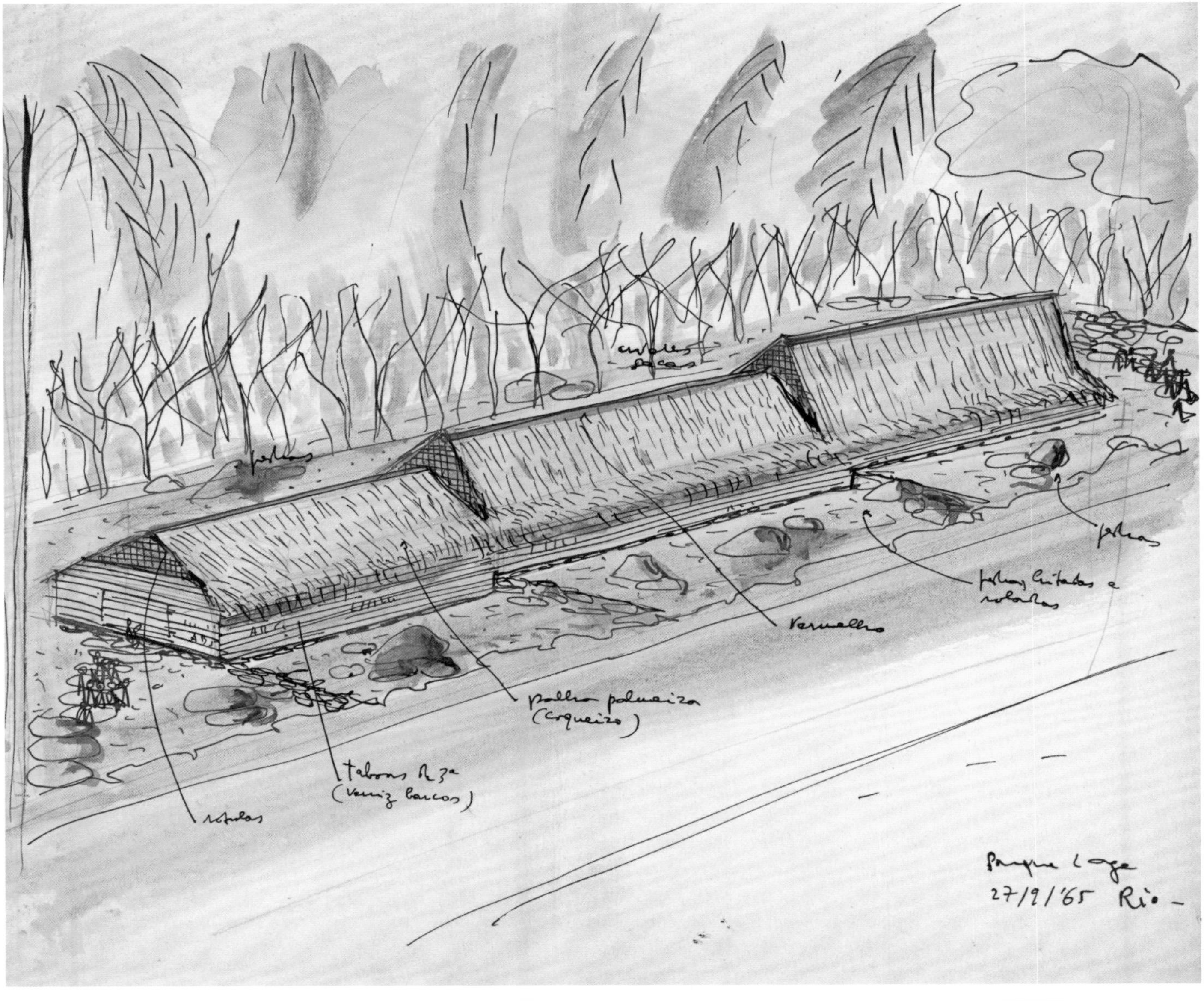

Church of Espírito Santo do Cerrado

Uberlândia, Minas Gerais
1976–82
With the collaboration of André Vainer and Marcelo Carvalho Ferraz (Architectural project)

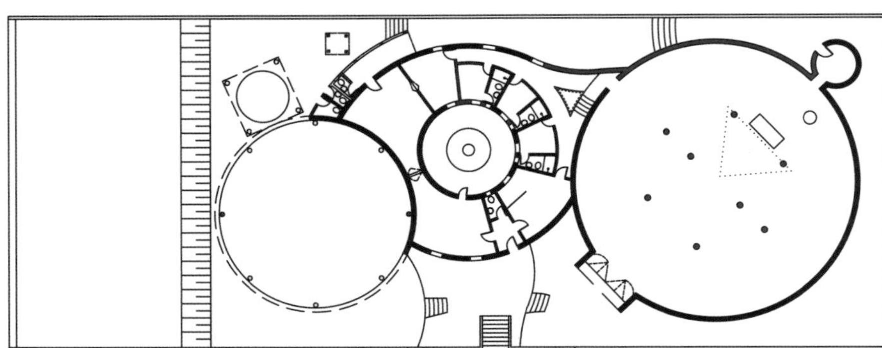

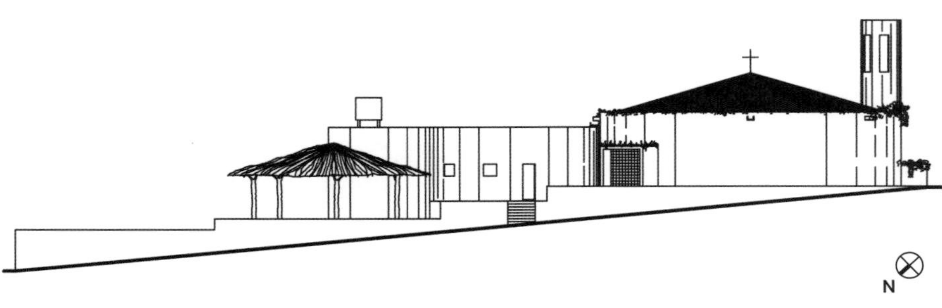

FIGS. 308–309
Plan and elevation of the Church of Espírito Santo do Cerrado

Located in the working-class neighborhood of Jaraguá, on the outskirts of Uberlândia, Minas Gerais, this church arose from the contact between the architect and her collaborators with Franciscan friars from the Cerrado Mineiro region. Given the lack of public facilities in the area, the complex was planned as a community center, encompassing a small soccer field, a barbeque pavilion for events, a residence for three caretakers, and the church. The gently sloping rectangular grounds access the street on three sides. Four cylindrical structures comprise the building complex. In the lower section is the soccer field, an empty space that functions as an entryway to the structures above. The large covered pavilion references indigenous thatched houses and creates a transition between the open area of the soccer field and the enclosed spaces of the cloister and church. The fourth cylinder is the bell tower, whose exposed masonry construction maintains the project's rigorous unity. The symbolism of elevation suggested by the property's natural slope is enhanced by the intentional misalignment of the cylindrical structures that disrupts the uphill axis. Further, the church is accessed along the side street, pointing to true north, respecting the tradition of religious buildings that provide sun exposure to the main facade throughout the day. A garden/gutter crowns the church cylinder with plants from the *cerrado* (savanna).—DJ

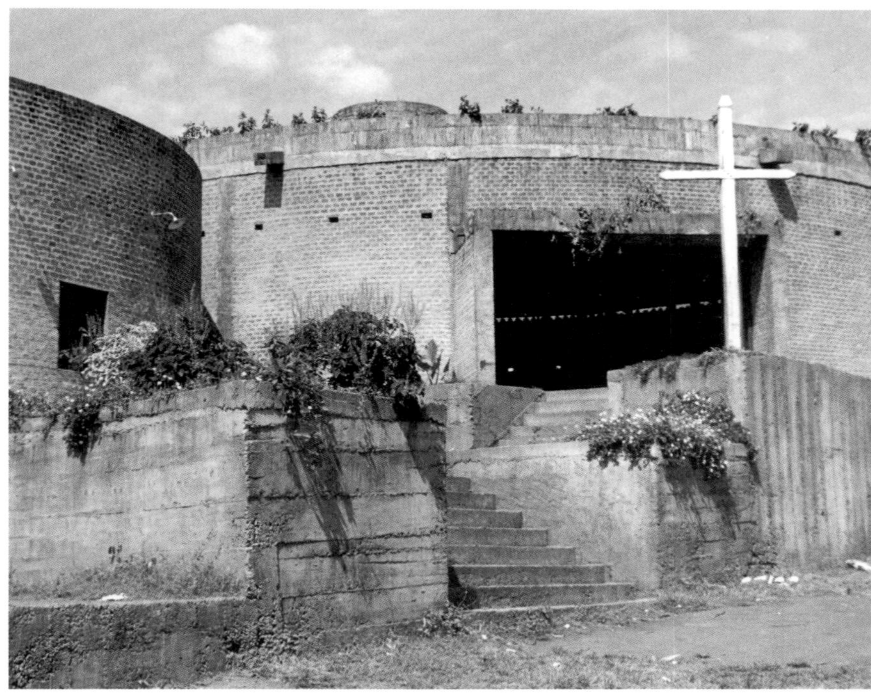

FIG. 310
Exterior view of the Church of Espírito Santo do Cerrado, 1980s

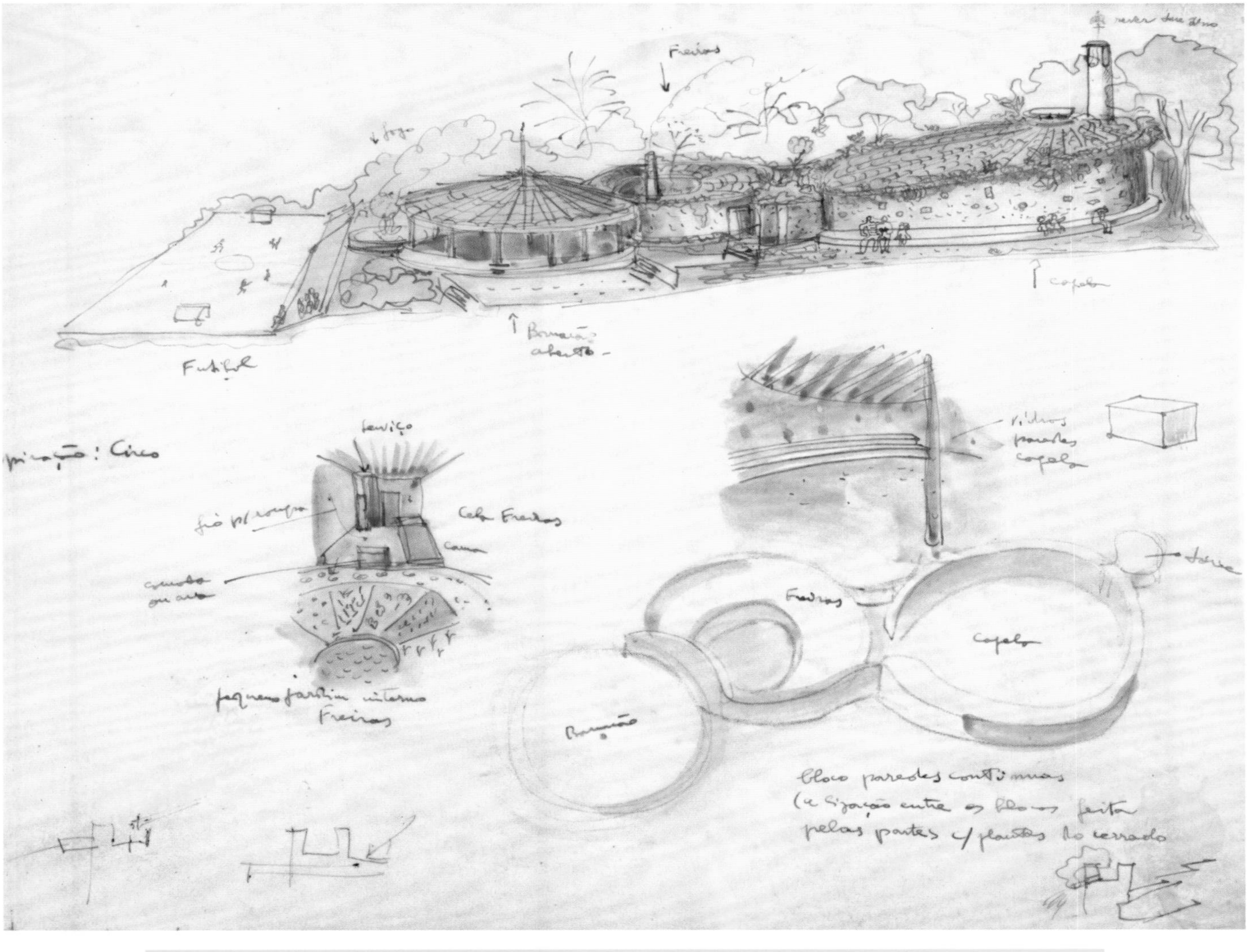

FIG. 311
Lina Bo Bardi, *Perspective drawing of the complex*, 1976. Watercolor, graphite, ink, and collage on parchment and offset paper, 23.5 x 32.5 cm. Collection of the Instituto Bardi/Casa de Vidro, São Paulo

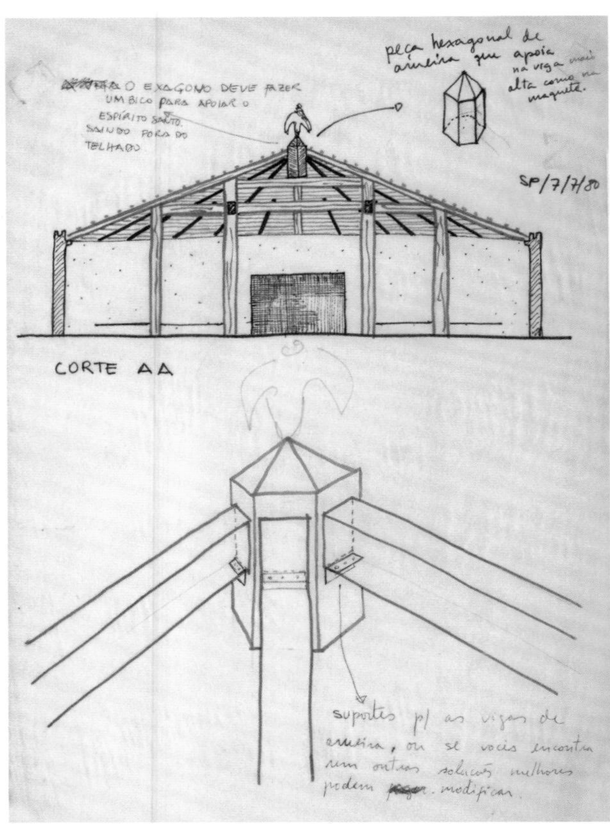

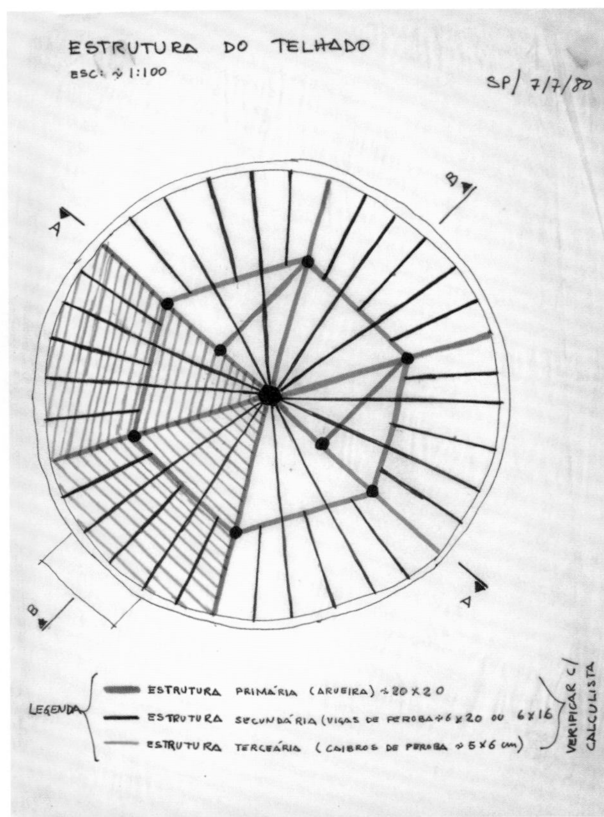

FIG. 312
Lina Bo Bardi, *Section of the roof structure*, 1976. Ballpoint pen, graphite, and ink on parchment paper, 35 x 25 cm. Collection of the Instituto Bardi/Casa de Vidro, São Paulo

FIG. 313
Lina Bo Bardi, *Plan of the roof structure*, 1976. Ballpoint pen, graphite, and ink on parchment paper, 35 x 25.5 cm. Collection of the Instituto Bardi/Casa de Vidro, São Paulo

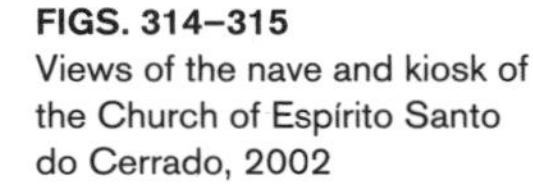

FIGS. 314–315
Views of the nave and kiosk of the Church of Espírito Santo do Cerrado, 2002

FIG. 316
View of the altar of the Church of Espírito Santo do Cerrado, 1980s

FIG. 317
Exterior view of the Church of Espírito Santo do Cerrado, 2002

Sesc Pompeia

São Paulo
1977–86
With the collaboration of André Vainer and Marcelo Carvalho Ferraz (Architectural project)

The ensemble of buildings that comprise Sesc Pompeia carries a symbolic relationship between programming and architecture. Maintained by a trade association, the complex is housed in a former drum factory in the Pompeia neighborhood of São Paulo. The factory was slated for demolition, and the decision to preserve it was defended by Bo Bardi, whose proposed use subverted the industrial plant's serial logic of labor with activities considered unproductive, focused mainly on relaxation, leisure, and well-being. The facility's program is divided between the cultural section, which occupies the structure of the old factory, and the sports section, concentrated in two new towers. The service road became the main axis of the complex: the "citadel of freedom" street. The largest of the warehouses was converted into a multipurpose space qualified by poetic incisions: a meandering reflecting pool dubbed the São Francisco River and a large open fireplace. The library is situated in a reinforced concrete mezzanine, framed by but deviating from the preexisting structure. A restaurant, studios, and an auditorium are arrayed along the internal street and occupy other warehouses. The preservation of the factory limited the area on which to build at ground level, which is bifurcated by a stream (now covered) and—at the time—protected by an undeveloped perimeter. A 30 x 40–meter rectangular tower, aligned with the factory axis, houses the pool and four floors of multisport courts. Across the stream, a smaller tower contains the stairs, elevators, changing and exercise rooms. Bridges of exposed concrete, forming an eloquent fan when viewed from above and below, cross the airspace between the towers.—DJ

FIG. 318
Lina Bo Bardi, *Perspective drawing, Sesc Pompeia Factory*, 1977–86. Watercolor, ballpoint pen, and ink on card stock, 49 x 35 cm. Collection of the Instituto Bardi/Casa de Vidro, São Paulo

FIG. 319
View of the entrance to Sesc Pompeia, 2002

FIG. 320
Lina Bo Bardi, *Perspective drawing of the internal road, Sesc Pompeia Factory*, 1977–86. Watercolor, ballpoint pen, and graphite on card stock, 28.5 x 38.5 cm. Collection of the Instituto Bardi/Casa de Vidro, São Paulo

FIG. 321
View of the workshops at Sesc Pompeia, 2002

FIG. 322
View of the living area and the exhibition space at Sesc Pompeia, 2002

FIG. 323
View of the reading rooms in the library at Sesc Pompeia, 2002

FIG. 324 ↗
Lina Bo Bardi, *Perspective drawing of the warehouse interior, Sesc Pompeia Factory*, 1977–86. Watercolor and graphite on card stock, 28.5 x 38.5 cm. Collection of the Instituto Bardi/Casa de Vidro, São Paulo

FIG. 325 →
View of the living area and exhibition space at Sesc Pompeia, 2002

FIG. 326
Lina Bo Bardi, *Study of the walkways for the sports block, Sesc Pompeia Factory*, 1977–86. Marker and graphite on parchment paper, 50 x 75 cm. Collection of the Instituto Bardi/Casa de Vidro, São Paulo

FIG. 331 →
View of the warehouses, solarium, and sports block at Sesc Pompeia, 2002

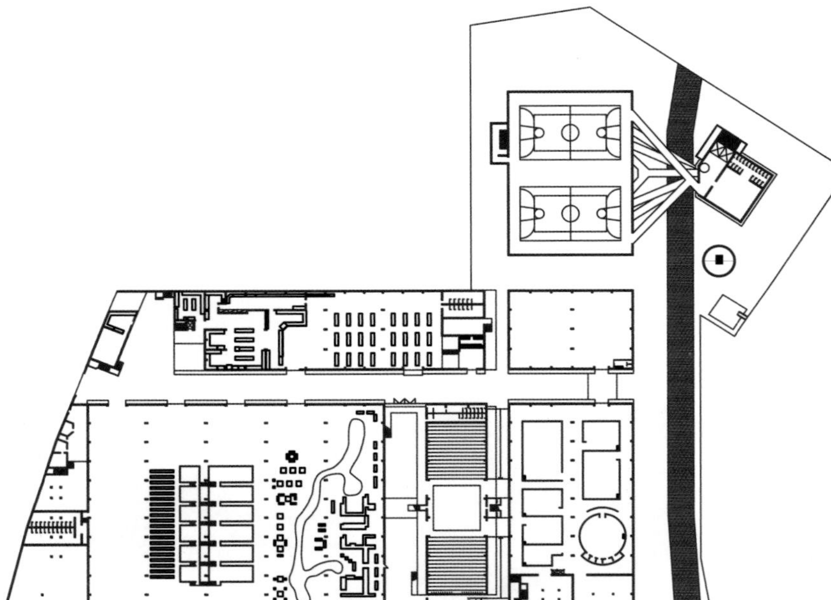

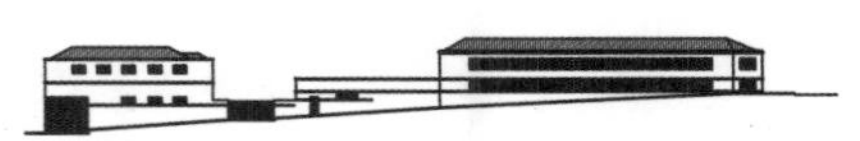

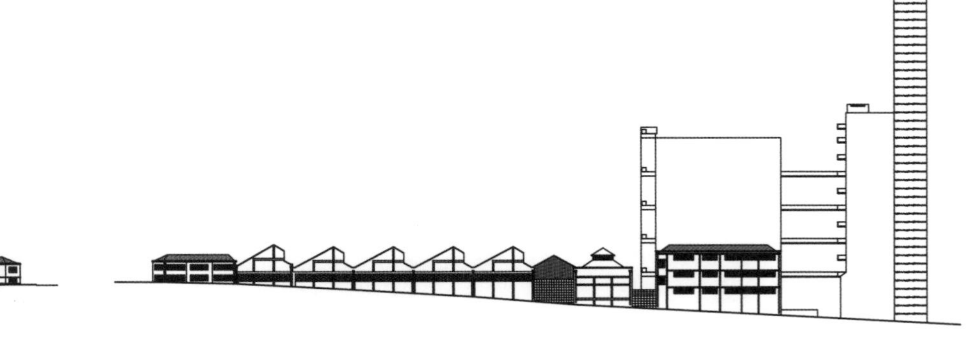

N ⊕ 0 5 10 20 50 m

FIGS. 327–330
Section of the sports block, plan of the complex, elevations of Rua Clélia and Rua Barão do Bananal, Sesc Pompeia

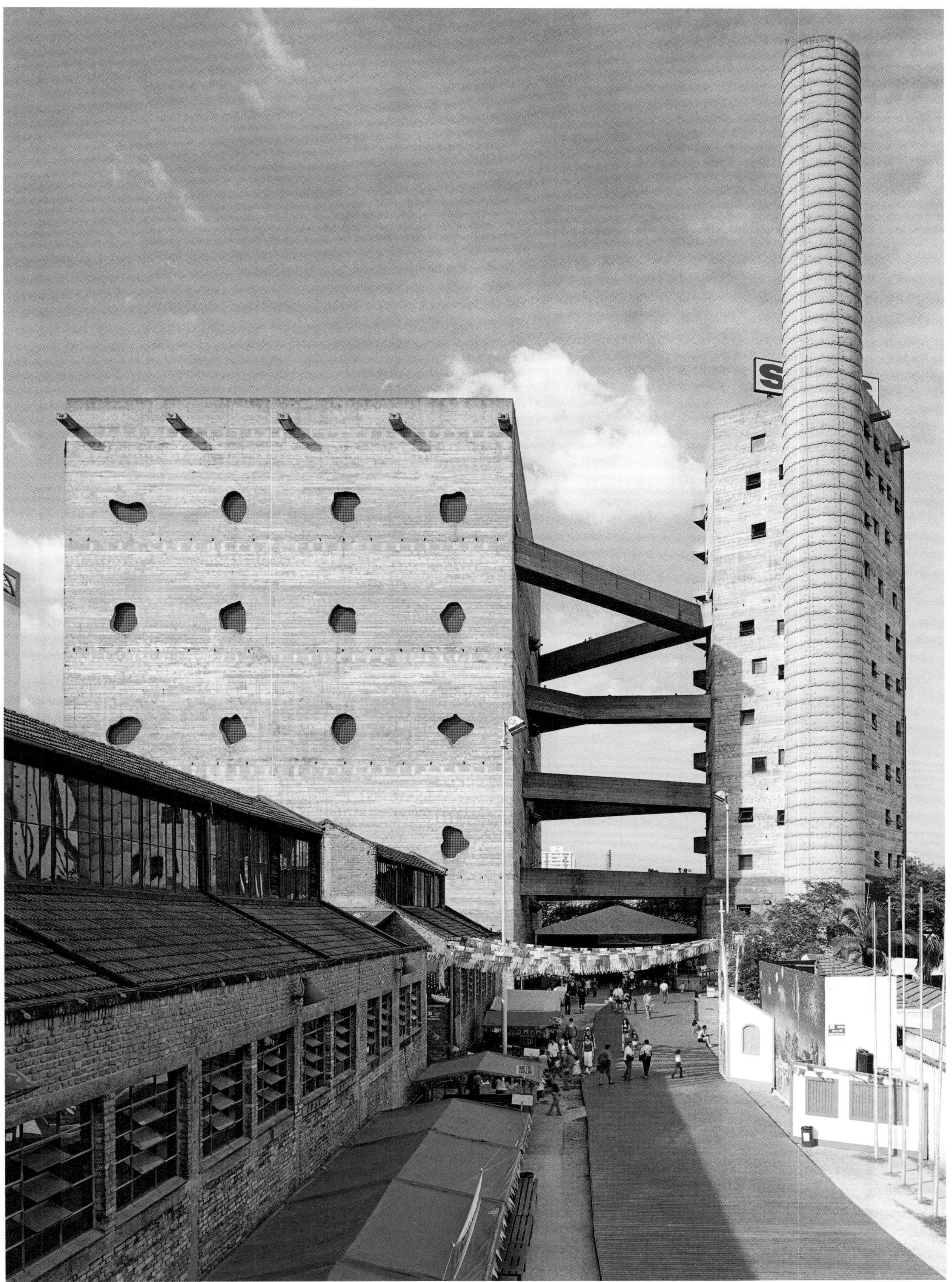

FIG. 332 →
Lina Bo Bardi, *Walkways in the sports block, Sesc Pompeia Factory*, 1977–86. Ballpoint pen and marker on parchment paper, 31.5 x 21.5 cm. Collection of the Instituto Bardi/Casa de Vidro, São Paulo

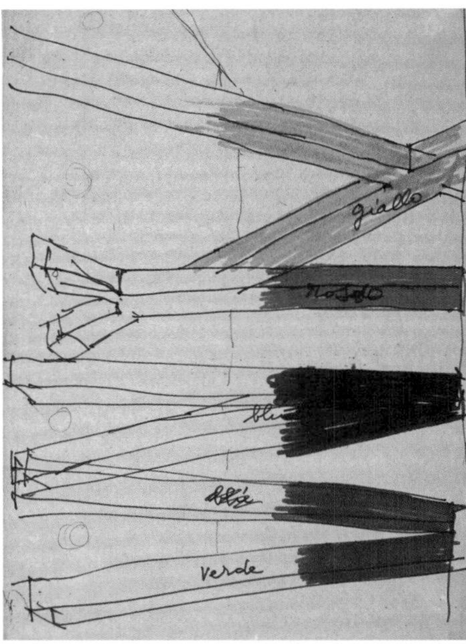

FIG. 333
View of the walkways of the sports block at Sesc Pompeia, 2002

FIG. 334
View of the tower with access to the sports block at Sesc Pompeia, 2002

FIG. 335 ↗
View of the multisport area at Sesc Pompeia, 2008

FIG. 336 ↗↗
View from a "window hole" of the sports block at Sesc Pompeia, undated

FIG. 337 →
View of a walkway of the sports block at Sesc Pompeia, 2002

QUADRA 2

Benin House in Bahia

Salvador
1987
With João Filgueiras Lima and the collaboration of Marcelo Carvalho Ferraz and Marcelo Suzuki (Architectural project)

The Benin House in Bahia is located at the foot of Pelourinho Square, next to the church of Nossa Senhora do Rosário dos Pretos, in Salvador's historic center. A product of diplomatic relations between Brazil and Benin—a country on the West African coast from which the majority of enslaved black people in the Bahian Recôncavo came—the project's original program included a cultural exchange center with lodging for Beninese representatives, a restaurant, and exhibition spaces for the collection of ethnologist and photographer Pierre Verger. The complex consists of large houses connected by an internal garden, in which a cabana with a communal table serves the restaurant. Bo Bardi retained the original facades of the mansions and the internal concrete reinforcement, incorporating new elements such as the staircases and precast panels developed in partnership with architect João Filgueiras Lima, known as Lelé. The cladding of the beams and concrete pillars with fabrics and hand-thatched coconut fronds added lightness to the exhibition room, where an open staircase, parallel to the wall of rough stone and scraped plaster, is supported by a single pillar. Thus the space blends temporal periods and techniques, establishing relationships and frictions between materials typical of modernism and artisanal production.—VM

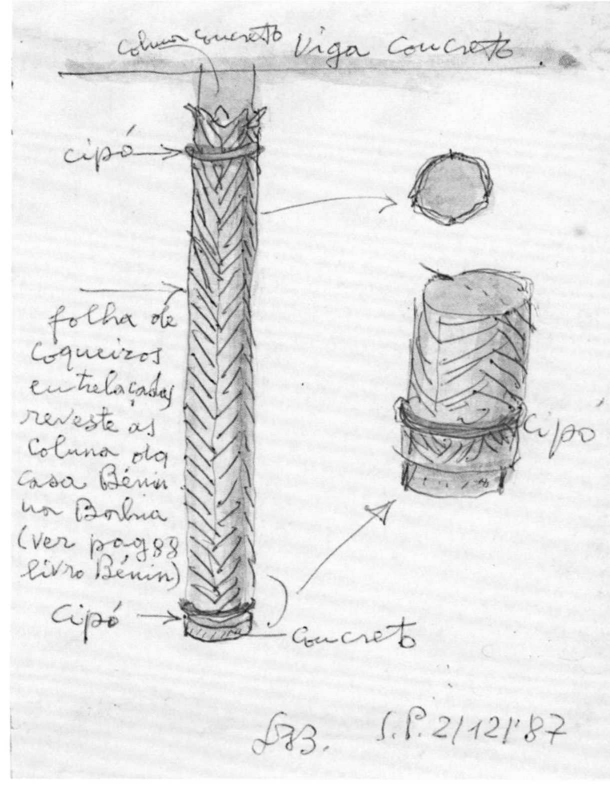

FIG. 338
Lina Bo Bardi, *Benin House in Bahia: thatch covering of pillars*, 1987. Ballpoint pen and gouache on offset paper, 19 x 28 cm. Collection of the Instituto Bardi/Casa de Vidro, São Paulo

FIG. 339
Interior view of the Benin House in Bahia, 2002

FIG. 340
Exterior view of the Benin House in Bahia, 2018

FIG. 341
Lina Bo Bardi, *Elevation: restaurant*, 1987. Ballpoint pen and gouache on offset paper, 32.5 x 49 cm. Collection of the Instituto Bardi/Casa de Vidro, São Paulo

FIG. 342
Interior view of the Benin House in Bahia, 2002

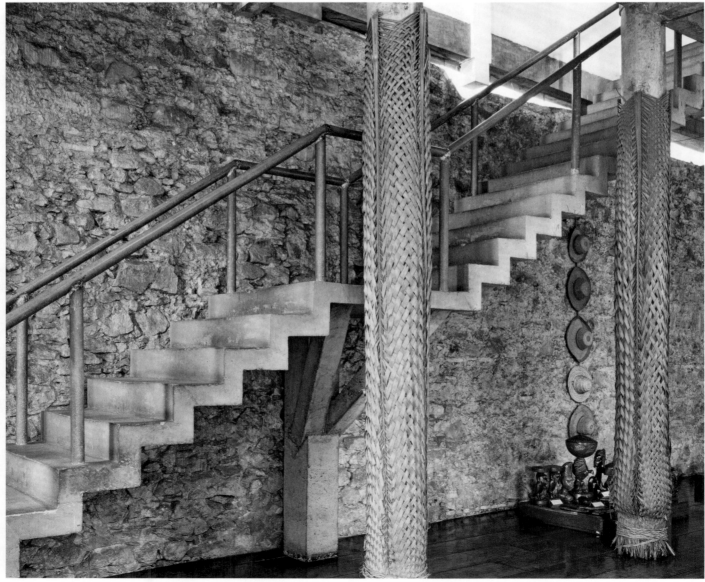

FIG. 343
View of the restaurant at the Benin House in Bahia, undated

FIG. 344
Lina Bo Bardi, *Plan of the table and chair arrangement in the restaurant*, 1987. Colored pencil and reprography on offset paper, 19.5 x 29 cm. Collection of the Instituto Bardi/Casa de Vidro, São Paulo

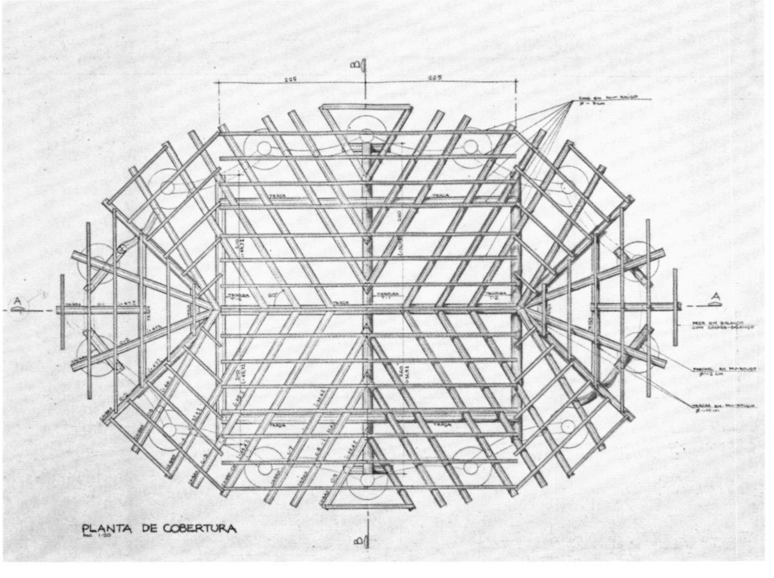

FIG. 345
Lina Bo Bardi, *Plan of the restaurant roof structure*, 1987. Marker, graphite, colored pencil, and reprography on paper, 19.5 x 29 cm. Collection of the Instituto Bardi/Casa de Vidro, São Paulo

Brazil House in Benin

Uidá, Benin
1989
With Marcelo Carvalho Ferraz and Marcelo Suzuki
(Unrealized project)

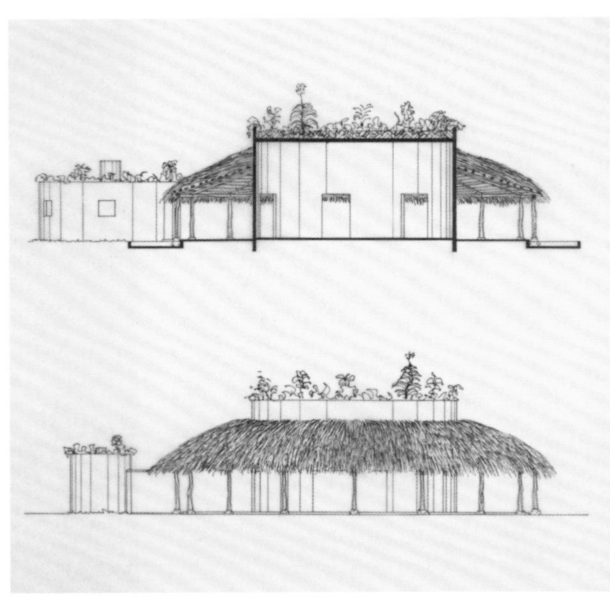

The Brazil House in Benin was one of a group of projects incorporated into a general plan of interventions for the historic center of Salvador that Lina Bo Bardi prepared at the invitation of Gilberto Gil, president of the Gregório de Matos Foundation. They included the Cuba House in Bahia, the Bahia House in Cuba, and the Benin House in Bahia. The Brazil House would have been located in Uidá, a city on the West African coast that was a hub of the transatlantic slave trade. The project envisioned the renovation of a French colonial mansion to accommodate housing for Brazilian representatives and students, a library, and an exhibition space. A new building, sited next to the mansion and surrounded by a sandy expanse of coconut palms, would make room for a restaurant. The mixing of materials such as straw and concrete with structural elements such as the balcony and a reflecting pool, as well as the fluidity of the circular plan expressed in the project sketches, contrast with the rigid colonial-era layout, which compartmentalizes and hierarchizes the space into several rectangular rooms.—VM

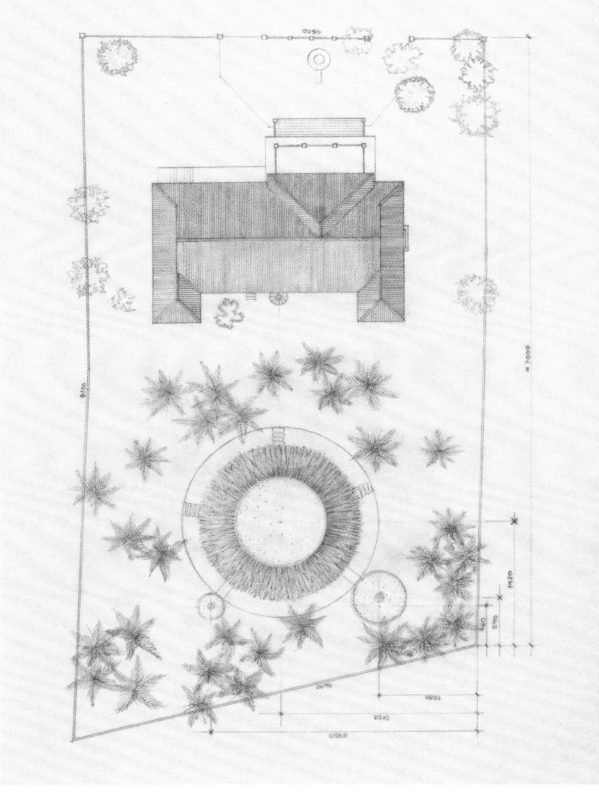

FIG. 346 ↑↑
Lina Bo Bardi, *Section and elevation*, 1989. Ink on parchment paper, 30 x 43 cm. Collection of the Instituto Bardi/Casa de Vidro, São Paulo

FIG. 347 ↑
Lina Bo Bardi, *Plan*, 1989. Ballpoint pen, marker, and graphite on offset paper, 31.5 x 21.5 cm. Collection of the Instituto Bardi/Casa de Vidro, São Paulo

FIG. 348 →
Lina Bo Bardi, *Plan and perspective drawing*, 1989. Ballpoint pen, marker, and graphite on offset paper, 31.5 x 21.5 cm. Collection of the Instituto Bardi/Casa de Vidro, São Paulo

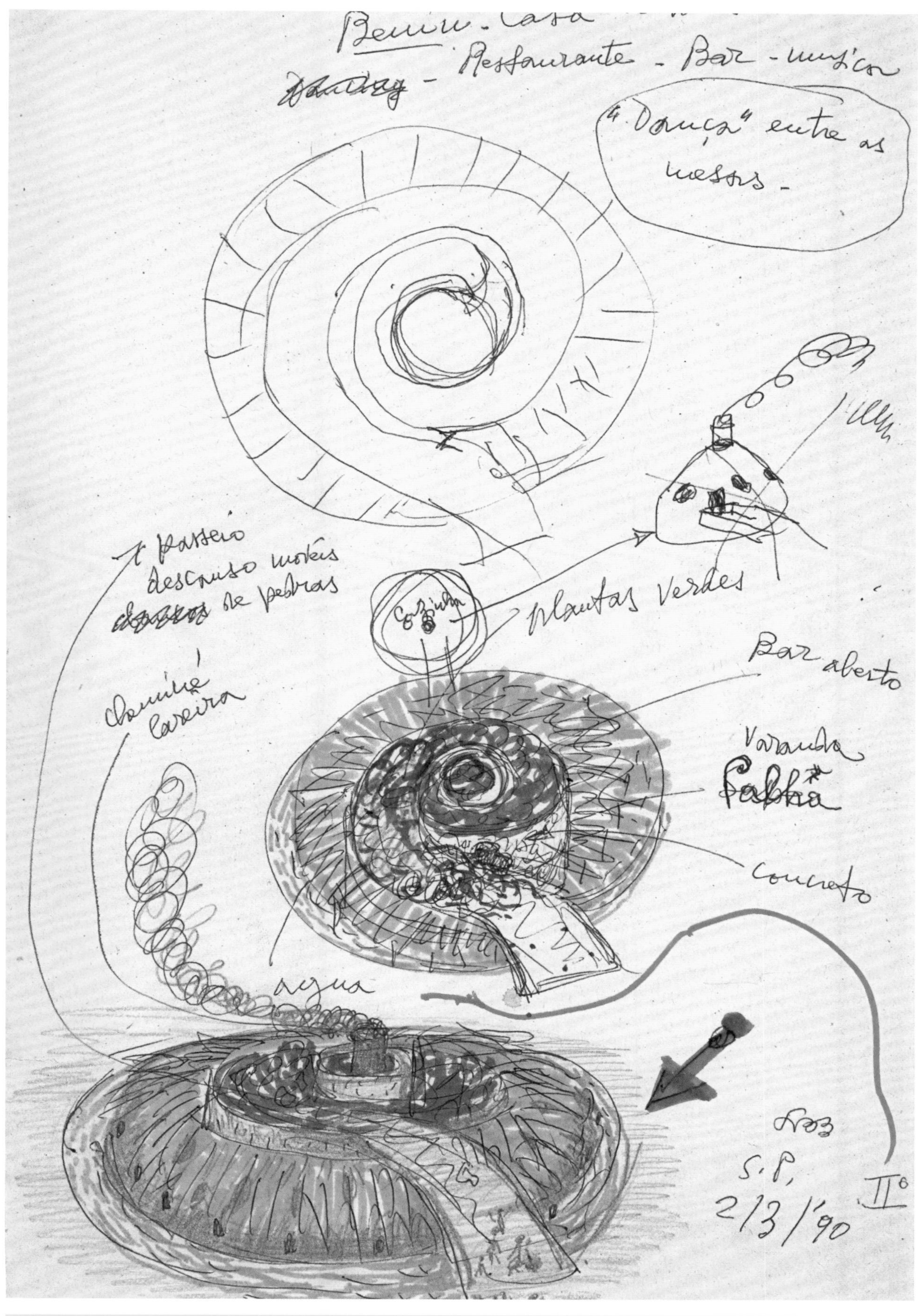
Benin - Casa
Restaurante - Bar - música
"Dança" entre as mesas
Cozinha
plantas verdes
Bar aberto
Varanda
Concreto
água
S.P.
2/3/'90

Ladeira da Misericórdia

Salvador
1987–90
With João Filgueiras Lima and the collaboration of Marcelo Carvalho Ferraz and Marcelo Suzuki (Architectural project)

The Ladeira da Misericórdia (Mercy Slope) experience was conceived as a pilot project for the entire historical center of Salvador. The five lots chosen for intervention were representative of the conditions that marked the Ladeira da Misericórdia, the city's historic street: decaying houses, the ruins of eighteenth-century buildings, and abandoned spaces. The project was carried out in partnership with architect João Filgueiras Lima, called Lelé, widely recognized for his work with prefabricated reinforced mortar. Using this material, the duo developed components that were added as buttresses to the existing buildings—staircases, slabs, and walls. These elements endowed the group with an architectural unity. The generation of Italian architects of which Bo Bardi was a part developed a certain sensitivity to historical heritage that was very different from the Brazilian scene at the time of her arrival in 1946. The relationship between the buildings' rehabilitation and their proposed use is as crucial in this project as in Bo Bardi's work at Sesc Pompeia. The three old mansions—renamed House 1, House 3, and House 7—were refurbished into seven affordable residences on the upper levels and commercial shops on the ground floor. The ruin received the open-air Three Arches Bar, and the vacant lot a new circular structure to house the restaurant Coatí. The recuperation effort, which maintained popular housing, was designed as an antidote to the recurring museification of historic centers in which tourist activity erased the urban memory that preservation sought to recover.—DJ

FIG. 349
View of the Bar of the Three Arches at Ladeira da Misericórdia, 1989

FIG. 350
Lina Bo Bardi, *Principal elevation (Ladeira da Misericórdia), wall elevation (bastions)*, 1987. Watercolor, marker, and ballpoint pen on offset paper, 48.5 x 98 cm. Collection of the Instituto Bardi/Casa de Vidro, São Paulo

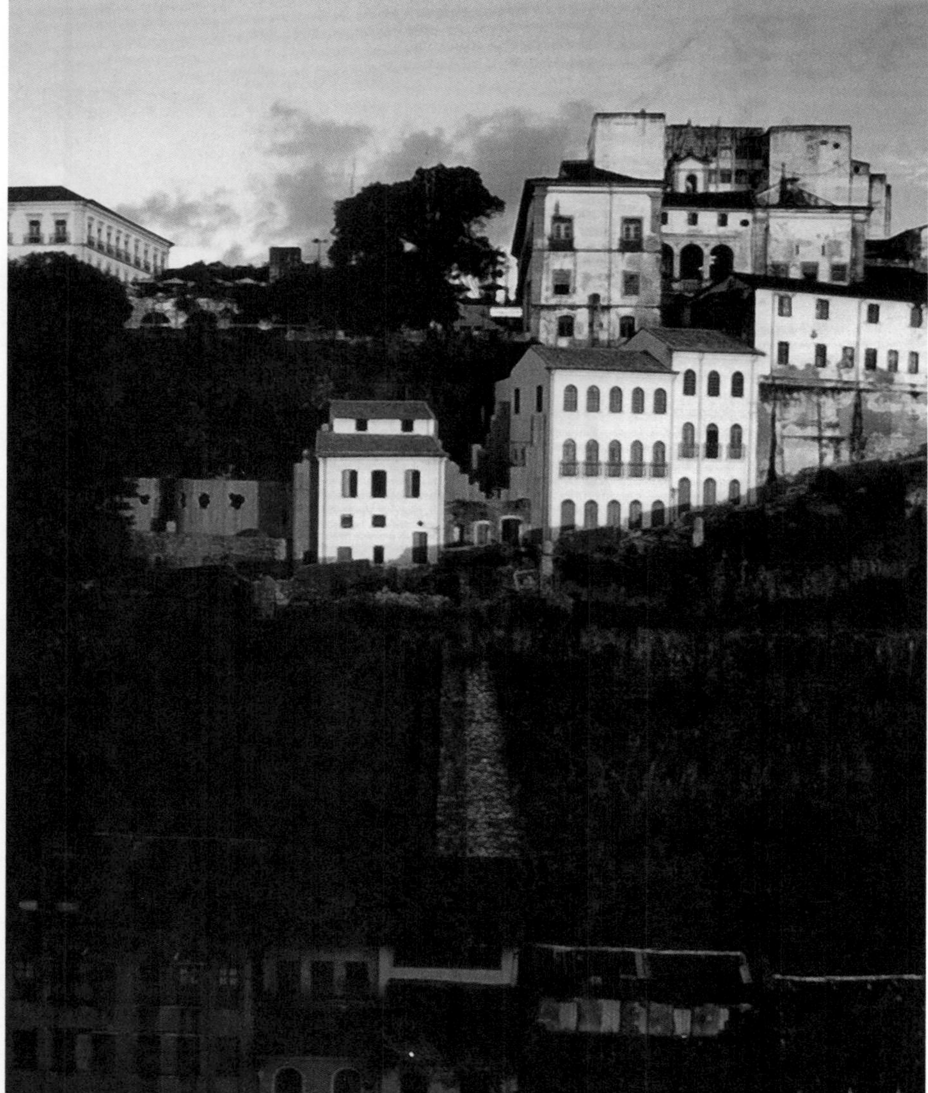

FIG. 351
View of Ladeira da Misericórdia, after the recuperation project, 1989

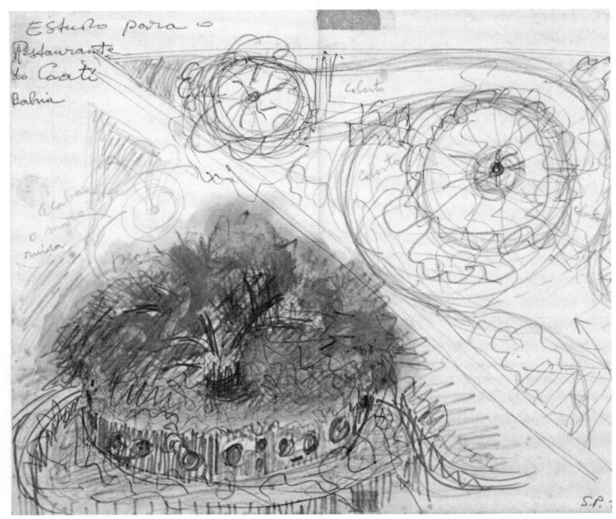

FIG. 352
Lina Bo Bardi, *Plan: Coatí restaurant*, 1987. Watercolor, ballpoint pen, graphite, and colored pencil on offset paper, 29.5 x 41 cm. Collection of the Instituto Bardi/Casa de Vidro, São Paulo

FIG. 353
Interior view of Coatí restaurant on Ladeira da Misericórdia, 2002

FIG. 354
Exterior view of Coatí restaurant on Ladeira da Misericórdia, 2002

THEATER

MASP Auditorium

São Paulo
1957–68
(Architectural project)

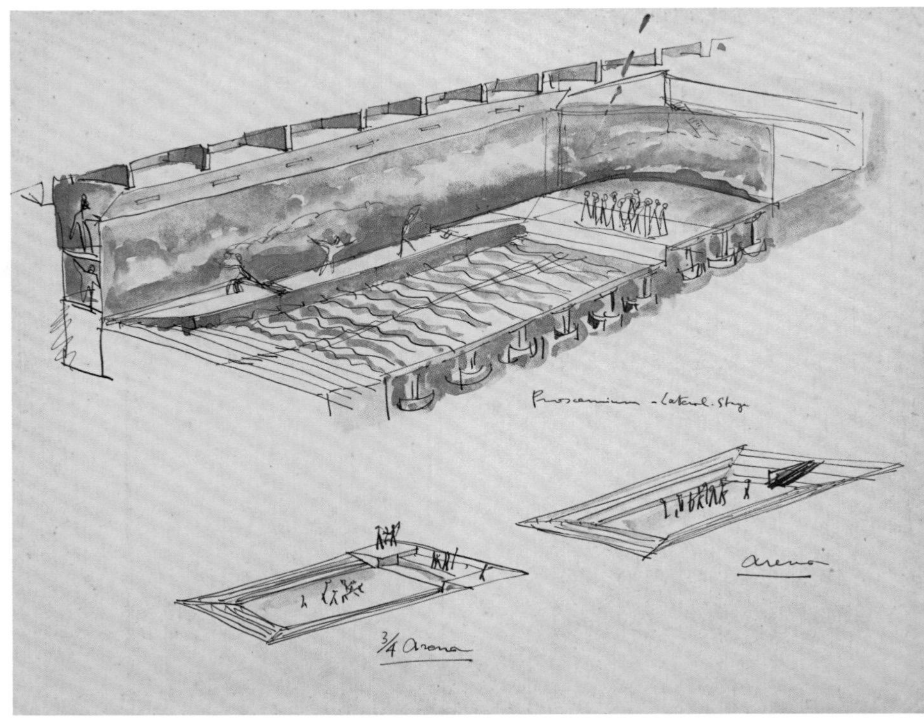

MASP's large auditorium is located on the first basement level below Avenida Paulista. According to theater director José Celso Martinez Corrêa, Bo Bardi's design was conceptually based on the text "The Scene—The Room" by French writer and theorist Antonin Artaud. Here, Artaud defined the "action theater" as a space in which the action develops in the four corners of the room, with spectators positioned in the middle of the scene in portable chairs that allow them to follow the spectacle happening around them. Bo Bardi's drawing explores possible relationships between theater space and staging, with a structure that extends the scene to the sides of the room. In the executed project, the walls and exposed concrete floor extend the boundaries of the stage, allowing simultaneous actions to take place at different levels around the audience. Lina had created studies for mobile seating and developed a prototype of a fixed-base wood armchair for the theater, which has not yet been implemented. After undergoing some adaptations, such as the installation of fixed armchairs and curtains on the stage, the museum auditorium currently hosts performances, seminars, workshops, and other events.—VM

FIG. 355
Lina Bo Bardi, *São Paulo Museum of Art: perspective of proposed proscenium, side stage, 3/4 arena, and arena*, 1957–68. Watercolor and ink on card stock, 29 x 39 cm. Collection of the Instituto Bardi/Casa de Vidro, São Paulo

FIG. 356
View of the auditorium at MASP, Avenida Paulista, without seating, 1969

Castro Alves Theater

Salvador
1960
(Unrealized project)

FIG. 357
Lina Bo Bardi, *Perspective drawing of the feasible lateral and grandstand structure*, 1959–64. Watercolor, graphite, and ink on card stock, 38.5 x 50.5 cm. Collection of the Instituto Bardi/ Casa de Vidro, São Paulo

FIG. 358
Lina Bo Bardi, *Perspective drawing of the feasible lateral and grandstand structure*, ca. 1960. Watercolor, marker, graphite, and ink on card stock, 38.5 x 56.5 cm. Collection of the Instituto Bardi/ Casa de Vidro, São Paulo

Days before its inauguration in 1958, the Castro Alves Theater, designed by architect José Bina Fonyat, suffered a fire that destroyed the building's grandstand and stage. Two years later, the foyer and other spaces of the theater were occupied by the Museum of Modern Art of Bahia, founded and directed by Bo Bardi, who organized onsite exhibitions and educational activities. The designs for the theater's auditorium and temporary bleachers were elaborated by Bo Bardi between 1960 and 1963, while MAM-BA was in residence. On the access ramp to the bleachers, between the foyer and the theater hall, a "cinema auditorium" was established for conferences, classes, image projections, and debates. Using materials at hand, Bo Bardi designed the wood and natural leather chairs adapted to the ramp's angle of incline. The improvised bleachers on wood boards, mounted atop the ruins of the stage, served as seating for performances of *The Threepenny Opera*, by Bertolt Brecht and Kurt Weill, and Albert Camus' *Caligula*, directed by Martim Gonçalves. The lateral structures that appear in the sketches are also present in Bo Bardi's studies for the reconstruction of the Castro Alves Theater, which, as prescribed by her, should follow modern and popular conceptions of theater.—VM

The Threepenny Opera

Castro Alves Theater, Salvador
1960
(Set design)

FIG. 359
Scene from *The Threepenny Opera*, 1960

The Threepenny Opera, written and composed by Bertolt Brecht and Kurt Weill in 1928, was staged with set design by Lina Bo Bardi and direction by Martim Gonçalves in 1960, in the context of the provisional installation of the Museum of Modern Art of Bahia at the Castro Alves Theater in Salvador. Satirizing the traditional format of opera, the play is a blistering critique of bourgeois capitalist society. Bo Bardi's set design incorporated the dilapidated showroom (destroyed in a fire), with its soot-streaked exposed concrete block walls. The whole space was reconfigured in order to facilitate the viewer's active critical attention to the drama, in accordance with the premises of Brechtian theater. The drawings and project plan show the relationship between the structure assembled for the public and the spaces that would serve the movement of actors and the composition of the scenes. The temporary seating and scenic architecture were mounted on the rubble of the original stage so that the opera could unfold at different levels and depths. In the staggered structure in front of the bleachers, a few meters from the audience, the scenic area was defined through the use of everyday objects distributed in space.—VM

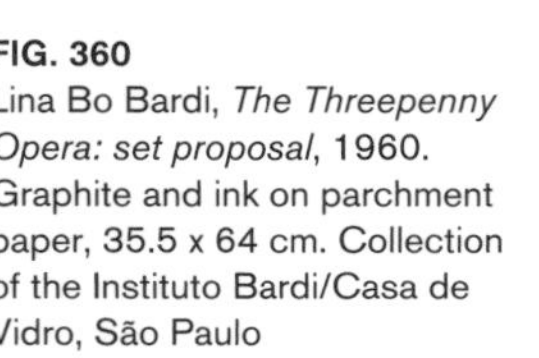

FIG. 360
Lina Bo Bardi, *The Threepenny Opera: set proposal*, 1960. Graphite and ink on parchment paper, 35.5 x 64 cm. Collection of the Instituto Bardi/Casa de Vidro, São Paulo

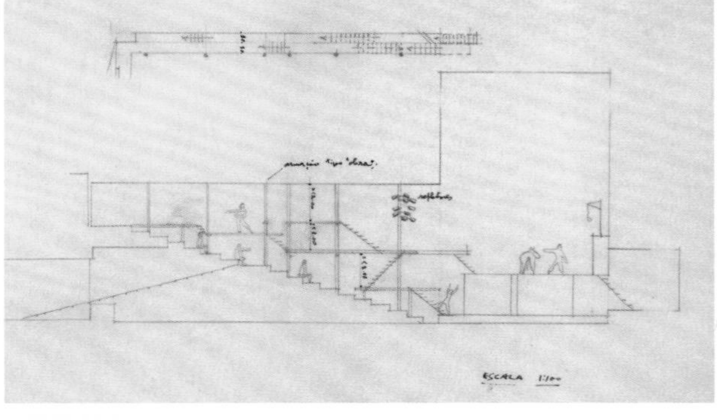

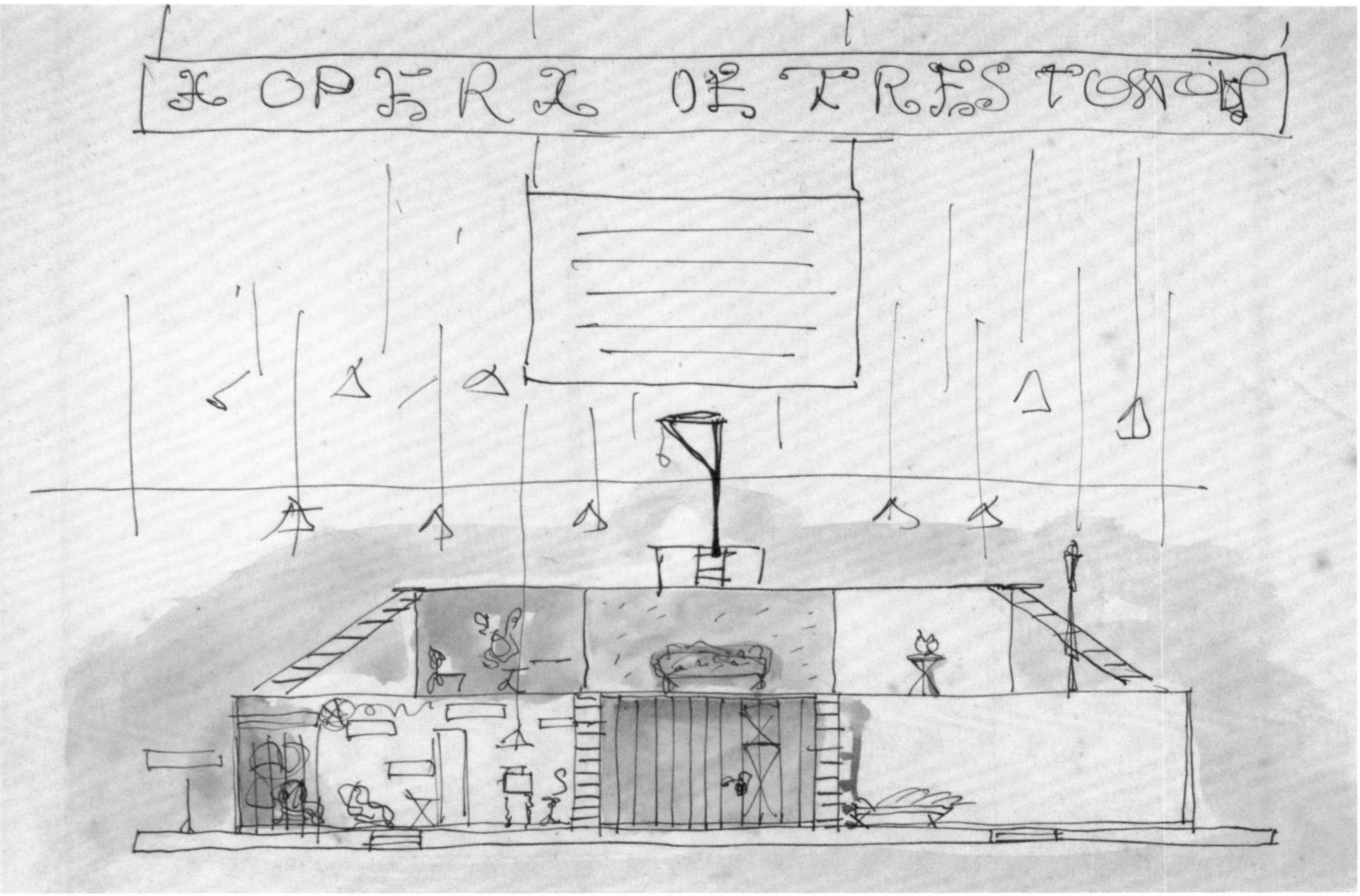

FIG. 361
Lina Bo Bardi, *Set design for The Threepenny Opera*, 1960. Watercolor, marker, and ink on offset paper, 22 x 33 cm. Collection of the Instituto Bardi/ Casa de Vidro, São Paulo

FIG. 362
Scenic architecture for *The Threepenny Opera*, 1960

In the Jungle of Cities

Teatro Oficina, São Paulo
1969
(Set design and costumes)

FIGS. 363–364
Lina Bo Bardi, *Plan and perspective drawing: In the Jungle of Cities*, 1969. Watercolor, ballpoint pen, and graphite on offset paper, 32.5 x 47.5 cm. Collection of the Instituto Bardi/Casa de Vidro, São Paulo

In 1969, the Teatro Oficina, directed by José Celso Martinez Corrêa, mounted a production of Brecht's *In the Jungle of Cities*. Bo Bardi, who had been introduced to Celso by Glauber Rocha, was invited to design the set and costumes. The play chronicles a metaphorical boxing match between two men in Chicago in 1912 and addresses the big-city battle for survival. The Oficina used the theme as an opportunity to implement a revolutionary scenography: the stage was constructed as a boxing ring that, with each performance, the actors and audience gradually destroyed. Such a scenario allowed Bo Bardi to fully activate her notion of "poor architecture." The set was built with debris collected in the theater district itself, which at the time was being violently transformed by the construction of elevated freeways. The countless demolitions promoted by the government and the installation of public works such as a viaduct provided the material to relate the Chicago jungle of Brecht's text to the tragedy of the developmental spectacle rehearsed in São Paulo during the "years of lead" under the military dictatorship. The cathartic destruction of the set extended through the floor of the theater to the dirt of Bexiga, the neighborhood where the building is located. This experience led to a reformulation of the entire theater based on Bo Bardi's designs.—DJ

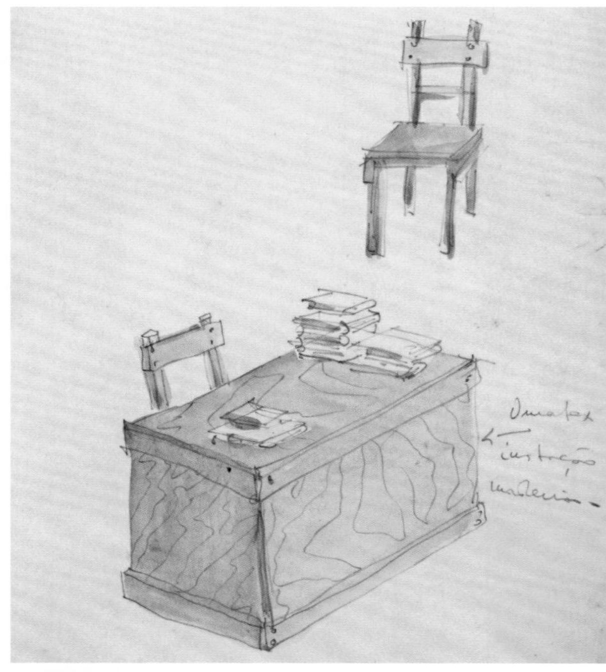

FIG. 365
Scene from *In the Jungle of Cities*, 1969

FIG. 366
Lina Bo Bardi, *Plan and perspective drawing: In the Jungle of Cities*, 1969. Watercolor, ballpoint pen, and graphite on offset paper, 32.5 x 47.8 cm. Collection of the Instituto Bardi/Casa de Vidro, São Paulo

FIG. 368
Lina Bo Bardi and Edinízio Ribeiro, *Woman's costume: cropped lace dress, pink socks, white chicken feather hat*, 1969. Marker, gouache, and graphite on newsprint, 31.5 x 22 cm. Collection of the Instituto Bardi/Casa de Vidro, São Paulo

FIG. 369
Lina Bo Bardi and Edinízio Ribeiro, *Man's costume, viewed from the front, accessories: gray flannel suit with white stripes, high-collared shirt, waistcoat, hat, patent leather shoes*, 1969. Ballpoint pen, marker, gouache, and graphite on newsprint, 31 x 21.5 cm. Collection of the Instituto Bardi/Casa de Vidro, São Paulo

FIG. 367
Lina Bo Bardi, *Plan and perspective drawing: In the Jungle of Cities*, 1969. Watercolor, ballpoint pen, and graphite on offset paper, 32.5 x 47.8 cm. Collection of the Instituto Bardi/Casa de Vidro, São Paulo

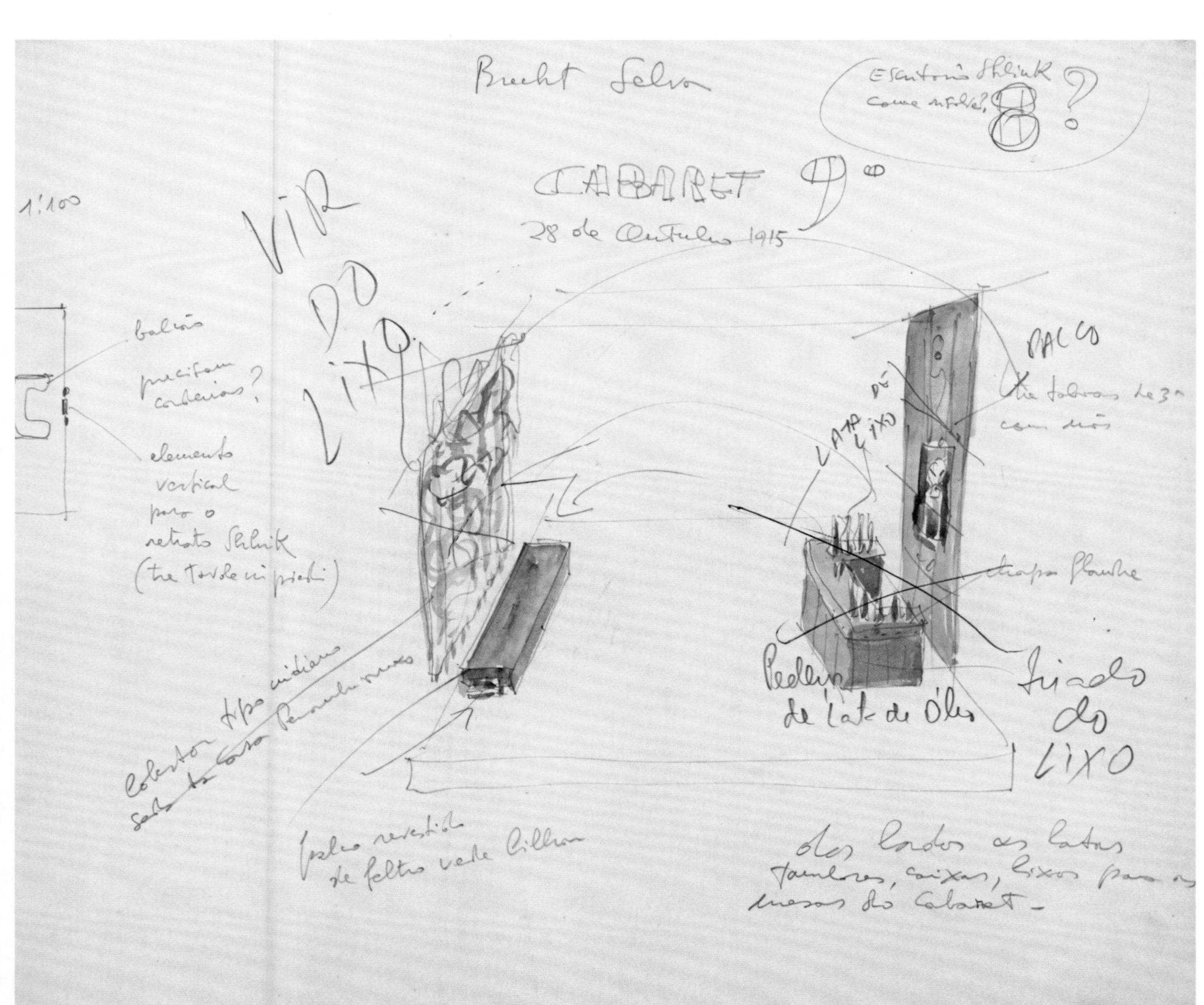

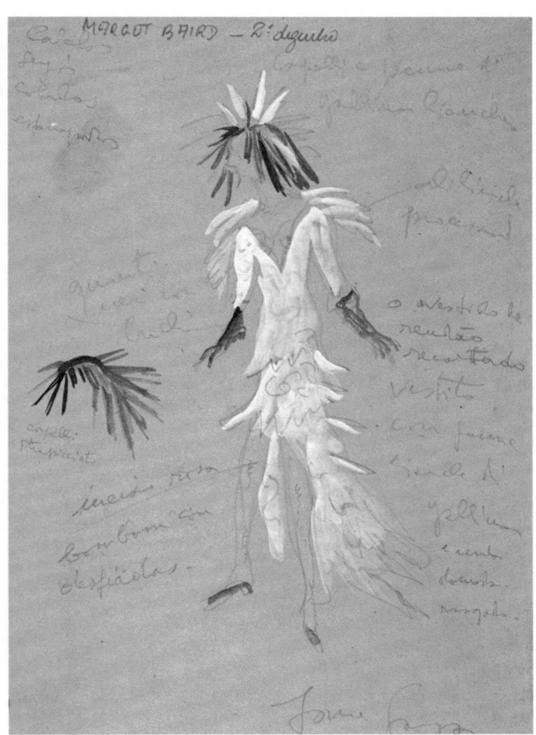

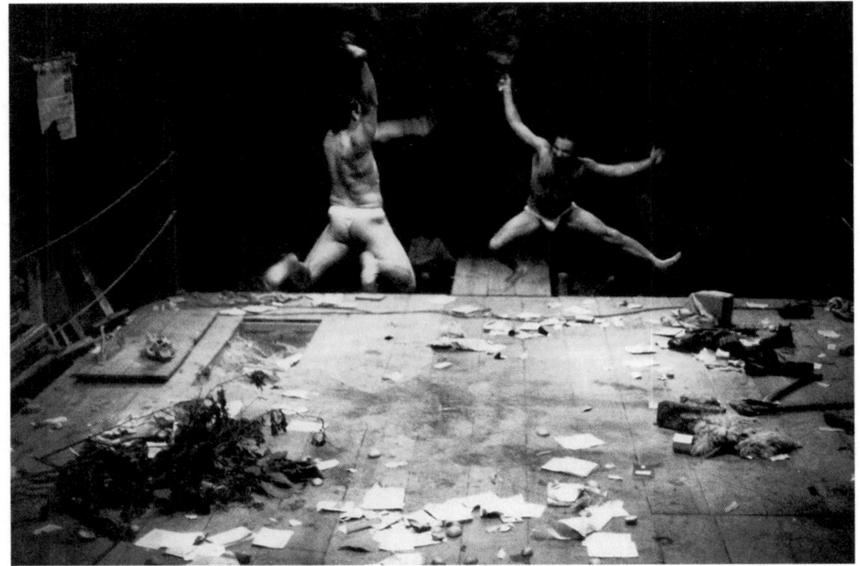

FIG. 370
Ítala Nandi during the staging of *In the Jungle of Cities*, the first fully nude performance in Brazilian theater, 1969

FIG. 371
Othon Bastos and Renato Borghi during the staging of *In the Jungle of Cities*, 1969

Sesc Pompeia Theater

São Paulo
1977–86
In collaboration with André Vainer and Marcelo Carvalho Ferraz (Architectural project)

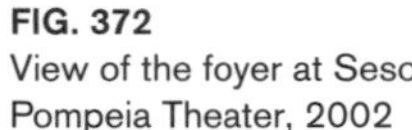

FIG. 372
View of the foyer at Sesc Pompeia Theater, 2002

FIG. 373
View of the stands and stage of the Sesc Pompeia Theater, 1983

The Sesc theater occupies the only isolated structure of the former Pompeia drum factory, and the building was subjected to the bluntest intervention in the entire complex. The secondary road that linked the warehouse to the large factory pavilion became the theater's foyer, with a new roof sealed by glass tiles. Wood *mux-arabis* form large sliding panels that enclose the foyer without nullifying the ambience of an exterior space. Access to the theater is made through an exposed concrete structure, which encases the old factory building like a modern prosthesis: a bridge crosses the foyer and ends in a staircase that leads to the first seating area; parallel to it, a transversal volume houses the dressing rooms and service areas, and at the far end of the foyer, another staircase leads to the second seating area. In the interior, two seating areas span the width of the warehouse at either end, sloping down to a central stage. The position of the stage controverts illusionism. It is a theater without a proscenium, closer in character to the Roman arena. The austerity of the chairs, specially designed for the theater in bare wood, confirms Bo Bardi's intention to establish Brechtian detachment: more than mere seating, chairs should be uncomfortable enough to prompt, in her words, "distanced engagement."—DJ

FIG. 374
Lina Bo Bardi in the Sesc Pompeia Theater, 1986

FIG. 375
Lina Bo Bardi, *Perspective drawing, Sesc Pompeia*, 1977–86. Watercolor and ballpoint pen on card stock, 37.5 x 57.5 cm. Collection of the Instituto Bardi/Casa de Vidro, São Paulo

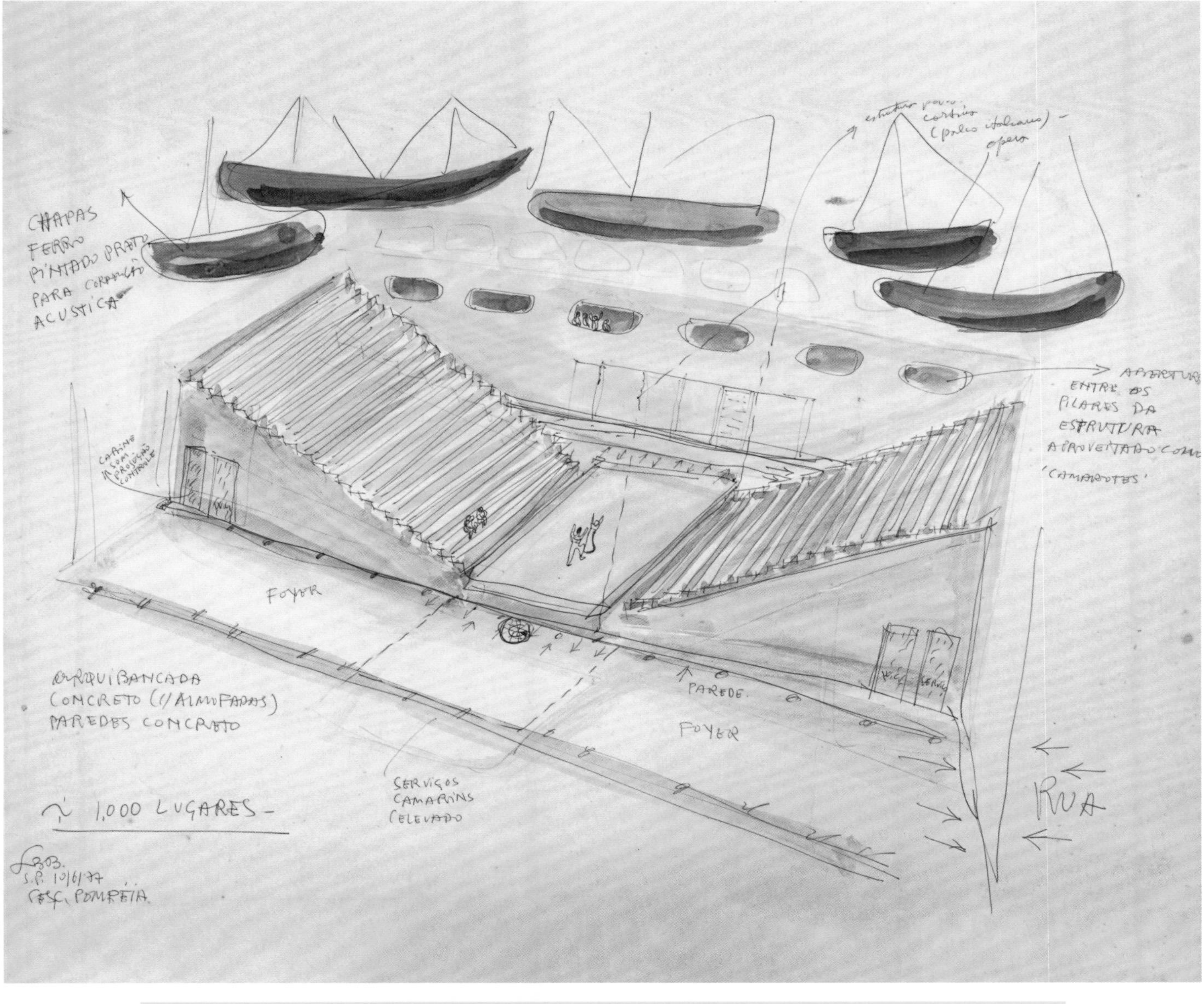

Teatro Oficina

São Paulo
1980–91
With Edson Elito and the collaboration of Marcelo Carvalho Ferraz and Marcelo Suzuki (Architectural project)

Teatro Oficina's first location was the result of a renovation undertaken in 1958 by architect Joaquim Guedes in an early twentieth-century building in the Bexiga neighborhood of São Paulo. After a fire in 1966, the theater was rebuilt the next year by Flávio Império and Rodrigo Lefèvre. Beginning in 1969, Bo Bardi staged some of the group's plays, led by José Celso Martinez Corrêa. Based on these collaborations, architect and director began to rethink the theater's layout, eventually leading to a complete reconstruction. For the redesign, only the old facade and the exposed brick walls of the 9 x 50–meter building were retained. The new theater is constituted as a strip of walkway that runs the length of the available space. The old shell is treated as a historical relic, and a delicate metal structure supports all contemporary interventions, highlighting their temporal distance. Collapsible scaffolding lines the side galleries that hold the public and all the supporting infrastructure of the plays. Everything is exposed, as if the entire theater were a stage, in an unprecedented mix of actors and audience, scene and backstage, front and back. The theater strip begins on a ramp and reaches a wide stage that brings together the Four Elements: a garden with soil from Bexiga, a waterfall, a gas network that permits the lighting of a fire—a pyre in the geometric center of the building—and finally the retractable roof, which allows the city's air to flow in. Traffic noise, sun, and rain also participate in the "contamination" promoted by the Oficina.—DJ

FIGS. 376–377
Interior views of Teatro Oficina, 2002

FIG. 378
Exterior view of Teatro Oficina, 2017

FIG. 379
Lina Bo Bardi and Edson Elito, *Teatro Oficina*, 1985. Graphite and marker on parchment paper, 100.5 x 70 cm. Collection of Edson Elito, São Paulo

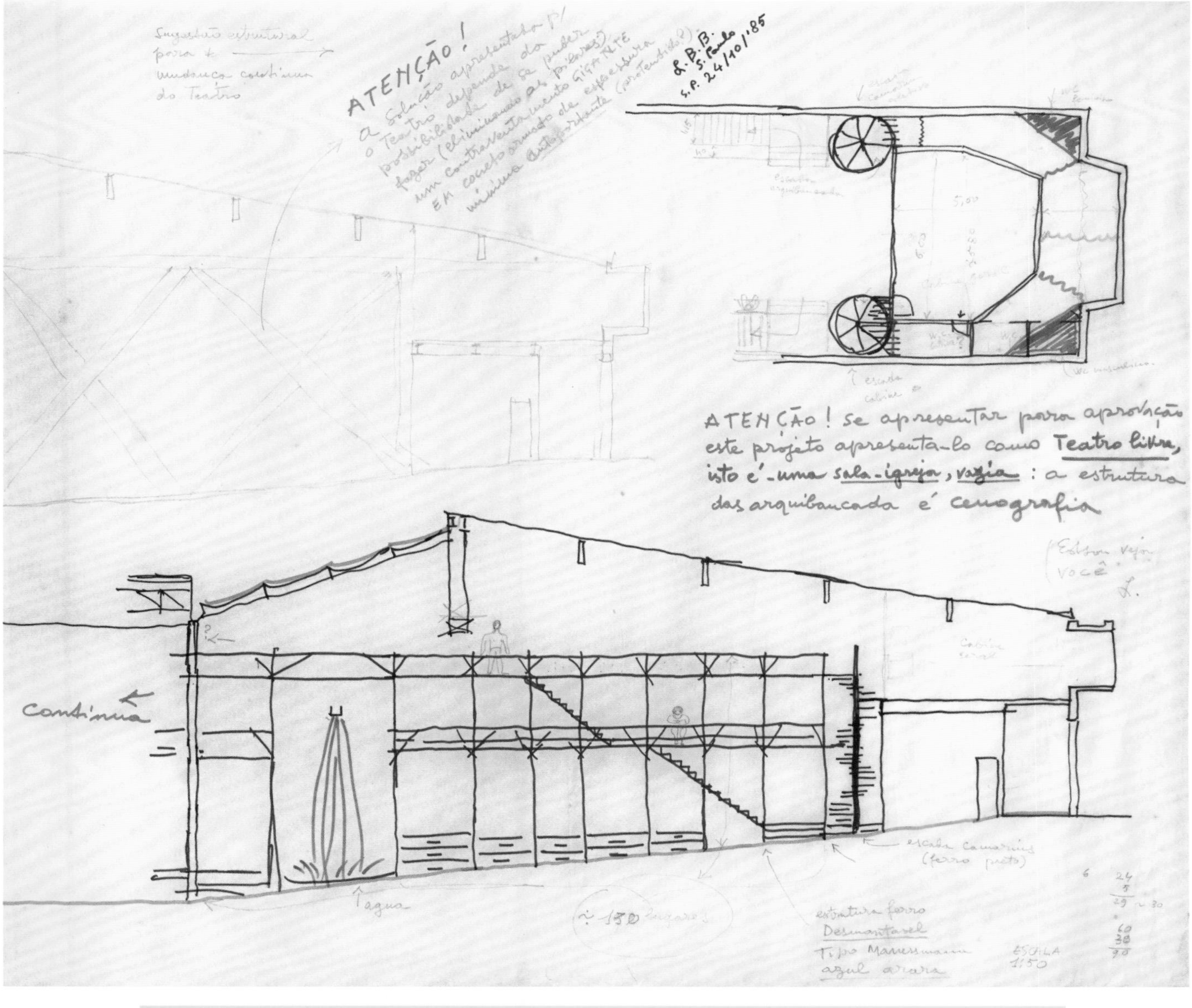

FIG. 381
Staging of the play *Ham-let*, directed by José Celso Martinez Corrêa at Teatro Oficina, 2001

FIG. 380
Lina Bo Bardi, *Perspective drawing, Teatro Oficina*, 1984. Watercolor, ballpoint pen, marker, and graphite on card stock, 32.5 x 51 cm. Collection of the Instituto Bardi/Casa de Vidro, São Paulo

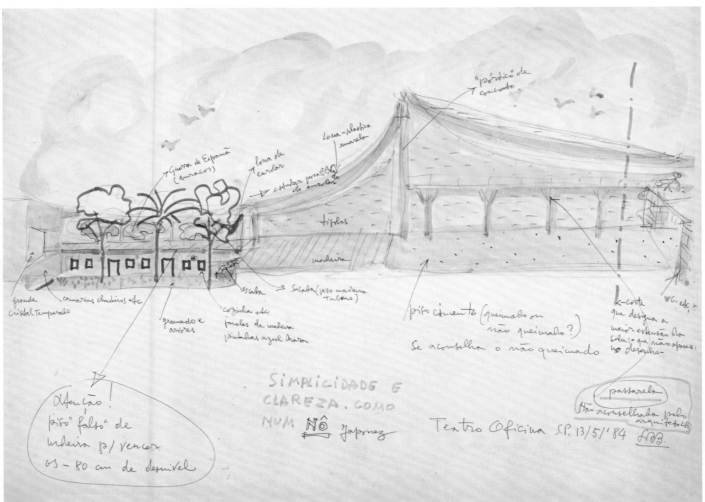

FURNITURE

1947–1987

Initially aligned with modern Italian design, the first pieces of furniture by Lina Bo Bardi were developed at Studio Palma (1948), in partnership with architect Giancarlo Palanti, a fellow Italian immigrant. The pair sought to combine modern design with local materials such as Brazilian woods and chintz from Casas Pernambucanas. But Bo Bardi's appropriation of the local context soon encompassed not only a material and productive reality but also a cultural one. In this way, she investigated a particular Brazilian posture, incorporating gestural informality into her furniture, such as an indigenous hammock, in the wood and iron versions of the Tripod Chair. The objects she designed from the 1950s broke with so-called good taste in modern furniture and gained a specificity that brought them closer to local artisanal production than to the industrialization project advocated in Europe. The Roadside Chair (1967), made with three branches and a piece of tree trunk tied together with liana vine, is Bo Bardi's most radical proposition in this regard—improvised with found material, it proposes a new way of sitting. In another example, the multidirectional articulation of the Bardi's Bowl Armchair (1951) takes on the playfulness of the Chaise LC4 by Le Corbusier and Charlotte Perriand, as do the lounge chairs in the Sesc Pompeia living area. The latter, made of padded crate segments, are composable modules on wheels that invite the user to reconfigure their spatial arrangement. Bo Bardi's broad understanding of the role of furniture is best demonstrated in the chairs she designed for the Sesc Pompeia auditorium (1977–86): purposely uncomfortable, they serve to stimulate the viewer's active attention.—DJ

Auditorium Chair for MASP, Rua 7 de Abril

FIG. 382
View of the auditorium at MASP, Rua 7 de Abril, with chairs designed by Lina Bo Bardi, 1947

FIG. 383
Lina Bo Bardi, Folding chair for the auditorium at MASP, Rua 7 de Abril, 1947. Jacarandá paulista wood and leather, 89.5 x 45 x 59 cm. Collection of the Instituto Bardi/Casa de Vidro, São Paulo

Iron Tripod Chair

FIG. 384
Protoype of the Iron Tripod Chair, 1948

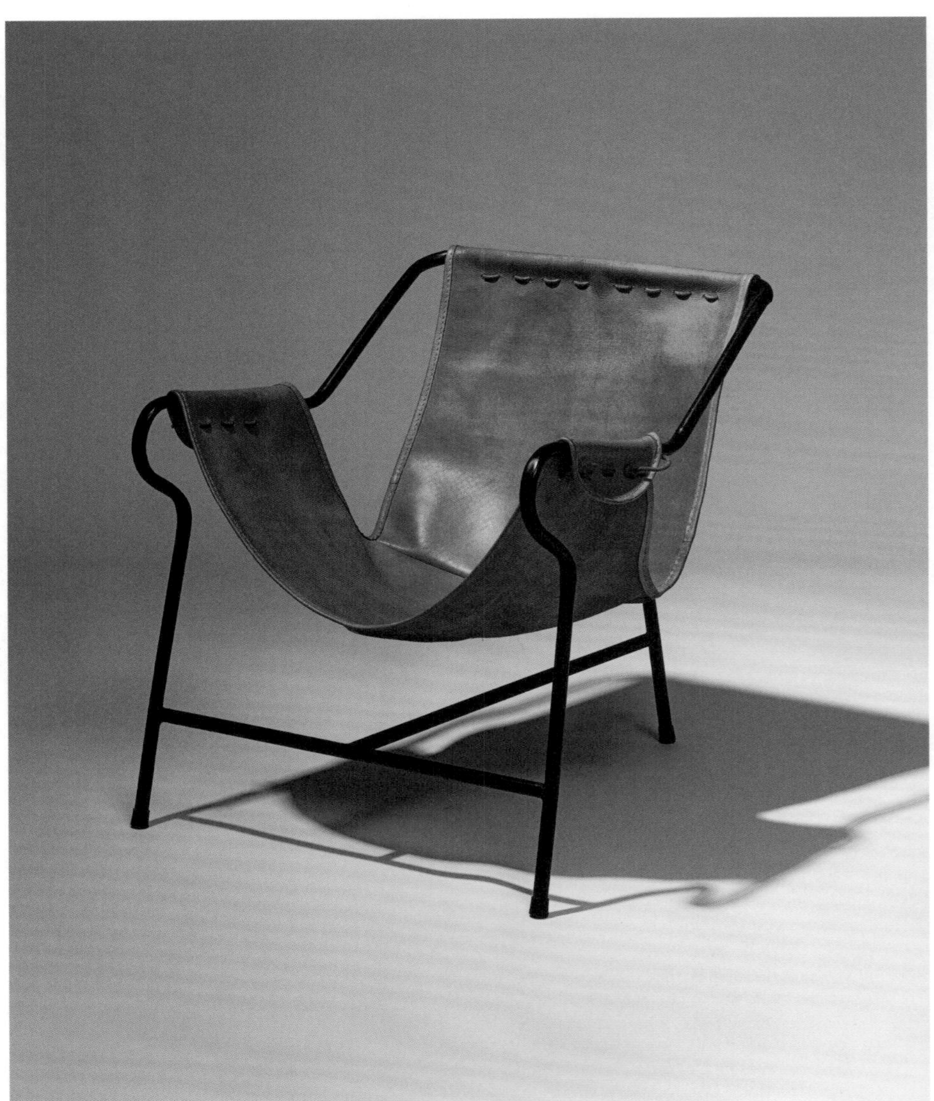

FIG. 385
Lina Bo Bardi, Iron Tripod Chair, 1948–85. Tubular structure in iron and leather, 75.5 x 68 x 81 cm. Collection of the Instituto Bardi/ Casa de Vidro, São Paulo

Wood Tripod Chair

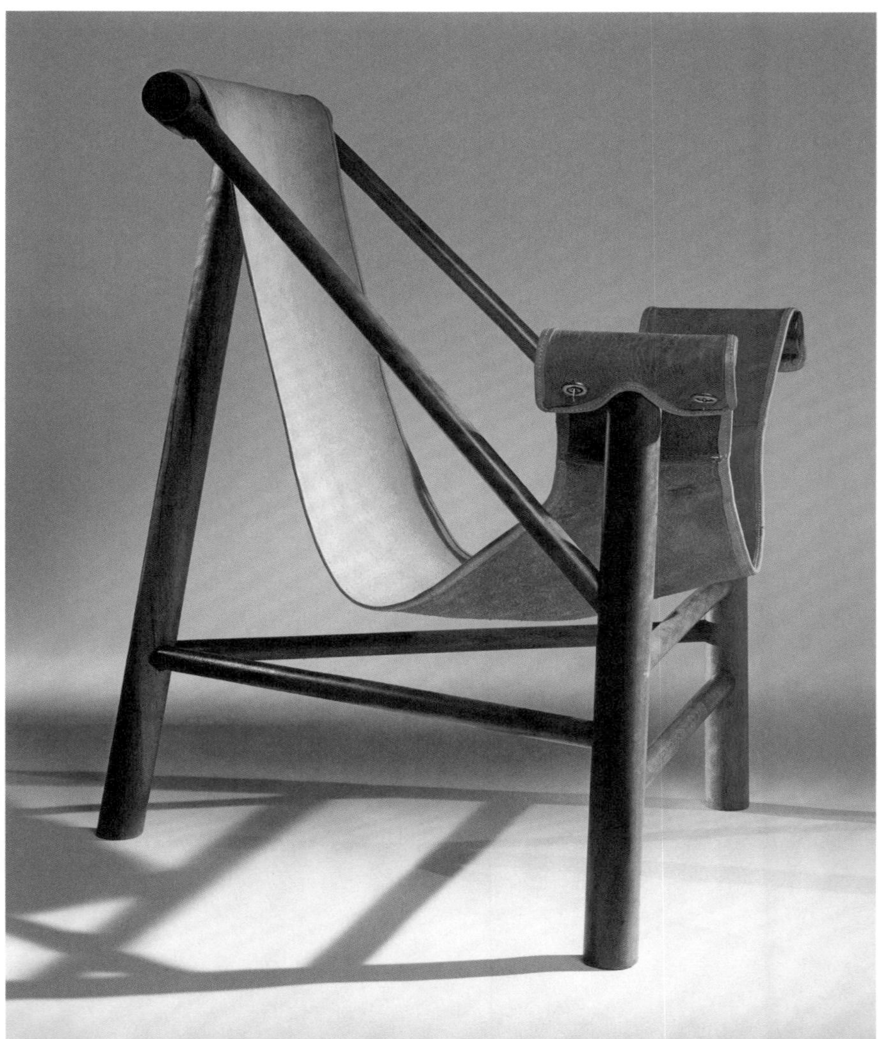

FIG. 386
Lina Bo Bardi, Wood Tripod Chair, 1948. Tubular wood structure (possibly cabreúva wood) and leather, 90.5 x 71 x 70 cm. Collection of the Instituto Bardi/Casa de Vidro, São Paulo

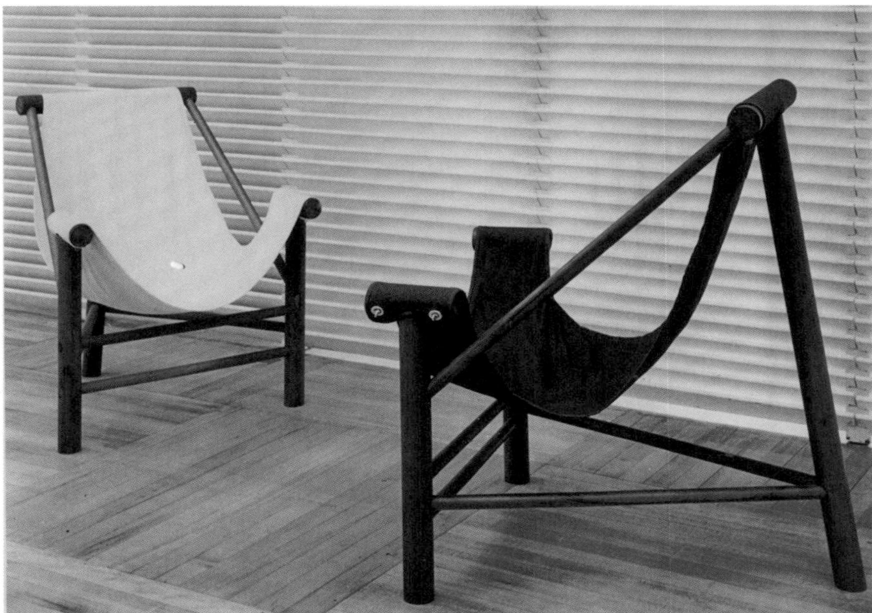

FIG. 387
First prototypes for the Wood Tripod Chair, 1948

Bowl Armchair

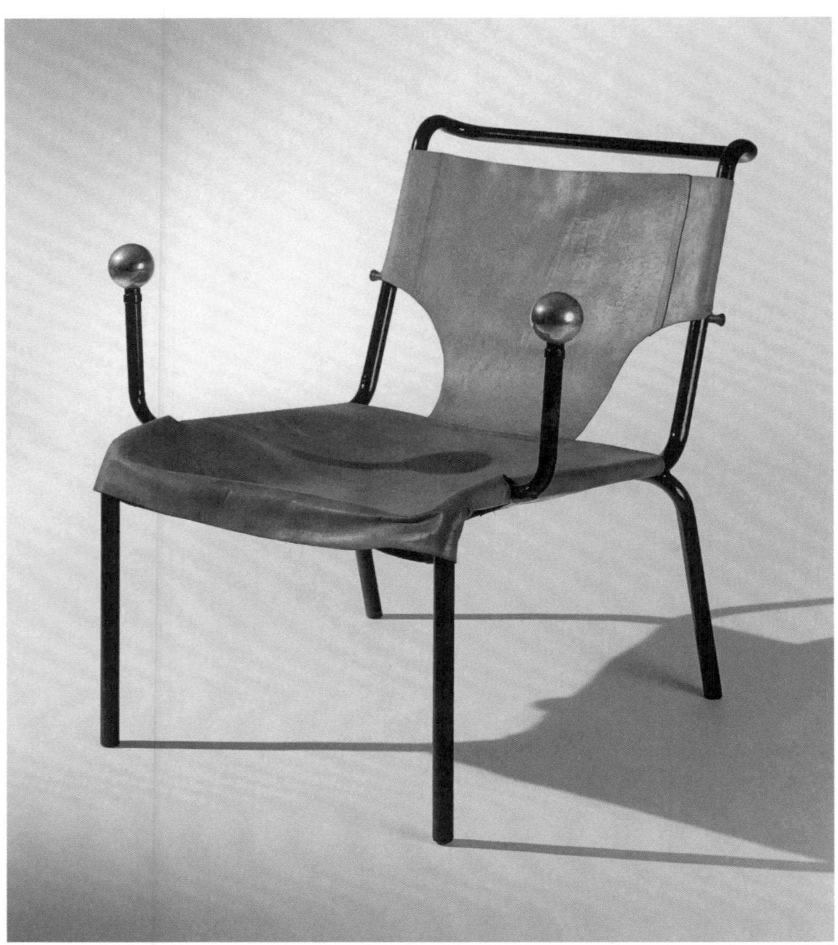

FIG. 388
Lina Bo Bardi, Bowl Armchair, 1951. Tubular iron structure, polished brass, and tanned leather, 76 x 72 x 83.5 cm. Collection of the Instituto Bardi/ Casa de Vidro, São Paulo

FIG. 389
Interior view of the Glass House with a group of Bowl Armchairs, 1951

Bardi's Bowl Armchair

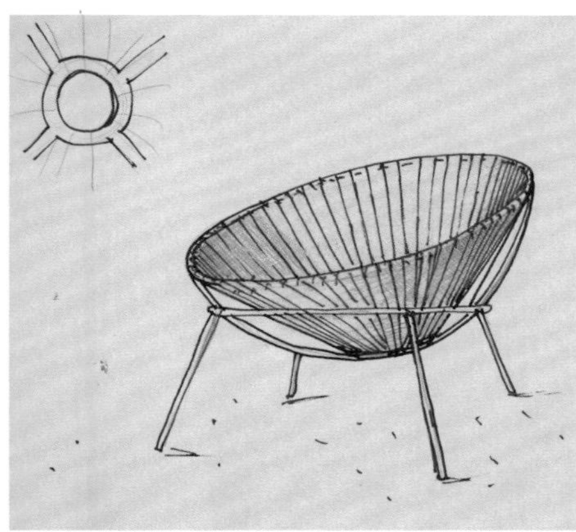

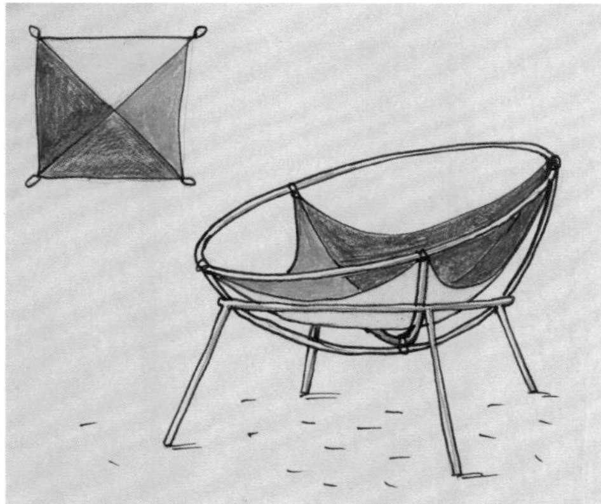

FIG. 391
Lina Bo Bardi, *Perspective*, 1951. Graphite, ink, and crayon on offset paper, 21.5 x 31.5 cm. Collection of the Instituto Bardi/Casa de Vidro, São Paulo

FIG. 390
Lina Bo Bardi, *Seat plan and perspective*, 1951. Graphite, ink, and crayon on offset paper, 21.5 x 31.5 cm. Collection of the Instituto Bardi/Casa de Vidro, São Paulo

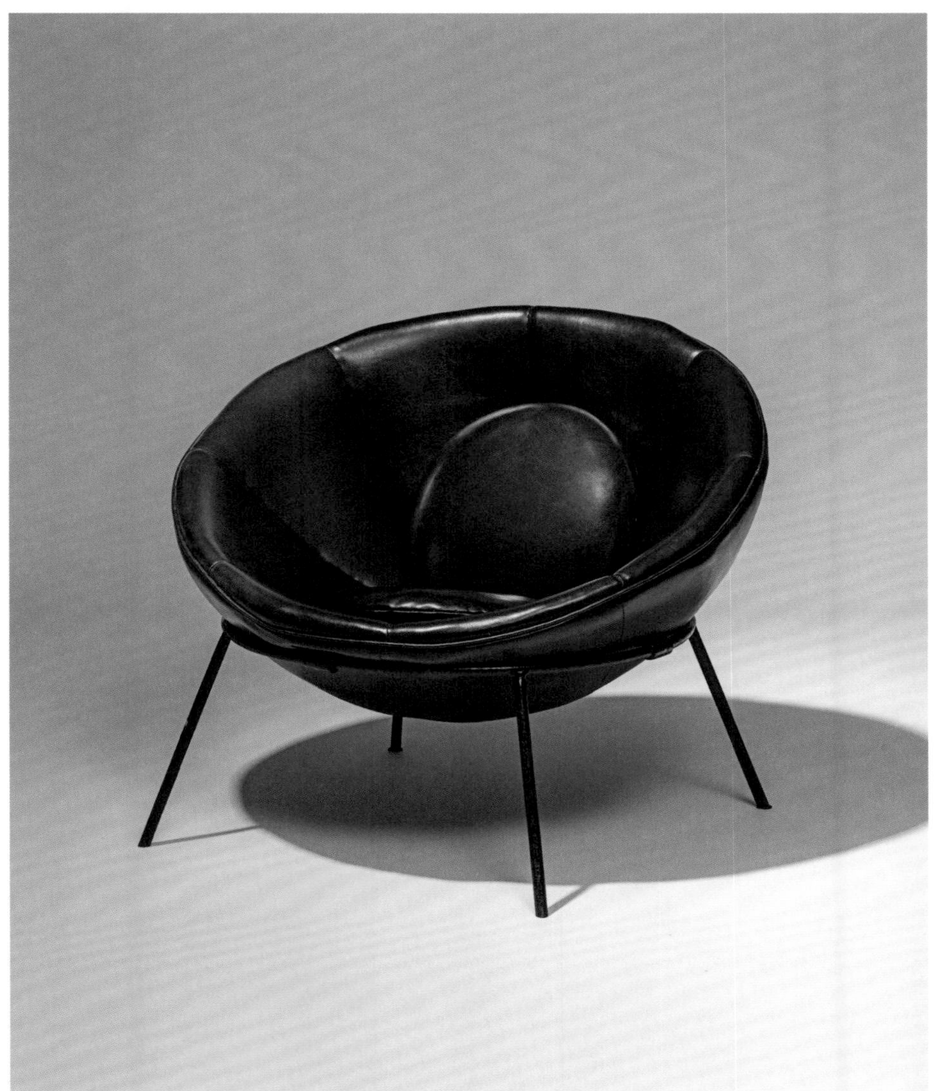

FIG. 392
Lina Bo Bardi, Bardi's Bowl Armchair, 1951. Tubular iron and leather structure, 70 x 84 x 84 cm. Collection of the Instituto Bardi/Casa de Vidro, São Paulo

Chairs for the Castro Alves Theater

FIG. 393
View of the Castro Alves Theater with chairs designed by Lina Bo Bardi, 1960s

FIG. 394
Lina Bo Bardi, Chairs for the Teatro Castro Alves, 1960/1994. Wood and leather, 82 x 124 x 50 cm. Collection of the Instituto Bardi/Casa de Vidro, São Paulo

Chairs for the MASP Auditorium, Avenida Paulista

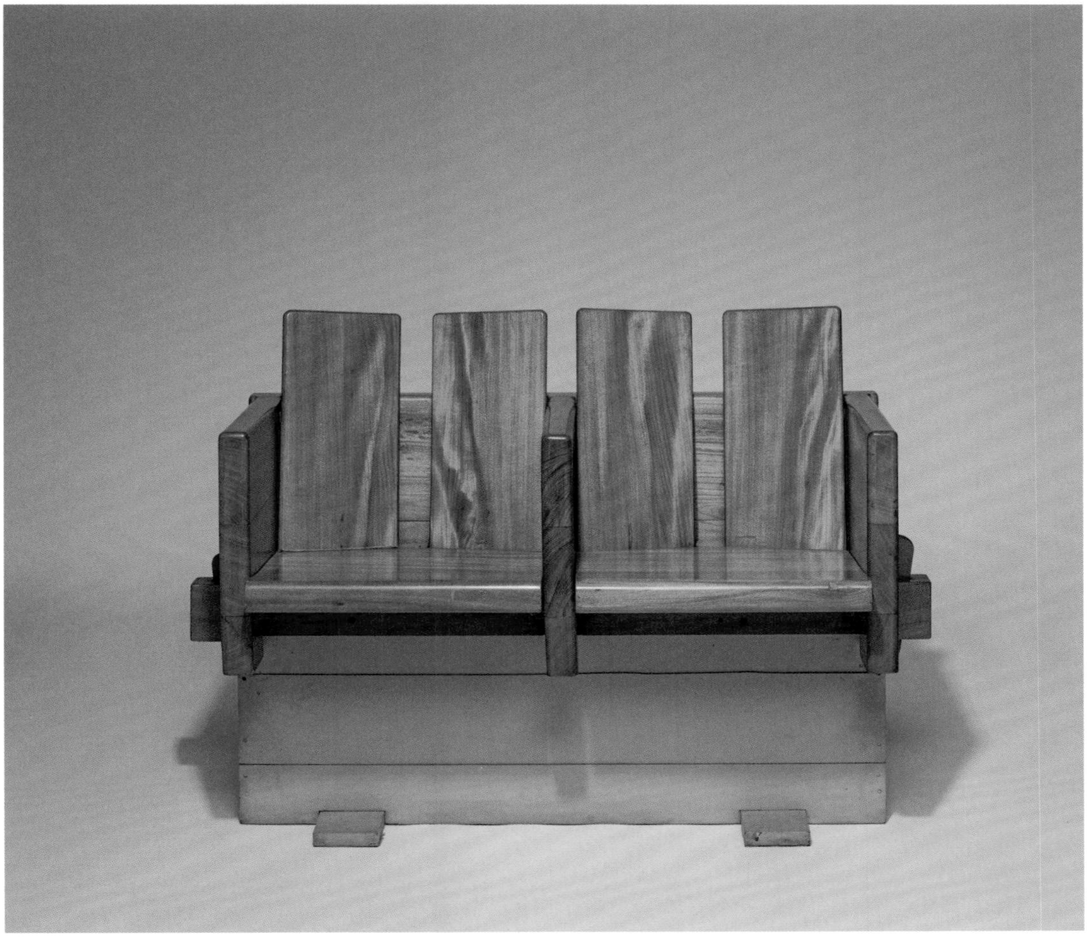

FIG. 395
Lina Bo Bardi, Prototype chairs for the auditorium at MASP, Avenida Paulista, ca. 1970. Wood and concrete, 84.5 x 120 x 60 cm. Collection of the Instituto Bardi/Casa de Vidro, São Paulo

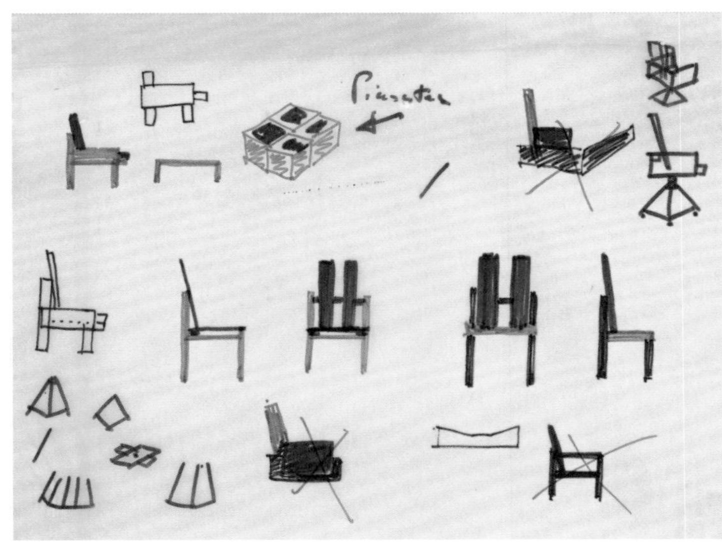

FIG. 396
Lina Bo Bardi, *Front and lateral elevations, São Paulo Museum of Art*, 1957–68. Marker on parchment paper, 17 x 25.5 cm. Collection of the Instituto Bardi/ Casa de Vidro, São Paulo

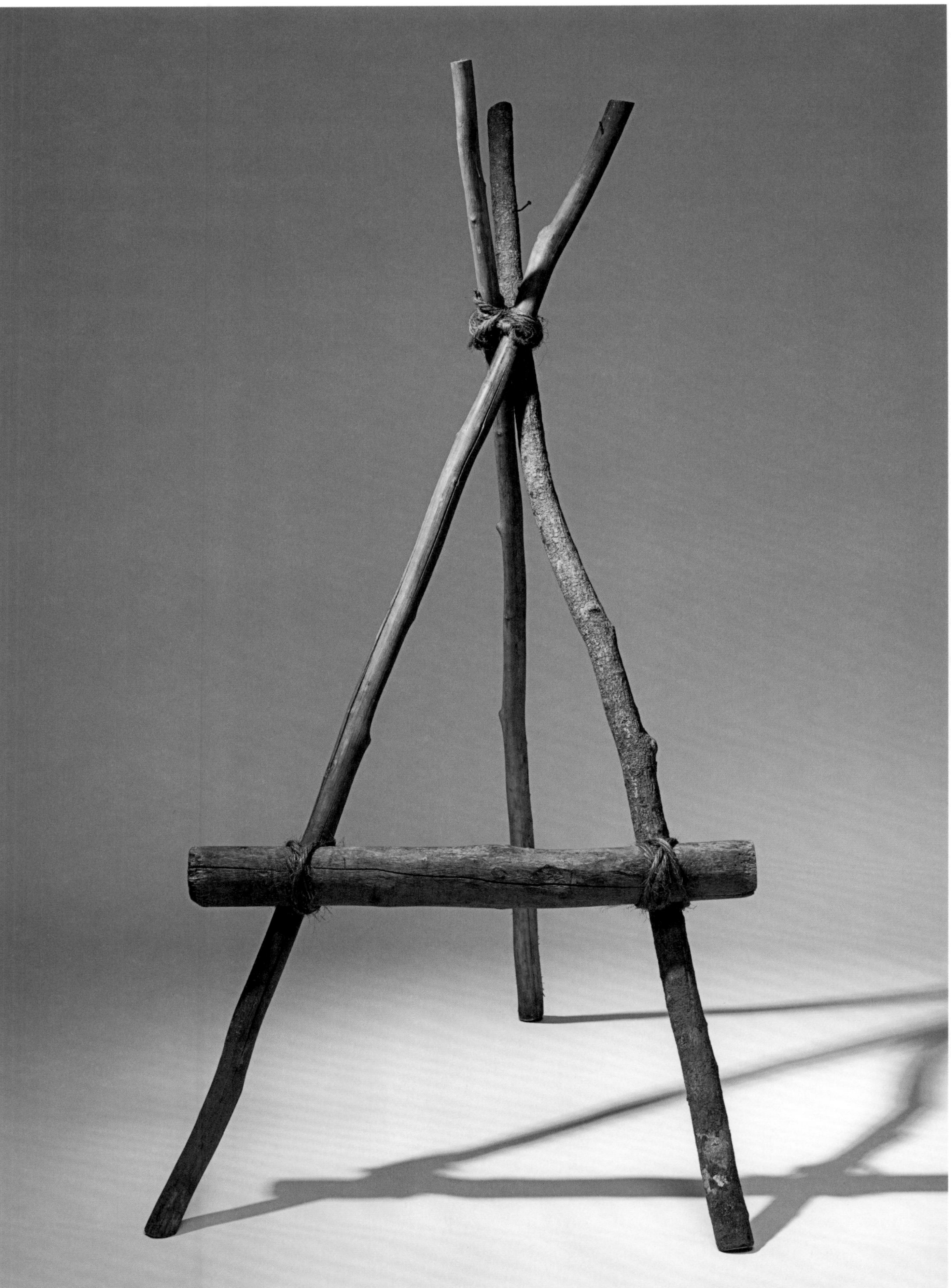

Roadside Chair

← **FIG. 397**
Lina Bo Bardi, Roadside Chair, 1967. Wood branches and cord, 190 x 97 x 145 cm. Collection of the Instituto Bardi/Casa de Vidro, São Paulo

FIG. 398
Lina Bo Bardi seated in the Roadside Chair, 1967

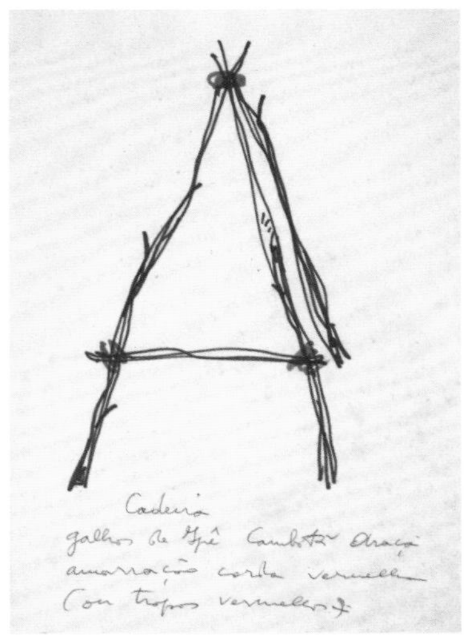

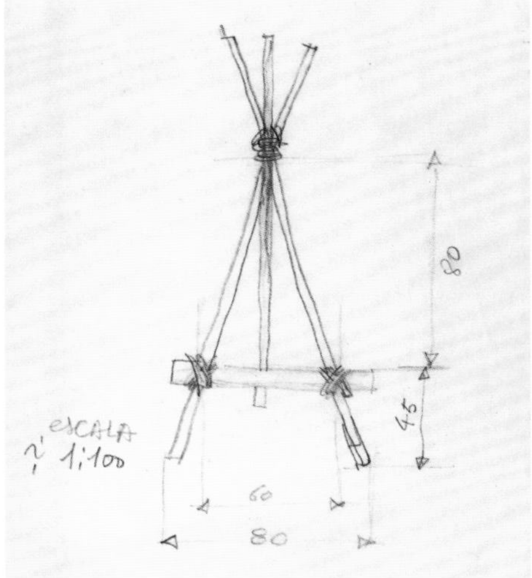

FIG. 399
Lina Bo Bardi, *Perspective drawing, Roadside Chair*, 1967. Marker on offset paper, 25 x 15.5 cm. Collection of the Instituto Bardi/Casa de Vidro, São Paulo

FIG. 400
Lina Bo Bardi, *Roadside Chair*, 1967. Graphite on parchment paper, 32.5 x 23 cm. Collection of the Instituto Bardi/Casa de Vidro, São Paulo

Sesc Pompeia Chair

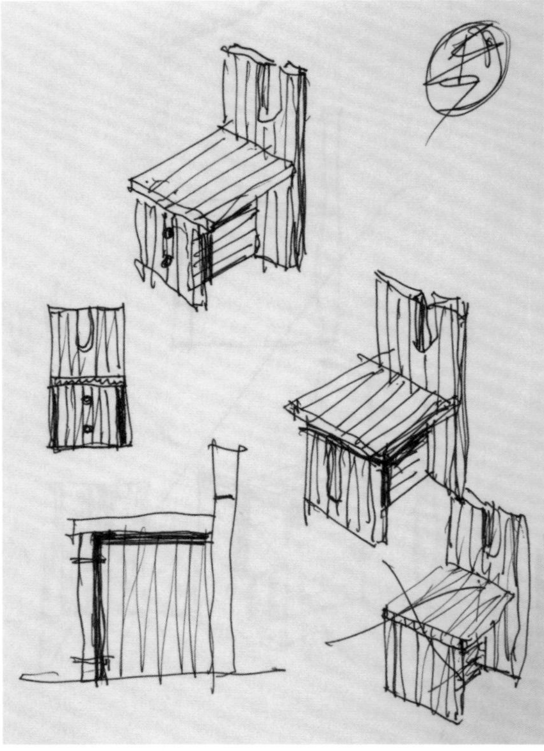

FIG. 401
Lina Bo Bardi, *Perspective drawing, Sesc Pompeia Chair*, 1977–86. Ballpoint pen on offset paper, 21 x 14.5 cm. Collection of the Instituto Bardi/Casa de Vidro, São Paulo

FIG. 402
Lina Bo Bardi, Sesc Pompeia Chairs, 1980. Madeira wood, each 69 x 39.5 x 52.5 cm. Collection of the Instituto Bardi/Casa de Vidro, São Paulo

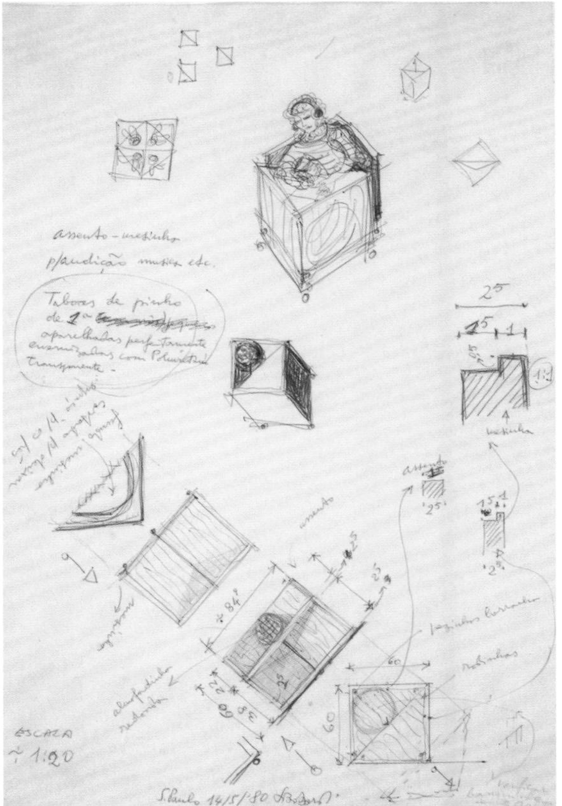

Little Box for Sesc Pompeia

FIG. 403
Lina Bo Bardi, Prototype of the Little Box for Sesc Pompeia, 1977–86. Wood, melanylene laminate in red, and castors, each 66 x 58 x 58 cm. Collection of the Instituto Bardi/Casa de Vidro, São Paulo

FIG. 404
Lina Bo Bardi, *Elevation, plan, and perspective for a child's chair and desk, Sesc Pompeia*, 1977–86. Ballpoint pen, marker, and graphite on offset paper, 31.5 x 21.5 cm. Collection of the Instituto Bardi/Casa de Vidro, São Paulo

Frei Egydio Chair

FIG. 405
Lina Bo Bardi, Marcelo Carvalho Ferraz, and Marcelo Suzuki, Frei Egydio Chair, 1986. Araucaria wood, 84.5 x 44 x 44.5 cm. Collection of the Instituto Bardi/ Casa de Vidro, São Paulo

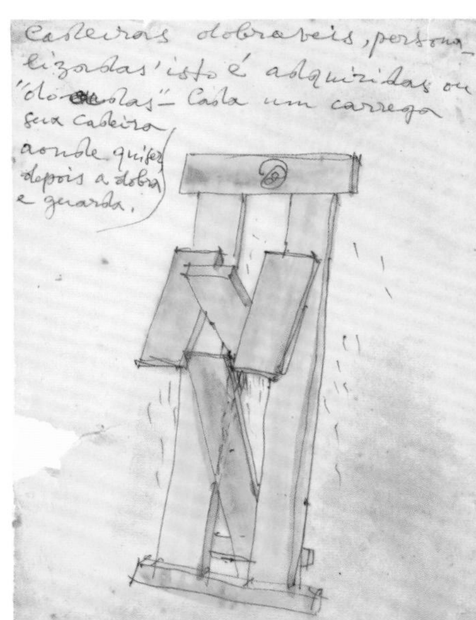

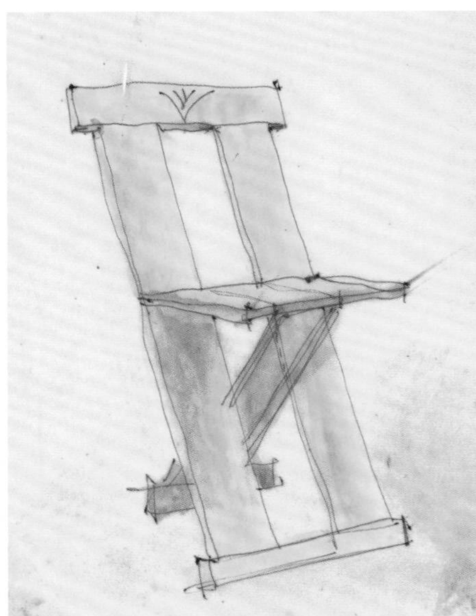

FIG. 406
Lina Bo Bardi, *Perspective of closed chair, Barroquinha Project*, 1986. Watercolor and ballpoint pen on parchment paper, 22 x 16 cm. Collection of the Instituto Bardi/Casa de Vidro, São Paulo

FIG. 407
Lina Bo Bardi, *Perspective of open chair, Barroquinha Project*, 1986. Watercolor and ballpoint pen on parchment paper, 22 x 16 cm. Collection of the Instituto Bardi/Casa de Vidro, São Paulo

Giraffe Chair

FIG. 408
Lina Bo Bardi, Marcelo Carvalho Ferraz, and Marcelo Suzuki, Giraffe Chair, 1986–87. Araucaria wood, 72 x 39 x 38.5 cm. Collection of the Instituto Bardi/Casa de Vidro, São Paulo